'Entertaining . . . a fascinating insight into life lived to the full and thoroughly enjoyed and reveals the private man behind the public personality.' *Birmingham Post*

'It is peppered with anecdotes which his father would have clearly enjoyed and has a name dropper's dream list of acquaintances from John F Kennedy and Neville Chamberlain to Denis Compton and Bud Flanagan. Very comprehensive.' *Yorkshire Post*

'Anecdotal evidence of the broadcaster's beaming zeal for life is crammed between the covers like a Test player's cricket chest . . . the book radiates warmth, pride and humanity. What's more, it is a rollicking good read.' *York Evening Press*

'A moving biography. It is a wonderful portrait of a full and vigorous life against the backdrop of most of the major events of the 20th century.' *Halifax Evening Courier*

'Moving . . . This definitive and intimate portrayal is definitely a must-have for all fans of cricket.' *Devon Today*

'Barry Johnston's fondly written record of his father's full life is a must for cricketing enthusiasts and a fitting tribute to a national treasure.' *Kent Messenger*

Edited by the same author:

An Evening with Johnners

Letters Home 1926–1945

A Delicious Slice of Johnners

Another Slice of Johnners

A Further Slice of Johnners

BARRY JOHNSTON

Johnners:
The Life of Brian

CORONET BOOKS
Hodder & Stoughton

Copyright © 2003 Barry Johnston

First published in Great Britain in 2003 by Hodder & Stoughton
A division of Hodder Headline

The right of Barry Johnston to be identified as the Author
of the Work has been asserted by him in accordance with the
Copyright, Designs and Patents Act 1988.

1 3 5 7 9 10 8 6 4 2

A CIP catalogue record for this title is
available from the British Library

ISBN 0 340 82471 9

Typeset in Plantin Light by Palimpsest Book Production Limited,
Polmont, Stirlingshire
Printed and bound in Great Britain by
Clays Ltd, St Ives plc

Hodder and Stoughton
A division of Hodder Headline
338 Euston Road
London NW1 3BH

For Fiona,
Olivia and Sam,
with all my love

Contents

Foreword by Richie Benaud ... ix

Prologue ... xi

Introduction by Barry Johnston ... 1

PART ONE: 1912–44

1 Golden Days ... 7
2 Tragedy at Bude ... 14
3 Temple Grove ... 23
4 Floreat Etona ... 30
5 Most Popular Boy ... 38
6 A Real Live Wire ... 48
7 Home and Away ... 60
8 Something in the City ... 69
9 An Awful Lot of Coffee ... 79
10 Peace for Our Time ... 89
11 Breaking All the Rules ... 98
12 Determination Under Fire ... 109

PART TWO: 1944–72

13 A Job with Auntie ... 123
14 The Telephone Rings ... 132
15 Let's Go Somewhere ... 140

16 In Town Tonight   147
17 Jack of All Trades   156
18 Game for Anything   165
19 BBC Cricket Correspondent   175
20 Staff Commentator   186
21 Down but Not Out   199

PART THREE: 1972–94

22 It's Been a Lot of Fun   211
23 Test Match Special   223
24 Down Your Way   237
25 This Is Your Life   247
26 From Tests to Trivia   261
27 Father Figure   272
28 Friends and Neighbours   285
29 It's Been a Long Time   295
30 Aggers, Do Stop It   306
31 An Evening with Johnners   316
32 The Light Fades   325
33 End of the Innings   332
34 Summers Will Not Be the Same   340

Epilogue   347
Acknowledgements   348
The Brian Johnston Memorial Trust   351
Index   352

Foreword

I had the good fortune to start my working life in England forty-three years ago when the BBC asked me to be part of the radio commentary team. Additional good fortune was to be interviewed by Brian Johnston and Peter West on television. A little more than six months later, I was greeted in Aden by the cry of 'Benners!' because Brian had taken himself and a small television crew to meet my Australian team and produce a scoop when scoops were rare on English TV.

Don't ever think of him as simply a happy-go-lucky sports commentator who ad-libbed his way through a maze of happenings which by accident turned into success on radio or TV. He was meticulous in his preparation in each medium and was unfazed by anything unexpected. That later translated, for me, into the wall plaque by Australia's David Hill which said 'Assume Nothing'.

Brian was a cricket lover, and a wicket-keeper of sorts, and he had a wonderful sense of humour, underneath what on the surface was something more schoolboyish. Nothing I have seen has been better than at Edgbaston in 1993 where, after being beautifully 'done' by a colleague, he then constructed his own brilliant response.

He was a great friend to Daphne and me over forty years, as indeed the family are, and it is a privilege to pen a few words for the book.

Richie Benaud
31 January 2003

Prologue

It was a summer morning in late August 1922. Nine-year-old Margaret Edwardes-Jones was enjoying a quiet breakfast with her family at their holiday home, 'Garthmyl', by the seaside at Brancaster, in Norfolk. The house had been built by her father George and the family used to spend their holidays there every year.

Suddenly, through the window, Margaret saw the 'telegraph boy' cycling up the garden path. Their house, like many rural homes in the early 1920s, had no telephone, so the telegraph boy on his old Post Office bicycle was a familiar sight. It was exciting to receive a telegram, whether it contained good or bad news, and as Margaret was the youngest of the five Edwardes-Jones children, she begged to be the one to answer the door.

The small brown envelope was addressed to her mother Gaie, so Margaret handed it to her at the breakfast table. As Gaie opened the envelope and read the contents she turned pale, and Margaret later told me that her mother looked as though she might faint. The message was brief and to the point: TERRIBLE ACCIDENT JOHNNO DROWNED.

As Gaie would discover soon afterwards, her younger brother, Lieutenant Colonel Charles Johnston, had been swept out to sea in a swimming accident and had drowned while on holiday at Bude in North Cornwall. He was only forty-four years old and left a wife and four children.

Many lives were changed on that fateful day, but the most unexpected and the most extraordinary would be that of Charles's ten-year-old and youngest son, Brian Alexander Johnston.

Introduction

Since my father died nearly ten years ago there have been a number of books published about him, several of them edited by myself. So why a new biography, and why now, and why written by me – his eldest son?

First of all it is a desire to put the record straight. Whenever people talk to me about Brian, they inevitably mention his famous fit of the giggles on *Test Match Special* after Jonathan Agnew remarked that Ian Botham 'couldn't quite get his leg over'. It is a wonderful way to be remembered, but there was more to Brian Johnston than an infectious giggle.

Second, he wrote three volumes of autobiography, but none of them told the full story. In fact he hardly touched on the last fifteen years of his life, when he became a national institution on *Down Your Way* and *Test Match Special*. His own books also contain some notable omissions. For example, he devoted only three paragraphs in his first autobiography to the death of his father and he dismissed his war experiences in France and Germany with typical modesty.

While I was researching a book of my father's letters five years ago, I spoke to many of his oldest friends who had known him since he was a schoolboy at Eton and uncovered a lot of new information. Sadly several of those friends have since died. It occurred to me that if anyone were going to write a definitive biography of Brian, they would need to do it soon. Many of his contemporaries are in their nineties, and in a few years' time there will be no one left who knew Brian before the war.

When I mentioned this to Hodder & Stoughton, they suggested that I should write the new biography. As his eldest son I knew

Brian better than most; I researched his early life when compiling his letters and I have already edited three anthologies based on his writings.

I felt a great responsibility to make sure that it was accurate in every detail. I talked to dozens of Brian's friends and colleagues and thought the hardest task would be to come up with some fresh anecdotes. I need not have worried. I lost count of the number of times people said to me, 'Of course, you know the story about . . .' and I would have to quickly reach for my pen.

It was impossible to mention Brian's name to anyone without receiving a smile. 'He was the most reliable and faithful friend I had,' said Sir Edward Ford, who knew him for more than sixty years. 'He was so good at keeping in touch.' Several people described him as a life-enhancer. One colleague told me that you always knew when Brian had arrived at a party because laughter followed him around the room.

The most illuminating remark came from Lord Carrington, who served with Brian in the Grenadier Guards. 'The one thing you must remember,' he stressed, 'is that underneath it all he was a serious man.' That is really the key to Brian's character. He may have given the appearance of being a light-hearted practical joker, but throughout his adult life he was always totally professional.

The hardest part was writing about him as a father. Now that I have children of my own I realise how disappointed he must have been by my failure at Eton and my lack of interest in cricket. Talking to my brothers and sisters also made me aware of how little Brian was around during our childhood. At the time we did not know any different: we thought all fathers were away a lot. As I point out, however, he more than made up for it when he was at home.

This book is an affectionate portrait but it is also an honest one. I have not attempted to hide his faults, not that there were many. For most of his broadcasting career he put his work before his family; he was a notoriously fussy eater and he kept his emotions well hidden. But his kindness and good humour were legendary, and it was not an act; he was exactly the same in public and in private.

The more I learned about my father, the greater the respect I gained for him as a man and as a broadcaster. His broadcasting achievements were considerable; no one has enjoyed such a long and varied career. Gillian Reynolds, the radio critic of the *Daily Telegraph*, once described how she gave the audio cassette of *Johnners at the Beeb* to a young friend who did not remember Brian on the air.

'What a great man,' he told her later, 'what a life!'

Barry Johnston
February 2003

PART ONE

1912–44

I

Golden Days

In later years Brian Johnston would express surprise at the lifestyle he enjoyed during his childhood. He grew up in a world of Edwardian luxury and privilege far removed from his ultimate career as a broadcaster. Before the First World War the Johnston family were among the most respected members of the banking community in the City of London. Brian's grandfather Reginald Johnston was Governor of the Bank of England and a director of several City companies. Brian's father Charles was chairman of the family coffee business, E. Johnston & Co., as well as a director of the London & Brazilian Bank and the Midland Bank, and his godfather Alex Johnston was deputy chairman of Atlas Assurance and a director of the National Provincial Bank.

Brian was proud of his Scottish heritage and always wore a signet ring with the Johnston family crest of winged spurs – as do his three sons today. The motto is *Nunquam Non Paratus* – Never Unprepared – and Brian's family liked to believe they could trace their roots back to the Scottish borders in the twelfth century.

After researching his family tree I did some simple arithmetic. I do not suppose Brian ever worked it out for himself, because he never mentioned it, but in fact he was three-quarters English and only one-eighth Scottish and, more surprisingly, thanks to his great-grandmother, one-eighth Dutch.

The surname Johnston is derived from the original 'John', a Norman lord who arrived in Scotland in the mid-1100s and was granted lands at Annandale in Dumfries. The family name gradually evolved into Johnstone or Johnston, spelled with a 't', as opposed to Johnson, a surname which is unrelated. For the next few hundred years the Johnstones farmed their lands, fought with their neighbours, and gained a reputation as 'reivers' or cattle thieves, carrying out frequent raids south of the border.

One of the problems in tracing one's Scottish roots is that most family records were destroyed in the religious wars of the seventeenth and eighteenth centuries. The oldest verifiable member of Brian's family is therefore Francis Johnstone, who was born in about 1665 at Cummertrees near Annan, Dumfries. Previous generations have claimed that he was related to the Marquis of Annandale. This may well be true but there is no written proof of it.

Francis Johnstone was a gardener and had about six children, including a son, James, who was born in 1699. James also became a gardener and moved to Dailly, Ayrshire, where he married the daughter of a local farmer. By then he was fifty-two, but they had five sons and three daughters.

Their third child, Francis Johnstone, was born in 1757, and he was the first member of Brian's family to leave Scotland. He left home when he was about sixteen and obtained a position in the service of Lord Napier of Merchiston. Soon afterwards he sailed to America, and at the age of only eighteen fought at the Battle of Bunker Hill in 1775. On his return to England, he settled in London and Lord Napier helped him to secure a job as a clerk in the Navy Pay Office at Somerset Place with a salary of £75 per year. By now Francis was signing himself Johnston, and it is thought to have been a custom of the time that Johnstones who left the Lowlands of Scotland dropped the 'e' from the end of their name.

Francis Johnston and his wife Elizabeth had seven sons and two daughters. Their fourth son was Brian's great-grandfather Edward, who was born in 1804 and was the founder of the Johnston family fortunes. At the age of seventeen Edward went to Brazil, where he married Henriette Moke, the daughter of a Dutch coffee plantation owner. In 1842 he founded his own company, Edward Johnston & Co., to export coffee from Brazil. The company flourished, and within a decade they had offices in Rio de Janeiro, Bahia, Liverpool, New York and New Orleans.

Edward Johnston moved back to England, and in 1862 he established a new head office for the business in the City of London. He had a large family of thirteen children, and his sixth son was Reginald Eden Johnston, Brian's grandfather, who was born in 1847. When Edward died, Reginald and his elder brother Charles took over the running of the company and expanded it even further. Reginald developed his own reputation in the City and went on to become chairman of two insurance companies, Guardian and Thames & Marine, as well as being as a director of the Bank of England from 1893 to 1909. He was also a Justice of the Peace.

The pinnacle of his career was when he was appointed Governor of the Bank of England in 1909, a post he held for two years. The Bank's historian, R. S. Sayers, has described Reginald as having 'considerable personality and experience'. His business mind and warm personality were said to be exceptional.

Reginald Johnston married Alice Eyres, daughter of the Reverend Charles Eyres, and they had four sons and three daughters. Their eldest son was Brian's father, Charles Evelyn Johnston, who followed his father Reginald to Eton College and New College, Oxford. He was a keen oarsman and rowed in the University Boat Race in 1899 and 1900. Unfortunately Cambridge won in both years, and in the latter year by the all-time winning margin of twenty lengths.

As the eldest son, Charles was expected to follow his father into the family business, and went to Brazil to learn about coffee before becoming a partner in E. Johnston & Co. In 1905 he married Pleasance Alt, the youngest daughter of Colonel William and Elizabeth Alt. The Alts were a well-established upper-middle-class family whose members included various explorers, academics and military officers.

Charles and Pleasance had four children, Anne (born in 1907), Michael (1908), Christopher (1910) and Brian Alexander, who was born on 24 June 1912 at the Old Rectory, Little Berkhamsted, in Hertfordshire. Brian was named after his mother's elder brother, Brian Alt, who had been killed in the Boer War. His second name, Alexander, was possibly taken from his godfather, Francis Alexander Johnston, who was known by the family as Cousin Alex. He was a happy child. In his baby book, Brian's mother wrote: 'He laughed at a fortnight.'

A year after Brian was born the family moved to an elegant Queen Anne house called Little Offley, near the village of Offley, about halfway between Hitchin and Luton. It had a farm of about 400 acres and a large garden, and Brian's elder brother Christopher remembers it as 'heaven'.

In his autobiography *It's Been a Lot of Fun* Brian admitted to having 'only vague recollections' of his early childhood. He recalled having to walk one and a half miles to church and one and a half miles back every Sunday. They would leave their Sealyham terrier in the little village post office and pick him up, along with the Sunday papers, on the way home. The boys had to wear sailor suits, and if they didn't giggle during the sermon they were rewarded by being given sticky brown meringues for lunch. Otherwise the family's main form of transport was by dog cart or pony-trap, pulled by a temperamental pony called Raffles, who sometimes refused to move and on one occasion tipped them all out on to the ground.

One of the big treats was when the children were taken to stand on the platform at Hitchin station to watch the Flying Scotsman go thundering through, with huge clouds of steam belching from its funnel.

Little Offley was a working farm, and Brian was brought up among animals. There were pigs and cows and bulls and two big farm horses called Boxer and Beauty who used to pull the farm wagon. Brian used to look forward to the harvest, when an enormous steam engine would arrive hauling the threshing machine. One year, when he was six years old, he fell off the top of the haycart and suffered severe bruising to his shin. The doctor diagnosed it as periostitis – the bruising of the membrane around the bone. X-rays were still in the early stages of development, so when he had his leg X-rayed at a medical facility all the doctors crowded round because they had never seen one before.

Not long after Brian's second birthday, war was declared against Germany and his father was mobilised as a Territorial officer. For the next four years Brian hardly saw his father except on the few occasions when he was allowed home on leave.

Charles Johnston had a heroic but tough war. His youngest brother Geoffrey was killed at Ypres in 1915. Charles served in the 7th London Regiment of the Territorial Army and rose swiftly to the rank of Lieutenant Colonel, an indication both of his ability and the number of casualties among the senior officers in the trenches. He was awarded the Distinguished Service Order and the Military Cross. His DSO was given for: 'Conspicuous gallantry in action. Under heavy machine-gun fire he personally reorganised his battalion with stragglers from other units, and when all his Officers had become casualties, he went forward himself and dealt with any remaining nests of machine guns. He displayed great coolness and composure under intense fire, and his example had an excellent effect on his men.'

Back home the war passed uneventfully, apart from a bomb being dropped by a Zeppelin near Hitchin, about three miles away. Brian was taken to see the hole, but the only casualty was a chicken. It might have come in handy because, although they lived on a farm, there was strict rationing in force during the war and Brian's mother insisted that they stick to the rules. They had to eat maize bread and maize pudding, and instead of lettuce they used dandelions, which they grew under inverted flower pots. Finally the Great War ended and Brian watched a victory torchlight procession through the village.

His father came home to find the family business in danger of collapse. On top of that the farm was also losing money. Lieutenant Colonel Johnston had to work long hours at his office in the City to keep his company afloat. He owned a house in St James's Court where he resided during the week and saw his family only at weekends.

Meanwhile life returned almost to normal for Brian at Little Offley. His two brothers went off to boarding school at Temple Grove in Eastbourne, but Anne stayed at home and shared a succession of governesses with Brian. Christopher says it was Anne who was responsible for the high turnover of about two or three governesses a year.

Their standard of living improved considerably after the war. The dog cart and pony-trap were replaced by two cars – a two-seater Ford, one of the original Tin Lizzies, which took his father to the station, and a coach-built Fiat Landerlette, which went at the then unheard-of speed of 52 mph. There was a chauffeur called Wakefield, a cook, housemaid, parlourmaid, 'tweeny', groom, a gardener and his boy, and a butler, who used to get drunk and 'was lovely to watch as he swayed in with the vegetables'. I mentioned to Chris that this seemed to be a very large staff, but he reminded me that wages were so low in those days that it was possible for someone with an annual income of only £1,000 to staff a house and raise a family and still have some change.

Life at Little Offley may have been very comfortable but for most of the time that the Johnstons lived there the house had only gas lighting and no electricity. In one of only a handful of his letters to survive, Brian's father wrote to him in February 1922: 'The men are busy putting in the electric light and I believe they hope to have it working by next Sunday in the house but not in the outbuildings. I am having it put in the stables and cowhouses as well.'

Occasionally Brian would be taken to visit his grandfather Reginald at Terlings Park (which they pronounced Tarlings), his large Victorian mansion with thirty-seven acres at Gilston in Hertfordshire, a few miles from Harlow. The retired City banker lived in some style and employed a large staff which included a butler called Morgiste Ottea – pronounced Otter – who was a local legend. According to Christopher Johnston, Ottea had been found as a baby in a burned-out West African coastal village by the crew of a Royal Navy ship. They had brought him back to England, where he grew up to be a coachman in London before he came to the attention of Reginald Johnston.

After Reginald hired him to be his butler, Ottea worked at

Terlings for the rest of his life. He was probably the first black man that most of the family, including Brian, had ever seen, and Brian remembered being waited on at table by Ottea wearing immaculate white gloves.

Brian related how one day someone rang the local otter hunt and told them that there was an 'otter' up at the big house. The hunt duly turned up at Terlings and were rather taken aback when Ottea answered the door and asked whether he could help them. Ottea married a local girl and was respected by all who knew him. When he died the whole village turned out for his funeral.

Brian's cousin Margaret Blyth (née Edwardes-Jones) said that whenever her family drove through the gates at Terlings the staff at the lodge would come out and curtsy. The Edwardes-Joneses were not quite as well off as their Johnston cousins and were not used to this kind of treatment. The River Stort ran through the grounds and Margaret said her grandfather used to row her in a boat up and down a moat at the back of the house. 'I wasn't afraid of him,' she confided, 'so he loved me.' His grandchildren called him GrannyPa and Christopher describes him as being a serious man, which is only to have been expected of an Edwardian gentleman in his position, but he was 'very genial and very kind'.

In May 1921, when Brian was eight and three-quarters, this idyllic childhood came to an abrupt end. It was time for him to leave home and join his brothers at Temple Grove School.

2

Tragedy at Bude

I asked Christopher Johnston why his father chose to send Brian and his brothers to Temple Grove School, and he thought it must have been because the school had a good record of sending boys on to Eton. Temple Grove was founded in 1810, and was said to be the oldest preparatory school in the country. It was in Eastbourne, near to the old Saffrons cricket ground, and the school buildings were rather rambling, with narrow staircases and dark corridors, and in a poor state of decoration.

The boys were certainly not sent there for the food. Chris described it as 'filthy' and said his father was appalled by the quality of the food when he came to visit his sons. 'I suppose it was all right before it was cooked,' muttered Chris, 'but it was certainly not enough!' Brian used to wolf his food down at tremendous speed which he always blamed on having to be first in the queue for second helpings.

The family used to send Brian food parcels from the farm containing items like butter, Marmite, biscuits and cakes, which were devoured the moment they were opened. Marmite had recently come on the market and was very popular. Almost every boy had his own pot labelled with his name. Brian loved Marmite, which he pronounced in the old-fashioned way as 'Marmeet', and used to have it with everything.

An official report into the quality of the school food concluded that everything was done for the benefit of the masters and very little for the boys. Parents sent their sons back to school each term with huge quantities of jam, usually about a dozen two-pound pots per term, which was shared out among the other boys on their table at teatime. Any birthday cakes would also be divided among the boys. One of the most famous cakes was received during Brian's first year at Temple Grove in 1921 by Gaekwar major, who later became the Maharaja of Baroda. It was alleged to have been about two feet in diameter. The fees were less than £50 a term, and Chris feels that it might have been better if the school had charged a little more money and improved the quality and quantity of the food.

The headmaster was the Reverend Harry Waterfield, known by all the boys as Bug, and his wife was Dame Bug. She was not in good health and possibly suffered from arthritis, because she used to walk bent forward nearly parallel to the ground.

While Brian was at Temple Grove Waterfield was hit in the eye by a ball during a game of racquets in the school holidays. He lost the sight of one eye, and one of Brian's earliest jokes was:

'Do you know that Bug has a glass eye?'

'No, how do you know?'

'Oh, it came out in the conversation!'

He was still telling that joke in his one-man show, 'An Evening with Johnners', more than seventy years later.

Brian was always puzzled as to how Waterfield came to be known as Bug, but while searching through the school archives I discovered he was originally called Waterbug. Other masters had equally colourful nicknames, such as Buffer, Bowler, Burbug, Helgy, Doodah and Daddy Sharp.

Brian described Temple Grove as 'a pretty tough school', and his brother Chris remembers it as 'hard'. Brian was teased about the size of his nose and called 'Beaky' by the other boys. He was also subject to 'the usual amount of petty bullying'. As if all that weren't bad enough the new boys had to take part in an initiation ceremony in which they had to sing or recite something in front of the senior boys. If they failed to please they were hit hard on the head with a heavy book by a prefect standing behind them.

There was certainly a lot of physical punishment. Waterfield kept a collection of canes under the settee in his study, including a thick, short cane 'which looked like a rhinoceros whip'. Brian was once given two of the best and 'my goodness it hurt'. During the summer term the boys used to swim naked in the outdoor swimming pool and several of them would display black and blue stripes on their bottoms as a result of being 'swished' by the headmaster. Remarkably Brian described Waterfield as being 'a kindly man', and he seems to have been liked and respected by the boys.

It was during Brian's second year at the school that something happened which was to change his life for ever. Every summer the Johnstons used to spend their holidays at Bude in North Cornwall. It was a family tradition. Brian's grandmother had gone there for her summer holidays, and after the war ended his mother carried on with the custom. Every year she would rent the same house, belonging to a Mrs Curtis at number 15 Flexbury Road. The Johnstons were obviously creatures of habit. Chris Johnston says that when he was grown up he took his own children to Bude, and more recently his daughter took her children there too.

To the outsider Bude can appear a little bleak and uninviting. It has a rugged coastline and is exposed to the winds coming in off the Atlantic. The sea is often very rough. But the Johnston children loved it. They used to travel down on the Atlantic Coast Express, carrying white mice in tins with them on the train. Once on the beach they would 'dig trails, tunnels and bridges in the sand and then let the mice loose', and large crowds would gather to watch the free show. There were rock pools in which to go crabbing and saffron buns or cake to eat after bathing. In the afternoons they would be taken by a wagonette drawn by two horses to one of the local beauty spots for tea, which always finished with their favourite – splits and cream.

During the summer of 1922, when Brian was ten years old, his father had been spending time with the family on holiday. He was due to return to work in London on Sunday, 27 August. But on the Sunday morning the weather was so pleasant that the colonel decided to stay on for an extra day and the family organised a picnic excursion to Widemouth Bay, a few miles south of Bude. They were quite a large party: as well as Lieutenant Colonel and Mrs Johnston, their daughter Anne and two younger sons, there was Lieutenant Colonel Marcus Scully, an old army friend of Colonel Johnston's; a cousin, Lieutenant Walter Eyres, RN; Paymaster-Lieutenant Barclay and Captain Leame; two more cousins, Sheila and Dodo Annesley; and another boy, possibly named Anderson, who was staying at a house near them.

At about 4.30 in the afternoon they decided to go for a swim. Before they went in the colonel warned Lieutenant Barclay not to go out of his depth. The currents were very strong and Barclay had not bathed in English waters for some years. It was low tide and the sea was on the turn. They waded about 150 yards out to the west of a ridge of rocks, behind which they undressed.

After Marcus Scully had been in the sea for about ten minutes he came out, and had nearly dressed when Captain Leame came running up to him and shouted, 'They can't get back!' Anne Johnston and one of the Annesley girls, probably Dodo, were out of their depth and appeared to be in great difficulties. Scully had been badly wounded in the war and according to Chris 'his stomach was full of shrapnel', but he removed his clothes again and went back into the water.

Meanwhile Walter Eyres, who was the farthest out of the swimmers, noticed Anne Johnston close to him. She told him she could not get back, but she could still swim and did not appear frightened. It was only when Eyres looked back at the beach that he realised they were being carried out to sea, so he took Anne's hand and they started swimming back together.

Soon afterwards Anne's father, the colonel, came alongside them and told Anne to put her hands on each of their shoulders. The three of them started swimming together towards the shore, but the waves were getting rougher. The colonel lost touch with them and started to drift away. Eyres struggled on with Anne and they caught up with Lieutenant Barclay, who tried to help them, but he was exhausted. After a couple of minutes he too began to fall behind, so Eyres carried on with Anne until he was able to hand her over to the Annesley girl, who was now in her depth.

After that Walter Eyres had to stand for a minute to catch his breath, but then he went back in with Marcus Scully to try to rescue Barclay. On the beach there was a life-saving rope on a wheel and they struggled to undo it. Then they discovered that it was too short, so they tied two ends of rope together and, taking one end, Scully swam out with Eyres to rescue Barclay. The rope was still several yards too short. Those behind in the shallows hauled on the rope and pulled Scully under the water. He lost the rope. When he grabbed hold of it again he shouted, 'Don't pull!' but they misheard him and dragged him under again. By now Scully's war wounds were hurting him so much that he was doubled up in pain and was unable to continue. Meanwhile Eyres had managed to rescue Lieutenant Barclay, who was so battered by the sea and the rocks that he had to be taken to Stratton Cottage Hospital.

Only now did they begin to look for Lieutenant Colonel Johnston. At first they could not find him, but then they spotted him well out to sea. He appeared to be swimming, but the waves were getting higher and they kept losing sight of him. Eyres tried to reach him with the rope by climbing over the rocks but the surf made it impossible. The rescuers hoped that, as he was still swimming, they might be able to catch him farther to the north. But, as Brian and Chris watched helplessly with their mother on the beach, the colonel was slowly carried away out of their sight.

His body was recovered farther along the coast the next day.

The headline in the *Western Morning News and Mercury* read: COL. JOHNSON'S (sic) BRAVE SACRIFICE.

The coroner's verdict was that he had accidentally drowned while bathing. He continued, 'I shall try and get a notice board fixed on the Marhamchurch end of Widemouth Bay warning people that it is very dangerous to bathe at low water.'

At the inquest Lieutenant Eyres said: 'I think [the colonel] was feeling bad when he left me, but he dropped silently behind us to save us from embarrassment, as I think he realised the danger more than we did.'

Lieutenant Barclay added: 'I consider that he must have realised the danger of the situation but on account of the others he kept quiet.'

The implication was that the colonel realised the seriousness of the situation they were all in. He felt himself tiring and rather than risk hindering the safe return of his daughter to the shore, he let go. In other words he sacrificed himself in order to save Anne. In a letter written to Brian's grief-stricken grandfather after the inquest, Walter Eyres declared: 'The only consolation in the whole terrible business is that Charlie couldn't have died a finer death.'

Curiously, in his autobiography Brian described a completely different sequence of events: 'A friend of the family named Marcus Scully, who had been badly wounded in the war, got into difficulties. He was caught in the drag and slowly washed out to sea. In those days there were no beach guards or life-saving equipment so my father, who was a strong swimmer, went to the rescue but got caught himself in the strong current. Somehow Marcus was rescued by the other bathers but by the time they had helped him my father was washed right out to sea.'

Brian's cousin Margaret Blyth remarked that her mother Gaie, the colonel's elder sister, 'could never understand about the accident because Charlie was such a good swimmer'. He does appear to have kept swimming for quite some time, and it may be that the rescuers did not help him initially because they thought he would be able to save himself. Aunt Gaie blamed Anne for the whole affair and said she was always a bit of a show-off.

Christopher Johnston is the only survivor of that picnic party and he agrees that it was Anne and not Scully who originally got into difficulty. But the tragedy was never discussed by the family. It was painful enough for Anne and her brothers that they had lost their father in such devastating circumstances. If they had pointed the finger of blame at Anne, Chris feels that she would have been unable to live with the weight of her guilt.

One unusual aspect of the inquest was the statement by Lieutenant Barclay, who said that he had requested to give evidence 'because of the number of quaint rumours which appeared to be in circulation'. It was not specified what those rumours were, but it has been suggested that Brian's mother and Marcus Scully were more than just friends at the time of the drowning and that perhaps

Scully did not try as hard as he might have done to rescue the colonel.

Chris Johnston thinks it unlikely. He says he was too young at the time to have noticed whether anything was going on between Scully and his mother, and the fact that she married Scully a year later provides no proof. The evidence offered at the inquest seems to indicate that everything possible was done to save the colonel, and Brian himself always believed that his mother married Scully because she wanted help in bringing up her four children. That has a ring of truth about it, and it would seem to be borne out by subsequent events.

Phyllis Welch lived as a child at 'Salthouse', a tearoom overlooking Widemouth Bay, where her mother prepared the teas. More than fifty years later Phyllis contacted Brian after she had recognised his face in a photograph. 'I often wondered if you were the son of Colonel and Mrs Johnston,' she wrote, 'and when I saw a photograph of you I was sure. You look so like your mother as I remember her.'

On the day of the tragedy the Johnstons had ordered a tea for eighteen people, which had been laid out for them on a long trestle table on the cliff in front of the house. 'How well I remember that day,' continued Phyllis. 'I also was ten years old then, but the one thing that stands out clearly is a mental picture of your poor mother sitting, for what seemed to me hours, on a little bank that runs out to the cliff edge just north of Salthouse. There she sat just gazing out to sea, long after her husband had disappeared.'

Brian never talked about his father. One can only imagine what he felt when he realised he would never see him again. The sense of loss must have been compounded by the fact that he never really had a chance to get to know him. When Brian was only two years old his father had gone off to fight in the Great War, and by the time he returned home four years later he was almost a complete stranger. After the war the colonel had been forced to spend long hours working in the City in order to save his business. So Brian had hardly ever seen his father.

The colonel's nickname at Oxford had been Johnno, which

suggests someone who was well liked and had a good sense of humour. But a photograph taken of him in uniform during the war shows a serious-looking man with a clipped military moustache. Chris says that his father was badly affected by his experiences during the war and the memory of it haunted him. After his death, his business colleagues said that 'he applied an austere diligence with a very high sense of duty'. Brian remembered his father as being kind, quiet and a fairly strict disciplinarian, who believed that little boys should be seen and not heard. Although, as Brian commented, even in those days he found that a bit difficult.

I was curious as to how his father would have reacted to Brian's wish to be an actor. Chris doesn't think the colonel would have approved. But if he had not drowned, the family circumstances would have been completely different. Chris had enormous respect for his father and believes he would have followed him into the family business, which would have left Brian free to pursue his own career. The business would eventually have recovered and they would have continued to live at Little Offley.

But now everything changed. The colonel's surviving younger brother Hamil Johnston was appointed as trustee of his estate and also Brian's legal guardian. There was enough money in the estate to pay for school fees but not enough to maintain their way of life. Little Offley had to be sold, and Chris recalls that he wept when they finally had to leave. He thinks it must have been extremely difficult for his mother to have to pack up all her belongings, sell her house and face the prospect of bringing up four children on her own. She rented a house near Weymouth called Upwey Manor, which was reputed to be haunted, and the family moved to Dorset to start a new life.

Then they received another blow. In November, three months after Charles's death, Brian's grandfather Reginald Johnston also died, at the age of seventy-five. His youngest son Geoffrey had been killed in the war, but his eldest son Charles had managed to survive. For Charles to drown in a senseless bathing accident only four years later was more than Reginald could bear. It was said that he died of a broken heart.

Reporting his death, the *Herts and Essex Observer* described Brian's grandfather as having been 'one of those great souls who does good by stealth. He was indeed the highest type of the "fine old English gentleman", one whose word was always to be relied upon, whose ear was ever open to the appeal of the necessitous and his purse ever open to alleviate their distress.'

In the space of three months Brian had lost his father, his grandfather, his childhood home and most of his financial security. He was still only ten years old. How he dealt with such an unexpected tragedy would shape his whole life and character. As the youngest son he naturally leaned on his mother for emotional support, but in many ways he was now on his own. From this moment on he seems to have been determined to put on a brave face, to be cheerful and to enjoy life while he could.

3

Temple Grove

Back at Temple Grove Brian had to put the loss of his father behind him. There would have been little sympathy for displays of emotion. He began to gain a reputation as a bit of a joker – one of his school reports complained that he was 'apt to be a buffoon'. Chris recalls that Brian was always cracking jokes, the cornier the better.

There were two elderly spinsters known as the Misses Beckwith who taught the piano and looked after the boys' pocket money. One of the sisters used to supervise the writing of letters home to parents every Sunday, and it was at Temple Grove that Brian got into the habit of writing to his mother almost every week.

The other sister played the organ in chapel, and Brian was often responsible for pumping the organ during the services. This involved sitting on a stool behind the organ and pumping a wooden handle so that a lead weight on a string stayed below a certain line. If it rose above the line it meant there was not enough air in the organ and no sound would come out. Sometimes Brian would stop pumping and watch with excitement as the lead slowly inched up towards the danger line. If he miscalculated, the organ would hiss into silence and Miss Beckwith would leap off her seat and glare around the corner, 'her eyes popping out against the glass of her pince-nez'.

Soon he graduated into the choir. John Crump used to sit in the front row of the congregation, a few feet away from Brian. 'The senior choirboy and leader during my first term was Brian Johnston,' he recalls, 'and I was most impressed with both his voice and his nose. It moved up and down slightly as he sang!'

Some of the other staff at Temple Grove sound like characters from a novel by Dickens. One of the masters, Mr Fritche, who was nicknamed 'Friddler', would knock boys hard on the head with his knuckles – painfully known as a Friddler Fotch – while Mr Bellamy preferred to use a heavy black ebony ruler. According to John Crump, who started at Temple Grove eight months after Brian in January 1922, one of the strictest masters was Mr Taylor – Taylorbug – who was very bad tempered and looked like a retired army major with a florid red face and white hair. He would make the boys in his class stand on benches in the middle of the room while he walked behind them brandishing a long narrow piece of wood sharpened to a point. If the boys on the bench did not answer his questions correctly he would give them a sharp jab in the backside. He also kept a cane under his desk, with which he would whack boys across the legs, until one day a boy called Corrie snatched the cane from him and broke it across his knee.

There was even a butler called Wilkins, who was responsible for the school post and for handing out the large number of comics, such as the *Boy's Own Paper*. He was always dressed in a tail coat, with striped trousers and a wing collar, and in the evenings he went round the school lighting the gas burners with a taper on a stick. This sometimes took him longer than usual when a gas mantle had to be replaced after suffering a direct hit from a pea-shooter.

Every night at about 9.30 'Bug', the headmaster, would make a tour of the boys' dormitories, smoking a pipe with rather strong tobacco and holding a large torch. He walked fast and very loudly and, as the boys could smell his pipe coming from afar, he usually found them 'asleep' when he shone his torch on them, which was presumably the intention.

The matron was called Katie Allen, known to the boys as 'Putty'. She had a club foot which caused her to walk with a limp. She also had strong forearms and a very loud voice, and could silence any noise in the dormitories with one shout of 'Will you be quiet on Underwood's!' She had a small 'cat's whisker' crystal set and introduced Brian to the joys of radio by allowing him to listen to it on her headphones.

The area behind the fives courts was the meeting place for

smoking sessions. The older boys would slip out of the school into the Old Town and buy cigarettes from a sweet shop known as 'Eighty-One'. They usually chose the cheapest brands such as Craven A, which were only sixpence for a packet of ten, but Brian smoked BDV, which were supposed to be especially mild. Later he confessed it was pure bravado because he hated the taste of the smoke. One day he noticed the matron smoking a BDV in a rather ostentatious manner, and when he searched his play-box he found that his cigarettes were missing. She never told the headmaster and Brian never smoked again.

Dame Bug, the headmaster's wife, used to help the matron out with medical matters. Boys were always coming to Putty with cuts and bruises, and Dame Bug's standard response was to instruct her to 'Paint him up, Katie', which meant that the poor victim had to have his wound painted over with the iodine brush. Iodine was used for almost everything and could be very painful on open cuts. Another of Putty's assistants was called Elizabeth. She had no voice and could speak only in a whisper. She supervised the boys' baths, but would always manage to raise her voice loud enough to insist strongly that the boys washed themselves 'halfway down'.

After Brian's death, the Temple Grove newsletter reported: 'Very little is recorded about Brian's academic progress, other than a comment in one report that "he talks too much in school".' A later comment was that 'he should take things more seriously'.

A lot of time at Temple Grove was spent cramming the boys to ensure that they passed their public school Common Entrance exams. But a Report of Inspection by the Board of Education published in 1930 heavily criticised the methods of teaching and the curriculum at the school: 'An excessive allowance of time is given to Latin ... it receives twelve periods out of a total of thirty-six.' The teaching of mathematics was described as 'uninspiring and tends to be mechanical', and in geography 'the equipment is meagre and in no class seen at work was any use made of wall-maps'.

It is perhaps not surprising that Brian preferred games to classes. It was at Temple Grove that he discovered his love of cricket. He vividly recalled the moment when his eldest brother Michael threw him a tennis ball one day and shouted: 'I'm Jack Hearne, you are Patsy Hendren.' From that moment on the Middlesex and England cricketer was Brian's hero and he had embarked on a lifelong passion for the summer game.

Brian began to develop an ability as a wicket-keeper. He had started to keep wicket, he admitted later, because he thought the hard ball would not hurt so much if he wore gloves, but when he was twelve he was good enough to be selected for the first eleven. The Temple Grove magazine in 1924 said of him: 'Kept wicket very successfully – a position which he should try to make his own. He is quick and watches the ball well, and is a great help to a slow bowler. If he perseveres he should be really good when he gets older. An eccentric bat and a bad judge of a run; he is, however, very keen and more than justified his inclusion.' Incidentally, the magazine also noted that on sports day that year Brian and his mother came first in the Mothers and Sons Race!

Two years older than Brian at Temple Grove was a boy called Bader minor, who excelled at all sports. He was a brilliant fly-half in the rugby fifteen and a dashing centre-forward in the soccer first eleven. His stocky figure and his head of black curly hair were a familiar sight as he dribbled the ball through the opposition defence. He was also a fine cricketer who scored a century in nearly every school match. This made him extremely popular with the other boys because, whenever he did so, the whole school was excused prep. Brian believed the young Bader was talented enough to have been a Test cricketer, if he had not lost both his legs in a plane crash after leaving school. He went on to achieve lasting fame for his courage and determination during the Second World War as fighter pilot Group Captain Sir Douglas Bader, DSO, DFC.

In 1925 Brian's cricket continued to make progress and he was described as: 'A very efficient wicket-keeper; he can take the ball well on both sides and has caught and stumped a good many victims. His batting has much improved, and when he can check his natural impatience better, he should make a lot of runs. A very useful member of any side, owing to his never failing keenness.' His top score was 32 against the Parents XI.

Brian was also turning out to be equally skilled at rugby, although he was never the most aggressive of players. Later he would recall: 'I could run quite fast and was an expert at selling the dummy. I wasn't too keen on tackling but somehow got away with it.' In the Rugger Notes for 1925 he was listed as being aged 12.8 and weighing 7 stone 1 lb: 'A wonderfully improved player with plenty of brains, works well with his partner and has played a good game throughout the season, his tackling being his weakest point. He should, however, make a useful stand-off half in the future.'

At the end of the winter term there was always a play or a variety show in which both boys and masters took part. In December 1923 Major Duffield-Jones presented a comic operetta in two acts entitled *The British Lion*. Brian played 'Clement Leipsic, editor and pirate'. The reviewer wrote: 'The acting and singing were good throughout.'

Major Duffield-Jones – 'Buffer' – was also in charge of the Cadet Corps. Squad drill was taken by Chief Petty Officer Crease, and Brian seems to have enjoyed it. In 1924 the Inspecting Officer reported: 'Platoon and Company Drill, under Sgt. Johnston and Sgt. Hampton, was excellent, distances and intervals being exceedingly well kept; marching was good, and the two sergeants showed a good knowledge of their work.'

The following year Colonel Mitford praised them again: 'Platoon Drill under Sergeant Johnston and Sergeant Hearn was very good . . . All the above NCOs knew their work well, had good words of command, and the Cadets worked very well under them.' I was surprised at Brian's apparent enthusiasm for the Cadet Corps and especially drill, but at that time the Great War was still a recent memory. Brian's father the colonel had been a twice-decorated war hero, and after his father's death in 1922 Brian may have taken a certain amount of pride in honouring his memory by joining the Corps, and symbolically following in his footsteps.

Brian also became quite a good rifle shot. In 1925 he was

awarded his shooting colours, and he was a member of the second shooting eight. Rifle practice was carried out under the guidance of CPO Crease. The shooting range ran along the high flint wall at the end of the playing field, and there was a golf course on the other side of the road. One year a human skeleton was discovered in the corner of the field by the rifle range, but it is not believed to have had any connection with Brian's target practice.

One of the main punishments at Temple Grove was extra drill, which was also supervised by CPO Crease and involved marching or walking round the cobbled quadrangle. The difference was that the boys had to carry a cast-iron dumb-bell in each hand and hold it above their heads. In the winter, when it was cold, the boys were not allowed to wear gloves, so the frozen dumb-bells would burn their fingers until they were warmed up.

At the end of the summer term in 1925 Brian was thirteen, and because of the financial circumstances prevailing after his father's death it was hoped that he would be able to get a scholarship to Eton College. Waterfield duly took him up to Eton, where he struggled for two days with the examination papers. He failed to gain a scholarship and was forced to take the Common Entrance exam. This time he passed, to everyone's relief, but he achieved only Middle Fourth – the third-bottom form.

Before Brian left, Bug had one final task to perform – to explain to him the facts of life. This talk was known as a pi-jaw. I remember my prep school headmaster warning me before I went to Eton that some of the older boys might want to 'play' with me, but I was to have nothing to do with them. I had no idea what he was talking about, but I thought it seemed a little unfair.

Brian fared no better. Bug asked him whether he knew where babies came from.

'No, sir,' said Brian, looking innocent. He was.

'Well,' said Bug, 'you know the hole that women have in front?'

Brian remembered seeing his sister's navel in the bath at home and replied, 'Yes, sir.'

'Well, that's where they come from,' said Bug, looking relieved.

'Goodbye, thanks for what you have done for us and good luck at Eton.' And that was that. It is hardly surprising that Brian had a slightly confused attitude towards the opposite sex for several years to come.

Brian finished at Temple Grove as a school prefect and a leading member of the cricket and rugby teams. More interestingly he had acquired a nickname – the Voice – not, as he admitted, because of its beauty but because of its constant use. He said later that he managed to enjoy himself for 'most' of his four years at Temple Grove. But he would describe the next five years as among the happiest of his life.

4

Floreat Etona

For some Old Etonians their schooldays were among the best days of their life. For others they were more like a nightmare. I confess that for me it was the latter. But Eton College was the perfect school for Brian. His elder brothers Michael and Christopher had already gone on from Temple Grove to Eton in the house of R. H. de Montmorency, known as 'Monty', at Coleridge House in Keates Lane.

The eldest brother, Michael, had a difficult and unhappy time at Eton, and Chris thinks now that he might have suffered from dyslexia, which was not understood in those days. Whatever the reason, it was decided that Michael would leave Eton early, and in September 1925 he went to study at a crammer.

Normally each boy at Eton is allocated his own room, but the tradition in those days was that two brothers would share, so Brian, or Johnston minor as he was now known, was placed in a room with his brother Chris. The rooms were fairly small and all contained the same basic furniture: a burry or bureau, a table, a Windsor chair and a wicker armchair, an ottoman, a washstand and a bed which folded up against the wall during the day. The ottoman was a low oblong box with a padded top on which to sit. It contained all the boys' dirty games clothes, usually caked in mud and sweat, and an assortment of smelly socks. If mine was anything to go by, after a few weeks it took a brave man to open the lid without having to gasp for breath.

R. H. de Montmorency was described by Brian as 'a kind and friendly man' who had got Blues for both golf and cricket when he was up at Oxford. He was married with two daughters, and thirty years later his younger daughter Ann would reappear in

Brian's life when she married his BBC colleague E. W. (Jim) Swanton.

Coleridge House was one of the older Eton buildings, having been built in 1826, and it was actually demolished three years after Brian left. It was 'an absolute rabbit warren', according to Brian, and there was only one bathroom for the forty boys in the house. Each boy was allowed ten minutes in the bath once a week, which was strictly timed by one of the senior boys, known as the KCB or Knight Commander of the Bath. During the winter months the boys would usually be covered in mud after an energetic game of football, so they would have to wash themselves in a tin bath in their room. Filling it wasn't too difficult but tipping the dirty water out again afterwards could cause quite a problem.

There was no central heating and each room had a small coal fire. But the boys were allowed to light a fire only on three days a week plus Sunday, which meant that on the other days they virtually froze. So two or three boys would 'mess' together and meet for tea each afternoon, and would choose the room which had the fire on that day.

Discipline was enforced by the senior boys in each house, known as the Library, and the Captain of the House was allowed to beat boys for any serious infringements of the rules. Some boys took advantage of this, and I remember being hauled up before the Library for 'looking cool'. More serious misbehaviour was dealt with by the Lower Master or the Head Master. The worst punishment was to be 'swiped' with a bundle of sharp birch twigs, which I can assure you was extremely painful. As if that weren't humiliating enough, the price of the battered birch was then added to your bill at the end of the term – literally a case of adding insult to injury!

The Head Master while Brian was at Eton was Dr Cyril Alington, 'a distinguished grey-haired figure with an imposing presence, greatly respected by the boys'. He was famous for his Sunday evening sermons in College Chapel and was Chaplain to the King from 1921 to 1933. Later he became the Dean of Durham and, surprisingly, was also a keen writer of detective stories. Brian became very friendly with his daughter Elizabeth. So friendly, in fact, that his great friend William Douglas Home used to claim that Brian and Elizabeth were engaged for a short time while he was at Eton, although Brian later denied it. According to William, Brian told him that he was in the rhododendrons with Elizabeth one Sunday morning when Dr Alington walked by in his surplice on his way to chapel and said: 'Come out of there, Elizabeth, you can do better than that!' As it happened, she did, because in 1936 she married William's elder brother Lord Dunglass, later to become the Conservative Prime Minister Sir Alec Douglas-Home.

At the beginning of 1927 Monty retired as a housemaster and he was succeeded by A. C. Huson, an old Wykehamist who had once made a hundred against Eton. He had red hair and a face that was almost completely purple, said to be caused by having one skin less than everyone else. He was a bachelor with a great sense of humour, and he appears to have become a kind of father figure to Brian. Later Brian would say that he owed Huson 'as big a debt as anyone else in my life' and described him as being 'as near the perfect housemaster as could be'.

Brian's favourite master, or 'beak' as they were called at Eton, was G. W. 'Tuppy' Headlam, who taught him history. One of the reasons Brian liked Headlam was because he was a very witty man who also enjoyed a good joke in others. One day Brian discovered the secret of comic timing. Tuppy was discussing the wives of an historical figure called Henry.

'His first wife died,' said Tuppy, 'and now let's talk about his second one, Henrietta.'

'Did he really?' said Brian, as quick as flash from the back of the classroom. It got a huge laugh and Brian learned a valuable lesson: however bad a joke or pun, if it is delivered at the right time it will usually raise a laugh.

When Brian first arrived at Eton there was a wonderfully eccentric biology master called M. D. Hill, who had been at the school since 1896. He had a faithful assistant in the science laboratories called Pendry, who would be required at a moment's notice to supply him with a frog's leg or a rabbit's tooth or even half a chicken. Pendry always seemed to be able to find what Hill needed and would emerge from the adjacent room a few seconds later clutching the required object.

One day Hill called out, 'Pendry! Bring me blood!'

'Blood, sir?'

'Yes, man, blood. Your blood, any blood. Bring me BLOOD, Pendry!'

After a short but dramatic pause, blood, though whose they never discovered, was duly brought.

By now Brian's domestic circumstances had changed considerably. In 1924 his mother Pleasance had married Marcus Scully, the man who had tried to rescue her husband little more than a year earlier. Pleasance was still only forty-four and Chris Johnston believes that she sacrificed her own happiness in order to provide security for her children. Chris says he never saw any sign of affection between them. 'A woman widowed that young needed help,' he explained, 'but they were different people. Marcus liked hunting, shooting and fishing, and she didn't. She loved her gardening.'

The family moved to a new house at Moreton, near Dorchester. Brian loved it there because, during the summer holidays, the boys had a tutor called Mr Grover, who used to take Brian to cricket matches on the back of his motorcycle. But it didn't suit Marcus Scully, 'a charming but irascible Irishman'. He missed his country pursuits, so at the end of 1924 they moved again to the small village of Much Marcle, in Herefordshire. They rented a large old Jacobean house called Hellens, where they stayed for the next four years. Among its former residents were said to have been the Black Prince and Bloody Mary.

Gradually life began to return to normal. Marcus did not interfere in the bringing up of the children; he left that largely to Pleasance. They had a gardener and a cook, called Mr and Mrs Powell, and a groom called Dean, who had enormous ears which he could tuck in.

Chris recalls 'an amusing game' that they used to play at Hellens. On bank holidays, when there was more traffic than usual, they would take their old bull-nosed Morris car and park it on the verge outside the lodge gates. Then they would make Anne lie down on the grass with tomato ketchup splashed over her face and arms. A large number of people would stop their cars to ask whether they could help and, according to Chris, the 'accident' always worked.

There was village cricket in the summer and a trip to the local parish church every Sunday. The 'splendid' village parson was the Reverend Duncan. After he had been at Much Marcle for a short time one of his lady parishioners told him, 'Until you came here, Vicar, we didn't know what real sin was!' Brian's mother ran the local Mothers' Union and the Women's Institute, and during the holidays the children took part in activities at the local village hall. One year in the annual village concert they performed in a sketch called *George's Ghost*, and Brian accidentally set fire to his brother Michael's fake moustache, which produced gales of laughter from the audience. They even formed a family jazz band with Pleasance on the piano.

Brian was beginning to develop a strong interest in the theatre. It had started in 1921 when he was nine years old, and was staying in London with his mother's elder sister Nancy and her husband Colonel Freddie Browning at their house in Lowndes Street. One night they held a bridge party at which one of the guests was the famous opera singer Dame Clara Butt. When it became her turn to be dummy she asked the butler, Ford, to telephone the Royalty Theatre in London's West End, where the Co-optimists were appearing. The show was a pierrot revue starring Laddie Cliff, Stanley Holloway and Phyllis Monkman, and according to Brian in those days it was possible to call up a theatre on the phone and listen to what was happening on stage. When Dame Clara was connected, she sat listening to the Co-optimists singing the Canadian folk song 'Alouette'. Then she passed the receiver over to Brian and at the end of the song he was able to hear a tremendous round of applause from the audience and shouts of 'Encore!' He was thrilled by the exciting atmosphere coming down the line and became hooked on the idea of the theatre from that moment on.

When he was fifteen and at Eton, Aunt Nancy took him to see his first West End play, *Interference*, starring Gerald du Maurier, at the St James's Theatre. Brian was fascinated by du Maurier's apparently effortless acting, but much more to his taste was their next theatre outing, to see Fred and Adele Astaire in the classic George and Ira Gershwin musical *Funny Face*. This was more like it!

During the remainder of his time at Eton, before he took the train back to school at the beginning of each half (as terms are known at Eton), Brian would use part of his journey money to buy a seat in the stalls at the latest musical, revue or comedy, especially the Ben Travers farces at the Aldwych, starring Ralph Lynn and Tom Walls. He had discovered the two great passions of his life – cricket and the theatre.

Back at school Brian was once again an enthusiastic member of the cadet corps, known as the Eton College Officer Training Corps (ECOTC). There was no conscription and boys were under no obligation to sign up to the corps, but it was obviously encouraged, and most boys joined when they were about fifteen. They had their own song which was sung to the tune of 'Old King Cole' and ended with the words:

> There's none so fair
> As can compare
> With the ECOTC.

The corps was divided into sections with the boys from one house forming one section. Some houses took the corps more seriously than others. Bernard Fergusson entered Eton a year before Brian and in his book *Eton Portrait* he recalled one house section with more than its fair share of would-be jokers (could it possibly have been Brian's?). They tried to get a rise out of the staff sergeant by 'numbering' down the rank: '. . . nine, ten, knave, queen, king, ace'. The staff sergeant had seen it all before and didn't bat an eyelid. Instead he swiftly gave the order: 'Remainder, stand fast. Court cards, double . . . march!'

Field days took place two or three times per half and were considered to be great fun. One gets the impression that they were not always taken as seriously as intended. After a field day during Brian's first half the *Eton College Chronicle* announced: 'The editors wish to apologise for the inadequacy of the following account. Unfortunately our special war correspondent fell into the hands of the enemy while disguised as a sheep.' The captive correspondent apparently took it upon himself to eat all his notes, but he was later reported to be well on the road to recovery.

In October 1929, when Brian was a lance corporal in the corps, he wrote to his mother: 'On Tuesday we had a Field Day, during which we got soaked, as it simply pelted the whole time; I was in charge of a rifle section, and charged on every possible occasion with great vigour and success: it was evidently all contrary to military tactics. Still great fun . . .'

In spite of Brian's rather over-enthusiastic approach to soldiering, or maybe because of it, he rose through the ranks to become a sergeant and then a cadet officer, which he was pleased to learn meant he was allowed to wear a belt and 'rather a nice sword'. In June 1930 the corps went up to Windsor Castle to be presented with their new colours by King George V. Brian arrived at the castle early before the rest of the corps and was delighted to see through one of the windows the King being fitted with his belt. It was a very important occasion for the boys, and for the school, and the corps obviously performed very well because they were all awarded an extra week's holiday.

In a habit that he had acquired at Temple Grove, Brian used to write a letter to his mother every Sunday, except that now they were addressed to 'Dear Mummy & Marcus'. Food seemed to play an important part in his school life. After he had been back home for one half-term, or Long Leave as it was known, he thanked her for sending them back with a hamper: 'Chris took the rabbit pie and I the pheasant, which I had roasted at Rowlands [the school tuck shop] and sent up for tea.'

His mother used to send him pots of clotted cream, although they did not always reach him. 'Thanks very much for cream,' he wrote in March 1929, 'though I think [it] must have been pinched by someone as I saw it on the slab when I wasn't going upstairs; however when I went to get it on my way up, the cream had gone: it will probably turn up.' (It didn't.)

Brian's letters from Eton also reveal an early interest in cakes. In November 1928 he requested: 'If Mrs Powell happens to have a spare bit of flour, currants, etc, she might make me a bit of cake: it is always so welcome.'

A year later he was still hungry: 'Thanks very much for the very good cake: can it be chocolate next time?'

5

Most Popular Boy

Sport at Eton played a vitally important role. During the summer boys had to choose between being a dry bob (cricket) or a wet bob (rowing). In the winter everyone had to play the Eton Field Game, and in the spring there was a choice of rugby or soccer, although in those days most boys preferred rugby.

The Field Game is unique to Eton and is a combination of soccer and rugby. The ball is smaller than a soccer ball and you may only handle it to put it into the 'bully' or scrum, or touch it down to score a 'rouge' or try. When Brian was at Eton the Field Game was played in the winter half, and nothing was taken more seriously than the inter-house Field matches, where sporting reputations were made or lost.

As Brian grew older and stronger he discovered that he could sprint quite fast over short distances. This proved to be an invaluable asset, and in October 1929, when he was seventeen, he was awarded his House Field colours. A year later, in October 1930, he was awarded his School Field colours first choice immediately after the opening match of the season, when Eton beat the Royal Military College 1–0. According to the *Chronicle*, 'Johnston at fly excelled himself.' In another Field match the *Chronicle* declared that there was 'none swifter than Johnston', and two days later: 'Fine running by Johnston [was one of] the features of this terrific game.'

He also enjoyed athletics whenever he could find the time. On the school sports day in March 1930 Mr Huson's house won their heat in the relay race. 'In the last heat', reported the *Chronicle* excitedly, 'Mr Slater's looked as if they would win until about three-quarters of the race had been run, when Mr Huson's made a great effort and Johnston won the race with a fine 220 yd sprint.' Unfortunately Huson's were disqualified in the final.

Between the wars Eton was an even more exclusive society than it is today, and while Brian was at the school sixty-four boys were either peers or sons of peers, so many of his friends were members of the aristocracy. With his ready wit and charm, Brian was a popular house guest, and he was invited several times to stay at Chirk Castle near Wrexham by John Scott-Ellis, who was the eldest son of Lord Howard de Walden. Christopher Johnston was also invited, and he recalled that Chirk Castle was so grand even the butler Harper had a footman. Lord Howard de Walden enjoyed staging a family pantomime every year at Christmas. He wrote them himself and took them quite seriously; he also wrote operas and plays and owned the Haymarket Theatre in London. In January 1928 Brian had a small part in *Puss and Brutes, or Cinderella Carabas: a 'crook' pantomime.*

One of the other house guests that Christmas was the celebrated French poet Hilaire Belloc, author of *Cautionary Tales* and *The Bad Child's Book of Beasts.* With his sombre clothes and elastic-sided boots he was sometimes mistaken for the butler, and was delighted when someone once tipped him ten shillings. At night Belloc was frequently spotted going up to bed with a bottle of the Howard de Waldens' best port tucked under his arm.

Another regular house guest at Chirk was the actress Phyllis Neilson-Terry, who used to visit Brian and John Scott-Ellis at Eton. She would have lunch with the boys and their housemaster A. C. Huson in his private dining room and then take them out to tea afterwards at Fullers. Huson had met Phyllis when they were both guests of the Howard de Waldens, and he was such an admirer of hers that he once asked her to cry especially for him.

She was not the only celebrity that Brian met at Eton. In January 1931 Brian was invited to have tea with the author and playwright Edgar Wallace. At that time it was estimated that one out of every four books read in England was written by Wallace, most of them thrillers. Brian wrote to his mother that Wallace was 'very good fun last Sunday; we showed him round Eton and he was very amusing. He has asked us all to go to his play [*Smoky Cell* at Wyndham's in the West End] and then supper afterwards, all at his expense, at the end of the half.' Unfortunately Edgar Wallace was taken ill a few weeks later and so the trip to the theatre was called off. He died in Hollywood the following year, aged only fifty-six.

On 5 March 1931 Charlie Chaplin made a private visit to the school. The silent-movie star was in Britain for a few days to promote his latest film, *City Lights*, and was given a tour of the college buildings before being entertained to tea at Rowlands, the school tuck shop. According to Brian 'the whole street was packed with cheering crowds', and Chaplin had to make a short speech from an upstairs window, telling the enormous gathering that he wished he could shake them all by the hand personally. Then, in the words of the *Windsor Slough and Eton Express*, 'After some difficulty Charlie regained his motor car and left for London.'

During Brian's last half at Eton in June 1931 the Prince of Wales came to talk about his recent tour of Argentina to the Eton College Political Society, of which Brian was a member. They met in the Vice-Provost's study, and Brian sat about a yard away from the Prince, later to be the Duke of Windsor, whom he described as 'very amusing, and wasn't at all nervous after the first five minutes, although he speaks with a nervous cough the whole time'.

Two days later King George V and Queen Mary came down from Windsor to attend the Sunday morning service in College Chapel. There was confusion and embarrassment at the end, when all the boys sat down while the King remained standing, and Brian was amused to see that the Queen had to borrow a penny from the Earl of Harewood to put into the collection.

Between the wars the Eton and Harrow cricket match at Lord's was one of the social occasions of the year, with crowds of up to ten thousand parading around the ground. The men and boys wore top hat and tails while the women all had new hats and dresses. In fact the first cricket match at Lord's that Brian ever watched was the Eton v. Harrow match in 1926.

He did not get into trouble often at Eton, but when Brian was seventeen in 1929 he was handed one of the worst punishments he could imagine. He was banned from attending the first morning's play of the Eton v. Harrow match. He wrote apologetically to his mother:

> This is the reason: last Thursday was wet in the afternoon, and as there was no cricket till 4.15, we all returned to m'tutors [Huson's house]. What were we to do? Four of us decided to have a jolly good mob. So unfortunately mob we did. We began to throw water at each other and then at a boy called Lebus. At this point, after Lebus was rather wetter than any one of us, m'tutor [Huson] arrived on the scene. He was furious, as there was a moderate amount of water about, and a smashed glass or two. He also objected to us throwing water at Lebus as, though he is only one division below us, he came a year after us, and m'tutor didn't like us throwing water at anyone out of our own 'circle' so to speak. At any rate he complained to the Head Beak of bad behaviour in the house, and the latter has kept us here till 12.30, me and three others. I am most terribly sorry, but I think it hits me quite hard, missing most of the cricket before lunch.

Brian loved his cricket but, even so, he could never take it seriously for too long. George Thorne was exactly a week younger than Brian and had entered Eton with him in September 1925. Each summer they played club cricket together as they progressed through the different levels, on grounds with names such as Lower Sixpenny, Upper Sixpenny, Lower Club and Upper Club.

Thorne was an opening bowler and probably bowled more balls at Brian than anyone else during his schooldays. According to Thorne, Brian was usually worth two extra wickets to him because he would pretend to encourage the batsmen from behind the stumps. 'Don't worry,' Brian would reassure an incoming batsman, 'Thorne's no good. He'll never get you out!' The batsman would relax, and a few balls later he would be clean bowled.

'There was never a dull moment with Brian playing,' chuckled Thorne. In 1931, during their first year at Oxford, the two of them played together in an Eton Ramblers match against Windsor House Park, who were mainly cricket-playing Eton masters. Thorne took six wickets in quick succession, all of them clean bowled. After the fourth wicket Brian called out, 'Can't you think of anything else to do? It's hard work picking up these stumps!'

Because of Brian's speed as a runner he would always go for a quick single and his fellow batsmen had to be on their toes. If a ball was going to the left hand of a right-handed fielder Brian would often shout, 'Come five!', which so confused the fielder that he would return the ball wildly and Brian would get overthrows.

On one occasion Brian was batting with a boy called the Earl of Hopetoun at the other end who was slightly overweight and not very fit. Brian hit a ball towards the boundary and yelled at his partner to run. By the time Hopetoun was turning to start his second run Brian had already completed two and they ran down the wicket together. Brian soon left him behind and by the time he had run four poor Hopetoun was still only halfway through his third. By now the whole field was helpless with laughter, and when the ball was finally thrown in to the bowler's end no one could decide which batsman was out. Unfortunately the captain of the eleven had been watching near by and was not impressed.

One of the major disappointments in Brian's life was that he failed to get into the Eton first eleven and therefore never played at Lord's. All through his time at Eton Brian had been acknowledged as the best wicket-keeper in his year. At the end of the summer half in 1930 Huson wrote to Brian's mother: 'I think next summer should see the culmination of his and my desires. They certainly want him in the side.' Anthony Baerlein had kept wicket for Eton in 1929 and 1930, but was now eighteen and was expected to leave. Brian was the keeper of the second eleven, or Twenty-Two as it was called, so everyone believed that it would be his turn in his final summer.

When Brian returned to Eton after the holidays in January 1931 he received some devastating news. Baerlein had decided to remain at Eton so that he could play at Lord's for a third year, even though he would be nineteen years old. Brian wrote to his mother with typical understatement: 'I had a very gloomy piece of news last night: Baerlein is definitely staying on. A frightful bore.' His mother must have known how desperate he really felt because she broke all protocol and rang Brian at his house to commiserate with him. A week later he thanked her, 'M'tutor has forgiven you for ringing up, which it was very nice of you to do.' Later Brian would admit to feeling 'miserable about the whole thing'. But he was heartbroken.

Many of the boys, including George Thorne, thought Brian was a better keeper than Baerlein, and he had become a very popular character. Alfred Shaughnessy was four years younger than Brian and a Lower Boy at Eton when Brian was in his final year. 'It was the gossip of the Lower Boys,' he recalled. 'Would Johnston make it into the eleven? They were all disappointed when he didn't.'

Eton won the match by an innings and 16 runs, their second-biggest victory in fifty years, but Baerlein did not have a good game and conceded thirty-five byes. The *Chronicle* reported: 'Far too many balls were delivered down the leg-side, and of these far too many eluded the grasp of Baerlein, who must learn at all costs to be quicker on his feet. He took or neglected to take the ball again and again by a belated dive from his original position, so that he looked like a professional goal keeper failing to save a penalty kick.'

Brian could have allowed himself a small smile of satisfaction, but it was no consolation. He felt he had been cheated out of his rightful place in the Eton eleven and still talked of it with genuine regret more than sixty years later.

At the beginning of the summer half in 1930 Brian was elected to the Eton Society, better known as 'Pop'. Pop was, and still is, a self-elected group of about twenty-five senior boys, usually the most popular and successful in the school. They administer school discipline and have almost unlimited privileges. Instead of the normal Eton uniform of black tailcoat, black waistcoat and striped trousers they are allowed to wear black braid on their tailcoats, colourful – often garish – waistcoats, and 'sponge-bag' trousers. They are also the only boys permitted to sport flowers in their buttonholes and to carry a rolled-up umbrella.

The total effect is one of undisguised superiority, and as a young boy at Eton to see two members of Pop swaggering down the street towards you was – and probably still is – an awe-inspiring and often terrifying sight. Alfred Shaughnessy vividly recalls seeing Brian and his great friend Jimmy Lane Fox, who was then the President of Pop, walking arm in arm together, taking full advantage of their privileges.

To be elected a member of Pop is the highest accolade an Etonian can receive. The elections are often bitterly contested and have been known to last for hours, as unsuccessful candidates are blackballed by the other members. For many an Old Etonian being a member remains the high point of their lives and yet, apart from using its headed notepaper, Brian never even mentioned it in his letters home. The exclusivity of Pop creates a bond between its members, and it is perhaps significant that many of Brian's best friends, such as Jimmy Lane Fox, William Douglas Home, Charles Villiers, John Hogg and Rupert Raw, were in Pop at the same time as him, and they all remained friends for the rest of their lives.

As his time at Eton drew to a close, Brian could not make up his mind what to do next. He wanted to join his brother Chris up at Oxford but he was coming under considerable pressure from his godfather Alex Johnston to go into the family business in the City. In June 1930 Brian wrote to his mother and stepfather Marcus, asking for their advice, and suggested that it might be better for him to undertake a course of intensive business training rather than waste three years at Oxford.

Later that year he confided to his guardian Hamil Johnston that he really wanted to go up to Oxford but he did not want to let his family down. His housemaster, Huson, decided to apply some gentle pressure. 'I very much hope he will go up to Oxford,' he wrote to Brian's mother. 'I believe him to be one of those to whom great benefit will accrue.' And so it was agreed, and Brian was given some extra work to do in the holidays to help him pass the entrance exam to New College.

Academically Brian was about average. He was obviously intelligent, but school work did not particularly engage him. His interests lay elsewhere. He also found it hard to control his natural sense of humour, as his housemaster made clear in his end-of-term report in July 1930:

> I am much relieved to see . . . that he has managed to cut out some of that levity of manner which the boy finds so easy, and which verges on bad manners. Of course Brian can say with some justice that his buffoonery, to give the worst, but not infrequently used, term, has stood him in good stead as far as his associations with his own kind are concerned. He must, however, learn to discriminate between what boys want, and what masters want. The lines beyond which one must not step are drawn in two widely different places.

But Brian could be serious if required, as his tutor W. G. Tatham pointed out: 'I should like to say something about his work in my O.T.C. company because it throws a light on his character. He is a commander, who is efficient, vigorous, cheerful and tactful – a combination more difficult than it sounds.' An assessment of Brian's character that would prove to be remarkably prescient ten years later during the war.

Brian appears at an early age to have had the ability to inspire and encourage those under him and, judging by this next report, even those above him. In December 1930 Huson was positively effusive about Brian's abilities as his Captain of Games, especially as he was now in Pop and also playing for the Eton Field eleven:

> He has been if anything more conscientious, and I cannot recall one single instance of his not being present to encourage, and instruct, any one of his teams, when it was even remotely possible for him to be there. The effect has been most marked, and should have carried its own reward.

It is a great gift this of Bri's, being able to keep up his

enthusiasms, and I have tried to tell him how much I have appreciated all that he has done. He has a very great power over his fellow creatures. I rejoice to think that I shall enjoy Bri's presence for some time longer.

Urged on by his housemaster, Brian took the entrance exam to Oxford and was accepted by New College, where his father had gone thirty-one years before. He always doubted whether he had actually passed the exam, but in those days the family connection was of equal importance.

Brian had triumphed at Eton. When he left in July 1931 he was a senior member of Pop, he had been awarded his school colours for the rugby fifteen and Field eleven, he was captain of the cricket second eleven and Captain of Games in his house. In a letter to Brian's mother in December 1930, Hamil Johnston mentioned that he had enjoyed a long talk with A. C. Huson, 'who remarked of Brian that he was probably the most popular boy in the school'.

That is quite some achievement out of a school of 1,200 boys, and might be expected to have gone to Brian's head. But Hamil continued: 'It was very pleasant to me to notice that success, so far from spoiling him, has rather had the effect of strengthening his character and increasing his sense of duty and responsibility.'

There was a distinct danger, however, that life after Eton would seem like an anti-climax. Cyril Connolly was a King's Scholar at Eton in the early 1920s. In his book *The Enemies of Promise* Connolly identified what he described as 'The Theory of Permanent Adolescence':

It is the theory that the experiences undergone by boys at the great public schools, their glories and disappointments, are so intense as to dominate their lives and to arrest their development. From these it results that the greater part of the ruling class remains adolescent, school minded, self-conscious, cowardly, sentimental, and in the last analysis, homosexual. Early laurels weigh like lead and of many of the boys whom I knew at Eton, I can say that their lives are over.

In some respects Connolly is correct, for Brian remained essentially the same character as he was at Eton for the rest of his life. Indeed, he was often described by those who knew him as the schoolboy who never grew up. But in his final observation Connolly was wrong. Brian's life was far from over.

6

A Real Live Wire

Brian used to say about his days at Oxford that he read history and P. G. Wodehouse and played cricket about six times a week. The latter might be a slight exaggeration but it wasn't far from the truth. He summed it up in a letter home: 'We're having a marvellous term and am doing just sufficient work.' Sometimes it is hard to see when he was doing any work at all. In a typical week during his first Michaelmas term he played golf on Monday, rugby on Tuesday, soccer on Wednesday and real tennis on Friday. During the summer he would play cricket for New College, the Allsorts, Eton Ramblers and the Butterflies – sometimes all in the same week.

At first he had a bedroom and sitting room up a 'rather draughty' staircase in the college. The scout on his staircase was called Sid Honey – soon renamed by Brian as Bunch. He had previously looked after Brian's brother Chris and always referred to him as 'our kid'. The scout's job was to clean the rooms and serve breakfast or lunch if required. But it was not all luxury. There was no running water and no central heating. If Brian wanted to have a bath he had to walk across the quadrangle in his dressing gown, whatever the weather.

Chris remembers Sid Honey as 'a splendid man' and recalls that when Brian had a lunch party in his rooms his scout would often enter and say, 'Sir, a lady stands without.'

'Without what?' Brian would enquire.

'Sir, without food or clothing.'

'Then give her food,' Brian would declare triumphantly, 'and bring her in!'

New College in the thirties was quite a cosmopolitan place.

The majority of undergraduates were from Winchester College, a brainy crowd who tended to look down on their less scholarly Etonian cousins, but there was also a smattering of Rhodes Scholars from America, Canada, Australia and New Zealand. Most of Brian's friends from Eton were now at Christ Church, Magdalen and Trinity, so he was pleased to find another Old Etonian at New College, William Douglas Home. William had been a member of Pop with Brian but was not the sporting type, so they had moved in different circles. Once at New College, however, they discovered that they shared a mutual interest in the theatre, a similar sense of humour and a love of practical jokes. William would become his greatest lifelong friend.

The Warden of New College was the eminent historian H. A. L. Fisher, known to all as Hal, who had been the Minister of Education in Lloyd George's cabinet in 1922. Brian found it amusing that Fisher started almost all his conversations with the phrase, 'When I was in the cabinet . . .', which caused great mirth among those of his colleagues who spoke French (*cabinet* means toilet in French).

The Dean was a charming but rather old-fashioned don called Henderson, who spoke with a broken German accent. One day Brian was summoned to his room after he was caught speeding by the police in a friend's new car at more than 75 mph. He and his friends decided to err on the side of caution, and when Henderson asked them how fast they had been going they answered innocently, 'Thirty-seven miles per hour, sir.' The Dean whistled under his breath. 'Ach,' he said in his guttural accent, 'if you go at such speeds you must expect to get into trouble!' and promptly gated them for a few days.

After passing his Pass Moderations exam at the end of his first year, Brian started reading for a degree in history. One of his tutors at New College was Wickham Legge, a friendly man with a humorous manner of speech. Brian shared his tutorials with William, who described their weekly hour with Mr Legge as having 'a faintly festive air'. Their tutor got an unintentional laugh one day when he was explaining how Henry VIII suffered from bad fevers. 'Personally,' said Wickham Legge, 'if I am in bed with a fever I toss off everything within reach.'

The workload does not seem to have been too demanding. Brian averaged about one lecture a day and read books suggested by his tutor. On top of that he had to write only one essay a week. The rest of his time was devoted to games. In fact during his final term, when he was supposed to be studying for his exams, Brian played even more cricket than before. He had to resort to a crammer run by a Mr Young, who taught his students the essential facts from each period of history and urged them to include them in their answers, irrespective of the questions. It must have worked because Brian got his degree – a third in history, one better than William, who got a fourth, which he was told was awarded to those who gave erudite and admirable answers to questions that had not been asked.

One of their new friends at Oxford was a big-hearted American Rhodes Scholar called Bill Crandall, who was almost completely bald and, according to William Douglas Home, had a 'round, cherubic countenance'. Crandall was full of charm and always tried to be nice to everyone, but it did not always work. One evening they were all invited to dinner by Mrs Tollemache, the mother of one of their old Eton friends, Tony Tollemache. Mrs Tollemache was rather a large lady, in possession of a formidable pair of bosoms. Crandall was carving the chicken when he called out, 'Oh, gee, will you have some more breast, Mrs T?' He turned round and saw that she was still eating, so he added quickly, 'Oh no, I can see you don't need any!' Unfortunately she took it the wrong way and was furious.

Freed from the restraints of being in Pop, Brian was able to indulge his love of practical jokes and schoolboy pranks. One night he and some friends stretched some wire across the garden quad from two of the top windows and ran chamber pots down from either end by their handles until they met in the middle and smashed. As he commented afterwards, 'childish but funny'.

In May 1932 Brian helped to organise a mock garden party in a little garden in New College Lane. All the guests wore full morning dress and top hats, and Brian even sported a fake waxed moustache to complete the picture. A crowd of more than fifty people gathered to watch the guests eating and making 'absurd' speeches. Soon there were so many onlookers that the police had to be called to unsnarl the traffic congestion.

After the garden party Brian and one or two others rode down the High Street in an open Victoria carriage and waved to the crowd. At places there were several rows of people on the pavement watching them ride by, and motorists raised their hats in salute as they passed them. The Warden was informed of the affair but dismissed it as being 'good, clean sport'.

Professor James Gibson from Vancouver was at New College with Brian, and also attended the mock garden party. Years later he recalled Brian as 'rangy, a shade raw-boned, a voice verging on hoarseness, but with an insatiable gentleness of spirit, an innate courtesy, and, lurking beneath, a mischievous sense of fun'.

Brian's delight at pulling the leg of anyone in a position of authority started at Oxford. One of his favourite tricks was to start a conversation with a friend in a loud voice:

BRIAN: What's your brother doing nowadays?

FRIEND: Oh, he's doing nothing.

BRIAN: But I thought he was trying for a job at New College as a don? [or scout, or gardener, or porter, depending on who was standing near by]

FRIEND: Yes, he got the job!

Brian wrote to his mother with glee: 'It's amazing how annoyed they seem!'

John (later Sir John) Hogg, the distinguished City banker, was a close friend of Brian's at Eton and Oxford and was given the nickname 'Pig' by him. According to Hogg, Brian was one of the most fertile-minded practical jokers that he had ever come across. No one could feel himself secure from his activities. 'However,' added Hogg, 'Brian had a miraculous gift in that he never seemed to give offence by his jokes, practical or otherwise; if anything his victims seemed to enjoy being part of the game.'

One Sunday night during a concert at New College Chapel Brian disguised himself as a tramp and sat outside on the pavement next to some old hunting pictures taken from his room. When the concert-goers began coming out he croaked, 'Please help me, I've a wife and six children to keep . . .' while one or two of his friends tossed some coins into a cloth cap, murmuring, 'Poor fellow' and 'What a shame'. After a while the university proctor and his two bulldogs were spotted approaching and Brian quickly fled. But not before he had collected about five shillings – the first money he had ever 'earned'.

Within a month of going up to Oxford Brian had founded a light-hearted sports club called the Allsorts with a group of friends including William Douglas Home. They challenged all-comers at any sport from horse racing to tiddlywinks. They played rugger against neighbouring schools and soccer against various town sides such as the local fishmongers, bus drivers and hotel waiters. In one match against the college servants Brian was pleased when he scored 'a beautiful goal, which gave the bath man no chance to stop it'.

As usual with Brian, the Allsorts involved a lot of dressing up. Before every match the teams would line up to be presented to a visiting VIP, who would be one of their own number disguised in a funny hat and false moustache. When Brian couldn't play in a soccer match at Eton because of rheumatism in his knees, he acted as the trainer and stood on the touchline with a little bag full of bandages, wearing a bowler hat and white spats and clutching a cigar.

On 21 December 1932 the *Tatler* featured a picture of the Allsorts and reported: 'Mr Brian Johnston is the club president, and a real live wire he is! On Port Meadow, Oxford, recently, they organised a flat meeting of four races, the winner in each to compete in a final race for the President's Cup. After much excitement and many "objections" and disqualifications, Mr W. A. K. ("Bushey") Carr won the cup on "Aubrey", a hot favourite. Good luck to the club!'

The article failed to mention that the favourite in the third race bolted and ran straight into the river, from which both horse and jockey had to be rescued.

In May 1933 the Allsorts were invited to play cricket against an eleven led by the Hon. David Astor at his family's Cliveden estate in Buckinghamshire. After the morning session they were waited on at lunch by four footmen and a butler, and were joined by David's mother, the formidable Lady Nancy Astor, who had been the first woman MP in 1919.

Brian told his mother: 'She's very nice, though she talks a lot, and it was wonderful value to hear us all agreeing with her about the scandal of taking the tax off beer. All round the table were murmurs of "monstrous", "wicked", "scandalous", "poor wives on Saturday night" etc – it was grand!'

Afternoon tea was served in exquisite porcelain cups and saucers, and Brian was pouring out the tea when he came to a chap 'who had been rather a bore' earlier in the day. Brian poured some of the tea over his thumb, knowing that his victim would not dare to drop the expensive cup. 'He was much nicer afterwards,' related Brian, 'even without the skin on his thumb.'

It has been said that for many upper-class students between the wars Oxford was 'like a country house with dinner at the Bullingdon Club'. Brian was more upper-middle than upper class, but he was an enthusiastic member of several clubs at Oxford, including the Bullingdon, which was mostly for Old Etonians and was famous for its bad behaviour. He was also a member of the Gridiron, a dining club for the social elite, and Vincent's, which was mainly for sportsmen. As Brian commented when he joined Vincent's: 'More subscriptions but a good tie.' What they all had in common apart from their exclusivity was their schoolboy food, especially scrambled eggs. Brian's culinary tastes were already firmly established.

One of the strictest rules for undergraduates while at Oxford was that they had to be back in their rooms by midnight. This was not always practical, especially if one had been invited out to dinner, or a dance up in London. So William and Brian searched New College inside and out until they discovered a possible emergency route. According to William, it involved climbing over two walls, the first a fourteen-foot sheer wall and the second a twenty-foot sheer wall, topped with iron spikes and broken bottles.

One night they were forced to try it when they were invited to dinner at Eton with their old history master, Tuppy Headlam. On the way back their hired car broke down about eleven miles out of Oxford. After an hour they managed to get a lift, but didn't make it back to the college until 1.45 a.m. They succeeded in clambering over the two walls and into the garden, but Brian tore his plus-four suit on the spikes. It was dangerous, but it had worked.

They continued to use their secret route until one night William slipped on the second wall and felt a rusty iron spike go through his shin. It bled profusely and he had to be patched up by their friend Bill Crandall. They decided it was time to develop a new plan. The pair had spotted a door into the college that was always kept locked. It led to a coal cellar. They paid a visit to the porter's lodge and guessed, by the size and shape of a certain key, that it was the one they wanted. William engaged the porter in conversation while Brian lifted the key, went outside, made an impression of it in some soap and then returned it to the hook. They had a skeleton key made and from then on they, and their friends, were able to come and go as they pleased. Their secret was never discovered.

During the summer vacation in 1933 Brian went with his sister Anne to see her young brother-in-law Hugh Carter at school in Eastbourne. On the way back they stopped for tea at Drusilla's Zoo, and Brian bought a three-month-old Sealyham terrier puppy for three guineas. The puppy had a black patch over one eye so Brian called him Blob. From then on Blob went everywhere with him and was an instant hit at every cricket match. He became known as the Honourable Blobington, but not everyone loved him quite as much as Brian. One week Blob was sent to stay with John Hogg's girlfriend Betty Norton, and he 'drew blood from her aunt as soon as he arrived'. Later John Hogg saved the dog's life when Blob was nearly run over by a car in Oxford. The ungrateful animal promptly bit him, and poor Hogg had to go the doctor to receive an anti-tetanus injection.

Brian tried to train Blob to hunt. He took him hare coursing on a friend's estate, but even though the greyhounds caught two hares, Blob ran off in the opposite direction. On another occasion he took Blob beagling, although they were soon separated from the hounds. On the way there Brian and William caused chaos when driving down a blocked narrow road by saying that they were late and had the hare in the back of their car. All the other vehicles had to swerve into the ditches to let them by.

This seems to have been a common ruse of theirs. Brian admitted that he and William once got into the Bath and West Show without paying by shouting 'Official!' as they drove into the show ground.

At the beginning of the Michaelmas term in 1933 Brian moved into digs at 50 High Street in Oxford with three of his Eton friends, Jimmy Lane Fox, John Hogg and Roger Wilkinson. The landlady, Mrs Bates, lived on the premises and had a son, whom Brian always referred to as Master Bates. She used to look after Blob whenever Brian had to go out, and he said it was a wonderful sight to watch her trying to catch Blob's fleas with 'some stuff called Death Beetle'.

Meanwhile William Douglas Home had moved into digs in Merton Street. Early in his final term he left his hired car outside the house one night, uninsured and without its sidelights on – an offence in those days. He was disqualified from driving for twelve months by the local magistrate, who happened to be the Mayor of Oxford, Miss Lily Tawney. So he hired a horse and phaeton – an open four-wheeled carriage – and suggested to Brian that he should be the groom. Brian was never one to resist a challenge and kitted himself out with a sawn-off top hat, an ill-fitting frock coat, a wisp of straw in his mouth and trousers tied around the knee with twine.

On their first excursion to buy an evening paper the horse went so slowly that a traffic jam stretched all the way down the High Street and over Magdalen Bridge, but soon they were proficient enough to go for drives in the countryside. William called the mare Lily, after the Mayor of Oxford, and he would drive to lectures in the phaeton, leaving Brian to look after the horse outside the Schools while he went into the lectures, which Brian himself should have been attending.

Lily became famous around Oxford, and there were even articles and photographs in the local press extolling this delightful return to a more civilised way of life. Lily's fame endured, and fifteen years later William's father, the Earl of Home, was visiting Oxford when an old lady approached him.

'Lord Home,' she said, 'I must ask you, how is Lily?'

The 13th Earl, who had left his wife Lilian in perfect health back in Scotland only the day before, replied, 'Very well, thank you, when I last saw her.'

'I'm so glad,' said the old lady, 'I used to love seeing her spanking down the High Street, with her harness glinting in the sun!'

At which Lord Home is said to have slowly raised his eyebrows and continued on his way.

William and Brian seem to have spurred each other on to even greater pranks. In February 1934 they both took part in a point-to-point race organised by the Bullingdon Club. They entered themselves in the New College Members Race, even though William had hardly ridden before. They hired two horses and practised for a couple of days beforehand at a nearby riding school. William was allocated what he described later as 'a gigantic black beast' called Nero, although Brian recalled the horse as being 'docile'. William's memory is probably the more reliable, because during the actual race Nero threw him off twice.

Brian fared slightly better. He had at least done some riding as a boy with the Tetcott Hunt, near Bude, so he had a rough idea of what was required. His horse was a 'pale, brown streamlined creature' called Tip Top, who was alleged to be the half-brother of the 1932 Derby winner April the Fifth. Tip Top was an ex-flat racer, and according to Brian had only jumped once before, and that was in its stall when the groom frightened it. As they cantered down to the start, William was in a highly nervous state. Brian rode up alongside him and shouted: 'To think that in a few moments we'll be hearing the merry jingle of ambulance bells!' William nearly fell off on the spot.

Nero finally refused at the sixth fence, much to William's relief, but Brian managed to stay on Tip Top and finished fifth out of eight runners, one ahead of his friend Jim Harmsworth, an experienced rider, on his own horse. The race was won by Jimmy Lane Fox, and afterwards Nero's owner received an offer for the horse – from a local undertaker.

Back in the unsaddling enclosure Brian was surprised to be greeted by one or two boos from the crowd, until he discovered that his friends had placed so many bets on Tip Top that the bookies had made it third favourite. The local tipster, Captain Dean, commented: 'There are jockeys here today who couldn't ride in a railway carriage unless the door was locked.'

Brian was captain of the New College cricket eleven for two years but was never selected for the university side, although he claimed that in his second year Brian Hone, the Oxford captain, played in a match for New College in order to assess his form. But as at Eton, the Oxford University eleven already had an excellent wicket-keeper in Peter Oldfield. Brian had to make do with being elected to the Oxford Authentics, the equivalent of the Oxford second eleven and eligible to those not quite good enough to get a Blue. The cricket writer E. W. 'Jim' Swanton, later to be Brian's colleague in the BBC commentary box, played against him in a match on the New College ground in the early 1930s, and his first memory of Brian was of 'that prominent proboscis hovering over the stumps'. Swanton, who was not known for mincing his words, described him as being 'a thoroughly capable wicket-keeper, always welcome in Eton Ramblers, Oxford Authentics, MCC and I Zingari sides'. Later he added that, in another year, Brian might easily have got a Blue.

Brian also played rugby for New College, and in one match against Trinity his shorts were ripped off when he was tackled. He had to retreat to the touchline while someone hurried off to fetch him a new pair, and he was given a macintosh to cover his embarrassment. While he was waiting, the ball came down the three-quarter line towards him, so he quickly yelled, 'Outside you!', and ran on to the pitch to take the pass. In the general uproar that followed, he ran towards the posts, still wearing his macintosh, and scored a brilliant try. The referee should have blown his whistle, because Brian had not been given leave to go back on, but he was laughing so much that he just went *pffftt*, and the try was allowed to stand. Later Brian would declare proudly that he was the only person in the history of rugby ever to score a try in a macintosh.

Once again Brian had to think seriously about his future career. He had half considered joining the army, but after a game of cricket against the Royal Military College in May 1932 he changed his mind. While Brian had been playing at Sandhurst a friend of his had been 'doing an extra drill in the steaming sun and had to stay in his uniform for five days because he only had 5d left in his food account and ate something worth 8d'. This was not the career for him. He told his mother, 'I've kept this dark from Chris.'

By now his elder brother Christopher had left Oxford and had joined the 14th/20th Hussars. Chris explained that there were several reasons why he chose to go into the army instead of the family business in the City. He could tell there was a war brewing, many of his friends were joining the cavalry, and he loved working with horses. His stepfather Marcus Scully, a former regular army officer, also helped to influence his decision.

A year before Brian came down from Oxford he was invited to lunch by his godfather Alex Johnston, who began applying pressure on him again to enter the family firm, E. Johnston & Co. In fact, he informed Brian, he had already told the company that Brian would probably be joining them after leaving Oxford. Secretly it was the last thing Brian had in mind. What he really wanted was to be an actor. He thought about having a film test. 'So many people say I ought to go on the stage,' he confided to his mother, 'I think they may be right.'

A week after their race in the point-to-point Brian and William went up to the Pathé Gazette offices in London to look at the newsreel footage, but they were disappointed to discover that the film included every race except their own. While they were there, Brian chatted up one of the newsreel announcers, who suggested that if he wanted to have a film test he should go to the BIP studios at Elstree. However, when Brian learned that all would-be actors had to wait in a queue there for several hours, he lost interest. It is not clear whether he ever did go for a film test, but he never referred to it again in any of his letters or his books, so it seems unlikely.

Instead he considered being a schoolmaster, and even applied for a job as an advance agent with a company taking public school pupils on foreign tours. But nothing came of it. After more family conferences and another City lunch with Alex Johnston and Arthur Whitworth, the chairman of E. Johnston & Co., Brian had to admit defeat. He was about to become the last member of the Johnston family to enter the family firm.

In different circumstances one would have expected the eldest brother Michael to have followed his father into the company, but Michael's health had never been very good and he was not business minded. He was more suited to life as a farmer in the wide-open spaces of Canada. As the second son, Christopher would probably have joined the family business if his father had not drowned. Chris had enormous respect for his father and would have considered it his duty to carry on the Johnston tradition. But after the colonel died he had felt no similar obligation to the company and the family agreed he should go into the army. Which left Brian.

7

Home and Away

In June 1929, while Brian was still at Eton, his mother and stepfather Marcus Scully had left Much Marcle in Herefordshire and moved to a new house called Homewell at Bude in North Cornwall. It was considerably smaller than their previous home, which had been rented, but Chris Johnston thinks that Scully had inherited some money after his father died in Canada and decided to invest it in a house for the family. Many people, including Chris, thought it strange that Pleasance Johnston should want to live in Bude, the scene of her husband's tragic death only seven years earlier. But as Brian later explained: 'It had always been where we spent our summer holidays and we loved it.'

There were several other families in Bude with children of a similar age to the Johnstons'. Among their closest friends were the Thomas family, who lived at the White House, the old vicarage at Stratton, just outside Bude. Major and Mrs Thomas had four children, Marjorie, Micky, Jane and Pat. Micky had been to Radley and was the same age as Brian. He was witty and very keen on games, especially rugby and cricket, and he and Brian became firm friends. 'They made a good pair,' recalls Micky's youngest sister Pat (now Mrs Scott), 'they bounced off each other.' When Micky left Radley he went up to Sandhurst and later joined the Wiltshire Regiment. He used to visit Brian while he was at Eton and Oxford and they would go to watch rugby internationals at Twickenham.

Micky's elder sister Marjorie was one year older than Brian and became his first girlfriend – although he later insisted that it was 'nothing serious of course'. Nevertheless they used to go to parties and picnics and go swimming together during the school holidays while Brian was in Bude. She even went to call on him once or twice during his final year at Eton and up at Oxford.

Pat assured me that Marjorie and Brian were just good friends. 'It wasn't so easy to be more than that in those days,' she chuckled, 'although Marjorie wouldn't have minded!' Marjorie was very attractive, and very outgoing when it came to boys. 'In fact,' says Pat, 'I wasn't sure who was taking who out.'

When Brian came into a room, you knew he was there. He was learning the piano at the time and he used to breeze into the Thomases' house, call out, 'Hello, Jessie, hello, Cyril!' and, without waiting to be invited, sit down at the Thomases' piano and crash out the chords to 'Auf Wiedersehen', one of the current musical favourites. Somehow her parents did not seem to mind. 'He was fun,' says Pat, 'you couldn't help liking him.'

They would play tennis together on the courts next to the cricket ground on the cliff tops at Bude. It was so windy that you could never hit a ball over the cliff because the wind blew it back. One summer Pat went for a picnic up on the cliff tops with Brian and their friends. They had brought a wind-up gramophone with them and for a laugh someone picked up one of the 78 rpm records and sent it whizzing over the edge of the cliff. It made such a marvellous tinkling sound as it smashed on the rocks below that soon, according to Pat, 'they all went mad and started throwing the records one after the other over the cliff'. She was horrified. They were new records and had cost one shilling each.

In 1933 Marjorie met an out-of-work actor from Liverpool Repertory at a party in London and invited him down to Bude for the summer holidays. He was short sighted and wore a monocle and spoke in a 'high squeaky voice with a slightly querulous tone'. Marjorie asked Brian to be nice to him, so Brian dutifully entertained the struggling young actor, whom he found amusing but 'not much good at table tennis'. Soon afterwards Marjorie and the young actor became engaged. She changed her name to the more exotic-sounding Collette and early in 1934 she became the first Mrs Rex Harrison.

Their son Noel was born in January 1935, but the marriage

was not a success. It ended in divorce in 1942 after Rex Harrison, now a successful stage and film star, admitted to an affair with the German-born actress Lilli Palmer. Collette tried to launch a new career for herself as an actress and singer and in 1943 she landed a small part as a maid in a musical called *Something in the Air*. After the war, in about 1946, Brian and his mother went to see Collette performing as an understudy in another musical and thought she was dreadful. According to Pat, Brian turned to his mother when they came out of the theatre and said, 'That wasn't very good, was it?'

As soon as the Johnstons moved to Bude in 1929 Brian joined the Bude Cricket Club and played for them whenever he could on their picturesque ground on the cliff tops above the sea. He captained the side on several occasions, and one of his proudest moments was when he made his highest-ever score of 79 for Bude in a match at Tavistock in Devon.

Later, during the long vacations from Oxford every summer, Brian would play as much cricket as he could. Some of his happiest memories were playing for Millaton, a team run by Lord Carrington, the father of the present peer. The club was named after the Carringtons' house in the little village of Bridestowe in Devon, and consisted mainly of retired clergymen, doctors and solicitors. There was a vicar called the Reverend Paine, whom Brian called 'The Ache', and another old parson who was the wicket-keeper and known as 'The Ancient Mariner' because 'he stoppeth one in three'.

But the most fun was always to be had with the Eton Ramblers on their annual cricket tour of country houses. According to Sir John Hogg, who was a regular member of the team, Brian was a good wicket-keeper but an indifferent bat. 'However,' he added, 'he taught himself to become a master of the short single, almost tip and run. It was all right if you knew about this, but woe betide you if you didn't know his form, or were a slow starter.'

In September 1932 Brian went to stay with his friend Jimmy Lane Fox at Walton House, near Boston Spa in Yorkshire. He drove there in his new car, a second-hand open Austin Seven which he had bought for £17 with some help from his mother. The journey was a nightmare. The car suffered a choked jet at Wincanton and at Bagshot the rear leaf of one of the back springs burst. A garage patched him up but he had to crawl the whole way to St Albans, where the lights fused and he had to stay overnight. Next morning he made it to his sister's house near Stevenage, before going on to Biggleswade, where he had to wait another three hours while the spring was mended. He finally arrived in Yorkshire at 9 p.m., 'an awful' two days after setting out from Cornwall.

Brian was a regular guest at Walton House over the years and would often join in the activities of the local Bramham Moor Hunt, such as riding in the gymkhana, going with the Lane Foxes to the point-to-point or dancing at the hunt ball at Harrogate. One winter he had 'a terrifying day out' with the Bramham Moor Hunt and found himself riding with the Princess Royal, the Countess of Harewood, who lived near by and came back to the house for tea afterwards.

Every summer as part of their annual tour the Eton Ramblers would stay for a week with the Baerlein family at Whatcroft Hall in Northwich, Cheshire, where they would play against local teams such as the Northern Nomads, Cheshire Gentlemen and Old Cheltonians. Brian's old schoolfriend Edward (later Sir Edward) Ford was a frequent member of the touring party. 'The first time we went there we didn't know the Baerleins at all,' he recalls, 'but within twenty-four hours we were firm friends.' Brian was not so convinced. 'Mrs B. is hopelessly nice,' he wrote home, 'but he's not so good.'

Edgar Baerlein was a former amateur tennis and racquets champion and the father of Anthony Baerlein, the boy who had kept Brian out of the eleven at Eton. Edgar was famous for being a tough competitor and never admitting defeat. One evening Brian filled some of his favourite chocolates with toothpaste and after dinner he offered one to Edgar, who was in the middle of a heated conversation. He carried on talking even when he began to froth at the mouth, and swallowed it without missing a beat. Brian had finally met his match.

Colonel 'Buns' Cartwright was the secretary of the Eton Ramblers and was frequently the butt of Brian's practical jokes. At one house party Brian placed a 'whoopee' bag under the cushion on Cartwright's dining-room chair, and when Buns sat down there was an almighty explosion. The hostess calmly summoned the butler and ordered him to open a window.

After leaving Cheshire the Ramblers would often spend a day in Blackpool, where they liked to go on the switchback rides and look at the sideshows along the Golden Mile. In the early 1930s Blackpool Central Beach featured some extraordinary freak shows. For only twopence a time you could see a man hanging crucified on a cross or 'The Woman with the Lobster's Claws'. Brian recalled paying sixpence to look at the ex-Rector of Stiffkey in Norfolk, who had been defrocked for immoral conduct with teenage girls, sitting in a large barrel.

The most infamous attraction was 'The Starving Brides and Bridegrooms', in which a couple would lay side by side in two coffins and agree to fast for thirty days. If they survived they were paid £250. Thousands paid to see them, including Brian when he was there in August 1934, but after a public outcry the attraction was banned by the council two months later.

During the Easter vacation in 1934 he was invited by William Douglas Home to stay at the Hirsel, the Earl of Home's estate at Coldstream in Berwickshire. Brian thought it was an amazing household: 'Lord Home just goes about shouting at the top of his voice the whole time. He sometimes shouts for someone for about ten minutes and when they yell back he just says, "How are you?"' Later Brian tried his hand at salmon fishing, but without success. His first cast caught a fisherman in the face – a cast in the eye, said Brian.

The following year he stayed with William at Douglas Castle, in Lanarkshire, another of the Earl of Home's estates, which was used mainly for shooting. They went out on the moors and Blob retrieved a grouse, which surprised everyone, including

Brian. Then they played croquet with Princess Juliana of the Netherlands, who was visiting the castle for lunch. Even the princess was not safe from Brian's terrible puns. She had rather a husky voice so he told her she had a 'croquet' voice, which she quite liked. Afterwards Brian wrote home: 'We all bowed and scraped: she was very nice with a built up area [a large bust].'

On his first visit to the Hirsel, Brian and William planned an elaborate practical joke on an uncle and aunt who lived near by. They persuaded Lady Home to invite them over to tea to meet a strange clergyman who was staying at the Hirsel. He was half blind and almost totally deaf. Of course, Brian was the clergyman. He parted his hair down the middle, wore a thick pair of horn-rimmed spectacles and found a dog collar and some black clerical clothes in the dressing-up chest. At the time the guests were expected, he walked up and down the drive reading a Bible and pretended not to hear their car approaching. They were forced to stop and hoot at him until he stepped aside, and were soon convinced that he was an eccentric.

At tea Brian was seated next to the aunt and proceeded to make amorous advances towards her, putting his hand on her knee. She became rather flustered and even offered him some clothes for his mission. William shouted loudly at Brian, but he pretended not to be able to hear any of the conversation. So the guests, believing that he was deaf, started to make rude comments, muttering, 'He's quite mad. Why on earth did you ask us?'

Meanwhile the Home family were being nearly ill trying not to laugh, especially after William deliberately tipped a hot cup of tea over Brian, who let out a very unclerical expletive. When they all went into the drawing room after tea, Brian pretended not to be able to see very well and sat down on the aunt's lap on the sofa. She let out a yelp and became even more hysterical when the clergyman invited her to come for a walk in the shrubbery. By this time her husband was getting increasingly angry, grumbling, 'What the hell does the lunatic think he's up to?' and threatening to take his wife and their daughter home if they did not behave better.

At which point Brian asked to be excused and left the room. He did a quick change into his sports jacket and flannels, took off his glasses, parted his hair normally at the side and then strolled back into the room. William introduced him to the uncle and aunt and explained that Brian had been into Edinburgh. It was several minutes before they realised what had been going on, but fortunately they took it very well.

Brian had been telling jokes for years, but he made his stage debut as a comedian in September 1935, after a cricket match at Little Marlow in Buckinghamshire. In the evening he did a cross-talk act with John Hogg during the village concert. All of Brian's friends were used to being a part of his corny routines, and Sir John laughed as he recalled a particular old favourite from their double act at Little Marlow:

'I say, I say, I say. I call my dog Carpenter.'

'Why do you call your dog Carpenter?'

'Because he's always doing odd jobs around the house. Oi!'

Brian told his mother: 'The jokes went frightfully well. The whole village goes about shouting "Oi!" now wherever they go.'

Brian did not only play cricket for the Eton Ramblers. One year he turned out for his friend Nigel Turner's team against a local side at Hungerford. As usual he was the wicket-keeper. The opening batsman for the opposition methodically blocked almost every ball and the bowlers simply could not get him out. It was dull to watch and even more boring to play against, and after several overs Brian had had enough. Next time the batsman went to play the ball back defensively and missed, Brian leaned forward, pushed the batsman over and stumped him!

Brian loved watching cricket almost as much as playing it. When he was at Oxford he had made friends with an Old Harrovian called Jim St John Harmsworth, who had 'a wonderful sense of humour and a very funny, pompous way of talking', and went on to become a highly respected stipendiary magistrate at Bow Street Magistrates' Court in central London.

Every year, during the Eton and Harrow match at Lord's, Brian would gather with a group of his friends in the old Block G – the open stand to the right of the sight screen at the Nursery End. At about 5.30 on the afternoon of the second day, usually a Saturday, men would be seen leaving their seats and boxes in all corners of the ground and making their way towards Block G. There Brian would greet the Old Etonians on one side of the stand, while Jim Harmsworth welcomed the Old Harrovians at the other end. Once they had all assembled, a succession of childish insults and bad jokes would fly across from one side to the other, usually involving the age, ability and nationality of members of the opposing team. Brian always paid particular attention to anyone in the Harrow team with a foreign-sounding name.

This went on throughout the 1930s and into the 1950s. John Pawle was a regular member of the Harrow crowd and recalls a typical exchange which took place in July 1949. That year Harrow had a new South African pace bowler called M. Kok. When Brian was around, a name like that could not be allowed to pass without comment.

> BRIAN: I say, Jim, I've lost my scorecard. Can you tell me the name of your number-ten batsman?
>
> JIM: Certainly, Brian. It's Kok.
>
> BRIAN: Sorry, Jim, I didn't quite catch that. What did you say his name was?
>
> JIM: (louder): Kok!
>
> BRIAN: Ah, Kok, is it? Thank you! By the way, do you know how he got his name?
>
> JIM: No, I don't, Brian. Why don't you tell me.
>
> BRIAN: Well, it's quite simple really. You see, he was walking down the High Street in Harrow on his first day at school when he bumped into the headmaster. Well, of course the headmaster didn't know his name because he was a new boy, so he said, 'Hello, cock!' and he's been called Kok ever since!

Eton won that match by seven wickets – their first victory over Harrow since 1937. But Kok had the last laugh when he took three Eton wickets in one over.

It has been alleged, by Jim Swanton in particular, that Brian's membership of the MCC was officially delayed for a year 'because he was picked out as a ring-leader of a disorderly lot from both schools who used to trade badinage and genial insults with one another' at the Eton and Harrow match. Swanton was frequently on the receiving end of Brian's jokes at the BBC and used to get his own back by taunting him about having incurred the displeasure of the MCC. According to Swanton, 'he never positively denied it'. Whatever the reason, Brian's name was put down for the MCC in 1928 by his 'Uncle Freddie', Lieutenant Colonel Frederick Browning, and he qualified as a player in the mid-thirties, but his MCC membership did not eventually come through until during the Second World War.

8

Something in the City

After a summer spent playing cricket with the Ramblers, in October 1934 Brian had to exchange his white flannels for a new pinstripe suit and report for work at E. Johnston & Co. in the City. His great-grandfather Edward Johnston had founded the family business in 1842 with offices in Rio de Janeiro. At first the company exported coffee to Liverpool and also imported codfish, flour, wine, lumber, salt, coal and iron. After two years Edward returned to live in England and expanded the company substantially, opening offices in London and Liverpool, New York and New Orleans.

When he died in 1876, two of his sons carried on the business, and in 1881 they made the crucial decision to open a new office in the up-and-coming port of Santos, sixty miles from São Paulo, which gradually became the chief centre of the firm's activities.

Santos was an island port in the estuary of the Cubatão river and was infamous for yellow fever, known as 'Yellow Jack'. Indeed, for many years the wreck of an old steamer could be spotted rusting in the Cubatão estuary. Its crew had all died of 'Yellow Jack', and when a replacement crew was dispatched from England they too had all perished from the disease.

The Johnston family was also affected. Edward Johnston's grandson Bertram joined the business in 1886, was sent out to Santos and died there of yellow fever four years later. In an effort to save lives, E. Johnston & Co. built a barracks for the European crews on a small island called Ilha das Palmas at the mouth of the estuary, and it came to be known as 'Johnston's Island'.

Brian's father Charles became a partner in the firm in 1904, after serving his apprenticeship in London and Brazil, and two years later the firm was converted from a partnership into a private limited company with its head office in London. When Reginald Johnston was appointed Governor of the Bank of England in 1908, Charles took over the responsibilities of the company along with Edward Greene, who had been running the Brazilian office.

After the Great War broke out in 1914 Charles and his younger brother Geoffrey took leave from the company to enter the army, and Edward Greene became managing director. Geoffrey was being groomed to be a future director of the business but he was killed at the age of twenty-six in 1915. The war had a devastating effect on the company's fortunes. Most of its European market disappeared, and in 1917 Greene arranged for E. Johnston & Co. to be taken over by the Brazilian Warrant Co. Ltd, although it kept its trading name.

In the years following the war the company continued to struggle. The Brazilian government had accumulated large stocks of unsaleable coffee, its economy was in a state of near-collapse, and the value of the Brazilian milreis would more than halve over the next few years. The business was finally rescued in 1922 when the banks entrusted E. Johnston & Co. with the job of selling four and a half million bags of Brazilian coffee through their contacts in the United States and Europe.

It was while Charles Johnston was overseeing this enormous operation that he drowned in Bude in 1922, the accident being followed three months later by the tragic death of his father Reginald. This left on the board of the company only Francis Alexander Johnston, another grandson of Edward's and the younger brother of Bertram, who had died of yellow fever. When he retired three years later he was the last Johnston to be involved with the family business.

So when Brian left Oxford in 1934 his relations saw him as a symbolic connection with the founder of the company, his great-grandfather Edward, and that is why he came under such immense pressure to join the business.

In the end Brian felt powerless to resist, and in October 1934 he moved reluctantly up to London. He went to live with his father's cousin Francis Alexander Johnston, known as 'Cousin Alex', who was also his godfather. Alex Johnston was the chairman of Atlas Assurance and deputy chairman of the National Provincial Bank. He was a very good-looking man, and said by many to be the best-dressed man in London; some of his relations even called him 'Piccadilly Johnston'. According to Christopher Johnston, Alex 'made a lot of money but didn't spend it', although he was chauffeured around London in a brand-new Minerva – 'the Belgian Rolls-Royce'. He may have been careful with his money but he knew how to enjoy it.

Alex and his wife Audrey lived in a large house at 56 Queen's Gate in South Kensington. They had no children but compensated for this with staff, employing a butler, footman, housemaid, under-housemaid, 'tweeny', cook and chauffeur. Targett the butler was a wonderful old character who was very keen on the horses and would whisper hot betting tips to Brian as he was serving him the vegetables at dinner. One evening Chris Johnston was a dinner guest when Cousin Alex had just bought a new overcoat. Alex ordered the butler to put on the overcoat and walk up and down the dining room, so that he could see how it looked.

Audrey was a formidable woman who liked to know exactly what everybody else was doing. When Audrey's niece Anne Hankey and her cousin Joanah used to stay with her at Queen's Gate, Audrey would attempt to listen in to their telephone conversations with their boyfriends. She also liked to intercept Brian's telephone calls and chat to his friends, so Edward the footman would rush to answer the phone first to tell them when it was safe to ring back.

Audrey was a bit of a hypochondriac. According to her niece Anne (now Mrs Hanbury), she loved having operations and being fussed over afterwards. She was forever taking to her bed with some malady or other, and had a favourite doctor who would sit on the bed with her and tell her racy stories. He even took her out to the theatre.

Alex was over seventy but he still had an eye for the ladies and, unknown to Audrey, for several years he had kept a mistress in

Golders Green. One summer Alex and Audrey went on holiday to Sidmouth in Devon, where they were introduced to a Mrs Balfour, wife of one of the local dignitaries. Eve Balfour was a very attractive blonde, much admired by the local men and much distrusted by their wives. One day Alex Johnston announced that he was going out for a walk. When he had not returned after several hours Audrey feared he had fallen off a cliff and called the police. They found Alex having tea with Mrs Balfour.

It was not uncommon, at a time when families socialised together more than they do today, for brothers and sisters to marry their in-laws. So it was that Alex Johnston's younger sister Mildred had married his wife Audrey's elder brother Percival Hankey. Their daughter Anne Hankey was therefore Brian's cousin, but also a niece of both Cousin Alex and Cousin Audrey. When Anne was in London she used to stay with her uncle and aunt at Queen's Gate and saw quite a lot of Brian in the early 1930s. They were the same age and would go to the theatre together or to dances at society venues such as the Hurlingham Club, and even to the Richmond Horse Show.

Not long after Brian had gone up to Oxford, Anne invited him to the South & West Wilts Hunt Ball near her home at Stourton in Wiltshire. Brian motored down in his old car, which he told Anne was called 'Constipation', because it strained and strained and passed nothing. Brian stayed with the Hankeys on several occasions for parties and dances. 'He kept the whole party going,' says Anne. 'He made the most hideous-looking girls think they were the belle of the ball.' Anne's father Percival used to enjoy Brian's naughty jokes, although her mother Mildred was very Victorian and, perhaps fortunately, did not understand most of them.

Anne had never known anyone to be less shy than Brian. He could walk into a room full of strangers and within seconds he would be chatting away as if he had known them for years. The Hankeys had an old cook called 'Hurdie', who was very temperamental, so whenever Brian arrived he would be sent into the kitchen to cheer her up. Within minutes, related Anne, gales of laughter would be heard coming from the kitchen and all would be well again.

As a spare young man just down from Oxford, Brian was invited to many debutante dinners and dances, but it was not really his scene. Now that he was living in London he preferred to go out several nights a week to see a film or a show, with the emphasis on musical comedies, revues and the music hall. He particularly enjoyed going to the London Palladium, the Holborn Empire and Chelsea Palace, where he would see up-and-coming comedy stars such as Flanagan and Allen and Max Miller.

He loved to sit in the balcony at the Café de Paris, where he could get a plate of his favourite scrambled eggs and a glass of lager for about five shillings, and watch cabaret entertainers such as Sophie Tucker and Douglas Byng. This was the era of the great British dance bands, and he also spent many happy hours listening to the music of Roy Fox and Lew Stone at the Monseigneur, Ambrose and Harry Roy at the Mayfair and Carroll Gibbons at the Savoy.

He even went to the notorious Windmill Theatre, where nude girls had to stand perfectly still in carefully staged tableaux. He would admit later that the real reason he went there was to watch the comedians, especially John Tilley, who did a hilarious act as a scoutmaster. It is not that he was not interested in girls, but he was fascinated by the art of comedy. After he died I found a folder marked 'GAGS' tucked away in a drawer of the Wellington chest that stood in his study. It contained pages and pages of handwritten jokes and double-act routines, many of them on headed notepaper dating back to the 1930s.

According to his friends, in those days Brian was more comfortable in male company. He enjoyed the formal atmosphere of a gentleman's club like Boodles, and he was also a member of the Bachelors' Club in South Audley Street. One night in January 1935 he was in Pratts Club when he met Winston Churchill, who had come from doing a broadcast on the BBC about India. Brian was having a drink with Buns Cartwright, the Secretary of the Eton Ramblers, who knew Churchill and invited him to join them at their table. The day before there had been extraordinary scenes in the House of Commons during a debate on unemployment. *The Times* reported that the Scottish Independent Labour MP for Glasgow (Gorbals) had been 'moved to passionate personal abuse' of the Prime Minister, Ramsay MacDonald. This was followed by shouts of 'Down with the National Government' from the Strangers' Gallery, and the whole gallery had to be cleared. Churchill had not been in the Commons but he told Brian that he was angry about the outburst and 'even though he himself thought Ramsay a rotter, someone ought to have got up at the time to back him up'.

The nightlife may have been fun but the daytime was certainly not. On 1 October 1934 Brian arrived for his first day of work, equipped with a new bowler hat and rolled umbrella, in the offices of E. Johnston & Co. at 20 King William Street. He had a starting salary of £150, which he described to his mother as 'excellent'. His hours were from '9.30 till anything between 5 and 6 p.m. everyday, every third Saturday off and up to 12 p.m. on the other two'.

His first job was working in the cable office. Coded messages would come in on the telex from the company's agents in Europe. These would usually be orders for bags of coffee, which the office then had to put into a fresh code and forward on to Brazil. Brian had to learn how to type, but never progressed beyond two fingers at a time. He was taught how to taste the samples of coffee by swilling it round in his mouth and then spitting it out into a large spittoon. He tried to understand the City jargon such as 'draft at ninety days sight' and 'cash against documents less 2½%', but failed miserably.

He filled in time by writing to his mother with the latest office jokes: 'My telephone bell rang here the other day, so I took the receiver off and the operator said, "It's a long distance from Scotland." I said, "I know it is, but why the hell ring up and tell me."'

He was bored stiff. His brother Chris told me, 'Brian saw the fun in anything – but he couldn't see the fun in coffee.' One day

Brian arrived at work late and was reprimanded by one of the senior staff.

'Mr Johnston,' he said, 'you should have been here at nine-thirty.'

'Why,' replied Brian, 'what happened?'

He still found time for fun and games with William Douglas Home, and in July 1935 the intrepid pair chartered a small aeroplane from Croydon and flew down to Portsmouth to see the two hundred warships of the fleet, gathered at Spithead for the Royal Naval Review. It was probably Brian's first flight, and they were airborne for about eighty minutes. Afterwards he wrote: 'It was very thrilling, though we were pretty frightened as there had already been two crashes that day.'

After serving a year's apprenticeship in the London office, Brian was sent to Hamburg to learn more about the European side of the coffee business. He flew from Croydon to Amsterdam, where they stopped for breakfast, and from there to Hamburg, in a Douglas aircraft that 'went at an enormous pace, right above the clouds'.

E. Johnston & Co.'s German agent, Herr Korner, was an ex-U-boat captain from the First World War and his assistant was a keen member of the Nazi Party. Brian lodged with around six other young Germans and Norwegians in a pension run by a family who had been well off but had fallen on hard times. He had a sitting room, bedroom and a balcony for five shillings a day. He found everything extremely cheap in Hamburg and told his mother, 'one can spend a very good evening in a restaurant for about 1/- or 2/-'. He was also impressed with the dozens of nightclubs on the Reeperbahn, and particularly enjoyed a Bavarian restaurant 'where they all get up and dance on the tables when they happen to like a tune'.

The office staff were rigidly formal. Brian would have to shake hands all round on arrival at the office every morning, on going to and coming back from lunch, and again when he went home in the evening. One of his main problems was that he could not speak the language; he knew only about ten words of German. Soon after he arrived he was taken by Herr Korner to a business meeting with one of their buyers. Brian managed to say 'Hello' and 'Goodbye' in German and spent the rest of the meeting nodding in all the appropriate places. The buyer never realised that Brian had not understood a single word.

He went for German lessons twice a week to 'a rather aristocratic Frau' who lived in a large house. She taught forty-three pupils free of charge and handed out wine and cigarettes with the lessons. 'She must be mad,' wrote Brian, 'but is very nice and we get on with her.'

He used to practise his newly learned German phrases on an aunt of the family who lived at his pension. She spoke no English, so Brian would deliberately say the most awful things to her in German and pretend he did not realise that he had said anything wrong.

His grasp of German was obviously tenuous. One night he was dining out in a restaurant when he asked the waiter whether he had any bananas – or so he thought. The waiter replied, 'Yes, certainly, sir,' hurried away and asked the band to play 'Yes, We Have No Bananas'.

In a letter to his mother, Brian passed on his first Hitler joke: 'Someone said "Hail Hitler" to him the other day, so he said, "How dare you hail me when I am reigning".'

Brian found the German hospitality rather overwhelming. 'It's awful,' he wrote home, 'they won't let one refuse anything and are very hurt if one goes home after a dinner before 2 or 3 a.m. It's most exhausting.' On 19 November 1935 the Nazi Party member in his office took Brian to hear a speech by Dr Josef Goebbels, Hitler's Minister of Propaganda and Public Enlightenment. It was at a Nazi Party rally held in an enormous hall in Hamburg, where about 25,000 people sat on hard wooden benches while Goebbels spoke for nearly two hours. Brian felt very conspicuous in his City pinstripe suit among the hordes of Nazi brown shirts. With his limited knowledge of the language he hardly understood a single word of the speech, but at one point Goebbels' voice rose to a high-pitched scream. He was offering the German people a famous choice: guns or butter. Everyone in the hall sprang to their feet, gave the Nazi salute and shouted one word. Even Brian could tell it was not 'butter'.

At the end of it, said Brian, there was probably only one person more exhausted than Goebbels, and that was him. Later he confessed that he had felt obligated to shout '*Heil*' along with the Germans, and summed up the experience as 'very interesting, if rather nauseating'.

In mid-December he moved on to Bremen, where he spent a week with one of the company's other German agents, and then returned home to England to spend Christmas with his family. In January he was sent off to France and sailed to Le Havre, where he stayed at the Hotel Frascati for three weeks. The hotel was almost deserted, and after a few days he had still not spotted another guest. He ate alone in the dining room every evening, surrounded by about seven waiters 'ready to pounce at the slightest fall of the knife or fork'. When it came to food he was a creature of habit, and soon the waiters knew exactly what he was going to eat at every meal and had it ready for him, even down to his orange juice, 'which shook them a bit at first'.

He spent most of his days visiting the company's buyers in the region and once again struggled with the language. At first he found himself speaking to everyone in German. One day he went down to the port to see the ocean liners *Ile de France*, *Normandie* and *Paris*. When a ship called the *Largo* came in he turned to a man next to him and said, 'I expect that's a pretty difficult ship to Handel.' He told his mother later: 'I don't think he saw it.'

At the end of February he spent a couple of days in Antwerp with the company's Belgian agent before returning home. He now had three months in England in which to cram as much as possible. During one week in May he played in two cricket matches, went to a dance at Claridge's, and saw two plays and a musical in the West End. At Whitsun he went to Lord's Cricket Ground for the annual match between Middlesex and Surrey and saw an eighteen-year-old from the Lord's ground staff making his first-class debut. The young batsman went in at number eleven and made 14 runs, and Brian was suitably impressed. When Patsy

Hendren retired a year later, Brian 'adopted' Denis Compton as his new cricketing hero.

Then, after a final flurry of cricket, parties and extended farewells, came the moment Brian had been dreading. On 27 June 1936 he set sail from Southampton on the Royal Mail liner *Almanzora* for Brazil, to spend the next two years learning about coffee in the Santos office of E. Johnston & Co. He was extremely unhappy about having to leave his friends, his cricket and his London life, but he was resigned to his fate.

9

An Awful Lot of Coffee

The voyage on the *Almanzora* took about seventeen days, with stop-offs at Lisbon and Madeira en route. There were not many first-class passengers on board, so Brian spent most of his time reading or playing ping-pong. The liner had 'quite a good' dance band, he told his mother, 'though the material to dance with is somewhat absent'. The best moment happened at Cherbourg, when the boat bringing out some French passengers fouled a line in its propeller and was unable to move for an hour, resulting – to Brian's great amusement – in 'streams of French excitement'.

He arrived in Santos in the middle of a tropical thunderstorm and felt miserable and homesick. Even worse, he discovered that his work permit was not in order, so he was hurriedly sent 'up-country' while the authorities sorted out the red tape. He had to spend a month at Gallia, about four hundred miles inland and eight thousand feet up, on one of the company's fazendas, or coffee plantations.

Once his papers were in order Brian returned to Santos and moved into a rented house overlooking the beach with three other Britons, Fred Duder, Rex Davies and Robert Hunt. The owner of the house was Jock Munro, the local manager of Anglo-Mex, who had returned to England on leave for six months. The tenants inherited his cook and his maid, but they had to look after his Scottish terrier, for which Munro deducted 100 milreis (about £1) a month from their rent. Brian worked out that it cost him a total of 700 milreis (about £8) a month to live in Santos, including everything from laundry to drinks. His salary was only £150 a year but this meant he still had more than £50 left over. Drinks were an important part of his budget, he admitted, because in the tropical climate, 'though one swallow does not make a summer, summer seems to make a good many swallows'.

He tried to make the best out of being in Santos but his heart was really not in it. For a start he had to learn another language – Portuguese. He was supposed to have lessons with a woman called Frau Keller but he seldom went and usually rang up to say he could not make it. Brian's accent was 'atrocious', according to Fred Duder, and his rotten Portuguese became a kind of running gag. After eight months he gave up the struggle and switched to improving his German instead.

Fred Duder worked in the coffee room at E. Johnston & Co. in Santos. He was British, but had been born in Brazil and his family had lived there for many years. He was a year older than Brian and shared a similar sense of humour, and they soon became great friends. They used to play tennis together and even won the doubles trophy in the local club tournament, although Fred told me it was impossible playing tennis with Brian because he was always telling jokes and making a lot of noise. More surprisingly Brian also won the men's singles trophy, which he put down to 'some stupendous handicapping and some pretty good cuts and spins'.

They used to travel to and from work together on the tram, and Brian would often make funny comments about their fellow passengers. One of the regulars was a German businessman, whom they learned was called Herr Köhl (pronounced 'Curl'). You can imagine Brian's delight when one day the German took off his hat and revealed that he was completely bald. Brian suspected Köhl of being a Nazi spy, and when the *Graf Zeppelin* airship made a propaganda flight over Santos, Brian joked with Fred that the German was flashing secret signals to the airship from his bald pate.

Brian still could not see the fun in coffee. In fact the more he saw of it the less he liked it. After five months in Santos he was promoted to the coffee room, to learn more about the different types of bean. Later he confessed that he was never able to tell one bean from another, nor taste any difference between the various types. A week before Christmas 1936 he wrote home despondently: 'I look hopefully for snow to fall as the festival approaches, but the only flakes are gold and smell even worse here than in England.' Four months later he sounded even more disillusioned: 'It's funny one talks of a lively person being full of beans, yet so is a coffee bag, and it looks as dull and dead as anything you could imagine.'

He was also beginning to suffer from the dreaded Santos liver and was losing weight at an alarming rate. Almost every Briton in Brazil contracted jaundice after about two or three years there, but Brian's condition was not helped by his diet. He was a fussy eater who liked plain English cooking, and he refused to eat many of the local fruit and vegetables. His favourite meal in Sântos was risotto. He had always been on the thin side – one of his Oxford friends described him as 'raw-boned' – but photographs taken in Brazil at this time show him as hollow cheeked and gaunt.

His mother was obviously concerned about his health, but he told her not to worry. There's only one cure, he added: don't live in Santos. The doctors had advised him not to eat anything yellow, such as eggs or oranges, which only served to limit his diet even further. But as he explained, he was actually much better than several of his friends in Santos, including his house-mate Fred Duder, who had such a bad case of jaundice that he looked 'like Anna May Wong's husband'.

The climate did not help much either. Brian described it as 'lowering' and 'a very tiring atmosphere'. During February 1937 there was an unseasonal heatwave, which he complained was 'the hottest weather they've had here for years. I'm rather like a burst balloon. Everything sticks to one all day and then one just goes and sits in the sea.'

At least there was a good social life among the many expatriate English and Americans in Santos, especially at the weekends, and everyone seemed to drop by Brian and Fred's beach house for drinks on a Sunday morning. It was a very close-knit society, and Brian had soon met most of the 'elite' of Santos, although he was not overly impressed. 'Some very nice,' he commented, 'some not so good, being rather hearty and common, an awful mixture.'

The main centre of activity was the Anglo-American Club, and after a few months Brian was appointed Chairman of the Entertainments Committee. Cricket was played on matting about twice a month, although it was hard to find any competitive opponents. The main fixtures seem to have been Married v. Singles, Fathers v. Sons, and Gentlemen v. Ladies. The latter was not as straightforward as it seems because the Gentlemen had to bat, bowl and field left handed, which meant they usually lost quite heavily. On a more serious level Brian was selected to play for the State of São Paulo eleven in a three-day match against the State of Rio. His side was beaten, although Brian was praised for his wicket-keeping in the local English newspaper, which also noted his individual hit-and-run batting style: 'He taught both sides the art of running short runs.' In fact he made the second-top score with 22.

To make up for the lack of cricket, every Sunday morning the English colony used to take on the Americans at baseball on the beach. One weekend there was great excitement when an American cruiser came into port and a proper baseball match was hurriedly organised on the cricket ground. Brian was thrilled when he scored his team's only home run.

Back in England, during the summer of 1936 Brian's mother Pleasance and his stepfather Marcus had to leave Homewell, their house in Bude, for financial reasons. They put the house up for sale and moved temporarily into the Royal Hotel at Ascot, in Berkshire. According to Pat Scott (née Thomas), Brian's former friend in Bude, the estate agent's details described Homewell's garden rather grandly as having two lakes, which caused much amusement among the locals. They were actually two small fish ponds.

In October 1936 Brian heard the news that his sister Anne was getting a divorce. Her husband John Carter had met another woman, Margaret Astil, whom he wanted to marry. To everyone's surprise

Anne said that if she approved of Margaret as a stepmother for her children, she would agree to a divorce. This she did, and almost immediately Anne left her three eldest children with John, taking their one-year-old baby, Howard, with her to Rhodesia, where she moved in with a policeman called Terry Sharp, her mother-in-law's younger brother, whom she had met in England.

Brian was very upset by the break-up of his sister's marriage. Three months later he received an even greater shock. His mother Pleasance was also going to be divorced. She and Marcus Scully had not been getting on well for some time and there had been frequent rows between them. On New Year's Eve in 1936 they were at a party at the Royal Hotel in Ascot when Scully suddenly got up and walked out, leaving Pleasance on her own amid all the festivities. He never came back.

Brian was distraught. He walked into the office of Cecil Gledhill, the manager of E. Johnston & Co. in Santos, waving his mother's letter in his hand, and exclaimed, 'Now there are *two* divorces!' Gledhill told Vera Duder, Fred's youngest sister, that Brian was terribly unhappy about being away from home at such a time. Curiously, she says Brian never spoke about it with her, even though they were close friends. He was of a generation that did not like to display their emotions, especially at such a vulnerable moment.

Later, when he heard that Scully was planning to get remarried, Brian wrote to his mother in dismay: 'I'm afraid all this divorce and remarrying sounds incredible to me and much too like the films to be true – but I suppose it is. I can't see where it leads to, as it's so awful for everyone concerned.'

There was another problem too. Since Brian had been in Brazil, his beloved Sealyham terrier Blob had been looked after by his mother and Marcus at Homewell. Now that they were selling their house and getting a divorce he had to find a new home for the dog. Eventually it was arranged that Blob would live with Jimmy Lane Fox and his sister Felicity at their house in Yorkshire, where he settled in well, although it seems he still missed his old master. Brian used to take Blob to cricket matches, and whenever he came off the field Blob would rush on and proudly carry his master's wicket-keeping gloves in his mouth. One day the Lane Foxes found that Blob was missing and searched everywhere for him. After a while they discovered him sitting on the edge of the village green, watching a cricket match.

At the end of 1936 the nation was shocked by the abdication of King Edward VIII. The British press were limited in how much they were allowed to print, but there was no such restriction on the American media and Brian followed avidly the latest gossip about Edward and Mrs Simpson in *Time* magazine and on the radio. After the abdication he joked: 'I feel sorry for Ted but he had to go. Rumour has it that Lord Nuffield [the millionaire philanthropist] has bought Mrs Simpson and presented her to the nation.' Brian was fascinated by the whole affair and in particular the speeches by Queen Mary and Prime Minister Stanley Baldwin, which he learned by heart. He involved all his friends in re-enacting the events as he imagined they had happened at Buckingham Palace and 10 Downing Street.

There was a succession of cocktail parties in Santos over the festive season, which gave Brian a chance to try out some of his new 'knock-knock' jokes: 'Sonia – Sonia rumour'; 'Butcher – Butcher coat on or you'll catch cold'; 'Thunder – Thunder the bed if you want to use it'. They were dreadful, especially the 'Thunder' one, which Fred Duder revealed was one of Brian's favourites. In the normally genteel atmosphere of a Santos cocktail party anyone else would have been thrown out, but Brian had such an infectious sense of humour that somehow he got away with it.

Not all of his jokes went down so well, however. One day Brian went with some friends to the dockside to see off his house-mate Robert Hunt, who was being transferred to Pernambuco, farther up the coast in northern Brazil. A press photographer took some photographs and asked them for their names. Brian told him they were Lord Shufflebottom, Lady Kissmequick and one or two others, and said they were going off to help at the coronation of King George VI. Next day the story appeared in the local paper, along with their photograph, causing a great deal of adverse

1. Edward Johnston, Brian's great-grandfather, who founded the family coffee business in Brazil in 1842.

2. Marcus Scully with Brian, his mother and father, and brothers Christopher and Michael at Coombe Mill, near Bude in Cornwall.

3. 'A very efficient wicket-keeper' at Temple Grove.

4. 'None swifter than Johnston': the athlete at Eton.

5. In fancy dress for the Wall Game on Ascension Day at Eton, 14 May 1931. (*Back row, left*) William Douglas Home; (*middle row, second from left*) Brian, (*right*) Jimmy Lane Fox.

6. Off to a lecture at Oxford with 'Lily': William Douglas Home (*second from left*) and Brian as the groom, May 1934.

7. Going nuts in Brazil. Brian (*top*) with his best friend in Brazil, Fred Duder, and Frank Fussell at Bõa Vista Beach, Santos, 1937.

8. Recuperating after his illness at an Eton Ramblers match with 'Buns' Cartwright, at Windlesham Moor, 23 July 1938.

9. *Below*: 'I say, I say, I say!' Entertaining the troops with Charles Villiers at Castle Cary, Somerset, October 1940.

10. *Right*: New boy at the BBC. Planning the broadcast of another West End musical with John Ellison, c. 1947.

11. *Below*: Brian and Pauline are married at St Paul's, Knightsbridge, on 22 April 1948.

12. The first *Let's Go Somewhere* in the Chamber of Horrors at Madame Tussauds, 23 October 1948. Brian sits in front of waxworks of the murderers Frederick Seddon, Arthur Devereux and H. J. Bennett.

THE PEOPLE

SUNDAY, MAY 20, 1951   No. 3628 –70th Year

- **They advertised for girls who wanted "adventure"**
- **It was a hoax for "In Town Tonight"**

B.B.C. STUNT STARTS A GIRL STAMPEDE IN PICCADILLY

QUITE THE SILLIEST STUNT THE B.B.C. HAS EVER TRIED CAUSED A STAMPEDE IN PICCADILLY CIRCUS, LONDON, LAST NIGHT. POLICE HAD TO RUSH TO THE SCENE TO CONTROL THE CROWD.

Over five hundred girls started it. They responded to an advertisement in the " personal " column of an evening newspaper asking for " young ladies seeking adventure " to meet there a " well-set-up young gentleman."

The result—as might have been expected—was alarming. For not only did the girls turn up in their hundreds, but hundreds of sightseers also rushed to the scene to see what was happening.

With the result that traffic was held up and four police sergeants and eighteen constables were needed to control the jam.

All this was the result of " a lark " by the B.B.C.'s Brian Johnsten, who thought it would produce a bit of fun for the " In Town Tonight " programme.

He did it by inserting this advertisement in the personal column of a London evening newspaper on Friday:—

WELL SET-UP YOUNG GENTLEMAN with honourable intentions inviting young ladies seeking adventure to meet him on the steps of the Criterion Restaurant, Lower Regent-st., 7.15 p.m. Saturday, May 19. Identified by red carnation and blue and white spotted scarf. Code words.—"How's your uncle?"

Half an hour before the time announced, the girls began to roll up. Soon there was a stampede.

They began fighting and jostling to get near the steps of the restaurant. Police whistles blew as screaming women were pushed against the windows of near-by shops.

Then a middle-aged woman went down in the crowd as her shoe was stamped on and smashed. A protective circle was formed around her, but still the crowd swelled.

' It's only me '

At 7.21 the " young gentleman " ......ed. He had been hiding ...... screen inside the restau...

Back cover p...... ......sion saw the ...... " It's

---

13. CRUEL HOAX: the famous 'Piccadilly Incident', 19 May 1951.

comment among the British colony. This time Brian had gone too far. They were *not* amused.

In May 1937 Jock Munro returned from leave and Brian moved farther along the beach into another house owned by a friend called Macpherson. Brian described it as being in 'the best position in Santos'. He was joined by Fred Duder and his two sisters, twenty-eight-year-old Helena, who taught the English children living in Santos, and twenty-five-year-old Vera, a dancing teacher. Vera was dark and pretty and her family nickname was 'Nip', because she was small and always nipping about. Fred told me that Brian was 'very keen' on his sister and that she and Brian developed quite a crush on each other. I asked Vera (now Mrs Franks) about their relationship in Santos and she described it as 'propinquity', suggesting that they had become close friends through being thrown together. Nevertheless, for a time it seems to have been quite serious.

One of the few good things about being in Santos was that it enabled Brian to develop his love of the stage. In November 1936 he helped to organise a revue for the British Legion which was attended by about two hundred people. He was the compère and 'told silly stories in front of the curtain'. He also acted in a thirty-minute comedy and took part in a cross-talk act with Mike Bolsover, who worked at Western Telegraph. Brian wrote the script for the cross-talk act and included many of his favourite music-hall jokes from the Holborn Empire, which shocked some of the more sensitive ladies in the audience. A new British consul, James Joint, had just arrived in Santos. That inspired the old chestnut – 'My brother is doing nothing.' 'Oh, I thought he was trying for that job as consul in Santos.' 'Yes, he got the job!' – which earned a huge laugh.

About six months later, in May 1937, Brian co-produced *Nuts in May*, a revue in two acts, at the Santos Athletic Club. He took part in several sketches, including a solo turn as the Mystery Man from Newmarket in 'I've got a Horse', and performed a double act with John Miers as the Two Jays in 'Spot of Trouble', which ended with them pelting each other with pudding, eggs and flour.

(Incidentally, Fred Duder informed me that Brian was known by almost everyone in Santos as 'Jay' – but *never* Johnners. That would come later.) The revue attracted a record crowd of 220 people, which filled the club and resulted in a clear profit of £10. It was said to have been the funniest show they had ever seen there.

His next performance was at a cabaret-dinner-dance held at the Santos Athletic Club in August. Brian wrote and performed a song about some of the people in Santos, to a tune from the musical *The Country Girl*. One of the verses was about the American colony and went:

> Yanks, Yanks, we give you our thanks
> For coming tonight all so jolly
> And for giving our Ted, a partner in bed
> In the shape of the thrice-married Wally.

In November Brian made his acting debut in a production of Arnold Ridley's West End favourite *The Ghost Train*. He had one of the leading roles as the silly-ass character Teddie Deakin, who turns out to be a policeman in disguise. He wore a monocle and spoke in a high-pitched voice. On the opening night all was going well until he came to the scene in which he had to reveal himself and to explain how the gun-runners had worked the train. Brian stepped forward dramatically. 'What they did was . . .' he started, but that was as far as he got. He dried up completely, causing the biggest laugh of the evening, which is not exactly what the author had intended.

There is a picture of Brian on stage during *The Ghost Train*, and he is almost unrecognisable. He is extremely thin and was obviously not very well. Sitting in the audience was his mother, who had come out to Brazil on the *Almanzora* to stay with him, perhaps concerned about his health. She stayed in Santos for about two months, before returning to England in early January 1938.

The annual Carnaval was held in February, and it seems to have been almost as colourful an event in Santos as in Rio de

Janeiro. The dancing in the streets went on for three days and ended with a huge ball at the Parque Balneario Hotel, which, reported Brian, 'literally never stops from 11 p.m. to 6 a.m. as they have two orchestras which pick up the time from each other. They only play about five tunes all evening and people just rush round doing this queer Brazilian dance, just like a gallop in England but with a sort of tango rhythm.' Brian and a group of his friends drove through the streets of Santos in a large open car, cheering and throwing streamers.

It was shortly after the Carnaval in 1938 that Brian became seriously ill. He had started a new job, working during the week at the E. Johnston & Co. office in São Paulo and returning to Santos, where he kept a room in a large house owned by Charles and Dorothy Deighton, at the weekends. Charles, known as 'Jerry', was the accountant at Johnston's and Dorothy was a doctor in Santos. One day Brian noticed he was beginning to lose the use of his arms and legs, and after two days he could hardly move. He was diagnosed as suffering from acute peripheral neuritis (a form of beri-beri) and was rushed back to Santos, where he was nursed 'like a child' for six weeks by Dorothy Deighton. By now he was almost completely paralysed and unable to do anything for himself; he even had to be fed. Fortunately there was a local doctor called D'Utra Vaz who had dealt with this disease before and knew exactly what to do. He prescribed a diet of raw vegetables, lots of tomatoes – which Brian hated – daily injections ('over ninety') in the bottom, lots of massage and hours of lying in the sun.

At one point it was not certain that Brian would ever regain the use of his legs, but one day, to cheers from the Deightons, he was able to wriggle one of his toes. He slowly improved, but he was so weak that he had to learn how to walk again. The cause of the disease was said to be a deficiency of Vitamin B, due to Brian's lack of any fresh vegetables, although the doctor added that it could also be brought on by excessive drinking or childbirth! Brian's mother rushed out to Brazil to be with him, and in May he was fit enough to sail home with her to England.

About a year later, in 1939, Brian heard that Vera 'Nip' Duder was back in London and arranged to meet her. He took her out to dinner at the old Berkeley Hotel in Mayfair but, whatever their expectations, it seems that away from the exotic atmosphere of Santos the magic had gone. Said Vera simply: 'There was no spark in the friendship any more.' They parted as just good friends.

10

Peace for Our Time

Back home in England in June 1938 Brian was prescribed a strict regimen of rest, exercises, no drink, injections and early nights. He was not even allowed to play cricket. He had lost a tremendous amount of weight and was still very frail, and it would be several months before he was well enough to return to work.

At first he moved back in with Alex and Audrey at Queen's Gate, where he was welcomed back by all the servants and treated as a semi-invalid. But after a few weeks he moved out to join William Douglas Home in rooms at 35 South Eaton Place. The lodging house was run by a wonderful couple called Mr and Mrs Crisp. Tom Crisp, or Crippen as Brian later called him, was a retired butler and 'the perfect gentleman's gentleman', while his wife, Gert, was 'an absolute saint and a super cook'. They had met while working as servants together for a peer of the realm.

They had two rooms vacant. One of their tenants, Jo Grimond, who had been in Pop with Brian at Eton, had recently left to get married, so Brian took over his old room and John Hogg, his former flatmate at Oxford, moved into the other. As luck would have it Crisp had a very good sense of humour. He needed it because Brian and William ribbed him constantly. Sometimes when they were having a dinner party Crisp would wait at table in a powdered wig and knee-breeches. Alfred (Freddie) Shaughnessy, who had known Brian at Eton, was invited to dinner at 35 South Eaton Place in 1938. He thinks William was trying to raise money to put on a new play in the West End. Shaughnessy told me: 'They teased Crisp like mad. If he got something wrong they would shout, "Crisp! Go down to your quarters where you belong!"' If there were strangers present they would ask innocently around the dinner table whether anyone knew of a good butler, and Crisp would pretend to be shocked and drop a plate loudly on the floor.

Sir Edward Ford was another dinner guest at number 35. He remarked that Brian was 'totally classless' and always treated Tom and Gert Crisp as friends and not servants. As a result the Crisps were incredibly loyal to him and never minded being the subject of his schoolboy humour. 'The Crisps were made to feel completely a part of it,' explained Ford. Crippen and Brian even used to go to Highbury to watch Arsenal together – Brian was a lifelong Gunners fan – and once saw the legendary Alex James score a sensational hat-trick.

Brian spent most of the summer of 1938 catching up with his many friends, going to the theatre and watching cricket, especially the touring Australians under Don Bradman. He was always proud that he was at Lord's to see Wally Hammond hit a 'majestic' 240 in the second Test against Australia, which he considered to be 'one of the greatest Test innings I ever saw'.

Brian was a confirmed bachelor in the old-fashioned sense and, while he enjoyed the company of women, he was a bit shy when it came to actual romance. This led to a practical joke being played on him during the Lord's Test. One night William was with his friend Michael Astor at the Bag O' Nails club in Soho, when they were introduced to a young 'lady of the night'. William persuaded her to come back to South Eaton Place where Brian was already fast asleep in bed, snoring soundly after a long day watching the Test. They quietly opened his bedroom door, ushered the young lady in and shut it again. After a few minutes they heard the murmur of voices and, unable to resist, sneaked the door open to find Brian sitting up in bed describing the day's marvellous cricket to his fascinated companion, perched innocently at the far end of the bed. After they had informed the girl it was time to leave, Brian shook her hand and thanked her for coming, and as his door closed, related William, the snoring gently resumed.

Brian was thinking seriously about leaving the family business. While he was in Brazil several of his friends in England had started to ask around for him. John Hogg had even arranged for him to be offered an interview by a firm of stockbrokers in the City – 'Solomon & Isaacs, or some such' – but as there was no guarantee of a job, Brian had felt it was too much of a risk to return to England.

In July 1938 he had lunch with Arthur Whitworth, the chairman of E. Johnston & Co., who persuaded him to stay on at the company for a while longer. They agreed that Brian would go to see clients in New York for about six weeks in October and then to Kenya for a similar time the following February. Brian was delighted. 'If after that things are no better,' he recounted to his mother, 'and there's nothing much for me to do, we agree it is best for me to try something else, and he supports the idea of the stage if I want it.'

His delight was short lived. On 29 September the Prime Minister, Neville Chamberlain, flew out for talks with Adolf Hitler in Munich in an attempt to avert war. At that time Brian was an ardent supporter of the Prime Minister, and after Chamberlain made his dramatic announcement in the House of Commons that he was going to meet Herr Hitler, Brian enthused to his mother, 'Neville really is great.' William Douglas Home's eldest brother Alec, then Lord Dunglass, was Chamberlain's Parliamentary Private Secretary. When he realised that he would be going to Munich with the Prime Minister, he rushed round to South Eaton Place to borrow a clean white shirt. Brian was happy to lend him one and afterwards he was able to claim that his shirt had met Adolf Hitler. He went to Heston aerodrome with Alec's wife Elizabeth, Gert Crisp and William to cheer the Prime Minister off, and next day they returned to see Chamberlain wave his famous piece of paper and declare: 'I believe it is peace for our time.' For the moment it seemed true, and a few days later Brian felt honoured when it was announced in *The Times* that Mr Neville Chamberlain and Mr Brian Johnston had been asked to be joint godfathers to Alec and Elizabeth's daughter, Meriel.

As the situation in Europe grew worse, Brian volunteered to do some ARP (air-raid precautions) work. He acted as general transport, driving between various centres and helping to fit gas masks on to invalids. He had an ARP sign on his car and would 'dash through traffic looking v. important'. It was 'all great fun', he reported enthusiastically, 'but everything is wonderfully organised and we really are prepared.'

The Munich crisis and Hitler's subsequent invasion of Czechoslovakia put paid to Brian's overseas plans. In October 1938 he was pronounced fit enough to go back to work and he returned reluctantly to his old office at 20 King William Street. After the experience he was supposed to have gained in Brazil he was promoted to London manager with a salary of £500 a year and given an office of his own, with an enormous desk that had belonged to his grandfather Reginald.

He never did make it to New York or Kenya, but instead he was sent on a short tour of Europe. Over the next few weeks he visited the company's agents in Norway, Sweden and Denmark, as well as France, Holland and Belgium, from where he observed to his mother, 'They're all pretty scared of Hitler here and look to Chamberlain as their saviour.' He also looked in on his old colleagues at the Hamburg office, but found that the Germans had become noticeably more arrogant in their manner. 'I found this rather frightening,' he wrote later. 'They seemed far more intolerant of all those who did not support Hitler.' He was glad to get home.

Towards the end of the year he was invited by the Lane Foxes to the Bramham Hunt Ball in Yorkshire. During the evening he danced the military two-step with a pretty girl called Hester Loyd, known as Heck, who was Anne Lane Fox's younger sister. She was seventeen and more than eight years younger than Brian, but she liked his sense of humour and thought he was fun to be with. On another evening Brian and Heck went with a party to see the ballet at a theatre in Leeds, and she recalls that within minutes Brian had their whole row in giggles at the antics of the dancers on stage.

Back in London Brian began to see Heck Loyd on a regular basis; they would meet for lunch or dinner or to go out to the theatre. Heck had just turned eighteen and this was her 'coming out' year as a debutante. One day in the spring of 1939 Brian invited her to lunch at Rules restaurant in Covent Garden, and when she returned home her father was furious. She was supposed to have been at a debutantes' luncheon.

Brian still lived at 35 South Eaton Place with William Douglas Home and the Crisps, but almost every weekend he used to stay with his mother. Pleasance had moved into Elder Tree Cottage, a delightful black-and-white-timbered thatched cottage in the village of Chearsley, near Aylesbury in Buckinghamshire. The villagers thought she was very posh when she had an extension built on to the cottage to make room for her grand piano.

It was clearly only a matter of time before the country was at war. One day Brian was having lunch in the City with Jimmy Lane Fox and a group of his Eton friends when they agreed that they should try to get on to the reserve of a good regiment. They had all been in the Corps together at school and decided to aim for the top. They applied to the Grenadier Guards, the senior regiment of the Foot Guards, where Brian's cousin Tommy 'Boy' Browning was the commander of the 2nd Battalion. Brian always believed that Browning must have had some influence on the decision, because soon afterwards he learned that he had been accepted, along with his friends, for training by the Grenadiers. He was extremely proud to be a member of the regiment. 'Once a Grenadier,' he used to remind William Douglas Home for the next forty years, 'always a Grenadier.'

They were placed on the Officer Cadet Reserve, and in May they were told to report to Wellington Barracks for drill and basic training. For the rest of the summer, on one or two evenings every week, Brian and his friends would turn up straight from the City in their pinstripe suits and bowler hats. Freddie Shaughnessy was another of the new recruits and says it was highly embarrassing. 'We were marched around the parade ground by the drill sergeant,' he recalls, 'while members of the public used to look through the railings and laugh at us City gents in our bowler hats.'

Whenever Brian was in London for the weekend he used to go to St Michael's Church in Chester Square to hear Canon W. H. Elliott preach. One Sunday his sermon was about families in the North-East and how they were suffering owing to high unemployment, and he suggested that members of the congregation should adopt a family and help them. Brian volunteered and was allocated the Corbett family in Durham, a married couple with four children, whose husband was unemployed and in ill health. From then on Brian wrote to them regularly and sent them money or food and clothing. He referred to them as 'my Durham family'. Mr Corbett died in 1942 and Brian never met Mrs Corbett, although two of her sons visited him after the war in his office at the BBC, but he continued to send her a card and a small present every Christmas for more than thirty years.

During the summer of 1939 Brian played as much cricket as possible, mainly for the Eton Ramblers. Then in August, with war imminent, he had 'one final fling' when he met up with Jimmy Lane Fox and William Douglas Home for a week's holiday at the Cap Martin Hotel in the South of France. During their stay they were invited to dinner at the villa of the American ambassador, Joseph P. Kennedy. William had been going out in London with Kennedy's daughter Kathleen, known as 'Kick', and he and Brian had visited her several times at the US ambassador's house in Prince's Gate, Kensington. They had become great friends with her brother Jack, later President John F. Kennedy, who was then twenty-two and, according to Brian, seemed to enjoy even their worst jokes. After dinner with the Kennedy family they listened to the gloomy voice of the British Foreign Secretary, Lord Halifax, on the wireless. They were advised to return home as soon as possible, and next day the three of them managed to squeeze on to a packed train where, related William, 'Brian succeeded in silencing all conversation by the volubility and volume of his assaults on the French language.'

They made it back to England on the last day of August. When war was declared three days later on Sunday, 3 September, Brian was filling sandbags outside Westminster Hospital. William applied immediately to join the fire service, having already made clear his opposition to the war on political grounds, and Brian tried to join him, but was told to await orders from the army. William was very pessimistic about the outcome of the war, and in 1941 he even wrote a play called *The Little Victims* based on his conviction that Brian would be killed 'because he was such a good fellow', but it was never produced.

For a week or two Brian checked into his office but there was little work for him to do. It felt like the end of an era. Hitler had achieved what he had not been brave enough to do for himself. With mixed emotions of guilt and relief, Brian had made up his mind that once he joined the army there would be no going back for him. Whatever happened to him in the war, he would never return to the family business.

In October he received instructions to report to the Grenadiers for a medical inspection. All went smoothly until the eyesight test, when he had difficulty reading the letters on the card with his rather short-sighted right eye. The doctor simply opened the fingers of the hand covering Brian's left eye so that he could read the letters more easily, and he passed.

So did Jimmy Lane Fox and his other Eton friends. They were sent to the Royal Military College at Sandhurst, which was being turned into an OCTU – an Officer Cadet Training Unit – and they were to be its first 'victims'. Many of the other officer cadets were of a similar age and background, so at first it was like going back to school. The only difference was the reveille at 6 a.m. every morning and the emphasis on PT and drill. But Brian soon settled into the army routine and almost began to enjoy himself.

It was not long before he succumbed to his habit of giving people nicknames. One of the other officer cadets on the course was a young man called Goodfellow. Brian promptly renamed him 'Splendid Chap', and he was known as that from then on. But his sense of humour frequently got him into trouble.

One well-known incident happened during a TEWT – a Tactical Exercise Without Troops – during which the instructors used to take out about twenty cadets and give them various military problems to solve. They had stopped on top of a hill, looking down into the valley below. 'Johnston,' said the instructor, 'you and your platoon are defending this ridge. Suddenly at the bottom of the hill you see a troop of German tanks advancing. What steps do you take?'

'Bloody long ones, sir,' replied Brian, who was instantly 'put in the book' and told to report to the company commander next day for a reprimand. According to William Douglas Home, it was touch and go for some weeks whether Brian would actually make it into the Grenadiers.

Brian could never resist a practical joke. One Sunday the padre suggested that the cadets might be a little more generous with their contributions to the chapel collection. This was tempting fate. Next time they were in the chapel Brian and his friends filled up their pockets with pennies and halfpennies. The gold collection plates were soon overflowing and there was chaos up at the altar. The NCOs did not know whether to react with anger or disbelief. 'I was one of the collectors in Chapel today,' he wrote to his mother jubilantly. 'We made everyone bring in a lot of coppers: one row of six had 71 between them. The plate was so heavy when we had laid the bags on it that the padre had to do a strong man act to bless the money. Quite funny.' The padre never dared to criticise their generosity again.

In early February 1940 Brian went up to London to try on his new uniform. He was thrilled with it and looked forward to the day when all the NCOs who had been ordering him about would have to salute him instead. While he was at the tailors Brian noticed King George VI's field marshal uniform, which was there to be pressed. The tailor allowed him to try it on, and Brian revealed afterwards that it was 31½ inches round the waist and fitted him perfectly.

A fortnight later Brian was officially allowed to wear his new uniform and he left Sandhurst for the last time as a commissioned officer in the Brigade of Guards. He felt a bit of a fraud but, as he said, at least there was the one pip on his shoulder to prove his credentials. After a few days' leave, which he spent seeing all the theatre shows he could, he was sent to the training battalion of the Grenadier Guards at Windsor. Here life continued much as before, with drill in a special officers' squad and instruction in weapons and tactics, until Brian was considered sufficiently trained to be one of the junior officers on the guard at Windsor Castle. This was the wartime home of Princess Elizabeth and Princess Margaret, so he felt as if he was finally doing something to help the war effort.

Then, on 10 May, Hitler invaded Belgium and Holland, Neville Chamberlain resigned and Winston Churchill became Prime Minister. Brian was told to get the necessary injections immediately, collect his full fighting kit and report to Wellington Barracks, where a few days later he received his orders to join the 2nd Battalion in France. The training was over. He was about to go to war. In the heat of the moment he wrote a letter to Heck Loyd with a proposal of marriage. He told her that it would be reassuring for him to go away knowing that he was 'spoken for'.

His letter took Heck by surprise. When I asked her why, she explained that she had realised that Brian was fond of her but thought they were just good companions. They had never even kissed. Heck replied to Brian saying that she was sorry to turn down his proposal but, as she was only nineteen, she could not even consider getting engaged to anybody, especially in the middle of a war. It must have been an extremely difficult letter to write at such a time, but to her credit Heck seems to have found the right words. Brian wrote back to thank her for letting him down so sweetly, and they remained friends.

In his autobiography *It's Been a Lot of Fun* Brian never revealed Hester Loyd's identity but did admit that he had proposed marriage to a girl in 1940. 'Goodness knows what would have happened if she had said "Yes",' he reflected. 'I was in no position to marry anyone, nor was it a very good time to do so. Luckily for both our sakes she had the sense to say no.'

11

Breaking All the Rules

At the beginning of June 1940 the British Expeditionary Force had to be evacuated from Dunkirk and Brian's orders were suddenly cancelled. Instead of going to France, he was sent to join the Grenadier Guards at Shaftesbury in Dorset, where the 2nd Battalion was regrouping after its escape from Dunkirk. His first job was to help in the distribution of the stores as the battalion was re-equipped.

Brian was gregarious by nature and already knew many of the officers in the 2nd Battalion, so he was shocked at Shaftesbury to be on the receiving end of one of the traditions of the Brigade of Guards, designed to keep newly joined officers firmly in their place. For a fortnight he was cut dead by his fellow officers in the mess, even his friends, after which they finally spoke to him and welcomed him into the fold. Brian thought it made them look 'not only ridiculous but boorish and bad-mannered and I cannot believe it did anyone any good'.

The battalion was part of General Montgomery's 3rd Division and was being re-equipped in order to defend the south coast against a possible German invasion. In mid-June they left Shaftesbury to take up positions on the beaches near Middleton-on-Sea in Sussex, where they were billeted in a vacated hotel. Brian was put in charge of the mortar platoon, although he had never fired one, nor even seen one fired in practice, because they were under orders to conserve their ammunition. There were frequent air-raid warnings, although no bombs, and the only real excitement was when Brian celebrated his twenty-eighth birthday by going on the switchback ride at Littlehampton.

As the danger of an immediate invasion receded the 2nd

Battalion was moved to Castle Cary in Somerset, where Brian was given command of the motorcycle platoon. True to form he had never ridden one in his life. The platoon consisted of 'about twenty clapped-out second-hand machines which the Army had bought off the general public'. In the event of enemy action Brian was supposed to lead his platoon while riding in a sidecar armed with only a revolver. His men were intended to provide advance warning to the crack 3rd Division if the Germans invaded along the south coast. Their job was to go down the road the German soldiers were coming up and let the battalion know when they met them, but they were equipped with only a few rifles and had no radio. In September there was an invasion scare and all leave was cancelled. Brian wrote: 'We had to chase a supposed Nazi on a motorbike the other day on our motorbikes, but of course failed to find him.'

During the summer Brian helped to organise cricket matches between the 1st and 2nd Battalions, including one on the Duke of Norfolk's ground at Arundel. He also took part in a battalion concert at Castle Cary and performed a cross-talk double act with one of his fellow officers, Charles Villiers, who had been a member of Pop and had played in the rugby fifteen with him at Eton.

In the autumn the battalion moved again to Parkstone in Dorset and Brian was sent to Minehead on a Motor Transport Course, with a view to making him the Transport Officer. He commented later: 'It was obvious that my superiors felt I would never make a good fighting soldier.' This is being typically modest. Neville Wigram (now Lord Wigram) joined the 2nd Battalion as adjutant in 1941 and he believes that, on the contrary, Brian was singled out because of his outstanding personality. 'To be sent on an MT course after only three months with the battalion was remarkable,' he told me, 'especially to be given that much responsibility so early.'

Brian was not technically minded and later confessed that he only passed his MT exam after a friend showed him the questions the night before, but in December 1940 he was appointed Transport Officer, in charge of a small elite staff of fitters and storemen.

It was a very good job to have. Neville Wigram explained that the Motor Transport Unit were a law unto themselves and were not bothered too much by headquarters, mainly because his superiors were even less technically minded than Brian.

This independence may have suited Brian and his men, but it nearly led to a serious breakdown in discipline. As usual Brian had been unable to resist his practice of giving people nicknames, and members of his staff were soon rejoicing in colourful names such as Burglar Bill, Honest Joe and Gandhi. This was breaking all the rules. The Grenadier Guards were renowned for their strict discipline, and one of their oldest and most important traditions was that officers remained at all times on formal terms with the lower ranks. Officers were expected to refer to their men by rank only and never by Christian names or nicknames. This was believed to produce a stronger line of command and a tougher, more efficient fighting unit in battle.

Soon after Neville Wigram joined the 2nd Battalion in 1941 he was approached by the Regimental Sergeant Major, who expressed concern that Brian's drivers were getting a bit slack and were not as smart as they should be. Wigram had good reason to be worried. He had come from the 1st Battalion, where there had recently been trouble with too much familiarity between the ranks. This had led to a complete breakdown in discipline, resulting in a mutiny, a senior officer being removed, and the whole affair being hushed up by the army.

Wigram took his concerns to the commanding officer, Mike Venables-Llewellyn, and told him that he was worried that Brian was becoming too familiar with his men. To his surprise, the CO disagreed with him and assured Wigram that he was confident his Transport Officer could carry it off. Observed Wigram: 'What was equally remarkable was that Brian's men accepted this familiarity from an officer. They were trained to treat them as superiors. The fear was that discipline would fall apart once the bullets started to fly but, when it did happen, *there* was the discipline. Even when Brian's staff became bigger, they were one hundred per cent loyal and that was because of his power of leadership.'

But he was unique. According to Wigram, other young officers tried to copy Brian's easy familiarity with his men and 'it ended in tears'. They lost the respect of their men and discipline soon collapsed. They were ordered to revert to treating their men in the traditional Guards manner.

Lord Carrington was also in the 2nd Battalion Grenadier Guards and made the point that Brian would not have been allowed to behave as he did before the war. Indeed, to older serving Guards officers his informality was almost like treason. But the war meant he was allowed to bend the rules. 'He treated everyone the same,' explained Carrington. 'One couldn't see him being deferential to anyone. But he never went too far with his humour. Underneath it all he was very shrewd and knew exactly how far he could go.'

Sometimes it must have been a close shave. While they were stationed at Parkstone, William Douglas Home was invited to join Brian for luncheon in the officers' mess. After the meal they retired to the sitting room where Second Lieutenant Johnston offered his commanding officer a chair.

'Thanks, Brian,' said the unsuspecting colonel, but as he sat down Brian pulled the chair away.

Recalled William: 'I looked down at the floor but, much to my surprise, I saw the colonel laughing with the rest of us.'

The next few months were spent training at Parkstone and going out on manoeuvres. After one of these exercises Brian had another lunch with William, who related the following story in a letter to his parents. Brian told him that while out on manoeuvres he had been talking by field telephone to his Intelligence Officer, who was a friend. Brian was supposed to be passing on important tactical information such as 'Machine guns forward' and so on, but at that moment a pack of hounds came past and he started to give a commentary in the style of the BBC commentator Howard Marshall. 'Here comes the fox,' he burbled, 'slipping along the hedge. It's a lovely day . . .' Suddenly a crisp voice at the other end said, 'Come along, Johnston, less fooling please.' The company commander had taken over the telephone. Added William to his parents: 'I doubt if there's a word of truth in it.'

In March 1941 three press correspondents from *The Times*, the *Daily Telegraph* and the *Sketch* were invited to stay with the battalion for three days as part of a public relations exercise. When they visited the Motor Transport Unit Brian arranged for one of his clerks to ring his office every few minutes from a call-box. A few days later the newspapers wrote glowing reports about how hard an MT officer had to work!

Neville Wigram recognised that under Brian's jovial exterior there was an extremely kind man. 'He was never cruel with his humour and believed you could be rude to your contemporaries, but never to those older or younger.' Neville's father, Sir Clive Wigram, was Resident Governor of Windsor Castle during the war. 'I well remember his courtesy to my parents,' continued Neville. 'They came down to Bournemouth to escape the bombing at Windsor. They checked into the Canford Cliffs Hotel and bugger me if that night Bournemouth wasn't bombed! The hotel took a direct hit while I was taking them out to dinner. I'll never forget how sympathetic and nice Brian was to them afterwards.'

One night Brian walked into the Branksome Towers Hotel and was surprised to see his former stepfather Marcus Scully, whom he had not met since he walked out on Brian's mother four years earlier. Scully had remarried soon after the divorce and was staying at the hotel with his new wife. 'She seemed very nice,' Brian confided to his mother, 'and they looked happy, so probably all's for the best.' Scully died before the end of the war.

In mid-April 1941 a landmine fell near 35 South Eaton Place and the house was wrecked. The Crisps were badly shaken but unhurt, although the pub on the corner of Ebury Street had been completely flattened and the blast broke all their windows and blew in the door. Somehow Brian's room survived and he was able to rescue most of his belongings, but the house was no longer habitable. Tom and Gert Crisp had to move out and Brian found them a position looking after an old colonel in the village next to his mother.

This meant that he no longer had a place of his own. For the rest of the war, whenever he was on leave in London, Brian would stay at the Savoy Hotel. From a distance of more than sixty years this seemed to me at first to be an unnecessary extravagance, especially in wartime, but he was single and there was not much else to spend his army pay on. His regular room at the Savoy overlooking the river became a much-needed oasis of calm and a retreat from the rigours of war.

When Brian was not in London he would spend his leave with friends or staying with his mother at her cottage in Chearsley. His nephews Charles and David Carter, the two eldest sons of his sister Anne, stayed regularly with their grandmother Pleasance during the war. David recalls that there were two grand pianos back to back at Elder Tree Cottage – his and hers – and when Brian came home on leave he and his mother would sit and play them together. The cottage is only small, so it must have been quite a sight – and sound.

The major news in May 1941 was that a Guards Armoured Division was to be formed, and the 2nd Battalion Grenadier Guards was to be mechanised and transformed into a tank battalion. Brian was sent on an AFV – Armoured Fighting Vehicle – course to Bovington in Dorset, where he was to be groomed for the job of Technical Adjutant. As I have mentioned earlier, he was not highly technical, but the job of Technical Adjutant required someone with a very strong personality, who was a good organiser and administrator and had an ability to motivate a crew of mechanics.

The other battalions had sent along officers similar in age and personality to Brian, and among them was a reluctant William Douglas Home, who, against his better judgement, was now a lieutenant in the 7th Buffs – the Royal West Kent Regiment.

According to William, one morning he came across Brian trying to complete a test with Willie Whitelaw, who later became Deputy Prime Minister to Margaret Thatcher, and Gerald 'Daddy' Upjohn, who went on to be a highly respected Lord of Appeal. This unlikely trio had been given the task of stripping down and reassembling an engine. All the nuts and bolts had been placed on a tarpaulin and they had to put them all back again before the inspecting officer returned. William, intrigued, lit a cigarette and waited to see what would happen.

When the instructor came back he checked the engine and found that several of the nuts and bolts had not been replaced properly. 'Turn your pockets out,' he ordered, 'and let's see where them missing nuts and bolts is.' A picture of innocence, Brian and Willie Whitelaw promptly turned out their pockets and displayed that they were empty. Gerald Upjohn, who was older than the other two and took himself rather more seriously, protested strongly that this was completely unnecessary and he had nothing to hide. Still complaining, he turned out his pockets and, to his amazement, all the missing nuts and bolts fell out on to the floor.

'All right,' said the instructor. 'You two gentlemen can go off to the NAAFI while you, sir' – he turned to the horrified Upjohn with a look of contempt – 'will stay here until I'm satisfied that every man-jack of them nuts and bolts is back in place where they belong.'

Once they had reached the safety of the NAAFI and Brian had stopped laughing, he admitted to William that he and Whitelaw had slipped their nuts and bolts into Upjohn's overalls while he was not looking. 'Daddy' Upjohn was too much of a gentleman to sneak on his fellow officers, but he was not amused. Lord Whitelaw disclosed later that when the three men returned to their regiments their reports all contained the phrase 'These officers appear to be unsound under pressure'. Recalling their exploits on the AFV course together, Whitelaw added, 'We had a riotous time. One cannot help laughing all the time when one is with Brian Johnston.'

After ten weeks Brian had completed his AFV course and reported back to the battalion, and in September they moved to Warminster. Now Technical Adjutant, Brian was given a staff of about forty fitters and worked out of a commandeered civilian garage, where he was responsible for the maintenance and repair of about seventy-five tanks and over a hundred trucks and scout cars. It would become a proud boast of his men that they kept more vehicles 'on the road' than any of the other battalions in the division.

There was a lot of official interest in the new Guards Armoured Division. Winston Churchill paid a visit to the battalion and even General de Gaulle came to inspect their new tanks and gave a speech to Brian's men in French, which had to be translated sentence by sentence. He must have created a good impression because Brian reported afterwards: 'General de Gaulle was very good and the workers liked him a lot.'

During the winter Brian took part in numerous tank exercises on Salisbury Plain until in April 1942 he was badly injured when his scout car fell into an old shell-hole and he smashed his face on the armour plating. He needed a number of stitches over his left eye and on his nose, which was 'an awful mess'. His nose was already large before the accident but after the final plaster was removed it had acquired an extra bump, which gave Brian his famous and distinctive profile, and the scars would remain visible for the rest of his life.

More seriously, his great friend Charles Villiers was shot through the jaw during a combined exercise, when an RAF Hurricane fighter fired at the spectators' enclosure instead of dummy targets by mistake. Twenty-seven officers and other ranks were killed and seventy-one injured. Villiers had an operation on his jaw and was out of action for several months. At the inquest the coroner found that death was by misadventure and reassured the public that there was no truth in the rumour that the pilot was not of British origin.

Brian was promoted to captain and had only just had his stitches removed when he was back in hospital again. An army medical discovered that he had ruptured himself while helping his men change their heavy tank tracks. He was admitted to Shaftesbury Military Hospital where he underwent a hernia operation and had to spend six weeks recuperating.

By October he was fit again and went up to London for the E.

Johnston & Co. Centenary Lunch at the Savoy Hotel, where he was reunited with his friends Fred and Nip Duder from Santos. Fred was lucky to be alive. A month before, he had been on his way home from Brazil on the *Tuscan Star* when his ship had been torpedoed off north-west Africa. He lost all his belongings and thirty-three people went down with the ship. He was at sea for five days with about a hundred other survivors in three lifeboats, before being rescued by an American landing craft and taken ashore in Liberia.

It was in Santos that Brian had first displayed his natural talent as a compère and a comedian, and now he was able to develop it further. At the end of 1942 Brian and Alfred Shaughnessy, later to be the script editor of *Upstairs Downstairs*, were invited to devise and produce a Christmas revue for the 5th Guards Armoured Brigade. It was called *Come and Get It* and played for three nights to enthusiastic audiences in the well-equipped theatre at Warminster Barracks. As in Brazil, Brian was involved in all aspects of the production and appeared in five sketches as characters such as 'Meadows the butler', 'The Nuisance' and the MC of a South-Western Glamour Beauty Contest, which featured 'Lieutenant Fenwick as Miss Salisbury Plain'!

'Brian was marvellous to work with,' said Shaughnessy, 'because he was always so enthusiastic. He couldn't wait to get up on the stage.' The revue was such a success that they had to put on another five performances after Christmas and were thanked publicly by the brigadier.

After eighteen months in Warminster, the 2nd Battalion moved to Thetford in Norfolk, where they took delivery of their first Sherman tanks. Exercises with the new tanks were carried out in the local battle area, which became well known thirty years later when it was used for all the action scenes in the television series *Dad's Army*. The battalion was required to put on a number of demonstrations for visiting VIPs, including the King and Queen and the two princesses and, on one memorable occasion, the GOC Home Forces, General Paget. Paget had arrived immaculately dressed in breeches and highly polished riding boots, not really the most suitable outfit for inspecting tanks. He managed to climb up on to one of the Sherman tanks with great difficulty, but promptly slipped and fell straight back down the side, 'which provided a few laughs'.

As the summer progressed Brian helped to organise cricket matches for the 2nd Battalion against the 1st Battalion and local teams such as Thetford and Trinity College, Cambridge. The captain of the 1st Battalion team was a great friend of Brian's, Nigel Baker, who had played for the Eton eleven in 1930/31. One evening Nigel invited himself over to dinner in Brian's mess and unwittingly changed the course of his life.

He brought with him two BBC war reporters, a Canadian called Stewart MacPherson and an 'effervescent Welshman', Wynford Vaughan-Thomas, who had been seconded to the Guards Armoured Division to gain some military experience before the second front. As might be expected they had a lively evening at dinner and MacPherson said later that he thought Brian was 'quite simply one of the funniest men he'd ever known'. Vaughan-Thomas was also impressed with the young Guards officer. 'He could talk the turret off a tank,' he recalled. Brian saw a lot of the two BBC men over the next few weeks but never dreamed that they would play a key role in determining his future after the war.

Early in July the 2nd Battalion moved again, this time to Helmsley in North Yorkshire, where they were stationed in Nissen huts in the grounds of an eighteenth-century country house called Duncombe Park, owned by Lord and Lady Feversham. Most of their days were spent at West Lutton Camp or training with the tanks on the North York Moors, but there was still time for a little cricket at the weekends. They were only thirty miles from Scarborough and were even able to play one or two matches on the famous Scarborough Club cricket ground. Before the war, the Pavilion Hotel in Scarborough had been noted for the quality of its wines, but the tank manoeuvres must have been thirsty work, because during their regular visits to the town 'on recreation' the Guards drank the cellar dry. The hotel was unable to restock its cellar during the hostilities and, not surprisingly, the Guards were not too popular with the locals.

At the end of the year Brian and Freddie Shaughnessy put on their second Christmas revue called *It's All Laid On*, with Brian taking part in six sketches, as well as performing two solo spots. The show ran for four nights in the garrison theatre at Duncombe Park and was a tremendous success. Everyone agreed that it was at least fifty per cent better than the previous year's show and Brian received a personal letter of thanks from the brigadier.

As preparations for D-Day got under way in the spring of 1944, the battalion was paid another visit by Winston Churchill, who insisted on going for a ride across the moors in one of their tanks. He wore his trademark black Derby hat and, according to Brian, stuck his head out of the turret and tapped the driver on the head, urging him to go faster. A few weeks later General Montgomery came to give them an informal pep talk, but his hearty 'man to man' approach received a noticeably cool response from the strictly disciplined Guards, who expected a general to behave more like a general.

Then in early May the 2nd Battalion received their marching orders and left Yorkshire for Hove in East Sussex, where troops and vehicles were being prepared for the Normandy invasion. D-Day took place on 6 June 1944 and two weeks later the battalion transferred to a marshalling area at Waterlooville near Southsea, where Brian celebrated his thirty-second birthday. Before leaving, he had a last picnic supper with some fellow members of the battalion on the famous cricket ground at Hambledon, the birthplace of cricket. It was a poignant occasion. As he was to write later, they all shared the feeling that for some of them this would be the last time they would ever see England.

12

Determination under Fire

Shortly before Brian embarked for France he received a letter from Heck Loyd with the news that she was about to marry Guy Knight, who had served in North Africa with her late brother John. As soon as Brian arrived in Normandy he wrote to his mother and commented wistfully: 'A pity about Heck, but I knew it was going to happen.' Even so, it was not exactly the most encouraging letter to receive as he departed for the fields of war.

On 30 June the Guards Armoured Division finally loaded their tanks and vehicles on to the landing craft and crossed over in a large convoy from Portsmouth to Arromanches in Normandy. The weather was quite rough and Brian was seasick. Even worse, he lost nearly all his eggs. Since being stationed at Warminster he had kept three or four hens and they had travelled everywhere with the battalion in a toolbox in the stores lorry, providing Brian and his men with a steady supply of fresh eggs. Before departing for France they had reluctantly given the hens away, but had managed to save two buckets of pickled eggs to take with them. To their dismay, when the stores lorry rumbled down the steep ramp on to the beach in Normandy the eggs went flying, but they were able to salvage enough to enjoy their first meal on French soil.

As the Technical Adjutant, Brian had his own scout car, a Humber Mk 1, and rode into action with the battalion head-quarters tank squadron. His job was to stay in radio contact with the other squadrons and if one of their tanks was hit, or broke down, Brian was responsible for seeing whether there were any casualties and, if possible, for recovering the tanks and getting them repaired. Before leaving England he had asked a signwriter to paint the letters FUJIAR on the front of his scout car. They stood for the well-known army expression 'F*** you, Jack, I'm all right' and were accompanied by a picture of a small man with two fingers raised in a distinctly non-Churchillian V-sign. Before long FUJIAR was to become a familiar and welcome sight throughout the Guards Armoured Division.

At first the 2nd Battalion remained stationary in some orchards near Sommervieu, just east of Bayeux. It turned out to be a deliberate ploy by Montgomery to draw the fire of the Germans and enable the Americans, under General George S. Patton, to break out from the west. There was not much to do apart from eat the local butter and Camembert and drink the local wine. Meanwhile Brian had a chance to practise his dreadful French, surprising one poor Frenchman when he asked him whether he had '*une usine* [a factory] *dans la maison*'.

It was so quiet that he decided to drive round to see his friend Ken Thornton, who was stationed with the Coldstream Guards a few miles away, not realising that they were coming under heavy shellfire. Thornton disclosed that when he saw Brian rolling up in his scout car, he had to yell at him to 'Get out!' and Brian just had time to accelerate back up the road as the shells began to fall.

On 18 July the waiting was finally over and the 2nd Battalion took part in their first major battle at Cagny, near Caen. It was almost a disaster. They encountered unexpected opposition from German Tiger tanks and suffered a large number of casualties. Many of the battalion's Sherman tanks caught fire or 'brewed up' and Brian had to help rescue the burned survivors. By the end of the day twenty-two of their tanks had been knocked out. In his autobiography Brian described the battle as 'a bloody and chaotic affair', although in his letters he had to be more reticent. 'Have been a bit involved the last few days,' he related casually to his mother, 'but we are back again now.'

After regrouping, the battalion left Giberville, near Caen, and advanced south-west to St-Charles-de-Percy, coming under heavy mortar and shellfire. Seven of their Sherman tanks 'brewed up' and six others were damaged. In his official report the commanding officer, Lieutenant Colonel Rodney Moore, wrote:

> Brian Johnston, the Technical Adjutant, has had a tremendous time recovering tanks with all the unpleasantness that this involved when the tanks have been in areas in which it is impossible to move members of the crew who have been killed. He and his staff have worked like Trojans throughout.

Brian described finding 'friends wounded or killed, men with whom one had laughed and joked the evening before, lying burned beside their knocked out tank'. He may not have been directly in the front line but he was coming under continual shellfire. Freddie Shaughnessy was Technical Adjutant of the 1st Battalion and knew better than most what Brian was going through. 'He must have been horrified by what he saw and had to do as Technical Adjutant,' he observed, 'because he was so kind hearted. But he would always rise above it.'

He did more than that. He inspired all those around him. George Thorne also fought in France with the 1st Battalion and he told me: 'Brian was very well known in the division as being the outstanding TA. He had to deal with burnt bodies in the mud and the rain and often in freezing temperatures, yet he was always cheerful. He had the magic touch. The troops could be down, but as soon as he arrived, things felt better.' Lord Carrington was squadron leader of No. 1 Squadron in the 2nd Battalion and he agreed with this assessment of the effect Brian had on his men: 'During action when he arrived on the scene it wasn't "Here's the TA" – it was "Here's Brian!"'

Brigadier Peter Prescott was 'a very young and frightened ensign' in the 2nd Battalion in 1944. Brian used to call him 'Pranger' because he got shot out of so many of his tanks that Brian thought he was becoming an expensive liability. 'There *were* moments when we were frightened, cold and wet,' recalled Prescott. 'The arrival of Brian in FUJIAR with his wonderful humanity and seaside humour was the most wonderful uplift to us all, and we always looked forward to his frequent visits.

Guardsmen have an expression for such saints as Brian – "He was a lovely man" – and *this* was what Brian was to the Guardsmen.'

It was unusual for an officer to remain in the same job for so long without promotion, but Brian had created such a unique relationship with his staff of mechanics that he was virtually irreplaceable. 'He was wasted as a Technical Adjutant,' proclaimed Neville Wigram. 'With his powers of leadership he should have been in command of a company and led them into battle. But it was difficult to replace him. He had a spirit of genius in him as a morale raiser. He was never gloomy and kept everyone laughing, but when things were serious he had a great sense of duty.'

His men were intensely loyal to him. George Cross served with Brian for four years as his MQMS [Mechanical Quartermaster-Sergeant] and travelled with him in his scout car throughout the campaign. 'He was not like the other officers,' said Cross. 'He would listen to what you had to say to him. He wasn't the sort to tell you to do something, he would recommend it. He was a very pleasant man to be with in comparison to the others. He made friends so easily. You followed the other officers because of discipline but you didn't need discipline to follow Brian.'

As the fighting grew more intense in early August, several of Brian's closest friends became casualties. Jimmy Lane Fox and Ken Thornton were both wounded and sent home, while Micky Thomas, his childhood friend from Bude, was killed in Normandy commanding the 5th Battalion Wiltshire Regiment.

The Guards Armoured Division headed south and was involved in heavy fighting around Viessoix. During the night Brian became separated from the rest of the battalion and his CO reported: 'Brian Johnston had a very unpleasant couple of hours standing by the side of the road with a couple of scout cars, expecting any moment to be picked up by a German patrol, which we knew was between us and No. 3 Squadron.' He added, 'We have had little mechanical trouble with our tanks, largely due to the efforts of Brian Johnston and Bill Wells, our EME [Electrical and Mechanical Engineer].'

The battalion took up a defensive position at Presles and on a visit to brigade headquarters Brian, not wearing any badges of rank, was mistaken by the army commander for the brigadier. Afterwards Brian chuckled: 'He was very surprised when, on asking me how my men were, I said "Both of them are very well, thank you sir."'

After the frustration of Normandy, the 2nd Battalion suddenly 'made a mad dash' across France and Belgium and advanced a remarkable 440 miles in seven days. They left Presles on 25 August and advanced north-east to Vernon, where they crossed the Seine, and rapidly on to Amiens. By 2 September the battalion was at Douai Aerodrome near the Belgian border, where Brian wrote to his mother:

> Sorry not to have written for some days but we have been too busy travelling like hell with no sleep and a lot to do. It has been most extraordinary and the French people give the most tremendous welcome everywhere and can't do too much for one; they thank, kiss, throw apples, eggs, give champagne, climb on the vehicles, while the Maquis are superb: they've all risen against the Germans as we advance and tell us everything, where Germans are hiding etc. The Germans are utterly demoralised and but for the fact that war is the only hope of living for Hitler & Co there must have been peace long ago.

The next day, after an advance of a further 101 miles, the Guards Armoured Division liberated Brussels, where they were greeted by cheering crowds. They could only stay for one 'delirious' night before continuing their push forward. They also 'liberated' a secret German store of Krug vintage champagne, and every night for the next few weeks one of Brian's petrol lorries would deliver a bottle of Krug to each of the tank crews.

A fortnight later the Guards crossed the Belgian–Dutch frontier as part of Operation Garden. 'We are getting a great welcome in Holland,' declared Brian, 'especially as we are always in the lead.' The plan was to capture the vital Nijmegen Bridge and link up at Arnhem with British airborne troops under the command of Brian's cousin, Lieutenant General 'Boy' Browning.

As history relates, however, Operation Garden was a controversial failure. A troop of tanks led by Lord Carrington managed to capture Nijmegen Bridge but the British airborne troops met strong German resistance and were unable to join up with the 1st Division, who suffered heavy casualties.

The Germans cut the supply line behind them and the 2nd Battalion was ordered to withdraw. 'There were some very glum faces in the villages as we thundered back through them,' recalled Brian, 'and the flags and bunting soon disappeared.' Unable to advance, for the next few weeks they remained in woods near Grave, where they were reinforced with new tanks and personnel. Brian passed on two exciting snippets of news to his mother. The first was that he had just taken his first bath since leaving England more than three months earlier. The second, no less important, was that he had captured his 'first and only two' German soldiers. 'I was going along in my scout car the other evening,' he informed her, 'when two Germans leaped out of a ditch at me, luckily with their hands in the air.' He revealed later that he had pulled down his armoured hatch, fearing a grenade attack. However, when he heard the Germans shouting '*Kamerad!*' he ordered them to climb on to his scout car and carried them back in triumph to battalion HQ.

As the weeks ticked by, an officers' club was opened in Brussels and Brian was able to take the occasional forty-eight hours' leave, although he complained that there were no restaurants open and the hotels had no hot water. He sounded a bit happier, however, after he saw an ENSA show starring Noël Coward, Will Hay and Frances Day. One night he was in the Grand Place Hotel in Brussels when he literally bumped into Fred Duder, his former house-mate in Brazil, who was now a personnel officer with the RAF.

At the end of October Brian heard the shocking news that William Douglas Home had been sentenced to twelve months' imprisonment with hard labour. Two months earlier William had refused an order from his commanding officer in the Buffs to attack Le Havre, after the British had rejected a German offer to send out all the French civilians. When the battle took place, twelve thousand civilians were killed. After writing a letter to the British press to explain his motives, William had been court-martialled and found guilty of disobeying an order.

At the time Brian felt distinctly unsympathetic. 'Poor William,' he told his mother, 'cashiered and gaol, but he certainly asked for it.' He felt that everyone should do their duty in time of war, whatever their beliefs. After all, he commented later, if everyone had behaved like William, then Hitler would have won the war.

In mid-November the 2nd Battalion moved 125 miles south-east to Gangelt, north of Aachen, and so, for the first time, they were in Germany. The weather was wet and very cold, but they were making preparations for Christmas when, on 19 December, the Germans counter-attacked. In what became known as 'The Battle of the Bulge', German troops advanced more than thirty miles into Belgium, threatening to cut off the Allied supply routes. The Guards Armoured Division was hurriedly moved back to St Trond, north-west of Liège. Their new headquarters was located in a château at Velm, famous for its breeding of Percheron horses and owned by a wealthy old lady called Madame Peten.

On Christmas Day 1944 Brian awoke to find a stocking on the end of his bed. Somehow his mother had arranged for it to be placed there by his batman, Frank Ruston. Later the twenty-two officers of the 1st and 2nd Battalion Grenadier Guards sat down together along two sides of a long table in the dining room of the château, where they were served Christmas lunch and presented with a jeroboam of champagne by Madame Peten. The other ranks were served a gigantic meal by the nuns in the local convent.

The 2nd Battalion had to remain near St Trond for the next two months. The weather was freezing and there were several snowstorms, with drifts up to four feet high. In mid-February Brian was granted home leave and, after eight months abroad, he was finally able to go back to England for a well-earned rest. He stayed at the Savoy Hotel and saw as many shows as he could, including *Happy and Glorious* with Tommy Trinder at the London Palladium and *Strike It Again* with Sid Field at the Prince of Wales.

By the time he returned at the end of February, the battalion had moved into Germany and was holding a position north-east of Goch. He had arrived back with only days to spare. On 5 March the Guards Armoured Division, with the Grenadiers leading, began their advance towards Wesel on the Rhine. After meeting fierce opposition from the Germans, fighting desperately to protect their homeland, the Guards finally crossed the Rhine at Rees on Good Friday and battled their way slowly north towards Lengen. There they were faced with more fanatical resistance from Nazi paratroopers, and the Grenadier tanks and their crews suffered heavy casualties.

'It was a terrible time for our boys in the tanks,' wrote Brian later. 'They knew victory was coming any day for the Allies, but they also knew that death might be around the next corner for them – and so for many of them it was.' By mid-April the Guards Armoured Division were across the Weser, but now faced tough opposition from two German marine divisions. The Guards kept advancing and took Rotenberg and Bremen, before seizing Hamburg on 2 May. On the way they liberated a concentration camp at Zeven. Brian only looked into the camp from the outside but said later that what he saw was enough, and that fellow officers who had to go inside the camp were physically sick.

The Guards were advised by their corps commander, General Sir Brian Horrocks, to halt their advance, to save further unnecessary casualties, and two days later Brian and his men heard the announcement on the radio that the war in Germany was over. As soon as VE Day was declared Brian wrote an urgent letter to his mother: 'Could you send a parcel sometime containing: Wicket-keeping gloves, three cricket shirts, three pairs white socks . . . etc.'

The Guards Armoured Division was officially disbanded by Field Marshal Montgomery on 9 June at a giant farewell parade on Rotenberg airfield, and the Grenadiers returned to being an infantry division. As a consequence, Brian ceased to be Technical

Adjutant and he was put in command of the HQ Company, with special responsibility for welfare.

After several moves the Guards ended up at Siegburg near Bad Godesberg, where their officers' mess was in a 'large and luxurious' *schloss* (castle). Now that peace was restored in Europe, Brian could return to the two great loves of his life – cricket and the theatre. Cricket matches were quickly organised and the bemused Germans were even taught how to prepare a decent grass pitch. Meanwhile Brian and Freddie Shaughnessy began preparations for a new revue to be called *The Eyes Have It!* – the insignia of the Guards Armoured Division had been an ever-open eye. This was to be a much bigger production than their previous efforts and was devised, written and produced by Freddie Shaughnessy. Bad Godesberg possessed a very well-equipped theatre, so they were able to utilise professional sets and lighting and even a pit orchestra, and the show also featured two girls imported from Brussels.

The cast list included: 'Capt. Brian Johnston, ex-Technical Adjutant with 2nd Grenadiers, was something in the City and is now nothing in the Army.' As usual Brian featured in several sketches but scored his greatest success with his solo comedy spot at the beginning of the show.

'That was when we realised he was a first-rate stand-up comedian,' said Shaughnessy. 'His *métier* was handling an audience – that's what he was good at.' If Brian had so much talent as a comedian, I wondered why he never tried to pursue a career in comedy after the war. 'He probably couldn't have made it as a stand-up comedian because of his background,' explained Shaughnessy. 'He was too posh.'

Brian was usually careful not to be too blue, like his hero Max Miller, although his jokes were often quite naughty. But on the opening night of *The Eyes Have It!* he went too far when he told one of his favourite jokes: 'A man and girl riding a tandem bicycle came to the bottom of a hill. The man said: "Get off. We are going to push it up here." "Suits me,' replied the girl, "but what shall we do with the bike?"' There was a clatter of chairs as several uniformed women members of the ATS and other women's armed services stood up and marched grimly out of the theatre. The show was a huge success and played to packed houses for a week in July. At the end of the month Brian went home on leave, and after he returned to Germany he spent the rest of the summer touring with *The Eyes Have It!* round all the other units of the Guards Division.

In October he staged his final revue for the 2nd Battalion, called *What About It Then?*, devised and co-produced with Nick Allan. This time Brian performed a comedy double act with Alan Lightfoot and appeared in two sketches, including one called 'A Peep behind the Scenes in Hollywood' in which he played 'The Villain'.

By now his age group had received their demob papers and the last few days of October were filled with a hectic round of leaving parties. Brian's batman, Frank Ruston, was one of the first to leave and wrote to his wife: 'I shall be saying goodbye to "J" tomorrow morning while he is still in bed, I guess. Mrs Darling we have had quite a good time together really. He would rather I stayed on until he finished I know, but does not expect me to. He's been a good "boss" and we shall part on good terms, I know.'

During the summer Brian had been promoted to the rank of major but now he learned that he was to be awarded the Military Cross. This must have made him very proud, especially as his late father had been decorated with the same medal during the First World War. But he never talked about it. In all three of his autobiographies there is not a single word about his award.

This has been the subject of some discussion. My feeling is that Brian came from a generation which believed that it was not polite for a gentleman to boast. If questioned about his medal, he would dismiss it by saying that it had been 'handed out with the rations' at the end of the war. The military historian John Keegan has confirmed that during the war battalions were allotted a share of medals to be awarded at the CO's discretion, and that the Foot Guards were very good at seeing that their officers and soldiers were decorated. But there is more to Brian's medal than that.

The citation from his commanding officer reads:

This officer has been Technical Adjutant of the Battalion under my command since the Bn landed in France and, as such, has been responsible for the mechanical efficiency of the Bn. The outstanding results attained have been due to his energy, powers of organisation, and ability to inspire his staff of fitters, as well as by his mechanical knowledge and capabilities.

Since crossing the Rhine and advancing through waterlogged country, he has had the task not only of recovering tank battle casualties, often under fire, but also 'unbogging' a great many tanks. Often, had it not been for the efficiency with which this officer has recovered tanks, squadrons would *not* have been able to have gone into battle.

His own dynamic personality, coupled with his untiring determination and cheerfulness under fire, have inspired those around him always to reach the highest standard of efficiency.

It has been suggested that the Military Cross is normally awarded for acts of outstanding courage and that therefore this citation is somehow insufficient. Brian's fellow officers strongly disagree. Several of them assured me that the Military Cross was frequently awarded for continuous acts of bravery and leadership, rather than one particular act. As the citation points out, Brian often had to rescue soldiers and tanks on the battlefield while under enemy fire, and his cheerfulness and determination inspired all those who met him.

William Douglas Home once asked Brian how he received his Military Cross. With typical self-deprecation, Brian told him that he was sitting in his commanding officer's tent one afternoon while the colonel was writing out citations. Suddenly the colonel threw one over to Brian and said, 'I'm getting tired of doing these, so you can do your own.' According to Brian, his citation read: 'This officer, with incredible courage, went at the enemy with cold steel . . .'

I have the original citation in front of me, so this is demonstrably untrue, and having known both men with their teasing sense of humour, I would take the whole story with a pinch of salt.

The last word should come from General Sir David Fraser, who served with Brian after D-Day as a lieutenant in No. 2 Squadron of the 2nd Armoured Battalion Grenadier Guards, and wrote this moving tribute after Brian died:

> He was renowned throughout the Guards Armoured Division. Irreverent, gallant, irrepressible, impertinent to the exalted in a way which every recipient of the impertinence enjoyed, chuckling whatever the circumstances, cracking appalling jokes however hellish the war or the weather, Brian probably did more than any other human being to maintain morale in any circumstances, to encourage, cheer and induce laughter in soldiers however dark the day. He was widely and deservedly loved and among his men in the technical department he was a being entirely unique. It was impossible to mention his name to anybody, in any context, without an answering grin.

I do not think there is any doubt that Brian was entitled to his Military Cross. As Neville Wigram put it so forthrightly: 'No one could have deserved an MC more than Brian.'

He arrived back in England on 30 October 1945 and went straight down to his mother's cottage in Buckinghamshire. He needed to decide what to do next. He had survived the war, but he faced an uncertain future.

PART TWO

1944-72

13

A Job with Auntie

After a few days Brian put on his blue pinstripe demob suit and went up to London to have lunch with Arthur Whitworth, the chairman of E. Johnston & Co. Whitworth had worked with Brian's father and grandfather and was hoping to persuade Brian to stay on with the family business. He was in for a disappointment. Following their lunch he wrote a confidential letter to Brian's mother. 'It was a bitter blow,' he told her, 'to hear that his old love, the stage, was back upon him with ever growing strength. I had always thought it a possibility that the army might take him but was not prepared for this new resurrection.' Nevertheless he asked Brian to think carefully before making a final decision.

Brian was thirty-three years old. His experience entertaining the troops in Germany had fuelled his ambition 'to do something' in show business. He could carry off a slick stand-up routine and had developed a quick-fire cross-talk act but, as Freddie Shaughnessy pointed out, he was an Old Etonian, an ex-Guards officer and a City businessman. Not exactly standard comedy material. He might have made a good comedy actor, believes Shaughnessy, playing silly upper-class types on stage or in films, but apart from appearing in *The Ghost Train* and a few comedy sketches he had no acting experience. At his age he felt it would be too late to go to drama school or start at the bottom with a repertory company. The only alternative was to go into the production or management side of the business.

He came up to London and stayed at the Guards Club in Brook Street and made appointments to see a number of theatrical managers and producers. They were all very polite and understanding but gave him the same unequivocal response: they could not offer him a job without any previous experience. After about two weeks he began to lose hope. The thought of going back to his old job was too awful to contemplate, but what else could he do?

Years later Brian would say that he had been very lucky in life. This was the moment that proved it. He was sitting in the Guards Club feeling rather depressed and reading a newspaper one evening when an officer friend asked whether he would like to join him for dinner. He was entertaining two BBC types, whom he gathered Brian had already met. They were, of course, Stewart MacPherson and Wynford Vaughan-Thomas, back from their war reporting. During the course of the evening Brian mentioned that he was looking for a job in show business but was unable to find anything. Next day MacPherson rang him up to say that there was a vacancy in the Outside Broadcast department of the BBC, if he would like to go for an interview. 'What are his qualifications?' MacPherson had been asked. 'He's game for anything!' he had replied.

Brian's initial response was not enthusiastic. He had always thought of the BBC as being rather staid and stuffy and had never even considered broadcasting as a possible career. But everyone else had turned him down and he had nothing to lose, so he agreed to go. The head of 'OBs' was Seymour de Lotbinière, a six-foot-eight-tall Old Etonian known as 'Lobby' whom, by chance, Brian had met once before the war. Brian was a stickler for punctuality – a consequence of his Guards training – but he was given the wrong time by Lobby's secretary and arrived late for the interview. In the few minutes left, Lobby questioned him about entertainment and sport and in particular whether he was interested in people. He must have liked what he heard because at the end he told Brian that he would give him two tests and, if he passed them, there might be a job.

'He arrived one day,' Lobby was to recall later, 'saying he wanted to get into outside broadcasting. It was a tall order because a great many people wanted to get into the BBC at that time and indeed into outside broadcasting. But it seemed reasonable to give him a test.'

Lobby warned Brian that a job might only be temporary and it would not be well paid, but Brian had some of his army gratuity left and, anyway, he was not intending to make broadcasting his career. It was something to do.

His first test was to go down to Piccadilly Circus and write a five-minute report on what he saw there. On his way down Regent Street Brian spotted a sign in a record shop window advertising a 'record your own message' service. So he made a few notes, popped into the shop booth and recorded his five-minute report on a disc. He was shocked when he heard the sound of his voice for the first time but left the recording at Broadcasting House for Lotbinière, whom he discovered later was 'surprised and moderately impressed' at his initiative.

'He had the wit,' remembered Lobby, 'to get a recording done at some little place where I suppose the forces had been recording messages for their sweethearts. It seemed to me to have quite a bit in it, and he had a pleasant, warm voice – nothing too smart. It was the sort of thing the man in the street would warm to.'

The second test was more difficult. Wynford Vaughan-Thomas was going to be conducting some 'live' street interviews in Oxford Street, and after he had finished Brian was to record some interviews of his own. He watched Wynford carefully to see how it was done and then asked various passers-by what they were doing that evening, what they thought of the butter rations and so on. Wynford later described the result as 'rather like an atomic explosion – slow to start but ending in the crowd mushrooming to gigantic proportions. In the centre of the disturbance stood a tall and voluble figure. He wasn't just interviewing – he was talking a three-volume novel to his victim. It was a gloriously uninhibited conversation which would have gone on forever if I had not cut it suddenly short with my stopwatch.'

An admiring onlooker turned to Wynford and murmured, 'That fellow's got the gift of the gab, hasn't he? Has he been long in the BBC?' Wynford, dazed by Brian's performance, could only mutter, 'He joined us five minutes ago!' That was not quite true, of course, because there were still several hurdles to surmount, but on that cold December Saturday night Wynford Vaughan-Thomas was a hundred per cent certain that in Brian they had found that rare bird, the natural broadcaster.

Brian may have been ambivalent at first but now that he had learned more about the job he was determined to become a BBC commentator. After a few anxious days Lobby's secretary rang to say that he had passed the two tests and would have to go before a board consisting of five BBC officials, including the Appointments Officer and the head of the OB Department. He was offered the job. He quickly found some rooms in Gloucester Place, a ten-minute walk from Broadcasting House, and reported for work at the Outside Broadcast Department on 13 January 1946.

Robert Hudson, who became a member of the OB Department North Region in 1947, describes joining the BBC in those days as 'rather like being accepted by a Guards Regiment or a London club; OBs were the Household Cavalry'. In the days before television was available outside London and the Home Counties, radio broadcasters such as Raymond Glendenning, Stewart MacPherson, Freddie Grisewood, Rex Alston, Audrey Russell, Wynford Vaughan-Thomas and Gilbert Harding were famous in almost every home in the land.

If they represented the Household Cavalry, then Seymour de Lotbinière was their general. Every Monday morning Lobby would hold a meeting to review the past week's programmes and to plan future ones. Everyone had to attend and no one was above criticism. Lobby was a perfectionist and tried to listen to every outside broadcast, jotting his observations down in a little black notebook. He demanded an extremely high standard from his staff, but they respected his experience and his judgement. If he liked a broadcast he might say 'Not bad', which was praise indeed. But if he started thumping his right fist into the palm of his left hand, you knew that your programme was about to be ruthlessly dissected. As Brian put it later, it certainly kept everyone up to the mark, knowing that in addition to the millions of listeners tuning in there would also be a pencil poised over a black book at a house somewhere in Hampstead.

Brian's first broadcast could hardly have been in more unlikely surroundings. Not long after he joined the BBC an unexploded bomb was found in the lake at St James's Park. It was not far from Marlborough House and Queen Mary had to be evacuated. The BBC decided to do a 'live' radio broadcast of the bomb being blown up by the Royal Engineers, and Lobby thought it would provide the perfect opportunity for Brian to try his hand at some commentary. The plan was that he would stand on one of the bridges over the lake, but the police told him it was too dangerous, so he was moved to the nearby Ladies' lavatory, where he had to stand on a loo seat and peer out of the tiny louvred window. He managed to give a satisfactory description of the explosion but was disappointed that the blast was not very loud. Later he would joke that he 'came out looking a bit flushed'.

'My main recollection of the broadcast,' chuckled Lobby, 'is that, in his exuberance, Brian signed off saying, '. . . and next time I promise I'll bring you a bigger and better bomb!' In a lately war-torn London, I did not really think that was what London was after.' Lobby gave Brian a rap over the knuckles. 'How do you know the bangs will get better?' he asked him. 'For goodness' sake, stick to the facts!'

The Outside Broadcast Department, as the name suggests, was responsible for all broadcasts outside a studio and was divided into various sections such as Events and Ceremonials, Sport and Entertainment. Brian was assigned to the entertainment section as an assistant to John Ellison, a former actor who had been invalided out of the RAF after a car crash at the beginning of the war. Ellison was a delightful man with a lively sense of humour, who was in charge of organising radio broadcasts from the theatres and music halls.

'I was a bit pushed,' Ellison recalled, 'and I needed an assistant. When Lobby said he'd found me one I was delighted. But when I was told he had no professional experience and that his background was Eton, New College and the Brigade of Guards, my heart sank. Typical of the BBC, I thought, they *would* pick a damned amateur with a background like that.'

After that unpromising start, Brian went on to develop a close working relationship with John Ellison, whom he called 'Jolly Jack' because he laughed so much at his jokes. Later Brian would comment that he could not have wished for a better person to teach him his job. In those days the BBC would broadcast half-hour excerpts from West End shows – usually musicals or farces, because dramas were considered too visual for radio. The commentator would sit in one of the boxes and fill in the gaps for the listeners at home, describing the scenery and the action and identifying the actors and actresses. This was Brian's job, and it meant that he had to see a show two or three times beforehand in order to select the best part to broadcast; he also had to deal directly with the producers and managers and the stars themselves.

The first musical he broadcast was *Song of Norway*, and it was followed by countless others such as *Oklahoma!*, *Annie Get Your Gun*, *South Pacific* and *Carousel*, which he saw fifteen times and cried at every single time. His first non-musical commentary came from *Under the Counter* starring Jack Hulbert and Cicely Courtneidge, who went on to become good friends. He had achieved his ambition. He was now right at the heart of the entertainment world, seeing all the shows and meeting all the stars and, more importantly, working with them. He could not believe his luck.

Another main programme was a half-hour broadcast every Tuesday night called *Round the Halls*. Each week he had to select and introduce three acts from a different music hall around the country. These would usually be a singer, a stand-up comedian or cross-talk act, and a speciality act such as an impressionist, instrumentalist or animal impersonator. Once again Brian was in his element. He loved variety, especially comedians, and they warmed to him in return. He was soon working and making friends with established stars like Arthur Askey, Ted Ray and Tommy Trinder, and with up-and-coming newcomers such as Frankie Howerd and Max Bygraves.

When Lobby had interviewed Brian there had been no mention

of him doing any sports commentary. But after the war there was a shortage of soccer commentators, so he was encouraged to have a test. He had never played the game seriously at school, preferring rugby, but he had learned a lot from watching Arsenal, or so he thought. Geoffrey Peck, the producer in charge of football, took him to do a test recording at Loftus Road, where Queens Park Rangers were playing. Their centre-forward, McGibbon, had scored a hat-trick in the previous match and the press had labelled him '3-Goal McGibbon'. Brian had never seen him play but he was listed as number nine in the programme, so whenever he touched the ball Brian came out with: 'There goes "3-Goal" again, a typical dribble, would recognise his style anywhere . . .' and so on. Later he discovered to his horror that McGibbon had not played at all and the number nine was a substitute. It was his one and only soccer commentary.

Then came his second piece of luck. When Brian had played cricket for the Eton Ramblers before the war he had got to know an Old Harrovian called Ian Orr-Ewing, who was one of the regular 'Block G' crowd at the Eton and Harrow match. After he had been at the BBC for a couple of months the phone rang in his office and it was Orr-Ewing, recently out of the RAF and now head of TV Outside Broadcasts. They were planning to televise the Test matches at Lord's and the Oval against India, he said, and they needed someone to do the commentary. Brian knew about cricket, he could talk a bit, would he like to have a go?

We all know the answer. In June 1946, only five months after joining the BBC, Brian made his debut as a cricket commentator, and from then on he would divide his time every summer between his television cricket commentaries and his numerous radio commitments.

One of his responsibilities was an amateur show called *Work's Wonders*, which had started during the war and featured workers from different factories. Brian was the producer and also introduced it each week, and he had to be extremely careful about what he said. The BBC had very strict guidelines as to what constituted acceptable humour. Anything to do with sex, physical disabilities, politics, religion and even mothers-in-law was out – which did not leave an awful lot. Brian used to quote one joke which got him into trouble:

'Have you seen the PT instructress?'

'Oh yes, she's stripped for gym.'

'Lucky Jim.'

He was given a rocket for allowing that one to go out.

It was not all hard work. The OB Department shared a suite of offices at 55 Portland Place, across the road from Broadcasting House. They had been built as luxury flats and several of them contained bathrooms and kitchens, although Brian and John Ellison were not quite so lucky. As the new boys they were allocated the former maid's quarters, a large room without any carpet. Only Brian could have instantly seen this as a chance to invent a new game – office cricket, using a miniature cricket bat, a squash ball and the waste-paper basket as a wicket. There were three players a side and four runs were scored if the ball hit the wall, six runs if it hit the ceiling full pitch. The batsman could be caught off the ceiling or wall or if the ball landed in the 'in' or 'out' tray. There was also an LBW tray – 'Let the Blighters Wait'.

Their secretary, Polly Polden, was supposed to be the official scorer and umpire, although when the ball really started flying she would duck behind her typewriter. If they heard Lobby coming, they would quickly hide everything away, but more than once he caught them standing around in their shirtsleeves, red faced and breathing heavily. Stewart MacPherson and Wynford Vaughan-Thomas were regular opponents, but as the fame of the game spread they were joined by visiting England players such as Denis Compton, Bill Edrich and the Bedser twins. On more than one occasion the telephone rang in the middle of a game and a bemused caller was asked to 'hang on until the end of the over'!

Stewart MacPherson shared an office down the corridor. In the late 1940s the Canadian broadcaster was at the height of his fame. He had been a distinguished war correspondent and was the BBC's number-one boxing and ice hockey commentator, as well as being the chairman of *Twenty Questions* and *Ignorance*

Is Bliss. MacPherson had a great sense of humour, but would occasionally lapse into moments of self-importance, which was perhaps understandable considering his success. He was never likely to get away with it, however, with Brian around. He and John Ellison had a favourite routine whenever they thought 'Stewie' was getting above himself and others were in the office.

'I say, Jack,' Brian would start, 'did I ever tell you about the big retreat?'

'No,' Ellison would reply innocently, 'I can't say you did, Brian.'

'Well,' Brian would continue, 'we were going back like mad when one of my men said to his mate, "I say, Bill, isn't that the famous war correspondent Stewart MacPherson over there?" "Blimey, so it is," said Bill. "I didn't know we'd gone back that far!"'

'Now see here, Johnston,' MacPherson would protest, laughing. 'I don't want any talk like that!' But like most of the recipients of Brian's humour, in reality he used to rather enjoy it.

Another favourite trick of Brian's was to ring up his colleagues in the department and put on a funny accent. 'You never knew what was going to happen next,' admitted Lobby, 'but this was part of his contribution to the happiness of the department.' One day Brian convinced Geoffrey Peck that he was the French tennis player Jean Borotra and was threatening to sue the BBC. Peck rushed in to warn Lobby and Brian had to get him out of trouble by following him into Lobby's office and jabbering away in his phoney French accent until the penny dropped. Sometimes Lobby must have wondered if he had made the right decision in hiring this man.

14

The Telephone Rings

Brian was one of the first broadcasters to work on both radio and television, and it began to cause divided loyalties. Eventually an amicable agreement was reached whereby television would have complete priority over him for cricket while radio would have first call for everything else. He was still employed by radio OBs and had his office there, but television agreed to pay a percentage of his salary. The BBC had a very good deal. Brian was still on his original radio salary of about £1,000 a year, although they did condescend to pay him an additional clothes allowance for his television work – the princely sum of £25 a year.

One night in 1947 Brian was asked to perform his old army cross-talk act by royal command. He was at a 'rather posh' private party in Cadogan Square given by Charles and Nick Villiers, and the guest of honour was Princess Margaret. Charles prevailed on Brian to perform a double act – although one can imagine he did not need to be asked twice – and he persuaded a nervous Edward Ford to be his straight man. Ford had recently been appointed Assistant Private Secretary to King George VI, so he was understandably concerned that Brian would go too far and get him the sack. After a hurried rehearsal they stood in the drawing room and entertained the Princess with a string of Brian's oldest and corniest jokes. Fortunately most of those attending the party had never been to a music hall and did not listen to variety shows on the wireless, so the gags were new to them. Princess Margaret seems to have particularly enjoyed this old chestnut:

FORD: Where are you taking those plums?
BRIAN: I'm taking them to His Majesty the King.

FORD: Taking them to His Majesty the King? Why on earth are you doing that?

BRIAN: Well, it says in 'God Save the King', 'Send him Victorias!'

And Brian could not resist reviving one of his all-time favourites, which got a suitably big laugh:

BRIAN: What are you doing nowadays?

FORD: Nothing.

BRIAN: But I thought you applied for the job of Assistant Private Secretary to the King?

FORD: Yes. I got the job.

Afterwards Brian felt 'we went over remarkably well'. Sir Edward Ford was less convinced. 'I was awfully bad,' he declared. But at least he kept his job.

The demands of the OB Department left Brian little time for any social life. He would often be working in his office at Broadcasting House during the day and then doing a broadcast in the evening. Weekends were like normal working days, and public holidays such as Easter and Christmas were the busiest time of all for OBs. So Brian's life revolved around his work. His friends viewed him as a dyed-in-the-wool bachelor and doubted that any woman would ever put up with his irregular lifestyle.

On Monday, 1 December 1947, he was sitting at his desk when the telephone rang and an attractive female voice said: 'This is Pauline Tozer. I am working in the photographic section of the BBC and my brother Gordon told me to give you a ring.' Gordon Tozer had been Brian's Assistant Technical Adjutant in the Grenadiers from 1942 to 1945. Pauline was twenty-five years old, ten years younger than Brian, so Gordon had warned his sister that Brian would probably not be interested, but might be able to introduce her to some of his younger BBC colleagues.

Pauline Tozer came from Yorkshire and had grown up with her elder brother Gordon in a large house called Grange Cliffe at Eccleshall, on the outskirts of Sheffield. Her father, Colonel

William Tozer, had been a director of the family business, Steel, Peach and Tozer, and Master Cutler of Sheffield in 1936, but now worked as a stockbroker in the City.

Her first boyfriend, Michael Holdsworth, known as 'Flip', had been a sub lieutenant in the Fleet Air Arm and was killed in action in February 1942 after flying over Tripoli in his Swordfish plane. Pauline had trained as a nurse with the Red Cross and served as a Royal Naval VAD (Voluntary Aid Detachment) for three and a half years, ending the war at the Fleet Air Arm station at Worthy Down near Winchester. 'We were amateurs,' she says, 'but very efficient. They couldn't have done without us.'

After being demobbed in 1946 she had enrolled at the Regent Street Polytechnic School of Photography in London, and in August 1947 she had landed a job as a retoucher and finisher with the well-known society photographer A. V. Swaebe. On a train back from a holiday with her brother Gordon's new in-laws in Luxembourg, she had met Charles de Jaeger, a television newsreel cameraman, who suggested she apply for a job with the BBC Photographic Department. She took his advice and on 15 November 1947 she joined the BBC as a printer.

Two weeks later Gordon Tozer was home on leave from Germany, where he was still serving as a captain in the Grenadier Guards. Pauline told him about her new job and that his former senior officer, Brian Johnston, also worked at the BBC. Gordon offered to introduce them, adding that Brian was a bit of a misogynist and really preferred the company of men.

This did not deter Pauline. Gordon had to return to Germany that night, so the next day she rang Brian in his office at 55 Portland Place and explained that she worked a few doors away at the old Langham Hotel. Normally Brian would have made some excuse but, as he admitted later, there must have been something in that voice. He invited Pauline out to lunch three days later at the Bolivar, the BBC Club, and arranged to collect her from her office.

'I had heard him on the radio during the wedding of Princess Elizabeth and the Duke of Edinburgh,' recalls Pauline, 'but I didn't know what he looked like except that he had big ears, a bald patch and a large nose. Suddenly I bumped into someone in the corridor and when I saw "the nose" I said, "Oh, hello, you must be Brian!"' Brian found to his delight that Pauline was 'a very attractive blonde with blue eyes'. Wynford Vaughan-Thomas, Raymond Glendenning, John Ellison and Geoffrey Peck were also at the Bolivar, waiting to pull Brian's leg about his blind date.

Pauline admits that she got a bit merry and could not stop laughing at Brian's non-stop wisecracks. They arranged to meet again the next day and Brian took her to see the Crazy Gang at Victoria Palace; afterwards they had dinner and danced until 4 a.m. at the exclusive 400 Club in Leicester Square. They met again the next day and saw a film, and the next day for a drink. On 9 December Brian took Pauline with him to the Chelsea Palace, where he was doing a broadcast of a variety show with Dorothy Squires. When Pauline was introduced to her after the show, Dorothy asked: 'Are you two engaged?' They both looked rather embarrassed and explained that they had known each other for only five days!

Pauline was renting a top-floor flatlet in Bramham Gardens in Earls Court, and on 10 December her landlady complained about the noise on the stairs late at night and she was asked to leave. Pauline emphasises that there was nothing 'going on' between her and Brian at this stage but thinks that the giggles and laughter must have disturbed the people below.

They continued to see each other almost daily, and on 20 December Brian proposed, saying, 'I knew you were the girl for me as soon as I heard your voice on the phone.' Pauline could not believe he was serious, as by now they had still known each other only for sixteen days. Brian insisted that nothing would change *his* mind and it was up to her to decide. Pauline asked for more time. 'We hardly know each other yet,' she protested, 'though I love being with you and am very fond of you. Give me two to three months and then ask me again.' Brian agreed and they continued to see each other almost every day.

Soon it was every day, because Pauline found a room at 78

Gloucester Place, a few blocks down from Brian's room in the same road, and they walked together to the BBC every morning. After Christmas Brian began to introduce Pauline to his friends, and they celebrated New Year's Eve with Jimmy Lane Fox and his wife Anne at the Connaught Hotel.

Three days later Gordon Tozer's baby daughter Susan Pauline was due to be christened at East Grinstead Parish Church. His wife Germaine's brother could not attend so Gordon asked Brian to stand in for him. When Pauline saw him holding the baby in the church, her heart started to beat overtime. 'Somehow that just clinched my feeling for him,' she recalls, 'and I knew just how much I loved him.' They returned to London on a Green Line coach, cuddled together to keep warm.

The next day Pauline could not concentrate on her work. She had decided to accept Brian's proposal. To confirm her decision, she wrote a list of all the things they had in common and all the things they disagreed about. She must have thought it would be all right. On the bottom of the paper she wrote: 'I have decided to become his wife.' They became engaged on 4 January 1948, one month after they had met.

Brian did the right thing and two days later went to see Colonel Tozer at his office in the City to ask for his permission. Although surprised by the speed of their engagement, the colonel gave his approval. Pauline's parents wanted them to get married in June, but Brian objected because it would mean him missing the Lord's Test against Australia, so the date was brought forward to April.

Before then, however, Brian had a chance to fulfil his boyhood ambition to be an actor. In March he was invited to audition for a part in a film about the Guards Armoured Division, to be called *They Were Not Divided*. Terence Young, the writer and director, had been an intelligence officer in the division and had based some of his characters on officers he had known. He had written a part especially for Brian and had named his character Nosey. Brian went down to Denham Studios and did a film test with some other ex-officers in a hay loft, where they were supposed to be hiding from the Germans.

The test went well and he was offered the part at £50 a day. The BBC even agreed to give him six weeks' leave, but Brian discovered that the filming was going to clash with the Lord's Test match. He did not want to jeopardise his job as a cricket commentator, so sadly he had to decline. The part was rewritten, renamed Bushy, and given to the bewhiskered actor Michael Trubshawe.

Brian and Pauline were married on 22 April 1948 at St Paul's Church in Knightsbridge, four and a half months after that first telephone call. The OB Department decided to record the whole ceremony as a wedding present. Stewart MacPherson, Raymond Glendenning, John Ellison and Wynford Vaughan-Thomas formed an archway of microphones as Brian and Pauline emerged from the church, and MacPherson handled the commentary: 'This extraordinary-looking individual,' he began earnestly, 'who appears to have lost an argument with his tailor and who is now approaching us, must be the bridegroom . . .' The look of undying affection which Brian conferred upon him at that moment, added MacPherson afterwards, would linger long in his memory. There were no tape recorders in those days, so BBC sound engineer Oggie Lomas had to mix the commentary in the church vestry, while a colleague recorded it directly on to an acetate disc, which was later presented to the bride and groom. Raymond Glendenning took over the commentary for the going-away ceremony and described the couple's departure as if it were the Cup Final. 'It was magnificent!' said MacPherson.

The first week of their honeymoon was spent at the Grand Hotel in Eastbourne, which Brian knew well from his days as a schoolboy at Temple Grove. On the Sunday night Brian wrote to his mother: 'We've started on our letter-writing at last and have gone to bed early and are writing in bed. Everything perfect here and we're both frightfully happy. Lovely weather, marvellous hotel with the most perfect service, everyone very nice and friendly. We've been sitting out on beach a lot and up on Beachy Head this afternoon.'

For the second part of their honeymoon they spent a fortnight in a small hotel by the lake at Locarno in Switzerland. This was not such a success. After a few days Brian sent his mother a postcard: 'Just to let you know that in spite of me feeling sick on aeroplane, three days solid rain, and now I have a slight shaving rash on face – we are still very happy.' The rash got worse and he was unable to shave, so he had to grow a beard. A local doctor prescribed a course of injections and Pauline had to administer them twice a day in his bottom. Currency restrictions meant that they were only allowed £25 each in cash and the extra cost of the injections left them with no money for themselves. All they could do was sit around the hotel and then take the 4 p.m. steamer across the lake every afternoon to a tea house, where they blew what was left of their savings on a cream-filled meringue each. It was not exactly the start to married life they had planned.

When they returned to London they set up home in a small flat at 10 Westbourne Crescent in Bayswater, which had been found for them by Jimmy Lane Fox. It had almost no furniture, although the two mothers-in-law had done their best to make it more comfortable while they were away on honeymoon. At first Colonel Tozer did not recognise Brian with his beard and thought Pauline had come back with a different man. Fortunately, after a few days Brian was able to shave it off and he went back to work. Don Bradman and his all-conquering Australians had arrived in England and it would be a glorious cricketing summer.

In August he faced a new challenge when the first post-war Olympic Games were held in London. There had been no resources to build any new stadiums, so the track and field events were staged at Wembley Stadium, but traditional venues were used for the other sports. The equestrian events took place at Aldershot during the second week of August, and Brian was assigned to assist Lionel Marson with the commentary for the showjumping, about which he knew absolutely nothing. Pauline says he had a terrible time trying to learn the difference between 'fetlocks' and 'withers' and the exact height of a 'hand'.

The newly-weds did not want to be apart for five days so Brian and Pauline stayed in a caravan at the bottom of a friend's garden at Seale. It rained every day. The caravan was cold and damp and they had to dash up the garden into their friend's house if they wanted a bath. It was not exactly romantic. A few weeks later, however, Pauline discovered she was pregnant and, having checked her dates, she reliably informs me that the floor of their friend's bathroom in Seale may have had something to do with it.

With a baby on the way, it was obvious that they needed to leave their small flat in Bayswater. Brian was busy as usual, so he gave Pauline the task of finding them a house. He was not fussy, he said, except that it had to be near Lord's Cricket Ground.

15

Let's Go Somewhere

Television was in its infancy after the war. The BBC's transmitters only covered the London area until 1950, so TV audiences were small. At the time of the Coronation in 1953 there were still only two million television sets in the whole country. By contrast the wireless, as it was then called, could be heard by everybody, and radio audience figures in the 1940s were phenomenal. One of the most popular programmes was *In Town Tonight*, which was broadcast every Saturday night on the Home Service. It was an early version of the chat show, and each week film stars, politicians, businessmen or anyone in the news would queue up to be interviewed in the studio. It attracted a regular audience of over twenty million listeners, more than any television programme today.

There was an outside interview spot called 'On the Job', in which John Ellison talked to different people each week at their place of work. One night there was a technical hitch and Brian was asked to stand in for Ellison. The producer of *In Town Tonight*, Peter Duncan, must have liked what he heard, because when John Ellison took over as the studio interviewer he offered Brian 'On the Job'. As he later admitted, it was not the most exciting spot to do, partly because it was too similar to the interviews in the studio. Believe it or not, these had to be rehearsed and scripted. After all, the BBC could not risk an unscripted word from a member of the public across their airwaves! 'How are you, Mr So-and-so?' John Ellison would say. 'Very well, thank you, Mr Ellison,' they would read from their script, and so on. It may have been popular, but it was very dull. After a few months Peter Duncan agreed that the programme needed livening up. He thought Brian was just the person to do it and decided to revive a feature called 'Let's Go Somewhere', which John Snagge had originated before the war.

This was to be a 'live' three-and-a-half-to-four-minute spot, and in complete contrast to the studio interviews it was to have movement, excitement and even – as long as Brian did not go too far – a little humour. He broadcast his first 'Let's Go Somewhere' on 23 October 1948. By the time he ended the feature four years later he had carried out 150 different stunts and had become one of the most famous voices in the country.

It must have been difficult to find something different and exciting to do every Saturday night. In his first book, *Let's Go Somewhere*, Brian admitted that there were occasions when he was in despair over what to do next, and some of the broadcasts do sound more like interviews than actual stunts. When they worked, however, they were sensational, and unlike anything that had ever been tried before.

He wanted to start with something that would capture the public's imagination and would emphasise that this was going to be an amusing, interesting and sometimes exciting new feature. Vic Moody, known as 'Spud', was the brains behind more than seventy-five per cent of the ideas, and he came up with a brilliant suggestion for the first one, the Chamber of Horrors at Madame Tussauds. It had long been rumoured that Madame Tussauds would pay £100 to any member of the public who could spend the whole night there alone. It was said that those who had tried had either given up in terror or gone mad as a result. Brian contacted Reginald Edds, the PR man at Tussauds, and he assured him that there was no truth in the rumours. There was no offer of £100 and no member of the public had ever been in there alone after closing time at 7 p.m. It was agreed that Brian would be the first, although to his relief he would not be allowed to stay all night.

The Chamber of Horrors was an underground cellar, with a low vaulted ceiling and a stone floor, and was reached by going down a winding stone staircase and through a heavy iron gate. The chamber was filled with wax models of famous murderers, some of them wearing their original clothes. There was 'The Man in the Iron Mask', a model of the guillotine, instruments of torture such as the rack, and even the actual bath used in the notorious 'Brides in the Bath' case.

As the last member of the public walked up the stairs at 7 p.m., Brian entered the chamber and the gates were locked. For the broadcast all the lights had been turned off except for one dim bulb over a group of murderers which included Dr Crippen and Mahon, the Brighton trunk murderer. Brian was provided with a chair under the light in case he wanted to read. He had three London evening papers (they had them in those days) and a book about Lord's by Sir Pelham Warner. Pauline had made him some sandwiches and a flask of coffee and there was some whisky if he got desperate, even though he hated the stuff.

He tried reading but could not concentrate, so he walked around, but it was so dim that he could hardly see. At one point something brushed across the top of his head – it was a hangman's noose. By the time John Ellison cued over to him at 7.30 Brian was already sounding a bit shaky. He managed to get through the 'live' broadcast and informed the listeners that they could tune in again at eleven o'clock to see how he was getting on. For the next three and a half hours he was on his own and he insists that he was genuinely frightened.

Every sound seemed to echo around the chamber. He tried to eat an apple but it made such a noise that he had to stop. He tried another walk but the cold, staring eyes of the wax figures seemed to follow him round the room. What made things worse was that the chamber was directly over the Bakerloo Line on the London Underground, and every time a train passed underneath there was a low rumbling noise and the figures would start to shudder. In the end Brian sat rooted to his chair, shivering even though he was wearing an overcoat.

When the BBC came back to him at 11 p.m. he sounded immensely relieved, and when Reg Edds unlocked the gates he rushed up the stairs and into the arms of Pauline, who was waiting above. 'He was absolutely shaking,' she remembers, 'and white faced with fright.'

'Let's Go Somewhere' had got off to a tremendous start, and over the next few months Brian tried everything from serving behind the counter in a fish-and-chip shop to milking cows on a farm, playing a barrel organ in the street and even having a nude massage in a Turkish bath. One of the main attractions of the feature was that it was shrouded in complete secrecy. No one apart from Brian and the sound engineer knew where he would be or what he would be doing each week. If you wanted to find out, you had to tune in. This made it compulsive listening and meant that he could get away with having the occasional less than exciting episode. Oggie Lomas was the sound engineer on many of these early broadcasts. 'As engineers we really enjoyed it,' he said, 'because it was such a challenge.'

Whenever possible they would try to organise a stunt that had some movement, to provide a contrast with the static interviews in the studio. On different occasions Brian drove a hansom cab, a racing car and a tank; he rode on a penny farthing bicycle and aboard a fire engine. He broadcast from the driver's cab in a Tube train and he piloted a Moth trainer aircraft. He even tested an ejector seat and was shot sixty feet up a vertical tower. The acceleration was 'phenomenal' and he suffered a terrible pain in his backside for days afterwards from the tremendous blast under his seat.

No one had heard anything like this before. One of the reasons was the limited technology. 'One of our chief engineers had bought a load of American army tank transmitters after the war,' Oggie Lomas explained, 'and we converted them so that we could feed our microphones into them. This gave us good-quality sound for the first time and made it possible for us to do these stunts.' When Brian did a 'live' broadcast from the new Big Dipper roller-coaster at Battersea funfair, Lomas had to ride in the car alongside him, sitting with his feet on the transmitter to stop it from falling out.

As the series became more popular, Brian became more adventurous, and some of his stunts were downright dangerous. One night he accepted a challenge from a darts champion called Joe

Hitchcock, who performed an act at the King's Arms pub in Camden Town. Brian had to put a cigarette in each ear and then turn his back while Hitchcock threw six-inch sharpened nails at him and tried to knock out the cigarettes. It was one of Brian's most foolish stunts. An inch either way and the nails would have gone through the back of his head. On the recording of the programme you can hear Brian's heart thumping loudly, and he was not the only one to be scared. Pauline was there with him. She was seven months pregnant (with the author) and Brian's mother tried to persuade her not to watch in case the shock sent her into labour prematurely. Hitchcock had a couple of near-misses before he managed to hit the cigarettes successfully, and afterwards Brian rewarded himself with a stiff drink.

Two years later Hitchcock contacted him again to say that he was now doing the act with a blindfold. Would he like to have another go? Brian politely declined.

In another high-risk episode he rode on the back of a motorbike through a pyramid of empty beer barrels with a stunt man called Mad Johnny Davis. Later he was rescued by the Fire Brigade from the top of Bethnal Green Town Hall. He even went five miles out in a boat from Folkestone and swam in the English Channel while someone tried to feed him nuts and grapes. One Christmas he became a member of the Flying Ballet during a performance of the Ice Pantomime at the Empress Hall. He soared fifty feet over the ice rink while disguised as a large yellow bird, suspended from the ceiling by two very thin wires. Once again Pauline could hardly bear to watch. Newspapers began to refer to him as the 'daredevil broadcaster', 'radio's stunt man' and 'The Live-For-A-Thrill Man'.

There was a popular radio series in the early 1950s called *Riders of the Range*, which included a real-life Alsatian dog called Rustler. He had been trained by his owner Trevor Hill to do almost anything, so Brian thought he would test how good the dog was at catching a thief. He was informed that Rustler had been trained to attack the left arm only, and he was given a special coat with extra-thick padding on his left arm.

The broadcast took place on the BBC cricket ground at Motspur Park, and Brian's 'victim' was Pauline, now eight and a half months pregnant. Brian crept up behind her, snatched her handbag and ran off, and Pauline let out a convincing scream. Trevor Hill promptly appeared with Rustler and, after hearing Pauline's explanation of the 'robbery', set the dog after the thief. Brian had run about eighty yards when Rustler came pounding up to him, leaped in the air, and sank his teeth into the padding on Brian's left arm, knocking him to the ground. Brian could feel the teeth coming through the clothing and his cries of 'Ow!' were quite genuine.

As soon as he was on the ground Rustler let go and stood guard with his tail wagging, waiting for his master. After a few seconds Brian tried to get up, but Rustler seized him by the arm and pulled him down again, and he had to lie motionless on the ground until Trevor Hill arrived to put the dog on a lead. It was a frightening experience. If Rustler had bitten Brian anywhere except on the padding he could have caused him a serious injury.

Brian needed courage of a different kind when he dressed up as a tramp and tried being a street singer outside Charing Cross Station. He put on some filthy old clothes, smeared dirt over his face and pulled a battered hat down over his eyes. His microphone was hidden under a scarf and the microphone lead went down his trouser leg and off to a control van parked about fifty yards away down an alley. After receiving his cue from John Ellison, he shuffled out on to the street, carrying a small tin with some matches in it, and started to sing 'It's a Long Way to Tipperary' in a thin and quavery voice. As the crowds passed him by, he followed that with an even shakier version of 'Pack Up Your Troubles'. No one guessed that he was being heard by millions of listeners at home and he managed to collect twopence halfpenny from members of the public before handing back to the studio, with evident relief.

Surprisingly, when you consider some of his other stunts, Brian found the episode acutely embarrassing and one of the hardest things he had been asked to do. The American entertainer Danny

Kaye was the main studio guest on *In Town Tonight* that evening and refused to believe that the broadcast was genuine and actually 'live'. When assured that it was, he was said to have been most impressed, though more by Brian's nerve than by his singing.

The programme provided him with the opportunity to fulfil many of his ambitions, one of which was to appear in pantomime. He achieved his dream when he joined Tommy Trinder onstage at the London Palladium in *Puss in Boots* while wearing a donkey costume. He played a short scene with Trinder and described it as unbearably hot and difficult to breathe inside the fake donkey's head, but at least he could claim to have 'played' the Palladium.

On other theatrical occasions he was sawn in half and later floated in midair by the illusionist Robert Harbin, although he was sworn to secrecy as to how it was done. He was lifted upside down by strongwoman Joan Rhodes, until all the money fell out of his pockets and one of his braces burst. Quite a feat considering that he weighed nearly fifteen stone at the time. He also went onstage at the Adelphi Theatre during Jimmy Edwards' trombone act and sucked a lemon to see whether it would make him dry up. It did, although the audience was laughing so much it was hard to tell whether it was their laughter or the lemon that was to blame.

One evening in December 1949 he followed a young blind man with his guide dog Tessa through the busy theatre crowds in the Strand in London, to see how efficient the dog was at dealing with the crowds and the traffic. The blind man was Kenneth Spencer, and he went on to become Brian's piano tuner for about eight years. Fifty-two years later, in January 2002, I rang a number at random in the Yellow Pages, looking for a piano tuner in West Sussex. It was Ken Spencer. He recalled his appearance on 'Let's Go Somewhere' and said it was easy because he could hear Brian talking loudly into the microphone behind him, saying: 'He's coming up to some traffic lights now. Good, there's a gap in the crowd. He needs to be careful of that pillar box ahead . . .' and so on. Ken did not need the dog at all. I asked him what he remembered of Brian. 'A lovely man,' he said. 'He even let me feel his nose once!'

16

In Town Tonight

The BBC was viewed as a very strait-laced, sober organisation after the war, and audiences were not used to seeing BBC reporters making fools of themselves. So when Brian attempted to ride a horse bareback at Harringay Circus, the audience reaction was almost unbelievable. He had never tried it before and he had to be fastened into a harness attached to a pulley overhead, so that if he fell off he could be lowered gently to the ground.

He sat on the horse as it cantered around the ring and managed to get up on one knee and then two, breathlessly describing his efforts into a microphone strapped to his chest. Then he tried to stand up, lost his balance and swung out across the ring. Unknown to the audience, he had borrowed a pair of 'quick-release' trousers from one of the clowns and as he dangled over the ring he pulled a string and the trousers fell down. The screams of laughter from the audience were shattering. They simply could not believe they were seeing a man from Auntie BBC with his trousers around his ankles. Brian's bosses were not convinced that this was exactly the right image they wanted for the BBC but, as Brian admitted later, it was worth it for the laughs.

An even more uproarious performance took place when he joined the Crazy Gang onstage in their hit show *Together Again* at the Victoria Palace. He volunteered to play the part of a customer in their barber's shop sketch. They loaned him some old clothes, a macintosh and a waterproof wig, and told him that all he had to do was sit in the chair and keep talking into the microphone while they did their worst. As soon as he sat down Jimmy Nervo and Teddy Knox whipped off the wig and poured bottles of coloured shampoo all over his head. 'I spent an hour and a half getting the muck out of my hair,' Brian complained later. Next they lathered his face with an enormous brush and pretended to shave him, shoving the brush up his nose and in his mouth. He ended up on the floor cackling hysterically as they poured water down his trousers and tickled him, accompanied by loud roars from the audience. As a broadcast it was complete and utter chaos, but many people told him later it was their all-time favourite 'Let's Go Somewhere'. Back at home, according to Pauline, there was a multi-coloured rim round the bath for days.

Brian enjoyed it so much that he went back the following year for more punishment in their Butlin's holiday camp sketch. He had been a huge fan of the Crazy Gang since the 1930s, and had often watched Flanagan and Allen before they were famous at the Holborn Empire, where they used to finish their act with an unknown song called 'Underneath the Arches'. It became Brian's all-time favourite song, and one of only two that he could remember how to play on the piano – the other was 'We'll Gather Lilacs' by Ivor Novello. The piano tuner Ken Spencer used to listen to Brian thumping away on his baby grand piano at home and I wondered how good a player he was. 'His right hand was all right,' chuckled Spencer, 'but his left hand went anywhere it wanted!'

One of Brian's proudest moments happened in February 1950 when he wheeled an old upright piano into the side street by the Victoria Palace and Bud Flanagan came out of the stage door to join him in a chorus of 'Underneath the Arches'. Later he described it as 'one of the great moments in my broadcasting life'. The two of them obviously got on well together, and Flanagan contributed a reference as a foreword to Brian's first book *Let's Go Somewhere*, signing it 'Your old friend, Bud Flanagan':

> The bearer of this letter has worked for me many times. I have found him to have a lovely sense of humour, and as fearless as a Paris taxi driver. The things my colleagues and I in 'Crazy Gang' have done to him would have made a million other men lose all faith in mankind, but not so Brian. He has come back

for more, time and time again, which proves conclusively that
the man has no sense of feeling, no sense of responsibility, and
no sense. I would employ him again, only it hurts me more than
it hurts him.

Brian was always on the lookout for a good practical joke, and in
1950 he noticed that 1 April happened to fall on a Saturday. He
decided to play an April Fool's joke on John Ellison, even though
they are not really supposed to happen after twelve noon. Brian
auditioned various impersonators before he found one who could
copy his voice exactly. It was a young Peter Sellers, who was
beginning to make a name for himself in variety. Brian persuaded
Sellers to take his place doing interviews in Oxford Street, and
when Ellison cued over to him that night it was Peter Sellers
impersonating him. After a couple of hilariously bad interviews
Sellers said he was beginning to feel ill and the crowd were
pressing in on him and he handed hurriedly back to the studio.
At which point Brian crept up behind Ellison, tapped him on the
shoulder and said, 'April Fool!' Ellison looked as though he had
seen a ghost. Later he admitted that he had noticed Brian had
sounded a bit strange but reckoned he must have been drunk.

A few weeks after my first birthday Brian gave me a bath on
air. This may not sound like a particularly dangerous stunt but it
was one of the first times he had ever bathed me. The broadcast
was a complete failure. It may have been the shock, or the sight
of an engineer holding a microphone in front of my face, but I
remained totally silent throughout. Apart from a few splashes of
water, there was no evidence of a baby in the bath at all. 'The
little brat never made a squawk!' protested Brian afterwards.
Many listeners must have thought he was making the whole
thing up.

An even more unlikely episode happened two years later after
Oxford sank in the 1952 Boat Race. Brian had been due to
interview the university crews for 'Let's Go Somewhere', but
when the race was abandoned he had to come up with something
else at the last moment. That night he created his own Boat Race

by sitting in the bath at home and playing with my toy boats. Not one of his most memorable broadcasts.

One of his favourite stunts was the time he crouched between the rails outside Victoria Station. He had heard that about half a mile outside the station, on Grosvenor Bridge, there were deep pits between the lines where railway workers could crouch down if a train was coming. The idea was that Brian would describe the Golden Arrow passing overhead, but that evening it was running late and John Ellison handed over to him just as an electric train came rumbling towards him. When the engine was about twenty yards away Brian ducked his head down and had to shout into the microphone as the train thundered overhead. It was a thrilling moment. Afterwards he handed back to the studio but had to duck his head quickly once again because the Golden Arrow was on its way. It was a good thing he was not on air. As the express roared overhead someone 'washed their hands' and he got thoroughly soaked. His language would have turned the airwaves blue.

One of his most disturbing broadcasts produced a torrent of letters from the listeners. Some thought it was the funniest thing they had ever heard while others were shocked, horrified and even frightened by it. Brian had wanted to see whether he could make himself laugh hysterically by inhaling some nitrous oxide, known as laughing gas. He thought it would make a very funny broadcast, but the idea was discarded in case it caused some people to lose confidence in the use of laughing gas at the dentist's.

Instead he thought he would try to achieve the same effect through hypnotism and contacted a professional hypnotist called David Stewart. Shortly before they went on air, David Stewart hypnotised Brian into an early state of complete relaxation. When he was ready, John Ellison cued over to Henry Riddell, who explained to the listeners what was going on. Then Stewart told Brian: 'When you come round you will feel quite normal. You will feel fine and talk quite naturally to me. I will then point to Henry Riddell and when you look at him you will laugh and laugh as you have never laughed before.' He snapped his fingers and Brian talked normally to him for a moment until Stewart pointed at Riddell and Brian collapsed into shrieks of high-pitched and uncontrollable laughter. Brian admitted later that when he listened to the recording he thought the laughter sounded 'terrifying, at times even maniacal', and one listener wrote: 'It was as if your soul had gone into another world.' Pauline was genuinely concerned that Brian would never be the same again. 'I thought he'd "gone",' she says. The BBC decided to cancel the repeat broadcast because of the effect it might have on the listeners and Brian swore that he would never allow himself to be hypnotised again.

Two weeks before Christmas in 1950 he carried out the first ever 'live' broadcast from the coalface of a coal mine. It was at Snowdon Colliery in Kent, one of the three deepest mines in England. He went down over three thousand feet, descending in a cage at a terrific pace. At the bottom he walked for a few hundred yards and then travelled over a mile in a 'paddy' – an underground railway truck – before having to crawl on his hands and knees another fifty yards or so to reach the coalface, which was only three feet high. He did the broadcast half kneeling and half lying, and tried to hack at the coal with a pick. The temperature was over ninety degrees and he found the work back-breaking and almost impossible, although he did manage to dig out a few lumps.

He was down the mine for about two hours, but wrote later that it seemed like a lifetime. He felt 'trapped, shut in and completely at the mercy of nature', the only thing stopping him from being crushed by the weight of the coal above being the small wooden pit props. He could not imagine how miners could spend their whole lives in such an environment and asked one young miner what he thought about when he was working. 'Money,' was the reply. After that experience Brian had a much greater respect for miners. He believed that they were entitled to a special high wage, although he did not always approve of their methods in achieving it. More importantly he said that he would not take any criticism of the miners from anyone who had not been down a mine. 'Compare what they are doing with what you do yourself,' he challenged. 'Remember you are lucky even to be breathing fresh air. It does not smell so good three thousand feet down in the earth.'

The stunt that attracted the most publicity took place in May 1951 and became known in the BBC as 'The Piccadilly Incident'. The next morning it made the front page of the *People* with the one-inch high headline: BBC STUNT STARTS A GIRL STAMPEDE IN PICCADILLY.

> Quite the silliest stunt the BBC has ever tried caused a stampede in Piccadilly Circus, London, last night. Police had to rush to the scene to control the crowd.
>
> Over five hundred girls started it. They responded to an advertisement in the 'personal' column of an evening newspaper asking for 'young ladies seeking adventure' to meet there a 'well-set-up young gentleman'.
>
> The result – as might have been expected – was alarming. For not only did the girls turn up in their hundreds, but hundreds of sightseers also rushed to the scene to see what was happening.
>
> With the result that traffic was held up and four police sergeants and eighteen constables were needed to control the jam.

It had started as an innocent idea to see whether people actually read the personal columns in the newspapers and, if so, whether they took them seriously. On the Friday night before the broadcast Brian had inserted an advert in the London *Evening News*:

> Well set-up young gentleman with honourable intentions invites young ladies seeking adventure to meet him on the steps of the Criterion Restaurant, Lower Regent Street, 7.15 p.m. Saturday May 19. Identified by red carnation and blue and white spotted scarf. Code words: 'How's your uncle?'

Brian had included a password because he fully expected that no one would turn up and at least it would give him something to ask the passers-by. It might make quite an amusing broadcast.

On the Saturday Brian was doing a TV cricket commentary at Lord's and got to the Criterion at about 6.30 p.m. All seemed relatively normal and he went inside to be fitted with his microphone. Half an hour later, when he looked out of the front entrance, he could not believe his eyes. The whole of Lower

Regent Street was jammed solid. Traffic was at a standstill and police were linking arms trying to hold back a crowd of several thousand people. There were hundreds of young ladies – and quite a few middle-aged women – jostling around the steps of the Criterion. Brian also noticed several optimistic young men in the crowd wearing red carnations and blue-and-white spotted scarves. Police had to blow their whistles as screaming women were being pushed against the windows of nearby shops. It was chaos.

When Brian walked out on to the steps at 7.30 p.m. there was a roar of 'How's your uncle?' from the crowd. He explained to some of the disappointed young ladies that they were 'live' on *In Town Tonight* and managed to interview one or two of them, who all said that they had been intrigued by the advertisement and had come along to see what the 'adventure' might be. No one had known it was a BBC stunt beforehand, although as soon as they saw Brian with his microphone many of them had recognised him from television.

The next day the Sunday papers reacted with predictable outrage. 'Cruel hoax,' said one headline; 'Broadcast in worst possible taste,' cried another. Lobby called Brian into his office on Monday morning and, after hearing what had happened, he offered his full support. The BBC was always being criticised for being stuffy and staid, he said, but as soon as they tried something original their critics complained again. Lobby had only one reservation. Brian should have warned the police first.

A few minutes after Brian had left, Lobby received a telephone call from an angry inspector at West End Central police station. Brian was notorious for ringing up and pretending to be someone else, so Lobby told him to stop messing about and put the phone down. When he rang the police station later he discovered that it really had been an inspector, who was by now even more annoyed, but Lobby managed to calm him down. 'I don't know who had the last laugh on that,' sighed an exasperated Lobby afterwards, 'but I certainly didn't.' Brian had got away with it, but Lobby must have wondered once again what he had let himself in for.

For his one hundredth 'Let's Go Somewhere' in February 1951

Brian asked his producer Peter Duncan if he could be allowed to do something he had always wanted to do on the air – be a cross-talk comedian. Duncan readily agreed, and John Ellison was chosen to be Brian's straight man. The pair had swapped jokes ever since sharing an office together and had developed an almost intuitive sense of timing. Brian pulled out his file of old music-hall gags and, after crossing out some of his most treasured ones with a blue pencil, they put together a slick three-and-a-half-minute routine. The jokes were old and corny but delivered with such confidence and style that the normally subdued *In Town Tonight* studio audience greeted their double act with frequent laughter and – apparently unheard-of – loud applause at the end. Brian may have had to abandon his ambition to be a comedian but he had proved he could compete with the best.

Another memorable programme was aired at Christmas 1951 when he became the first person to broadcast from inside a letterbox. He was over six foot tall so an ordinary pillar box would have been impossible, but they managed to find a large wooden letterbox outside the main post office in Oxford. The idea was to help the Post Office by encouraging people to address their envelopes correctly. Before the broadcast Brian climbed inside the box and then reported 'live' to the listeners as letters and cards plopped down on to his head, picking them up to see whether they had been addressed properly. After a while he was unable to resist temptation and when he heard a lady coming up to post a letter he put his hand out and took it from her. She let out a scream and nearly fainted.

After three and a half years Brian and his producer Peter Duncan were finding it increasingly difficult to come up with new ideas. The slot was still immensely popular but Brian did not want it to become stale. 'It is better to kill a good idea while it is hot rather than flog it to death,' he said. He broadcast his 150th and final 'Let's Go Somewhere' on 17 May 1952 and finished in style by being rescued from a boat in the Solent by a Royal Navy helicopter.

The *Sunday Chronicle* declared that he would be sorely missed:

'Brian, more than any other broadcaster, has helped take the stuffiness out of the BBC. If he has more than once made the front pages of newspapers on the grounds of "sensationalism", what of it? Critics for years have been yelling for something new from the BBC and Brian provided it.'

He was now a household name, and even he admits that he allowed fame to go to his head. But not everyone approved. One day Brian was staying with John Ellison when his colleague had to leave early to drive up to London. Half an hour later Ellison came back to say he had driven his car into a ditch and could Brian help to pull him out with his Ford Pilot? When they got back to his car they found a nearby homeowner was standing beside it. He had recognised John Ellison from *In Town Tonight* and offered to help. 'You'll probably be interested to hear,' said Ellison, 'that the chap in the other car is my colleague from the programme, Brian Johnston.' As soon as Brian's name was mentioned the man said: 'Brian Johnston? I can't stand him. Yap, yap, yap, yap. Can't understand a word he says!' With that he turned on his heels and stormed back to his cottage, leaving Brian and John Ellison to rescue the car themselves. As Brian commented wryly, 'So long as this sort of thing can happen, a broadcaster should be able to keep the same size in hats.'

17

Jack of All Trades

While Brian was establishing his name on radio and television during his four years on *In Town Tonight*, his home life was also becoming more settled. In December 1948 he and Pauline moved out of their cramped Bayswater flat into a large Georgian villa at 1A Cavendish Avenue, about a hundred yards from the entrance to the Nursery End at Lord's. The house was so close to the cricket ground that you could hear the applause and oohs and aahs of the crowd whenever there was a boundary or a wicket or a dropped catch.

Then, shortly after midnight on Easter Sunday in April 1949, I emerged into the world, two weeks early, in the Lindo Wing of St Mary's Hospital, Paddington. Brian had driven Pauline to the hospital earlier that evening and then rushed off to interview a diver at Leabridge Fair for 'Let's Go Somewhere'. Pauline was listening to him on the wireless while she was in labour. 'That's my husband!' she gasped to the midwife, between contractions. Brian had been told not to expect anything to happen overnight, so after the programme he went straight home to bed. He was woken up by a telephone call with the news that he had a son. 'Jolly good,' he said, and went back to sleep.

As well as his cricket commentaries every summer, he was beginning to appear in other television programmes. In 1949 he made the first of four guest appearances as a straight man for Terry-Thomas in his TV show *How Do You View?* Each week Brian had to conduct an interview with Terry-Thomas as a different character, such as Captain Shaggers the lion-tamer, or the man who hit the gong for Rank Films, and they used to rehearse the sketches in the garden at Cavendish Avenue. The show itself went out 'live' from Alexandra Palace and Brian had great difficulty in keeping a straight face because Terry-Thomas would try to make him laugh. Many years later Terry-Thomas made a comedy LP featuring his favourite sketches from the series and asked Brian to re-create two of their interviews for the recording.

During one of the shows the newsreader at Alexandra Palace fell sick and had to go home. When an urgent news item came in about the Prime Minister Clement Attlee at Number 10 there was no one else available, so Brian had to borrow a dinner jacket from the bandleader Eric Robinson and read out the news flash. Fortunately the viewers saw him only from the waist up, as he was still wearing a pair of loud check trousers.

When 'Let's Go Somewhere' took its annual summer break, Brian started to introduce a new series called *Saturday Night at the London Palladium*. This featured major American stars such as Bob Hope, Jack Benny, Betty Hutton and Jimmy 'Schnozzle' Durante, who was famous for the size of his nose. At their first meeting Brian pointed to his own considerable nose and said, 'It's a bigger one than yours, Mr Durante.' Schnozzle looked suitably impressed and replied, 'It's the moick of distinction – the moick of distinction!'

Brian also started to do the commentary for the Royal Variety Performance every year, which meant that he had to attend all the rehearsals as well as seeing the actual show. He was being paid to do what he enjoyed most, and with so much of his job now divided between cricket and the theatre, he realised that he was lucky enough to have a job in a million – the only one of its kind.

Diana Davis (now Diana Fisher) had joined the BBC as a secretary in 1948 when she was seventeen. Later she was assigned to the OB Department at 55 Portland Place, where she shared an office with Wynford Vaughan-Thomas, Max Robertson and Henry Riddell. She had always wanted to be on the stage, so when Brian mentioned that he needed someone to go with him to take notes at one of his theatre broadcasts she immediately volunteered.

She had – and indeed still has – a bubbly personality, and with her love of the theatre she became his regular assistant on theatrical broadcasts. Brian called her Dizzy Di. 'Would you like to come and take something down in the dark?' he would ask her, and off they would go to see whether a new production was suitable for broadcasting. It became something of a ritual. 'There was always a glass of something and a plate of smoked salmon beforehand,' recalls Diana, 'and raspberries and cream after the show.'

Diana was also the captain of the BBC tennis team, so when Brian learned during the summer of 1952 that members of the cast of *Call Me Madam* played tennis in Regent's Park, he challenged them to a game of doubles. It became a regular event, and about once a week Brian and Diana would pop out at lunchtime and take on Anton Walbrook, Shani Wallis and other members of the cast. 'Brian was not very good at tennis,' says Diana, 'but he got things back. Unconventional is probably the best way to describe his style. When he served he looked just like the French comedian Jacques Tati in the film *Monsieur Hulot's Holiday* and the ball would simply plop over the net.'

Diana left the BBC after eight years to become an air hostess for BOAC. 'In those days you had to be a duchess's daughter or have good legs,' she laughs. 'I had good legs.' In 1959 she married Humphrey Fisher, the fourth son of the Archbishop of Canterbury, Geoffrey Fisher, a formidable man who believed that adultery should be a criminal offence. They asked Brian to give the speech at their reception. His opening remark complimented Diana on her wedding dress. 'I call it her religious dress,' he began, and all eyes turned to Archbishop Fisher, 'because it is lo[w] and behold!' Fortunately the gag had the Archbishop 'rocking on his heels', according to Diana, and everyone breathed a sigh of relief. Five years later Humphrey and Diana Fisher went to live in Sydney, Australia, where in the mid-1970s she would become almost a second mother to Brian's eldest daughter Clare.

Brian nearly missed Clare's birth in September 1950 because he was busy seeing the MCC team off on their tour to Australia. Pauline had decided to have her second baby in the nursery at home, with the help of a nurse and her mother Eileen. When she went into labour at about 8 p.m. the family doctor had to be called away from a dinner party and turned up in his dinner jacket to find Eileen offering Pauline words of encouragement, holding a cigarette in one hand and a gin and tonic in the other. Brian had to wait downstairs until he was told he could see the new baby. When he entered the nursery, Eileen was pouring the champagne while Clare lay in a wash hand basin in the corner.

The following year Brian had his second and final shot at film stardom when he received a phone call from the secretary of film producer and director Herbert Wilcox. They were filming *Derby Day* with Anna Neagle and Michael Wilding at Shepperton Studios and needed someone to do an 'interview' with Peter Graves on the racecourse. There was no script and Brian would have to make up his own dialogue. Oh, and did he have his own morning dress? He did, and the next day he showed up at Shepperton Studios, where Herbert Wilcox explained that he needed Brian to ask a key question at the end of the interview.

The scene lasted only a minute and he and Peter Graves got the giggles, but they managed to film it in one or two takes. I saw the movie when it was shown on BBC television in 1972 and was delighted to see a slim and youthful-looking Brian but amazed to hear how high his voice sounded. It all seemed very old fashioned, and one critic described the movie unkindly as producing 'far from happy results'. It was Brian's first and last film role, but it was worth it for a moment in Australia about twenty years later. He was at a party with Herbert Wilcox, by then an old friend, who introduced him to someone with the words: 'This is Brian Johnston. He once played for me in one of my films.'

The Royal Variety Show was always one of the highlights of the year for Brian, and in 1951 it led to one of the most unusual broadcasts of his career. In September King George VI had undergone a serious operation to remove his left lung and Archbishop Fisher had led prayers across the nation for his recovery. Princess Elizabeth and Prince Philip had to undertake a tour of Canada in his place. A month later the King was still recuperating and was not well enough to attend the Royal Variety Show, to be held on 29 October at London's Victoria Palace. Two days before the performance the BBC agreed to broadcast the second half of the show for the first time. They kept the decision secret because, in the days when millions would tune in to such a popular event, they were worried that attendances would be hit at theatres, cinemas and other entertainment venues around the country.

The Royal Variety Show was known to be one of the King's favourite events, so the BBC arranged a unique personal commentary. A special land-line was set up between the Victoria Palace and Buckingham Palace and Brian was positioned in a box, opposite the Queen and Princess Margaret, with a BBC engineer on one side of him and a telephone on the other. The King's customary souvenir programme, printed on blue handmade paper, bound in silk and embroidered in gold – with all the advertisements removed – had been delivered earlier in the day to Buckingham Palace.

In the *Daily Mail* next day, Cecil Wilson described Brian as 'the most important man of the evening'. He had to act as the eyes and ears of the King, who sat listening to the show in bed at Buckingham Palace, and to describe what was happening on the stage. It was a very sentimental occasion. At one point Bud Flanagan stepped up to the microphone and said, 'His Majesty is listening. Let us make him feel a bit better with some community singing.' He then led the audience of 1,500 in a hearty rendition of 'Daisy Bell'. King George VI died only three months later.

As a member of the OB staff Brian was often called on to take over a broadcast if someone else fell ill. His versatility was remarkable. One day he might be commentating on ballroom dancing, another day it would be showjumping at Olympia or the Brass Band Championships at the Royal Albert Hall. Robert Hudson says that Lobby expected his staff to be able to commentate on anything – a fly crawling up a wall, if necessary – and he had selected Brian, Wynford Vaughan-Thomas and the others with that express purpose in mind.

In January 1952 Max Robertson became ill and was unable to go on the Monte Carlo Rally. Brian was called in at the last minute and went as co-driver and co-broadcaster with Richard Dimbleby. They travelled in Dimbleby's touring Allard and the plan was to broadcast from various points along the route. The weather was fine when they started out but it soon turned to rain and then to snow. It got so bad that Brian had to get out of the car and push while Dimbleby steered. They fell miles behind the other competitors and never made it to Monte Carlo for their evening broadcast. Caught in a snowstorm, they had to send their report from a hotel bedroom in Digne.

In spite of their failure, Brian was to report on the Monte Carlo Rally for the next six years. Raymond Baxter took over the driving from Dimbleby and Brian used to join him in Monte Carlo to report on the finish. It was a welcome break from the English winter every January. In 1955 he even made a guest appearance as a commentator in the popular radio series *Hancock's Half Hour*, with Tony Hancock, Sid James and Kenneth Williams, in an episode where Tony Hancock was supposed to have entered the Monte Carlo Rally.

One year Brian and Raymond were sitting in the Restaurant César on their final night in Monaco when they realised they had not collected enough receipts for their expenses. By now the Maître d' was an old friend, so they explained their problem to him. '*Ah, oui, messieurs*,' he said with a smile, pulling out his pen with a flourish. 'Let me see, on Tuesday you dined with the mayor.' He filled out a bill. 'On Wednesday you entertained the manager of the casino . . .' At this point a man sitting at the next table leaned over and said, 'Hello, Brian, hello, Raymond, I thought I recognised your voices. I work for the BBC as well.' 'What a coincidence!' declared the pair. 'Which department?' 'Accounts,' said the man from the BBC. There was a stunned silence until Raymond managed to blurt out, 'Sorry, I didn't catch your name.' 'Mr Goat,' came the reply. 'Oh really?' said Brian, recovering quickly. 'How are the kids?'

Raymond Baxter shared an office with Brian at Broadcasting

House for several years, although they were rarely there at the same time. They used to send saucy seaside postcards to each other from different OBs around the country and the cards were pinned up on a green baize board on their office wall. By the time they retired from the BBC they had amassed one of the finest collections of naughty postcards in the country.

There are usually groups of autograph hunters outside Broadcasting House and in the days before Brian and Raymond Baxter became familiar faces on television they would often be mistaken for each other. Baxter says that, rather than disappoint their 'fans', they would simply sign each other's name.

One night the two of them were invited to a smart function which required them to wear dinner jackets. Baxter felt he looked quite smart until Brian wandered up to him, fingered his shirt and muttered: 'You know, you *can* get these shirts in white!'

Brian had made a name for himself as a versatile broadcaster, able to turn his hand to almost anything, but he was now about to face his sternest test. When King George VI died on 6 February 1952, Brian was told that he would be a part of the television commentary team for the funeral. Richard Dimbleby would be stationed in St James's Street and he would hand over to Brian at Hyde Park Corner. Brian had never been involved in such an important state occasion and he was determined to get it right. He learned that at the head of the procession would be five Metropolitan policemen mounted on white horses, so he wrote out his opening words, something he did not normally do, and practised them over and again.

On the day Dimbleby handed over to Brian as rehearsed. 'Yes, here comes the procession now,' started Brian, reading from his prepared notes, 'led by five Metropolitan policemen mounted on . . .' To his horror he realised they were not on white horses but black. His mind went blank. All he could think of to say was . . . 'mounted on [pause] horseback'. His producer, Keith Rogers, spluttered into his headphones: 'What on earth do you think they are mounted on? Camels?' Not exactly the most auspicious start, but Brian recovered and in the BBC archives you can hear him intoning solemnly: 'And . . . following the band of the Welsh Guards . . . comes . . . the detachment . . . from the Royal Air Force . . . junior of the three services . . .' It hardly sounds like him at all, and it was light years away from his normal upbeat personality. But he had proved he could be serious if required. From now on he would be a member of the radio or television commentary team for almost every major royal and state occasion for the next forty years.

For the Coronation in 1953 he was along the route of the procession in Hyde Park, sharing the television commentary with Bernard Braden. It rained for most of the day and they had to sit for hours huddled in their raincoats on a scaffolding platform, getting 'horribly wet', although not as soaked as the beaming Queen Salote of Tonga, who waved cheerfully to the crowds as her open carriage filled up with rainwater. Later that evening Brian reported from an open-air street party in Camberwell, where he joined the crowd in a rousing chorus of 'I've Got a Lovely Bunch of Coconuts'.

Perhaps because of his war experience Brian was often called on to perform the commentary at the big army reunions such as the El Alamein and Burma events. Over the years he developed quite a rapport with Field Marshal Montgomery, who would send for him before each broadcast to discuss the exact details of the event. 'How long have you allowed for my speech?' he would ask. 'Oh, about twelve minutes, sir,' replied Brian. 'You shall have it,' said Monty, and he would stick to the timing exactly. As Brian observed, he knew the value of good publicity.

One year Lord Mountbatten was unable to attend the Burma reunion at the Royal Albert Hall because he was going to be in India. The OB Department arranged for him to record a special message which they would play at the reunion, and it was copied on to two discs for safe-keeping. As the producer of the broadcast, Brian took personal responsibility for the discs and placed them in his desk drawer. On the morning of the reunion he went to collect them but to his horror he could find only one. The other disc was gone. Still, at least he had the one. He gave it to an engineer to take down to the Albert Hall for the rehearsals and warned him to be very careful as it was the only copy.

Half an hour later Brian's telephone rang. It was the engineer to say that they had accidentally scratched the disc with the needle and it was too bad to repair. Panic broke out. Broadcasting House was searched from top to bottom but the second disc was nowhere to be found. Brian decided to play the damaged recording rather than not broadcast the message at all, and listeners at home and in the Albert Hall were amazed to hear: 'I *click* am very *click* sorry *click* that I *click* am unable *click* to be with you *click* tonight . . .'

Brian confessed that he had rarely felt more embarrassed than when he listened to that broadcast, and afterwards he was given a reprimand by his superiors. He never did find out what happened to the missing disc.

18

Game for Anything

In 1955, four years after the end of the original series, Brian was invited to revive 'Let's Go Somewhere'. This time it would be fifteen minutes long instead of the old three and a half to four minutes but would still be 'live' and not recorded. This gave him a chance to expand some of the ideas from the original spots on *In Town Tonight*, and it was one of the first radio or television programmes to test the reactions of the public at large. As such it was an early version of *Candid Camera*, which came later on ITV.

The *Radio Times* featured a photograph of him on the front cover and described the new programme as 'Brian Johnston, out and about with his live microphone, looking for laughter, excitement, and anything else he can find'. His friends were thrilled at his success. Nico Llewellyn-Davies, an ex-Grenadier who had been with Brian in the revue *The Eyes Have It*, wrote to him: 'I've expected it ever since I saw you riding down the aisle in that pram with a cigar in your mouth . . . I can think of no one who I've known who has had such a big and rapid and deserved success, a success which can only delight his friends – a delight that leaves no room for envy of any kind.'

The seven-week series turned out to be a fascinating insight into the British character in the 1950s. People were so afraid of being embarrassed that they would do almost anything not to 'make a fuss' or attract attention. Brian's first 'experiment' took place at Victoria Station in London. He wore a false beard, under which he hid a microphone, and staged various incidents to see how people would react. He started by replacing the stop-press headline on a newspaper seller's placard so that it read: MAFEKING RELIEVED.

Having glanced at this headline, several people bought the paper, but no one seemed at all surprised that the placard was announcing something that had happened more than fifty years before.

Next he took a parcel containing a human skull to the left luggage office. He had deliberately torn the parcel so that the skull would poke through, but the man behind the counter simply looked at it and said: 'How long do you want to leave it, sir?' Then he arranged for the female announcer on the public address system, Mrs Giles, to declare: 'Will the passengers who took the six o'clock train to Brighton from Platform Fourteen this morning . . . please return it as it's needed first thing in the morning!' She repeated it several times but Brian could not spot a single person who had even noticed it.

By now slightly desperate, he went behind a pillar and put on a wolf's mask which one of his children had received for Christmas (I remember it well). He put his hat on over the top, pulled up his collar and walked around the station concourse wearing the brown wolf's mask. One or two people did a double-take but no one stopped and stared at him or asked him what he thought he was doing. In the end, as he handed back to the studio, he had to admit that on this occasion the celebrated reserve of the British had defeated him.

His second experiment, if anything, was even less successful. Brian arranged for his producer Doug Fleming, Henry Riddell and Cliff Michelmore to ask two people each to dinner at the famous Quaglino's restaurant. A microphone was hidden in a bowl of flowers on each table and Brian dressed up as a waiter called Alphonse, complete with a ginger wig and a dreadful French accent.

First he served some soup to Henry Riddell's table and tipped one of the bowls into Henry's lap. Henry created a terrible scene at the top of his voice, but his two guests pretended not to notice and carried on talking as if nothing had happened.

Next Brian served some sole to Doug Fleming's table. Doug and his female guest were each given a beautiful sole but her husband was served a bare backbone with only the head and tail complete. He was much too polite to complain, and when Doug asked him how his fish was he replied: 'Well, there's not too much of it, but it looks jolly good all the same, thanks very much.'

Finally Brian served some wine to Cliff Michelmore's table, where his guest was a wine connoisseur. Earlier he had added some Angostura Bitters, tomato ketchup and a pinch of pepper to a bottle of fine claret. He offered a glass to the wine expert. It must have tasted foul but he did not want to criticise his host's choice of wine. 'This is one I haven't met before,' he observed politely, 'but I am sure it will make a pleasant drink with our dinner.'

In the end Brian dropped a pile of plates and was given the sack in front of the whole restaurant. As soon as the broadcast was over he explained to his victims what had been going on and they were given a real dinner with some genuine claret. But the British stiff upper lip had won the day again.

Brian had first tried his clumsy waiter routine on the original series of 'Let's Go Somewhere' and there were a couple more episodes with echoes of that first series. In one programme he carried out a 'live' smash-and-grab raid on a jeweller's shop in Nottingham, and for the next fifteen minutes was chased through the streets by the Nottingham police force's new-fangled radio cars. One radio critic described it as 'exciting fun' and commented: 'It is quite astonishing that such a sober institution as the BBC should encourage that most pleasant of characters Brian Johnston to undertake adventures on its behalf which put even Dick Barton in the shade.'

In another programme he played an old upright piano – 'Underneath the Arches' as usual – in a street near Piccadilly Circus, to 'test the generosity of Londoners'. Kenneth Horne stood near Charing Cross Station and sang 'Comrades' for a quarter of an hour, while Raymond Glendenning played 'Knees Up Mother Brown' on a barrel organ in Leicester Square. They were all heavily disguised and none of them seems to have been recognised. Horne collected one shilling and fourpence and Glendenning just twopence halfpenny, but Brian emerged the winner after he managed to earn three shillings in fifteen minutes.

In a novel twist Brian's next programme involved trying to give money *away*. Once again he and Kenneth Horne disguised themselves and tried to hand out ten shillings (probably worth about five pounds in today's money) to passers-by outside Victoria Station. Brian was dressed as a tramp, saying that he had won the pools and wanted people to share his luck. Even though he was offering brand-new ten-shilling notes, everybody looked embarrassed or pretended not to hear him, apart from one soldier returning from leave who took the money gratefully. Kenneth Horne fared even worse and was unable to give one single note away.

My favourite episode from this series involved a return to Madame Tussauds. In the old entrance hall there used to be a grand staircase leading up to the main exhibits, and halfway up the stairs there stood a lifelike waxwork of a commissionaire in his smart uniform. Every time I went there, like thousands of others, I wondered whether he was real. For his broadcast Brian was fitted out with a commissionaire's uniform, side whiskers and a wax moustache to look as similar as possible to the famous dummy. He had a microphone hidden under his uniform and for ten minutes, 'live' on air, he stood on the staircase, ramrod stiff and staring straight ahead, as people prodded and poked him to see whether he was a waxwork. One woman even tweaked his moustache, so he gave her a slow wink with his right eye and she let out an hysterical scream.

If there was a major public event in the 1950s it seemed that Brian was involved in one way or another. He did the commentary for the Trooping of the Colour, which he found quite an ordeal because he knew that the slightest mistake would bring a flood of letters from irate colonels. He began a long association with the Boat Race as a commentator and interviewer, although his main experience of boats at Oxford had been rowing back with his friends from the Trout Inn after supper. He covered the Motor Show and the Lord Mayor's Show, which he always enjoyed. He also became one of the commentators at the Miss World contest, on which his verdict was: 'great fun reading out the statistics, but very frustrating'.

He was also making regular television appearances. He took part in a number of *Saturday Night Out* programmes, including one from a Turkish bath in Harrogate, of all places. He was shown lying on a Begoni cabinet, a kind of massage table, while electric shocks were administered to his bottom, which made him 'jump up and down like a yo-yo'.

Another stunt was described next day by TV critic Phil Diack as 'a heroic piece of fakery'. It happened during a Boys' Clubs Canoe Rally, attended by Prince Philip, which was being televised 'live' by the BBC from the Serpentine lake in Hyde Park. Suddenly Brian appeared at the water's edge, wearing a pinstripe suit, bowler hat and rolled umbrella. Handing over his hat and brolly, he lowered himself awkwardly into a small canoe and paddled out into the middle of the lake, where he pulled out a newspaper and started to read. Then he tried to stand up, ostensibly to get a better view of the Duke of Edinburgh, and promptly capsized into the water. He splashed around, yelling for help, and had to be 'rescued' by some young canoeists, who swam with him to the bank to demonstrate their life-saving skills.

When he clambered out he put on his bowler hat, picked up his brolly and a newspaper, and walked off through the crowd, still dripping wet, as if nothing had happened. Remarked Phil Diack: 'Without this wonderful bit of nonsense this canoe rally would have made dull viewing indeed. Instead it was a comic treat.'

Brian was now very much a family man, with four young children; his second son Andrew was born in March 1954 and Ian followed in May 1957. In what was becoming a Johnston family tradition, Andrew's birth was not without incident. Pauline started to go into labour as they were about to watch the Grand National on television. Brian had placed a bet on a horse called My Love, so he persuaded her to stay until the end of the race, which was won by Royal Tan, before rushing her off to the nursing home in Avenue Road.

When they got married Brian had made it plain to Pauline that the very nature of his job as an outside broadcaster meant that his career would have to come first. He would be required to work in the evenings, at weekends and on public holidays. He might also be away for days at a time during the summer. He would help when he could but Pauline would be responsible for bringing up the children. Later, when he joined the MCC on tour, Brian was abroad for two or three months every winter. My mother has confessed that it was quite lonely in their marriage sometimes.

To be fair, she did not have to manage alone and there was always a nanny and a housekeeper in the house to assist her, but it must have been a considerable strain. After Ian was born she had four children under the age of eight, and she had to make all the decisions about their welfare and their upbringing.

Brian hardly ever told the children off. That was left to Pauline, although sometimes he thought she was being too hard on us. Occasionally she would try to defer the discipline. 'Wait until your father hears about this,' she would threaten, but when he eventually did he would dismiss the offence with a joke. He only spanked me once, when I scribbled some pictures on the wallpaper in the spare bedroom. It was partly because he did not want to interfere with the way Pauline was bringing up the children but also because he hated to make a scene.

He liked to make his children laugh. My earliest memories are of sitting at the dining table while my father ran through his litany of corny jokes. 'I say, I say, I say!' he would start. 'My dog's got no nose.' 'How does he smell?' 'Dreadful!' or 'My car's called Daisy.' 'Why is your car called Daisy?' 'Because some days she goes and some days she doesn't!' It was like being one half of an old music-hall double act.

Now that he had a young family of his own, Brian started to become a regular presenter on children's television. His first children's TV programme was a quiz series called *Ask Your Dad*, in which he was given a 'family' of two and competed against the TV cowboy Ross Salmon and his 'family'. This was followed by *All Your Own*, which had originally been presented by Huw Weldon. Each week Brian would travel to the BBC studios in Glasgow, Manchester and Bristol and talk to children about their different hobbies and skills. I remember accompanying him to a

TV studio in about 1960 when he interviewed a young guitarist who could play the Shadows' hit 'Apache' left handed. Brian seemed suitably impressed, although I am not sure he had ever heard of Hank Marvin.

He also had a Sealyham terrier called Smokey, a successor to his beloved Blob from the early 1930s. This obviously qualified him as a dog expert and he presented a TV programme called *Dog's Chance*, where dogs were put through various obedience tests and celebrities were invited to bring their own pets to the studio.

Brian loved puns and playing word games and he always tried to complete the *Daily Telegraph* crossword every day. So he was a natural for radio panel games and quiz shows. He made his first appearance as a panellist on the popular *Twenty Questions* in 1954, when he filled in for Richard Dimbleby, and he went on to make many guest appearances over the next few years. He also made his debut as the chairman of a radio quiz called *What's It All About?* with a panel including Kenneth Horne, Celia Johnson and Dilys Powell. Listeners sent in cards relating an extraordinary incident which had happened to them and the panel had to guess what it was. 'Fairly childish,' according to Brian, but it became quite popular.

He was also being called on to do more interviews. The *Today* programme started on the Home Service in 1957 and about eighteen months later Brian was recruited to introduce a weekly spot called 'Many Happy Returns' in which he selected the outstanding birthday of the week. The interviews were about four minutes long and usually recorded at the home of the person concerned. He did about eighty of them altogether and his list of 'victims' was quite impressive – Sir Compton Mackenzie, Alfred Hitchcock, Stirling Moss, Gracie Fields and Field Marshal Montgomery, to name but a few. He interviewed Monty in one of the caravans that he kept in the garden of his Old Mill House near Alton in Hampshire. Brian was surprised to see a portrait of Monty's old rival Field Marshal Rommel hanging on the wall. 'Fine soldier,' said Monty in his familiar staccato accent, 'admired him . . . the Eighth Army gave him a bloody nose!'

Another radio series which went out on Saturday nights was called *Spot the Headliner*. This was half quiz and half interview programme, in which listeners had to guess the identity of a personality who had made the headlines during their lifetime. Brian would then conduct an interview with the headliner, such as Lieutenant Commander Kerans, who had rescued his frigate HMS *Amethyst* from a four-month siege by Chinese communists, or Arthur Bell, a survivor of the *R101* airship disaster.

At the same time he recorded more than sixty interviews for 'Meet a Sportsman', which was part of the *Roundabout* series on the Light Programme and featured an interview with a famous sportsman or woman along with recorded commentary on their most outstanding achievements. He had to display knowledge of almost every conceivable sport, from tennis to tobogganing, and among his interviewees was Henry Cooper, who revealed that he always had a glass of sherry before a fight because it was good for the wind!

Brian still liked to play cricket for the Eton Ramblers whenever he could find the time. In the summer of 1956 he turned out for the annual Ramblers match at Escrick, a delightful ground just outside York, along with Sir Edward Ford and another Old Etonian, Arthur Collins, the nephew of the Duke of Roxburghe. Collins was very proud of his family's close connections with the aristocracy and liked to remind people of it at every opportunity. During the luncheon interval he talked at great length about plans for the Duke of Norfolk to take a cricket team out to Jamaica in the New Year.

Brian arranged for a telegram to be sent from the local post office to the cricket ground. When Arthur Collins was batting in the afternoon, a messenger arrived with the telegram and took it urgently on to the field. It was handed to the umpire, Colonel Edward Lane Fox, Jimmy's father, known as 'The Squire', who stopped the game to pass the important message on to Collins. It read: 'MCC WOULD LIKE YOU TO TAKE A TEAM TO BORNEO AND SARAWAK NEXT JANUARY – AS MANY DUKES AS POSSIBLE. PLEASE CONFIRM SOONEST. SIGNED NORFOLK.' Needless to say, once the laughter had died down Collins lost his concentration and was out shortly afterwards.

One of Brian's favourite annual broadcasts was from the Bertram Mills Circus at Olympia on Boxing Day. He would get seats for his children near the ringside every Christmas, and one year he took me backstage to meet Coco the Clown in his trailer. For several years after that I held a secret ambition to be a clown in the circus.

In 1956 Raymond Baxter was handling the commentary at the ringside while Brian interviewed the performers outside the ring. One of the highlights that year was the Wall of Death, in which a motorcyclist had to perform stunts while riding around a large cage about twenty feet above the ring. It was vital that he maintain a steady speed, otherwise he would plunge to the sawdust ring below. 'He started to take off his shirt,' recalls Baxter, 'with both hands off the handlebars. The shirt billowed out behind him and I saw part of it get caught in the back wheel. I knew instantly what was going to happen.'

Baxter handed quickly over to Brian as the bike stalled and plummeted to the ground: '. . . and as the act finishes let's go straight back to Brian Johnston behind the scenes for some more interviews.' Fortunately Brian saw Bernard Mills walking towards him with a white horse and he had to spend the next five minutes trying to interview Mills about this unexceptional horse while the motorcyclist was carried out of the ring. 'I was criticised in the press the next day for not mentioning the accident,' added Baxter, 'but it was Boxing Day and there were children listening.' Charles Max-Muller, the new head of OBs, agreed that they had done the right thing.

In November 1956 Brian was admitted to King Edward VII's Hospital for Officers for a second hernia operation – on the opposite side to the one he had undergone during the war. When the surgeon examined him, he asked who had performed the original operation. 'Some army surgeon from London Hospital who operated on me at the military hospital in Salisbury,' answered Brian. 'I must have been in good form that day,' said the surgeon. Brian spent a fortnight in hospital and then had a short convalescence in Eastbourne, where his mother was now living in a private nursing home.

Pleasance Johnston had been suffering from rheumatoid arthritis for some time, and after a long illness she died on 13 April 1957 at the age of seventy-seven. It was four days before my eighth birthday and I remember Brian receiving a telephone call at lunchtime on Saturday at home. He left the dining room to answer the phone in the hall. It was the matron of the nursing home, telling him that his mother had died. He went and sat in the sitting room on his own. Brian had always been very close to his mother ever since his father had drowned, but what made the moment worse was that he was supposed to do some interviews that afternoon at his local garage for a record request programme. It was too late to cancel the broadcast, so after a few minutes he had to go out and chat up the motorists as if nothing had happened. As he reflected later, this was his first personal experience of the old theatrical cliché 'the show must go on', and he found it a painful occasion.

A few days later he caught the train down to Cornwall, where his mother was buried next to his father in the village churchyard at Stratton near Bude. Brian still retained fond memories of Cornwall. His brother Michael lived there and the family had spent their previous two summer holidays in Treyarnon Bay and Polzeath. In 1957, however, Pauline booked them into a bed-and-breakfast cottage near Swanage in Dorset. She had remembered the area after being sent there to convalesce for two weeks back in 1946. They liked Swanage so much that the following year Pauline bought a small holiday cottage in the tiny hamlet of Acton, among the Purbeck stone quarries at the top of the downs. It had a fabulous view overlooking Swanage Bay with the Isle of Wight on the distant horizon. Brian even had an outside toilet built in Purbeck stone, fitted with a special stable door so that he could sit there in the morning and look out at the view. For the next eight years, every Easter and summer, the Johnston family would spend their holidays at Quarry Cottage.

19

BBC Cricket Correspondent

Brian commentated on his first Test match at Lord's, against India, in June 1946. He knew nothing about television commentary, but then nor did anyone else. There had only been four televised Test matches before, in 1938 and 1939, so he had to develop his own technique as he went along. He shared the microphone with Aidan Crawley, who had been one of the commentators in the experimental transmissions from the two London Tests against the West Indies before the war. Crawley was described by Ian Orr-Ewing, then head of TV Outside Broadcasts, as being 'a little bit stilted', and over the next couple of years a number of other commentators were tried out alongside Brian, including the well-known cricket writers R. C. Robertson-Glasgow and E. W. (Jim) Swanton, and the former England captain Percy Fender.

Fender had a notoriously short fuse. 'He used to whistle through his teeth,' says Peter Dimmock, then a BBC TV producer. 'I asked him once in his headphones to explain why someone was out lbw and he bellowed on the air, "Don't tell me how to commentate!"' By 1949 the regular commentary team had become established as Brian, Jim Swanton and Robert Hudson.

There were no transmitters outside London so at first the television coverage was restricted to Lord's and the Oval. Facilities were primitive to say the least. Lunch at the Oval was taken in the open air with Brian and Jim Swanton eating their packed lunch at a small card table on the edge of the flat pavilion roof. Swanton had a thermos flask of tea which he always liked to keep close at hand. One afternoon John Woodcock, later the cricket correspondent of *The Times*, accidentally knocked the flask off the table and it tumbled over the side of the roof, almost knocking out a poor Surrey member sitting in the pavilion below. Brian went down to apologise and came hurrying back to report that the hapless spectator reeked very strongly of whisky. So much for Jim's 'cuppa'! Brian never let Swanton forget the incident, although Jim always insisted that the Surrey member received 'only a glancing blow'.

Some commentators found it difficult to make the transition from radio to television, but Brian seemed to adapt quite easily. Seymour de Lotbinière thought it was because Brian kept it simple. 'I don't think he was one of those broadcasters who coin great phrases and great descriptive passages,' reflected Lobby. 'Those were the ones who found, when there was a picture as well, that it was difficult to adjust their descriptive passages to pictures already doing the description. Brian, in his simpler approach to things, recognised that the picture was there and he was able to add to it, as and when it was wanted.'

Jim Swanton agreed. 'Television commentary is more difficult to do,' he observed, 'because everybody wants something differ-ent. The housewife wants a lot of chatter, which Brian was of course only too willing to provide, whereas the expert wants one to say practically nothing. We had to find a medium between those two extremes.'

It is impossible to please both audiences at the same time, of course, as Brian would discover, but at first he was given a free rein to develop the technique of television commentary in his own style. On one occasion England were struggling in a Test match at Lord's when a car outside the ground backfired. The viewers at home heard a loud bang, followed by Brian's swift riposte: 'That must be one of the selectors shooting himself!'

'Brian and I complemented each other on TV reasonably well,' maintained Swanton. 'I the technical, tactical half, he supplying the more jokey element. At Headingley once I had the mike when a man came into view for a few seconds with a lavatory seat around his neck. I, poor dimwit, could not think of the *mot juste*; Brian, frustrated, would have made a meal of it.'

The Sutton Coldfield transmitter was opened in 1950, enabling the BBC to televise a Test match from Trent Bridge for the first time. Television was such a novelty in the Midlands, recalls Robert Hudson, that even people living alongside the ground, with a free view of the game, preferred to sit indoors and watch the screen. At one point Brian suggested they should all come out on their balconies and wave to the cameras – which they promptly did. It was a typical example of Brian's original approach towards television commentary.

Peter West commentated on his first Test match in 1952, and for nearly two decades he alternated with Jim Swanton and Robert Hudson, and then Richie Benaud, as one of the regular commentary team alongside Brian and the scorer, Roy Webber. 'They were very happy days,' says West. 'There was nobody like Brian. He was always cheerful and buoyant, he never appeared to be depressed. I never met anybody who disliked him.'

Whenever he was asked which was his most memorable moment in Test cricket Brian invariably chose the last ball of the final Test between England and Australia at the Oval in 1953. It was Coronation year and many people were seeing cricket on television for the first time. England had not won the Ashes for nineteen years, so when they needed only four runs to win the match and the series the tension and excitement were almost unbearable. Finally Denis Compton hit a four towards the gas-holder and the crowd surged on to the ground. Brian was overcome with emotion along with everyone else and could only shout hoarsely, 'No! Is it? Is it the Ashes? Yes! England have won the Ashes!' It was a thrilling and unforgettable moment.

Brian believed that cricket should be enjoyed by the players and viewers alike and tried to reflect that view in his commentary. 'He had a marvellous understanding of the spirit of the game,' says West. The commentary box was often full of laughter and became even livelier after Denis Compton became the regular expert in 1958. 'He was a lovely man,' says Peter West, 'when he could remember to be punctual.' Compton's wicked sense of humour frequently got Brian into trouble. During one Test match at Edgbaston a mouse ran across the pitch and play was held up while the players tried to catch it. The cameras followed the small rodent as it was being chased around the field. 'They are bound to catch it soon,' declared Brian in the commentary box, 'it's got no hole to go down.' As an afterthought he added, 'Lucky it's not a ladies' match.' What he had meant to imply was that women were generally frightened of mice. But a snort from Denis Compton conjured up a completely different picture.

In those early days the technical equipment was extremely basic. There were only three cameras at each ground and no such refinements as replays or recordings. Communication with the producer in the control van outside was often difficult, so a system of codewords had to be developed. When the tea interval was approaching Brian would hear a voice in his headphones saying something like: 'Mention Freddie Trueman if you want a cup of tea.' Quick as a flash Brian would comment, 'You know, Denis, I think it's about time they brought on Freddie Trueman for a few overs.' 'One lump or two?' the voice would ask. 'I think he'll need at least two slips, don't you?' Brian would add, and a few minutes later a cup of tea and two lumps of sugar would magically appear in the commentary box.

By the end of the decade Brian had done the television commentary at every Test match in England since 1946, but he had never been on an MCC tour abroad. He felt his cricket education was incomplete and applied to the BBC to take some leave so that he could go to Australia to watch Peter May's tour of 1958/59. The BBC agreed to give him eight weeks' paid leave after Christmas, although he was informed that they would not pay for him to go. Brian promptly contacted the Australian Broadcasting Commission, who invited him to join their commentary team for the last four Tests, and he arranged to write some articles for the *Eagle* boys' comic. In a pattern that would become familiar the BBC said that, as he was now going to be in Australia, they would like to use him for their own reports and interviews, and eventually agreed to pay some of his expenses.

So he flew off to Australia for the first time on 27 December

1958. In those days the journey took forty-eight hours and he did not arrive in Melbourne until 30 December. Next morning he was feeling a bit jet-lagged and still trying to recover from the flight when he had to commentate on his first overseas Test match.

England were 7 for 3 as he took over the commentary. 'We have made another disastrous start,' he began, and then remembered where he was. He thought he had better explain himself and added quickly, 'Perhaps I ought to say that I am an Englishman.' Evidently this brought guffaws from many of the Australians within earshot. How could anyone with an accent like that be anything *but* an Englishman?

To add to Brian's discomfort a pigeon in the rafters overhead chose that exact moment to drop a message on to his wrist. Things could only get better, and fortunately they did. Over the next two months he grew to love Australia and would return many times over the next thirty years. He was impressed with the way he was made to feel so welcome. 'Australian hospitality,' he once quipped, 'is like a kangaroo with rheumatism. It knows no bounds!'

Brian's first overseas tour had gone well. He had arranged broadcasts and interviews that would never have been possible if he had stayed in London and had added greatly to his knowledge of cricket overseas. His boss, Charles Max-Muller, another Old Etonian, who had taken over as head of Outside Broadcasts from Lobby, agreed that the tour had been beneficial for both Brian and the BBC. For the next four years he would campaign tirelessly to have Brian appointed as the first BBC cricket correspondent.

In the summer of 1960 South Africa were the England tourists and Richie Benaud broke new ground by becoming the first Australian captain to work for the BBC while still captain. He covered the five-Test series on radio but was interviewed a number of times by Brian on television. 'This was great for me,' says Benaud, 'because I had already done a special BBC Television course in 1956, preparing for what I hoped would be a chance to be involved at a later date with sports television in Australia. Brian was extremely helpful at the end of each of those interviews and was happy to point out errors, or ways I might better have phrased something.'

Brian's next encounter with Richie Benaud came in 1961 when he brought his popular Australian team to England to defend the Ashes. In April Brian flew out to Egypt with a TV camera crew to meet them at Port Said. The idea was to travel with them to Malta aboard the liner SS *Canberra* for two days, filming interviews with Richie and the team. While Brian was waiting in Port Said for the ship to dock it started to pour with rain, so he popped into a shoe shop where he found a pair of brown-and-white corespondent shoes, similar to ones he had worn in Brazil in the 1930s. He tried on the left shoe and liked it so much that he told the Egyptian shopkeeper he would take it. After much gesticulating and general excitement Brian realised that the poor shopkeeper probably did not share his sense of humour, so he agreed to take *both* shoes.

He wore them at the first Test at Edgbaston and they attracted so much attention that he wore them at every Test match he attended for the next thirty-three years, in the expressed belief that they would bring England luck. The shoes became famous among cricket fans around the world, and when the original pair wore out he had two further pairs made especially for him by Barkers of Earls Barton. Shortly before he died Brian calculated that since he had started wearing the shoes in 1961 England had won sixty-two Tests, lost forty-eight and drawn eighty, so it is hard to tell whether they made any difference at all.

It was during the Headingley Test in 1961 that Brian made one of his most famous gaffes. Australia were fielding and Neil Harvey was standing at leg slip. Brian was always conscious of the need to tailor his words to fit the picture on the screen, so when the camera showed a close-up of Harvey, he had to think quickly of something to say. 'There's Neil Harvey,' he commented, 'standing at leg slip . . . with his legs wide apart . . . waiting for a tickle.' He would have got away with it if his fellow commentator, Jack Fingleton, the former Australian Test batsman, had not added drily: 'I beg your pardon. I presume you mean waiting for a catch.' For once Brian did not dare to speak.

One of Brian's most remarkable attributes was the speed of his wit. In the mid-1960s Ted Dexter was sharing the television commentary with Brian during a Test match when he observed, 'He drives well off the front foot.' Without a moment's hesitation, Brian responded, 'My wife drives well off the back seat!' Pauline had a few words to say about *that* when he got home.

When Roy Webber collapsed and died suddenly in 1962, Ross Salmon succeeded him as the regular TV scorer and statistician. His first Test was at Old Trafford, and he remembers trembling with fear at the prospect of working alongside such household names as Denis Compton, Peter West and Brian. On his first day Brian was commentating when Colin Cowdrey hit a boundary. Brian turned to Salmon and whispered, 'Is that his first boundary?' According to Salmon: 'I told him it was and Brian announced the fact to the world. Denis Compton behind us said, "How about that cover drive off the first ball?" Oh, heavens, I thought, I've made a terrible mistake already. Brian without any hesitation tells the world that it was *approximately* Cowdrey's first boundary. Or maybe his second. In that atmosphere of light-hearted good humour, all the clouds of apprehension and nervousness suddenly lifted. Because it was no longer a disaster to make a slight boob, I didn't make any after that.'

At the end of the year Brian flew out to Australia to cover his second Ashes tour. He was still not officially the BBC cricket correspondent, but Charles Max-Muller had persuaded his superiors that Brian ought to go on the tour. He flew out on 18 December, the first time he had missed Christmas at home with Pauline and the children, and joined Ted Dexter and his MCC team in Adelaide.

The Reverend David Sheppard was a member of the team on that tour and everywhere they went he was invited to preach a sermon at the local church. So every Sunday Brian, John Woodcock of *The Times*, Michael Melford of the *Daily Telegraph*, Colin Cowdrey and a number of other players would go along to the eleven o'clock service to support their friend and colleague. Colin Cowdrey used to delight in recalling how they all used to squeeze into the same pew, not too near the pulpit but not too far away. As soon as they had sat down Brian would produce a stopwatch, a Biro and a small notebook, in which he would write down everyone's initials. Against his own initials he would put, say, 7½ minutes. This was his estimate of the length of Sheppard's sermon. The notebook was then passed along the pew and everyone would write a different time against their own initials, such as 8¼ minutes, 10 minutes, and so on. The idea was that each of them put about fifty pence into the kitty and the closest to the correct time would scoop the lot.

As soon as Sheppard began his sermon Brian would start his stopwatch, and as the seventh minute arrived there would be mounting excitement. With thirty seconds to go, whenever Sheppard paused or reached the end of a sentence, Brian would reach for his hymn book and start to rise out of his seat, as if to say, 'Very good sermon, well done, David.' But when Sheppard continued he would sigh dramatically and sit down again until the next pause, when he would clear his throat and shuffle in his seat, encouraging Sheppard to finish.

This would go on several times, almost embarrassingly loudly, with people in the other pews beginning to look round to see where all the commotion was coming from. As the 7½ minutes went by a look of great despair would cross Brian's face, until the next target drew near and someone else looked like winning, when he would become excited all over again. 'It's yours, Wooders,' he would hiss hoarsely, 'it must be yours. Yes, I think . . . no, he's going past it . . .' and so on down the order. One Sunday Sheppard was so impressed with the enthusiastic turn-out for his sermon that he went on for a full twenty-eight minutes. A delighted Colin Cowdrey won the jackpot. As Cowdrey commented later, Brian could make even a church service seem like tremendous fun.

After Christmas, once we children were back at boarding school, Pauline flew out to join Brian in Australia. She would be the first to admit that she was never a huge fan of cricket, although her family had close associations with the game. Her great-grandfather, Edward Tozer, was one of the founders of

Yorkshire Cricket Club, and her maternal grandfather, Herbert Sykes, had his own cricket ground, where the great Wilfred Rhodes used to play regularly. Pauline enjoyed the social side of cricket, however, and this was the first of many overseas tours that she would share with Brian over the next three decades.

After Brian returned home in 1963 he was finally appointed as the first-ever BBC cricket correspondent. For the next nine years, until his retirement from the BBC in 1972, cricket would take precedence over his other broadcasting work. This meant that the BBC newsroom could call him at all hours of the day or night if they wanted his opinion on a late-breaking cricket story. It also meant that he would be expected to go on overseas tours with the MCC team whenever possible.

Brian was always prepared to try something new and in June 1963 he conducted a fascinating experiment with Richie Benaud, something that had never been attempted before on television. 'It was a Lord's Taverners against Old England match at Lord's,' recollects Benaud, 'and, with Brian in the BBC TV commentary box, Denis Compton and I were "miked up" out in the centre. Brian did a three-way conversation with me and Compton, in which I described what I would bowl, and then Compton would comment and say what he was going to do with the bat. Brian and the viewers could hear both of us but we could not hear each other. It was said at the time that it was wonderful to watch and great to listen to. These days it would be commonplace, with "red zones" and snickometers, but then it was ground-breaking.'

Richie Benaud joined Brian on the BBC TV commentary team in 1964 and worked with him for six years until 1969. 'The most important thing about Brian in the commentary box,' says Benaud, 'was that although he had the obvious reputation of being a humorous man, he was also one who prepared meticulously for every day's play. As he was the presenter of the programmes, this was of the utmost importance; so too was the fact that he had a wonderful memory for people and incidents, something that is priceless when the rain is falling and there is no immediate likelihood of a resumption of play. That early training stood me in good stead when I became the presenter of Channel Nine cricket in Australia.'

Brian started a friendly competition with Benaud and Peter West. As soon as a batsman hit the ball they had to say, 'That will be one run' or 'two', as the case might be. If they were able to predict a 'four' correctly, it was considered a minor triumph. Benaud was by far the best at this and seldom got it wrong. Brian used to be very bold and shout 'Four!' but then would frequently have to make an excuse when the ball was brilliantly fielded or stopped just short of the boundary.

It was during Richie Benaud's debut as a TV commentator at Trent Bridge in 1964 that Brian played one of his most famous practical jokes. Jim Swanton was the television summariser for the first Test against Australia and had arrived at the ground in a chauffeur-driven car. This was too much for Brian and Denis Compton, who composed a surreptitious message up in the box when Swanton was not looking. Compton took it down to the man on the public address system and at about midday, between overs, a voice over the loudspeakers declared: 'If Mr E. W. Swanton has arrived on the ground yet, will he please go to the back of the pavilion where his chauffeur has left the engine of his car running!' Brian said later that he had rarely heard such a roar of laughter on a cricket ground.

Swanton was well known for being rather pompous and was always having his leg pulled by Brian. A year earlier Brian was commentating in the exciting second Test match against the West Indies at Lord's while, at the same time in Rome, the Sacred College of Cardinals was meeting at the Vatican to choose a successor to the late Pope John XXIII. Crowds were gathered in St Peter's Square for the traditional signal that a decision had been reached – a puff of white smoke from a chimney in the Vatican. Suddenly Brian spotted black smoke pouring from the chimney of the Old Tavern at Lord's. The cameras quickly zoomed in. 'Ah,' said Brian, 'I see that Jim Swanton has been elected Pope!'

Now that Brian was the BBC cricket correspondent, Charles Max-Muller felt that he should not be used solely by television.

So from 1965 onwards he began to be heard on *Test Match Special* for the first time, doing three Tests each season for television and two for radio, with John Arlott and himself interchanging between the two. It was believed that this would also help to make Brian's voice more familiar to foreign listeners on the World Service in advance of his overseas commentaries in the winter months.

One of his last gaffes on television was also one of his most well known. New Zealand were the tourists in 1969 and during the first Test at Lord's Glenn Turner scored a defiant 43 not out in their second innings. Alan Ward of Derbyshire was playing in his first Test for England and was bowling extremely fast from the Pavilion End. Off the fifth ball of one of his overs he hit Turner with a sickening thud between the legs. Turner collapsed on the ground and the television cameras zoomed in to show him clutching himself in agony.

Mindful of his past indiscretions, Brian had to describe what had happened without mentioning exactly where Turner had been hit. He kept talking for about three minutes until Turner staggered to his feet looking pale and rather shaky and someone handed him his bat. Brian, relieved that he had managed to avoid saying anything rude, declared, 'Well, he's bravely going to carry on, but he doesn't look too good. One ball left!'

20

Staff Commentator

When Rex Alston retired from the BBC staff in 1961, Robert Hudson joined Brian and Raymond Baxter as one of the three BBC staff commentators in their office at Broadcasting House. In his book *Inside Outside Broadcasts* he describes the job as: 'a dream occupation, if ever there was one . . . There were no set hours and certainly no overtime. We did whatever was required, within the security (if not the riches) of a staff salary.' This latter point is vitally important. Brian himself revealed that against his name in the BBC personnel files were the initials SNF, which stood for 'Staff No Fee'. This meant that he could be booked by any BBC programme on radio or television at no extra cost. Whereas a freelance broadcaster might require a substantial fee, Brian was paid nothing more than his regular (and by no means generous) BBC salary. This is one of the reasons why he was hired so often as a stand-in whenever anyone fell ill or went on holiday. The other reason, of course, was that the producers knew they could rely on him to do a thoroughly professional job. Among dozens of other programmes in the 1950s and 1960s he stood in for Richard Dimbleby on *Twenty Questions*, for Peter Dimmock on *Sportsview* and for Jack de Manio on *Today*.

In those days there was only one presenter on *Today* and it was a much shorter programme than nowadays, with two separate editions on the Home Service at 7.15 and 8.15 a.m. Brian did his first stint as presenter in April 1963 when Jack de Manio took three weeks' leave. He found the early starts hard going as he had to do his normal work during the day, but fortunately he lived near Broadcasting House so he was able to set his alarm for 5.50 and be in the studio by 6.30.

Robert Hudson also used to present *Today* when Jack de Manio was away and says it was 'a very challenging' programme to do because you never knew who or what was going to be in the news each day, and you might have to interview a cabinet minister at seven o'clock in the morning. Between the two editions the production staff were provided with a light breakfast which Brian described as 'rather poor' and which included 'soggy toast' and marmalade. He objected strongly to the soggy toast but was told that the BBC would not supply a toast rack because it was always stolen. Brian made such a fuss that the BBC eventually paid out for a new one, which was known for ever after as the Brian Johnston Memorial Toast Rack.

I was surprised that Brian was chosen to present such a news-based programme, bearing in mind his reputation for more light-hearted fare. But Robert Hudson believes that Brian was a sensible choice because 'listeners wanted to have someone whom they could trust, whom they felt had integrity'. Nevertheless, even though Brian presented *Today* on several occasions, it was not really his cup of tea – with or without the toast.

Another programme that tested his versatility as a broadcaster was *Sportsview*, the popular television sports magazine hosted by Peter Dimmock. On his travels to America, Dimmock had discovered a new-fangled gadget called a teleprompter. It was a copy of the script on a revolving roller, which was projected on to the lens of the camera by a complicated system of mirrors. It enabled the TV presenter to look at the camera and read the script at the same time. In those days it was operated by the presenter with a foot pedal. The harder you pressed, the faster the script would go round. Brian described it as 'a nerve-racking operation'. 'It was tricky,' admits Dimmock. 'If you kept your foot down, the cue was gone and you couldn't remember what it said!'

In May 1960 Brian joined the television commentary team for his first royal wedding when Princess Margaret married Anthony Armstrong-Jones at Westminster Abbey. It was the first time that ITV had mounted their own coverage of a royal event and the BBC commentators were under pressure from their bosses and the television critics to prove that the BBC coverage was still superior. Brian was in a relatively unimportant position on Horse Guards Parade and had to cover the procession as it passed on its way to and from Buckingham Palace. By this point there was not a lot he could add to the picture as the previous commentators had already mentioned the main details of the procession. This led to a comment by the television critic Peter Black in the following morning's *Daily Mail*. 'By far the silliest remark of the whole day,' wrote Black, 'was made by Brian Johnston of the BBC, who when Princess Margaret passed a statue in Whitehall commented: "Princess Margaret is now passing the statue of the Second Duke of Cambridge. I am sure he would have waved at her if he could."'

At home, it turned out to be a memorable year for the Johnston family when Mrs Ella Callander moved with her children Jack and Ann into the downstairs flat at 1A Cavendish Avenue. Cally, as she was known, had answered an advertisement in the *Lady* for a new housekeeper and soon made herself indispensable, helping to look after the children, cooking, cleaning and answering the telephone. She even put up with Brian's practical jokes. He had a 'Dirty Fido', a realistic-looking plastic dog poo, which he used to delight in leaving around the house. One day he left it on the carpet and Cally was completely fooled. She went to clear it up, armed with a shovel and holding her nose, until she discovered it was false. Cally was always cheerful and became a real friend of the family, staying with Brian and Pauline for more than thirty-five years until she finally had to retire due to ill health.

In November 1960 Brian took part in one of the first breakfast television broadcasts after the US presidential election. John F. Kennedy, whom he had known socially with William Douglas Home before the war, had beaten Richard Nixon by the narrowest of margins and Brian conducted several interviews with American guests at the Savoy Hotel. He was fascinated by politics, but this was his only broadcast of a remotely political nature. As he commented afterwards, it was probably just as well because he would not have been able to disguise his political beliefs. Brian

once told William Douglas Home that he would have loved to
have stood for Parliament but he did not think he had the courage
to go and kiss all those babies. 'What party would you have stood
for?' enquired William. 'Right of any party there is at the moment,'
chuckled Brian. He was a lifelong Conservative voter, although I
suspect that it had more to do with his social background than
with any deep political philosophy. After all, in those days half
the cabinet were Old Etonians.

Raymond Baxter says that when he first shared an office with
Brian and Wynford Vaughan-Thomas, Brian leaned to the right
politically, Wynford to the left, while Raymond was somewhere in
the middle. Brian used to tease Vaughan-Thomas about his beliefs
but they were always careful to keep their opinions to themselves
in public. In fact BBC staff were under strict instructions not to
let their political views become apparent to the listeners. When
the Secretary of the BBC Staff Association announced that he was
standing as a candidate for Parliament, Brian and Raymond Baxter
promptly resigned from the Association on principle. Commented
Baxter drily: 'I don't think they missed us.'

Also that year Brian became the chairman of a new radio
quiz called *Sporting Chance*, devised and produced by Michael
Tuke-Hastings. This was a weekly competition between teams
from the New Towns who had to identify pieces of sports
commentary and answer questions about the laws and records
of different sports. It was instantly popular, and Brian was asked
by Paul Fox, then the Controller of BBC 1, to present a special
television version to go out every Saturday afternoon at the
beginning of *Grandstand*. This was essentially an early version of
the present-day *A Question of Sport*, and included film clips from
sporting events, photographs of well-known sporting figures and
a mystery personality each week.

After a couple of programmes Paul Fox thought it looked too
static for *Grandstand*, and had made the decision to drop it when
he was having a drink one evening in the BBC Club. Kenneth
Adam, then the head of BBC TV, approached him and said,
'That's a jolly good quiz you've got on *Grandstand*. I can't get

my two boys away from our set while it's on.' So *Sporting Chance* was saved and it continued on radio and television for some time. Richie Benaud recalls watching the programme during the 1961 Ashes tour. 'Television was new to us, it didn't begin in Australia until 1956,' he says. 'We used to watch *Sporting Chance* avidly in our hotel rooms.'

Two years later, in 1962, Michael Tuke-Hastings devised another radio quiz called *Treble Chance*, and once again Brian was invited to be chairman. This was more of a general knowledge quiz and featured a panel of three BBC experts, Nan Winton, Charles Gardner and Wynford Vaughan-Thomas, who would pit their wits against a team from a different seaside town each week. This proved to be extremely popular and the programme was to run for more than ten years. As *Treble Chance* became more successful, Michael Tuke-Hastings arranged ever more adventurous tours, and in 1964 they went on a six-week trip to the Middle and Far East, taking on teams from the three armed services in Aden, Bahrain, Nairobi, the Maldives, Singapore and Hong Kong. The BBC team was transported everywhere by RAF Transport Command and, according to Brian, they 'had a fantastic time and were royally entertained'. His only complaint was the oriental food, which he refused to eat. While the others tucked into local delicacies such as bird's-nest soup, Brian insisted on being served fried eggs and bacon. Nevertheless, over the next two years the *Treble Chance* team went on to tour the British armed forces bases in Cyprus, Tobruk, Malta, Gibraltar and Germany. As he observed later, it was turning out to be a case of 'join the BBC and see the world'.

Brian was not particularly interested in ballroom dancing but one of his regular radio commentaries during the 1950s was the annual Star Ballroom Championships. He became even more involved in the world of sequins and sambas in 1960 when he started an eight-year stint as the television commentator for the International Ballroom Championships at the Royal Albert Hall. Fortunately he was helped by his co-commentator Elsa Wells, who was also the organiser of the event and one of the judges.

Perhaps on the basis of this apparent knowledge of ballroom dancing, he was invited in 1962 to make his first – and last – appearance as a compère on the popular television series *Come Dancing*, which was introduced by Peter West. Brian had always thought it looked rather a thankless task, sitting at a table surrounded by 'a bevy of beauties' and having to appear enthusiastic as the South-East region competed in a foxtrot against the North-West. He appeared on one programme from a ballroom in Purley and received a polite note of thanks afterwards from the television producer but was not asked again. He was not disappointed.

A few years later Neil Durden-Smith was one of the compères on *Come Dancing*. His wife Judith Chalmers had just given birth to their daughter Emma, so Brian suggested to Peter West that he should congratulate Neil on the programme by saying: 'By the way, Neil, congratulations on the birth of your daughter Emma.' To which Neil would reply: 'Emma-so-many-thanks!'

All would have gone well except that on the programme Peter introduced Neil with the words 'Congratulations on the birth of your daughter', leaving out her name. As rehearsed, Neil replied, 'Emma-so-many-thanks,' but as no one knew that this was his daughter's name, there were some puzzled expressions among the viewers at home.

More to Brian's liking was a new television series called *What's New*, which was an early version of *Tomorrow's World*. It also featured Peter West, Polly Elwes and a young David Dimbleby, and each week they looked at new inventions and ideas. Brian found the programme interesting and fun to do, especially as they all tried to make each other laugh, and the series ran for several years.

In 1961 he was surprised to receive a call from the BBC TV Light Entertainments department asking whether he was doing anything that evening and, if not, could he stand in for Eamonn Andrews on *This Is Your Life*? Fortunately he was only required to introduce the programme while Andrews was trapping that night's 'victim' in another studio, because in those days the programme went out 'live', so anything was liable to go wrong, and it often did. That night, when the dramatic *This Is Your Life* signature tune started the programme, Brian had to walk out onstage at the TV Theatre in Shepherd's Bush and explain to the surprised audience what was happening until Andrews appeared with his subject – the actor Rupert Davies, star of the *Maigret* TV series. It would be more than twenty years before Brian himself was caught by Eamonn Andrews with the famous big red book.

The following year he was asked to do another interview series for radio called *Married to Fame*, in which he talked to the wives of well-known people to find out how their lives had been affected by their husband's celebrity and career. He visited a diverse selection of wives, including those of Sir Francis Chichester, H. E. Bates, Graham Hill and Humphrey Lyttleton. The series ended with a spoof interview with comedian Dick Emery, who put on one of his sexy female voices, lisping, 'Ooh, you are awful . . . but I like you!'

The summer of 1962 held a touch of nostalgia for Brian because it was the year I went to Eton College. Sadly, it was a mistake. Eton is a marvellous school but it was not right for me. Now that I have been able to read Brian's letters from Eton I can see why he enjoyed it so much. He was an extrovert personality and excelled at sports, which made him extremely popular. I was completely the opposite. I was hopeless at sports and my only interest was in music. After the Beatles burst on to the scene at the end of 1962, my only ambition was to play the guitar and write songs. It was a difficult time for both of us. Brian could not understand why I was not happy at Eton. I remember him being almost tearful when he read some of my school reports. Apart from anything else, my education was costing him a lot of money. On more than one occasion I came close to being expelled for being caught smoking or some other transgression. One day the Head Master asked me why I did not leave the school if I disliked it so much, but I told him that it would break my father's heart. I'm afraid it probably broke his heart anyway.

After four years I took my A-levels early at the age of seventeen and left without looking back. On my last morning I was summoned to see the Head Master, who banned me from going back to the school for a year because I was such a bad influence on the other boys. Brian was terribly upset. My brothers Andrew and Ian had been scheduled to follow me to Eton, but he was so disillusioned by my experience that he withdrew their names. Instead Andrew went to Westminster School and Ian to Bradfield College, where they fared much better.

This was not the only reason for Brian to have felt disillusioned. In a newspaper interview in 1961 he was asked whether he had any unfulfilled ambition. 'I'd dearly love to see one of my sons walking down the pavilion steps at Lord's to bat for England,' he replied. A few months later he sent me for coaching at Lord's Cricket School but I have never been able to bat, bowl or even catch a ball. It was embarrassing. The final straw was when I dropped an easy catch and one of my teammates shouted in disgust, 'And you call yourself the son of Brian Johnston!' They sent me home after three days and told Brian to save his money. To his dismay, Andrew and Ian were also useless at cricket. Worse than that, none of us even showed an interest in the game.

Brian's brother Christopher thinks it was because Brian tried too hard with us. There is a photograph of me at the age of four holding a miniature cricket bat, with Denis Compton trying to teach me how to bat. Andrew says Brian once took him to the Lord's Cricket School and stood behind the bowler's arm, yelling, 'Hit the bloody thing!' 'I'm trying to!' said Andrew, as he flailed at another ball. Ian recalls the England captain Colin Cowdrey bowling to him in the nets. It may have been that we felt under too much pressure to perform, but I think the real reason is simply that we were not any good at sports. It meant that Brian was not able to share his love of cricket with his three sons and it must have been a major disappointment to him.

The 'swinging sixties' were turning out to be a time of change in more ways than one. After Brian was appointed the official BBC cricket correspondent in 1963, his role as a jack of all trades gradually came to an end. He continued to be the chairman of *Treble Chance* and stood in occasionally on *Today* but the greater part of his time was now spent commentating or reporting on cricket. One exception was when he was invited to be a disc jockey for a week on *Housewives' Choice*, the popular radio request programme. He had to write his own links for each record and was unable to resist one or two dreadful puns, including one for the Seekers' hit 'I'll Never Find Another You'. 'Sounds the sort of song that a blind ram might sing,' added Brian shamelessly.

His television appearances also became mainly restricted to cricket, although he was given the job of commentating on a huge firework display in April 1964 to celebrate the start of BBC 2. Much to the embarrassment of the BBC, its electricians went on strike and blacked out the entire opening-night transmission, so the launch of the new channel had to be postponed for twenty-four hours. When it did eventually take place Brian's carefully prepared notes were rendered completely useless after the man in charge panicked and lit all the fireworks in the wrong order. But, as Brian observed, at least BBC 2 was introduced with a bang.

In March 1964 he travelled up to the Hirsel in Scotland for the wedding of his god-daughter Meriel Douglas-Home. Her father Sir Alec was then the Prime Minister, so there was a lot of media interest in the wedding and the press were desperate to find out where the happy couple were going to spend their honeymoon. After the reception Brian travelled with Meriel and her husband on the plane back to Heathrow Airport and, avoiding the reporters in their cars waiting to follow them, smuggled the couple out of the airport in the back of his Ford Zephyr.

Meriel's elder sister Caroline Douglas-Home recalls how Brian also saved the day at the wedding reception. They had recently installed a small lift at the Hirsel which was designed to carry four average-sized people. During the reception Nancy the cook, an 'extremely large' lady, squeezed herself and three others into the lift and promptly overloaded it, so that it became stuck between two of the floors. Fearing that the lift might plummet to the ground, Caroline and her brother David, Lord Dunglass, started to wind the lift down by hand. As the guests gathered round anxiously, Brian positioned himself with a glass of champagne outside the lift doors and began to give a running commentary on the rescue attempt: '. . . Yes, I can see the floor of the car and feet and it looks as though they are all managing to remain upright. No one has fainted. Another few inches and we will be able to revive these incredibly brave and calm people with glasses of champagne . . .' and so on for about fifteen minutes, until the four guests were released from the lift to cheers from the assembled partygoers. Many years later Caroline could still recite Brian's commentary and added, 'It was hilarious at the time and the one thing *everyone* remembered about the reception!'

Margaret Cormack joined the Outside Broadcasts Department in 1965. She had come from the BBC Overseas and Foreign Relations Office where the secretaries had to address their bosses by their surnames, so she was surprised at first by the informality of the staff commentators. She shared an office with Robert Hudson, next door to Brian and Raymond Baxter. They were not usually in the office at the same time, but when all three of them were together she says it was chaos, because they all wanted to use her services simultaneously.

By the mid-1960s Brian was trying to avoid going to the office at all if he could, and when it was a sunny day he would ring Margaret at the BBC and invite her round to Cavendish Avenue, where they would sit in the garden while he dictated his letters. Robert Hudson was often left wondering where his secretary had gone. Margaret says that Brian was very bad at keeping his expenses up to date, and when he returned from a foreign tour he would often present her with three months' worth of expenses to type up. (She says that he was always referred to in the office as Brian, BJ or Beejers – never Johnners.)

When Raymond Baxter left the department in 1966 and joined the British Motor Corporation, he took their secretary Margaret with him. Brian was rather annoyed. Next time they met he asked Baxter: 'Pinched any good secretaries lately?'

Even though Brian was now in his early fifties, he still liked to pull on his wicket-keeping gloves whenever he could find the time. One of his favourite annual fixtures was at the village of Widford in Hertfordshire, against a team run by his friend John Pawle. Three years younger than Brian, Pawle had played cricket and racquets at Harrow, where he had first heard tales of 'this hilarious chap called Johnston' at Eton. They had met through mutual friends and later Pawle had been one of the regular group of Old Harrovians who used to gather at Block G during the Eton and Harrow matches.

John Pawle's grandfather had created the cricket ground at Widford in about 1880. During the war it had been grazed by sheep, but after it was restored in the late 1940s Pawle invited Brian to bring a team to play the local village side. It was a perfect setting, surrounded by trees and gardens, and with a small thatched pavilion. The match became an annual fixture and was always held on the Sunday of the Lord's Test, which in those days was a rest day. This meant that Brian was able to invite his broadcasting colleagues, and his team would often include commentators like Peter West and Jim Swanton, as well as former Test cricketers such as Richie Benaud and Jack Fingleton, and even the film star Trevor Howard.

One year Jack Fingleton, known as 'The Finger', hit six sixes in one over off the Widford leg spinner Lou Bly. At the end of the over Fingleton walked up to a shattered Bly and shook his hand. 'Well done, boy,' he said, smiling broadly, 'you kept the ball up!'

In another match Jim Swanton was brilliantly caught and bowled low down by a young bowler from the village. Rex Alston was at the non-striker's end. 'Well caught!' he shouted, but Swanton stood his ground. 'I'm not going for that one!' he growled, and he didn't.

The fixture nearly became a victim of its own success, after the crowd swelled from about fifty spectators in the first year to more than two thousand, eager to watch the visiting celebrities. They had to call the match off for a while after the players complained that they kept being pestered by the fans.

On Midsummer Day in 1962 Brian's team created an extraordinary record when they were playing twelve a side. After four different bowlers had taken the first four wickets, Brian kept switching the attack so that by the end of the innings eleven bowlers had each taken one Widford wicket apiece. The last wicket fell to a superb leg-side stumping by Brian, who was thus able to also claim a victim. The umpires verified that Widford had not cooperated in the achievement of this remarkable feat, and it is unique in the annals of organised cricket.

There were no Sunday league matches in those days, so Brian was able to play in charity matches for the Lord's Taverners alongside some of the most famous Test cricketers of the time. He kept wicket to the bowling of Lindwall, Miller, Trueman, Bedser, Statham and Laker, to name but a few. Brian would seem to have missed more catches than he caught. 'Not a role model as far as the skills are concerned,' observes Richie Benaud.

Brian continued to keep wicket until the late 1960s when John Woodcock invited him to play for his team against the Rugby School Boys' Club at the Dragon School in Oxford. Richie Benaud was also in Wooders' team but missed the start of the game because he had to cable some stories early that morning. 'I arrived at the school ground,' recalls Benaud, 'and started badly by driving my car behind the bowler's arm, holding up play and causing near-apoplexy to Johnny Woodcock.' When Benaud came on to bowl Brian did his best to read his flippers, googlies and top spinners. 'I read them all right,' Brian used to say, 'they all went for four byes, but I read them well!' When the last man came in Benaud bowled him a leg break. The batsman went down the pitch, missed it and with all his old speed – or so he thought – Brian whipped off the bails. 'Not in the Alan Knott, lifting-one-bail school of stumping,' adds Benaud, 'but all three stumps down.' Brian was thrilled. There it was, inscribed in the scorebook for ever: stumped Johnston, bowled Benaud. As they walked off Brian asked Richie what he had thought of it. 'Neat execution,' replied Benaud laconically, 'and how very sporting to give the batsman so much time to get back!'

Brian used to say that it was the school bursar, Mickey Jones, who had made the remark. Whoever it was, he got the message and hung up his gloves soon afterwards.

21

Down but Not Out

By the spring of 1965 Brian and Pauline had been married for seventeen years. All four children were away at boarding school and Pauline was frequently on her own, especially during the winter months when Brian might be abroad for three months at a time. She decided, without telling him, that she wanted to have another child, 'to keep her company'. A few weeks after Brian returned from South Africa in early March, Pauline broke the news that she was pregnant again. She was forty-two and healthy and describes the next nine months as 'the happiest I can remember'. She admits, however, that she was concerned in case there might be some defect in the baby because of her age. Her friends told her not to worry.

On 28 November 1965 Pauline went into the nursing home. Brian waited nervously in the hall downstairs for about three hours until a nurse came down to tell him that he had a baby daughter. She added that Pauline was fine, but looked embarrassed and walked off before he could ask any questions. A few minutes later the family's GP, Dr Cove-Smith, arrived to say that the baby was in an incubator and he was not quite happy about her. He wanted the specialist to see her the next day. Brian went up to see Pauline in the delivery room. She had seen the baby only for a moment but was delighted to have had a daughter. Brian did not say anything to her but he suspected that something was wrong.

The next day a paediatric specialist from St Mary's Hospital examined the baby and asked for a meeting with Brian and Pauline. He informed them that their daughter had Down's Syndrome but in a milder form called Mosaic. This meant that she would be physically perfect but would be backward and not quite like other normal children. He added that she would be pretty, loving and a source of great happiness and, as Brian would confirm later, the doctor was right on all three counts.

After hearing the news, Brian had to leave Pauline to catch a train for Lancaster, where he was recording an edition of *Treble Chance*. They had decided not to tell anyone about the baby's condition for a while, so it must have been heartbreaking for him to be greeted by his colleagues with endless congratulations on his new daughter.

The specialist had explained that some parents might have to put such a baby into a hospital but pointed out that a happy home life was the best medicine. Brian and Pauline did not hesitate. 'We've had seventeen blissfully happy years,' Brian told her, 'with four lovely children, a lovely home and all the things we have really wanted. This, in a way, is a test for us. We must prove we are strong enough to overcome adversity. You can't go through life without some troubles and so far we have been so lucky in every way. This was meant to happen some time to us. We must be patient and persevering and all will turn out happily, I'm sure.' They promised each other that they would do everything in their power to treat Joanna – as they named her – as near as possible the same as any other child.

From then on, with the help of Pauline and the faithful Cally, Joanna was raised as normally as possible. Because her condition was so rare she was monitored closely, and for five years she had regular tests at Guy's Hospital and Great Ormond Street, which showed that she was making steady progress. Unfortunately they also discovered that she had diabetes, which meant that she would have to inject herself twice a day with insulin and watch her diet carefully.

Pauline arranged for Joanna to go to a Montessori nursery school in a local convent and then to the Gatehouse Learning Centre, a pioneering school in Bethnal Green which integrates normal and handicapped children. Then at the age of thirteen she went to Flexford House, a small boarding school for fifty girls near Newbury, where she was one of five girls with learning difficulties.

Finally Joanna spent three years at the Derwen Training College for the Disabled at Oswestry in Shropshire, where she learned the art of dressmaking. After she returned to live at home, Pauline found Joanna a part-time job hemming and tacking customers' skirts at a couturier's in Mayfair. But she found it hard work doing the same job for hour after hour and she began to wander off at lunchtime. Sometimes she would fall asleep on the bus and miss her stop. After six months it seemed kindest to all concerned for her to relinquish her job.

After that Joanna attended several training courses for the mentally handicapped, in which she studied everything from cooking and drama to computer skills. She is also a wonderful artist and her paintings have been shown in several exhibitions. In 1990, after being on the waiting list for thirteen years, she was offered a place at a house run by the Home Farm Trust in Biggleswade. She lives there with six other mentally handicapped young adults and is looked after by a devoted staff. This is now her home and she is very happy there.

When Joanna was about a year old, Brian and Pauline were forced to move house for the first time in their married life. The lease on 1A Cavendish Avenue was coming to an end, and once again Pauline was delegated by Brian to find a new house 'somewhere near Lord's'. Another reason for wanting to move was that a year earlier Paul McCartney had bought the house opposite. The Beatles were then at the height of their fame and there were always dozens of girl fans hanging around outside his house day and night in the hope of catching a glimpse of McCartney and his actress girlfriend Jane Asher.

He would occasionally emerge in his black-windowed Mini, to a chorus of high-pitched screams, but otherwise there was not much for anyone to see. The house was hidden behind a high wall, and for most of the time the blinds were drawn and it looked largely unoccupied. Brian used to meet McCartney's butler when he was out walking their dog, and he revealed that the Beatle tried to avoid the crowds by sleeping during the day and getting up for breakfast at 11 p.m. That did not deter his fans, however, and

Cavendish Avenue was no longer the peaceful little road it had once been.

Pauline succeeded in finding an impressive four-storey house at 98 Hamilton Terrace, about a quarter of a mile away, and the family moved in, along with Cally, during November 1967. 'Hammers T' – as Brian soon called it – was a broad, tree-lined avenue known locally as 'Millionaire's Row', and their new neighbours included the film actresses Lee Remick and Dame Anna Neagle and the politician Lord Lambton. The good news was that it was still only a ten-minute walk from Lord's.

It was about this time that Colin Cowdrey approached Brian with an unusual proposition. He asked him whether he would like to buy a one-quarter share in a greyhound. Brian thought it was a brilliant idea and persuaded his friends John Woodcock and Michael Melford, the cricket correspondents of *The Times* and the *Daily Telegraph*, to take up the remaining two shares. None of them knew anything about greyhounds, but they convinced themselves that they were on to a winner.

The dog was trained and raced in Kent, so they decided to call him Kentish Kipper, after Cowdrey's nickname. One evening Brian took the family down to Catford to watch him run but the dog was bumped on the first bend and trailed in last. Later he actually won two or three races although never when his owners were there to see him. After about a year the kennel and training bills began to mount up and they came to the conclusion that owning a greyhound was not as much fun as it had sounded.

When Cowders, Wooders and Mellers went on a tour to the West Indies, they handed Brian the job of finding a new owner for Kentish Kipper. By chance, Arthur Milton, the former Gloucestershire and England opening batsman, told Brian that he knew of a 'lonely little old lady in Bristol' who wanted a greyhound as a pet. Milton offered to pay them a hundred pounds for the dog and they were glad to see the back of him. A few months later a friend showed Brian a cutting from a West Country newspaper. The headline read: KENTISH KIPPER WINS AGAIN! Either the little old lady was a remarkably good trainer of greyhounds or Arthur Milton had got himself an extremely good deal.

At the end of the 1960s Brian was no longer the instantly recognisable figure that he had once been. He was remembered with affection by the older generation for his stunts on *In Town Tonight*, but when I told my friends at school that my father was a well-known BBC cricket commentator I would often receive a blank look. He was frequently mistaken for Michael Miles, the question-master on the popular ITV quiz show *Take Your Pick*, who was also tall and had a very large and distinctive nose. On one occasion we were eating as a family in a restaurant when a young boy approached our table rather sheepishly to ask Brian for his autograph. Brian signed it with a flourish, but as the boy walked back to his table he looked closely at the autograph and seemed a bit disappointed. When he sat down we heard him complaining, 'See, I told you it wasn't him!'

One day Brian flew to Northern Ireland to do a programme for the BBC. As he stepped off the plane he was greeted by an airport official who said, 'Well, here's someone who needs no introduction.' 'Thank you very much,' said Brian, suitably flattered. 'Yes,' said the official, 'I watch your programme every week, Michael. What's in Box Thirteen tonight?' Brian was too embarrassed to correct him so he had to pretend to be Michael Miles until the man had gone away.

The final indignity was still to come. In January 1970 Brian flew out to South Africa at the invitation of Charles Fortune to be the neutral commentator in a four-Test series between South Africa and Australia. This was the series in which Barry Richards and Graeme Pollock hammered Australia with displays of batting that Brian described later as 'pure perfection'.

He arrived back in England in the middle of March and was on his way to his office in Broadcasting House when he bumped into his friend Neil Durden-Smith. 'I had sat next to Jim Laker at a dinner a few nights before,' says Durden-Smith, 'and he told me he had heard it on very good authority that Brian's contract was not being renewed. So when I saw Brian I said I was sorry to hear that he was no longer doing the cricket commentary on television. He was flabbergasted. That was the first he had heard of it.'

Brian went to see the new head of Radio OBs, Robert Hudson, who confirmed that he had heard about the change but said that Brian should wait to be told officially by TV. He added that television's loss was radio's gain and he would like Brian to become a regular member of the *Test Match Special* team. This helped to soften the blow but Brian felt humiliated.

He was the BBC cricket correspondent. He had restarted cricket on television after the war and had helped to develop the technique of cricket commentary on television. He had commentated on every Test match in England for twenty-four years. The least he might have expected was a letter informing him that he was being sacked. A word of thanks for nearly a quarter of a century's contribution to cricket on television would also not have gone amiss. But he heard nothing.

'There is no doubt in my mind that he was very upset at being dropped,' says Peter West. 'It was such a surprise. I think they might have had the decency to give him a warning.'

The decision to replace Brian had been taken by the head of television sport, Bryan Cowgill, an outspoken North Countryman who had been brought in to toughen up the BBC's approach to sport. 'Television Outside Broadcasts *was* a bit like a garden party in those days,' admits Peter West. 'It was not as professional as it became later.'

Cowgill informed Peter Dimmock, then the general manager of Television Outside Broadcasts, that Brian had to go. He wanted to move away from the jokey approach to cricket commentary and believed that the commentators should stick to the game. Dimmock tried to dissuade him. 'It will break his heart,' he told Cowgill, 'and he has a very popular following.'

'I don't care,' replied Cowgill. He felt that it was wrong that Brian was a BBC staff commentator and not a professional cricketer, and he was determined to introduce former Test players such as Richie Benaud and the former Surrey and England bowler Jim Laker. 'I agonised over it,' says Peter Dimmock.

'I knew how upset Brian would be. It was no reflection on his ability.'

Robert Hudson thinks that Cowgill made a mistake in getting rid of the only man who had ever made television cricket commentary sound like fun. 'Even if the cricket was deadly,' says Hudson, 'it was never dull in the commentary box when Brian was on. The viewers were still enjoying themselves.' He suspects that pressure was applied on the BBC by the hierarchy at Lord's, who did not approve of Brian's light-hearted approach to cricket and wanted the commentary to be more serious and technical. He thinks the BBC were worried about retaining the television rights to cricket and did not want to offend Lord's, so in the end Brian was unceremoniously dumped.

Bryan Cowgill says that is absolute rubbish. 'If any such pressure had ever reached me,' he says, 'Brian would have stayed on television for ever, probably to the detriment of his career!'

The reality was more mundane. 'The traditional role of the commentator was being superseded,' explains Cowgill. 'Technology had improved vastly and the visual side had become so graphic. I genuinely felt that it was doing Brian no favour to keep him on television. He was a wordsmith. His personality and humour were better placed on radio than television.'

Peter Dimmock agrees that television equipment had become more reliable and efficient, which made it easier to train ex-sportsmen as commentators. It also meant that it was no longer necessary to have a professional broadcaster in the commentary box in case something went wrong.

'I am sure Brian regarded it as a slight,' adds Cowgill, 'and some people may have viewed it as a demotion, but that was balls.' So why did no one tell Brian that he had been sacked? 'It was probably a cock-up,' says Cowgill, 'a lack of communication.' I asked him whether it would not have been possible for him to have written a letter or to have picked up the phone to say thank you for all he had done for television. There was an awkward silence. 'It didn't work like that,' he said.

Brian was a loyal BBC man. He did not deserve to be treated in this way. It is the only occasion when his colleagues remember him being bitter about anything. He was rarely heard to say a bad word about anyone, but he never forgave Bryan Cowgill. Not for dropping him, which he had every right to do, but for not having the courage or the courtesy to tell him.

In the end Peter Dimmock wrote Brian a short note to say how much he would miss him personally. 'He was obviously upset,' Dimmock recalls, 'so I thought I should write him a letter. I never realised that no one ever told him.'

As it turned out, of course, Cowgill had done Brian a huge favour. Robert Hudson was delighted to snap him up for *Test Match Special* and the rota of commentators was increased from three to four in order to include him in the commentary team. 'His arrival had a huge impact,' recollects Hudson. 'From being a worthy but slightly dull programme, it became one to listen to. Brian took chances and no one else had the courage to do what he did. He was a breath of fresh air.'

Ironically, it was not long after he had moved from television to radio that Brian was portrayed in the cult comedy series *Monty Python's Flying Circus*. John Cleese was a great cricket fan and wrote a very funny sketch in which he played Jim Swanton, Graham Chapman was Peter West and Eric Idle impersonated Brian by wearing an enormous false nose. The three of them were surrounded by empty wine bottles, commentating on a Test match in which England had been batting for five hours but were still o for o. 'A superb shot of no kind whatsoever,' declared Brian's character, after the batsman failed to attempt a stroke, 'I well remember Plum Warner leaving a very similar ball alone in 1732.' 'Oh shut up, elephant snout,' said Jim, as a drunken Peter fell off his chair.

The following week *Monty Python's Flying Circus* began with a programme trailer for 'a whacky new comedy series' called *Rain Stopped Play* starring Peter West and Brian Johnston, about the gay exploits of two television commentators and featuring E. W. Swanton as Aggie the kooky Scots maid! Brian was highly amused.

Once he had settled into his new role on *Test Match Special* he had to face a new problem. He was going to be sixty on 24 June 1972. That was the official retirement age for members of staff at the BBC and he would have to leave the Corporation after twenty-seven years. He would also cease to be the BBC cricket correspondent. Robert Hudson was surprised when Brian did not apply for an extension of his contract for another year, but he had made the decision to go freelance. He was not a wealthy man. Early in his career he had chosen to stay on the staff of the BBC so that he could have financial security. He told the journalist Elkan Allan: 'I like my job as it is. I get enough money, and I can think of the job without worrying how I can make more out of it.' He may have had security but his final salary at the BBC was only £10,000; some of his freelance colleagues had been earning three times as much.

As he entered his final year with the BBC he flew out to Australia to be the neutral commentator on ABC Television for a Test series between Australia and a World eleven, which included a thrilling 254 by Gary Sobers at Melbourne. At the end of the series he flew to South Africa, where Pauline and their second son Andrew met him in Durban. They went to see Brian's sister Anne in St Lucia and then left Andrew, now almost eighteen, to spend a year working and travelling in South Africa.

Brian arrived back in England in mid-February 1972. On Thursday, 2 March, he was walking down the corridor to his office in Broadcasting House when Arthur Phillips, the producer in charge of *Down Your Way*, popped his head out of a door and asked Brian whether he had heard the sad news about Franklin Engelmann. Engelmann, known to his friends as 'Jingle', had been the presenter of *Down Your Way* for nineteen years and had died of a heart attack the night before, after recording his 733rd edition of the programme. There were no programmes held in reserve, so they needed someone to present the next recording at Hyde in Cheshire the following Wednesday. Would Brian be able to help out?

Brian felt obliged to say yes, although he felt awkward about stepping into Engelmann's shoes so soon after his death, and agreed to stand in for a week or two while they searched for a permanent substitute. He recorded ten programmes before he had to return to his duties as the BBC cricket correspondent in May. During the summer four different interviewers were tried out on the programme, but none of them had Brian's relaxed and friendly style, so he was approached again and invited to take over the programme full time from the beginning of October. He was to present it for the next fifteen years.

Brian always referred to this as another example of how lucky he was. If he had not been walking down the BBC corridor at that moment, he might never have been offered the programme. Although, with his reputation as a reliable pair of hands, it is likely his name would already have been near the top of the list. Brian liked to present himself as a happy amateur who always happened to be in the right place at the right time, but it is not possible to sustain a career of nearly fifty years unless you are extremely professional.

The BBC had agreed that he could stay on until the end of the cricket season and he retired as a member of the BBC staff at the end of September 1972. He was sixty years old and self-employed for the first time in his life. He went down to Swanage with Pauline to begin work on his autobiography *It's Been a Lot of Fun*. He still had *Test Match Special* to look forward to during the summer and *Down Your Way* to record every week, but it must have seemed as if his best days were behind him.

PART THREE

1972–94

22

It's Been a Lot of Fun

Brian did not have to wait long for his first job offer. In September 1972 he was asked by Thames Television to introduce one programme in a new television series called *A Place in the Country*, which visited a National Trust property each week. He presented the programme from Lacock in Wiltshire and admitted that he found it strange to be working for ITV for the first time in his career. The highlight of the day came while they were filming a cricket match. To Brian's obvious delight, Larry the Ram escaped from his pen and ran straight across the pitch, followed closely by half the village trying to catch him.

At the end of the year Brian went down to Swanage to spend Christmas with his family. Quarry Cottage had been sold in 1966 and for a while Pauline had rented a flat on the top floor of Kenfield Hall, a Queen Anne mansion at Petham in Kent, which they used for weekends and holidays. But they had all missed Swanage and in 1972 Pauline bought a new house on the edge of the cliffs at the north end of town, with a panoramic view of Swanage Bay. Brian loved it there and for the rest of his life he would escape down to Swanage whenever he could, to play golf and to relax.

After Christmas Brian flew out to South Africa for some winter sunshine and on his return in February he settled into his new life as a freelance broadcaster. During the summer he commentated on all six Test matches as well as a number of county, Benson and Hedges, John Player and Gillette matches. At the same time he had to squeeze in a recording of *Down Your Way* every week. He appeared on the popular television game show *Call My Bluff* with Frank Muir and Patrick Campbell, and his services as a commentator were also required at such ceremonial occasions as the Lord Mayor's Show, the Festival of Remembrance at the Royal Albert Hall and the wedding of Princess Anne and Captain Mark Phillips. Obviously his 'retirement' from the BBC did not mean he was about to slow down at all.

His first volume of autobiography, *It's Been a Lot of Fun*, was published by W. H. Allen in February 1974. John Arlott wrote a perceptive review in the *Guardian*.

> His performance on radio or television has a boyish character, friendly, humorous, at times verging on Wooster. Do not, though, underestimate him. Any man who remains twenty-eight years on the top performance-level of radio has an in-built survival gear and an ability to use it. In most fields some retrenchment is possible. In newspapers, films or the theatre, for instance, a man may lose a degree of standing and yet remain secure; even find a foothold for a subsequent climb. In broadcasting, though, he can only go upwards or maintain position. For any radio performer – the more since the move to exclude them from permanent staff appointments – the slightest downward movement leads directly to the discharge vent. Find a *Radio Times* of even a dozen years ago, or cast your listening or viewing memory as far back as that in sport or, indeed, general Outside Broadcasting – and count the man-wastage.

Arlott had made a very good point. One tends to take Brian's long career for granted, but at the time Arlott was writing in 1974, how many of his contemporaries had lasted ten years in broadcasting, let alone twenty-eight? What makes the observation even more remarkable is that Brian would continue at the peak of his profession for a further twenty years.

Brian embarked on a round of interviews to promote his new book. He appeared on a variety of radio programmes including *Today* and *Open House*, but the highlight was his guest appearance on *Desert Island Discs* with Roy Plomley. Brian had always wanted to be on the programme, which was viewed then as the ultimate accolade on the BBC. His choice of eight records and a book was honest, unaffected and in many ways completely predictable. His tastes in literature and music remained unapologetically low-brow throughout his life and he never tried to pretend otherwise. He enjoyed reading biographies or a good mystery novel and he was not interested in classical music; he used to say that he preferred a simple melody to which you could sing along. His eight records were:

'The Eton Boating Song' by the Eton College Musical Society
'All The Things You Are' by Leslie Hutchinson
'We'll Gather Lilacs' by Vanessa Lee and Bruce Trent
'Double Damask', a comedy sketch by Cicely Courtneidge
'Strolling' by Bud Flanagan
Elgar's *Enigma Variations* by the Philharmonia Orchestra conducted by Sir Malcolm Sargent
'Tie a Yellow Ribbon round the Old Oak Tree' by Dawn
'End of the Party' by Design

Most of his choices speak for themselves and reveal the unexpectedly sentimental side of his nature, although I feel the last two require some explanation. The record by Dawn had been a huge, and immensely irritating, hit the previous year, which Brian had found very catchy, and the song by Design was a novelty number written and sung by myself. In 1969 I had formed a vocal harmony group called Design with some friends, and soon afterwards we were fortunate to have been discovered by John Ammonds, the producer of *The Morecambe and Wise Show*. Over the next five years we would appear on more than fifty television shows, including those of Morecambe and Wise, the Two Ronnies, Tommy Cooper and Benny Hill. Brian loved to hear the showbiz gossip from behind the scenes; it gave us something in common at last, and it was the start of a real friendship and understanding between us.

He was a great supporter of my songwriting and was not above giving one of my songs a gentle plug whenever he thought he could get away with it, which is why it appeared on *Desert Island Discs*. His choice of book was also illuminating. It was *Funny Way to Be a Hero*, a collection of music-hall biographies and comedy routines, by John Fisher. Life on a desert island would not have been the same for Brian without plenty of laughter.

In mid-February he appeared on the television programme *Pebble Mill at One*, one of the few times we ever worked together. I was also on the programme with Design, singing a couple of songs from our latest album, and to my embarrassment the programme started with a close-up of my nose. 'Does this face remind you of anyone?' asked the presenter. 'How about this?' The camera then showed a close-up of Brian's familiar profile. I would not have minded but, to be fair, his nose was *much* bigger than mine.

It's Been a Lot of Fun reached number two on the best-seller list but its sales were hampered by the imposition of the three-day working week and subsequent general election, which meant that there were long delays in replacing stock in the shops. It probably did not help that Brian and Pauline flew out for a holiday in Barbados the week after it was published. Nevertheless it had established Brian as a successful author and he would publish thirteen more books over the next twenty years.

In August 1974 I appeared with Design for a week at the London Palladium. Top of the bill was Josephine Baker, the veteran French chanteuse, and the show also featured the impressionist Roger Kitter and cockney comedian Mike Reid. Brian came to see the first night of the show. He had trodden the boards of the Palladium himself, of course, in the early 1950s, when he dressed up as a donkey in a pantomime with Tommy Trinder. After our performance he told me that it had given him as much pleasure to see me walk out on to the stage at the London Palladium as it would have done if I had been walking down the pavilion steps at Lord's. From him, I felt that was a real compliment.

As usual, he went down to Swanage for a few days in September with Pauline and Joanna. Brian was very good with Joanna and treated her the same as his four other children, but she could be difficult at times. One afternoon they took Joanna, who was then twelve, to see a show in Bournemouth. Once they were seated,

Joanna refused to let Pauline see her copy of the programme. In the end Brian had to take it from her as the lights were going down. Joanna let out a piercing scream, hit Brian hard, and threw her glasses over the edge of the balcony. They landed on a poor couple sitting below and Brian had to hurry down to retrieve them. 'We had to have steel nerves on these occasions,' admits Pauline, 'as it was extremely embarrassing, especially with Brian being a public figure.'

Towards the end of 1974 he took part in a television series on BBC2 called *Reunion*, which was presented by Brian Redhead. The programme reunited old school friends to see how their lives had fared, and Brian was joined by his Old Etonian friends William Douglas Home and Jo Grimond. At the time of the programme, William had had sixteen plays performed in the West End, Jo had retired after being the leader of the Liberal Party for eleven years, and Brian was a household name as a broadcaster. Not bad for three old school chums. Brian Redhead encouraged them to talk non-stop for about forty minutes, which none of them found difficult to do, and at the end of the programme they reached the conclusion that all three of them had been very lucky and that Eton was the best trade union in the world.

On New Year's Day 1975 Brian flew out to Australia to promote his autobiography and to watch Mike Denness and his MCC team in the Ashes series. He stayed with Clare, who had been living in Sydney for two years, working for the New Caledonian Tourist Office, and he appeared on a number of TV and radio chat shows to plug the book.

When he returned to England at the end of January he found himself embroiled in two major controversies. The BBC was going through one of the regular upheavals that seize the Corporation from time to time. Tony Whitby, the Controller of Radio 4, had declared that his network was too old fashioned and had set about changing some of its most popular and long-running programmes. In February Brian was informed by his producer Richard Burwood that *Down Your Way*, which had been on the air since 1946, was going to be scrapped 'for reasons of economy'.

The news caused a tremendous public outcry and resulted in an unprecedented U-turn by the BBC, which I shall deal with in a later chapter.

Another of Whitby's targets was the panel game *Twenty Questions*, which had also been a popular favourite for nearly thirty years. The programme had become indelibly associated with its question-master Peter Jones and its regular panellists Anona Winn, Jack Train and Joy Adamson.

They all got the sack, apart from Anona Winn, who somehow survived the cull. Joy Adamson had been on the panel for twenty-five years and Norman Hackforth had been a panellist or the mystery voice for eighteen years. Brian was invited to join a new team with Terry Wogan as the question-master and a panel which consisted of Brian, an obscure Belgian actress called Bettine le Beau, Anona Winn and the humorist Willie Rushton.

Brian felt awkward about replacing the original panellists in such a manner and suspected that he had only been offered the job to compensate for the loss of *Down Your Way*. Nevertheless, he persuaded himself that as a freelance professional broadcaster he had to accept any opportunity offered, without allowing his personal feelings to interfere. According to Terry Wogan, however, Anona Winn seemed more concerned with ensuring that her stage lighting was correct. As Wogan commented drily: 'That's important, on radio.'

They recorded thirteen programmes during the summer, in front of an invited audience at the Playhouse Theatre near Charing Cross Station in London. The purpose of the game was to discover the name of the object written on the question-master's card, which could be animal, vegetable, mineral or abstract, by asking no more than twenty questions. The previous panel had honed their skills over many years, and inevitably Brian and his colleagues found it hard to be as quick witted at the game as their predecessors. The situation was not helped by the producer, Alastair Scott-Johnston, deliberately giving them a high proportion of abstract objects to guess, which made it harder for them to work out the answer.

After one recording two old ladies were overheard talking as they left the Playhouse Theatre. 'Did you enjoy it, dear?' enquired one of them. 'Yes, I did,' replied the other, 'very much indeed. But you know, I still prefer *Twenty Questions*!'

Brian was assumed by the public to have replaced Jack Train, a much-loved comedy actor who had been a member of the legendary radio comedy series *It's That Man Again*. According to Willie Rushton: 'The rest of us got away with it. Not so poor Johnners. For some months he became the recipient of vicious hate-mail. As vicious as only the British middle classes can get when they don't get their ball back.'

As usual, Brian glossed over the unpleasantness. 'It was all great fun to do,' he would recall later, 'and under Terry's cheerful guidance we were a very happy team.' But it must have unnerved him to have been on the receiving end of such vitriol for probably the first time in his life.

A happier occasion was a special edition of *In Town Tonight*. The Aeolian Hall in Bond Street, from where all the original programmes had been broadcast, was going to be closed down in July 1975. BBC Radio 2 decided to commemorate the event by recreating *In Town Tonight* for one night only. Brian revived his old 'Let's Go Somewhere' spot after a gap of twenty-three years and he broadcast 'live' from a sauna bath in Kensington, where he was heard in the hot room, under the cold shower and being 'slapped' on the massage table. Age had not dimmed his enthusiasm for such stunts and his broadcast was accompanied by a chorus of yelps, giggles and shouts. As he would observe later, at least *he* had enjoyed it.

At the end of the 1975 cricket season Brian and Pauline went on a two-week holiday to Corfu. It was the first time they had been to the island and they travelled with a party organised by Ben and Belinda Brocklehurst of the *Cricketer* magazine. The two couples were good friends; Ben Brocklehurst, a former captain of Somerset, was the owner of the *Cricketer*, and Brian was a director of the magazine for twenty years. One day they were walking along a beach in Corfu when they met a friend of the

Brocklehursts, called Paul. After they had been introduced, Brian said, 'Paul! I've been wanting to meet you for a long time. Tell me, did you ever get a reply to that long letter you wrote to the Corinthians?'

In the centre of Corfu town there was a cricket ground, where cricket had been played for more than 160 years after being introduced to the island by the Royal Navy. The Brocklehursts had arranged a series of cricket matches and Brian was 'persuaded' to play for the *Cricketer* against Gymnasticos, one of the three local Greek teams. He went in at number eleven, where he managed to score a 'stylish' single down to third man before being caught in the gully. But at least he could say that he had played cricket in Corfu.

One afternoon he was enjoying a quiet drink with Henry Blofeld in a local taverna when they were approached by a young Englishman, who asked hesitantly, 'Is that Henry Blofeld sitting there?' He was blind, but he had recognised their voices. The young man told them that he had been mad about cricket as a boy but had lost his sight at the age of eleven. He was now twenty and said that the sound of their voices kept cricket alive for him and he never missed a single word of *Test Match Special*. By the time he had finished Brian was practically in tears. 'It's blubbers time,' he sniffed. He was so moved that he invited the young man to join them at their next cricket match, and for the rest of the holiday he was welcomed as a member of their party.

Brian was well aware of the large number of blind listeners to *Test Match Special* and he felt a tremendous responsibility towards them. In 1976 he became the first president of METRO, the Metropolitan Sports and Social Club for the Visually Handicapped, and continued to support them for the next eighteen years. He used to refer to the club proudly on air as his 'blind boys'. He took his position in earnest: he worked tirelessly behind the scenes to get blind cricket taken seriously and would turn up whenever he could to watch one of their matches at Highgate Wood. His last after-dinner speech on 26 November 1993, less than a week before his heart attack, was at the twentieth-anniversary dinner of the Metro Club at Lord's.

He was also a great supporter of the Primary Club, which supplies sporting and recreational facilities to the visually impaired, and he raised thousands of pounds for the charity by giving it a plug on the Saturday of every Test match. Mike Thomas, the honorary secretary of the Primary Club, says that they used to receive applications for membership from all over the world after one of Brian's broadcasts on *TMS*.

The summer of 1976 was memorable for being the hottest for more than 250 years. Brian was kept busy with a non-stop routine of *Down Your Way*, *Test Match Special* and after-dinner speeches. Towards the end of the year, however, he became involved in a new departure for him, as the part-owner of a racehorse.

The former Warwickshire and England fast bowler David Brown and his wife Tricia had started breeding horses at their farm near Kidderminster. Big Dave, as he was called, asked Brian whether he would like to buy a share in a 'strapping roan colt'. Brian brought in his Old Etonian friend Sir Martin Gilliat, the Queen Mother's racing manager, and there were five other partners, including the Warwickshire cricketers Jack Bannister and Bob Willis.

First they had to name the colt, which was by Grey Mirage out of the Browns' mare Santa Marta. Brian wanted to keep a cricketing connection and jokingly suggested the name W. G. Greys. To his surprise it was accepted by Weatherbys and the horse was sent for training with the Midlands trainer Reg Hollinshead.

W. G. ran in six races during 1977 and improved gradually with each outing. In August Brian accompanied David Brown and Bob Willis to see him race at Chester. As soon as one of the bookmakers saw Brian and Bob Willis approaching he thought the owners must be planning a betting coup and wiped W. G.'s price off the board. 'I'll have you reported to the Jockey Club, my man!' cried Brian, to the amusement of the other punters. He need not have worried. In a portent of things to come, W. G. led all the way to the final bend, but when the horses turned into the home straight he was nowhere to be seen.

A month later I travelled with Brian and Pauline to watch W. G.

run at Newbury. We were assured confidently by Big Dave before the race that the horse was in with a great chance. Any lingering doubts were dismissed when Brian declared that we would have no trouble in the event of a photo finish because he had been at Eton with two of the stewards and in the Guards with the other two. It would have made little difference. We all lost a packet after W. G. led for most of the race but once again faded at the end to finish seventh.

At York he finished third and then, during the last week of the flat racing season in November, W. G. Greys won his first race, over six furlongs at Teesside Park. Brian was working that day and sadly he had to miss his moment of triumph.

The following year it looked as though W. G. might be on to a winning streak when he won his first race of the season in April. We descended on Newmarket a fortnight later in high spirits and bet heavily on W. G. to win, but, to quote David Brown, 'he ran an absolute stinker' and finished well down the field. He never won another race. Brian was not one to be downhearted. 'I was a bit disappointed,' he told Brown at Newmarket, 'until I bumped into a friend of mine who had just had his first winner after owning horses for thirty years, so I suppose we are lucky.' Not quite lucky enough, however. A year later Grey Mirage sired another foal that went on to win a race or two. He was called Desert Orchid.

Along with most of the cricketing world, Brian was shocked when the Australian television magnate Kerry Packer announced in May 1977 that he was launching World Series Cricket, a rival to the established game, and that he had signed up about fifty of the world's leading players. Brian was terribly distressed by the affair. What upset him most was not that the players wanted more money but that it had all been carried out in such secrecy. He felt it was deceitful, disloyal and a betrayal of all that cricket stood for. 'It put a severe strain on old friendships,' he wrote, 'and introduced argument, resentment and rancour into the dressing-rooms.' He was particularly outraged that the captain of England, Tony Greig, should have played a leading part in the signings.

'I think I was more realistic about it than he was,' remarks

Trevor Bailey. 'Brian was very pro-MCC. He felt that the players had betrayed their country for cash.'

Another of the prime movers behind World Series Cricket was Richie Benaud, who was to be the leading commentator for WSC on Kerry Packer's Channel 9 television network in Australia. Brian felt so strongly about the Packer affair that he made a pact with his friend Richie not to talk about it. 'When I saw Brian in 1977 at the MCC v. Australia match at Lord's,' says Benaud, 'he told me he was very much against World Series Cricket. That was his firm opinion, but he hoped our friendship would not be altered in any way. Nor was it over the following seventeen years.'

Brian had commentated on almost all the major royal occasions since the war but he made broadcasting history in 1977 by becoming the first commentator to actually take part in a royal procession. It was the year of the Queen's Silver Jubilee, and 7 June had been declared Jubilee Day and a national holiday. The official celebrations started with a service of thanksgiving at St Paul's Cathedral. After the service the Queen and the Duke of Edinburgh conducted a walkabout through the thousands of cheering people who lined the streets from St Paul's to Guildhall, where she was due to take lunch with the Lord Mayor, Sir Robin Gillett. For the first time the BBC had been granted permission to join the royal procession, and for half an hour Brian walked a few yards behind the Queen, describing the scene to radio listeners as she stopped to talk to the crowds. After the Queen had moved on he asked a few of them what she had said and was amused to discover that it was either 'Where do you come from?' or 'How long have you been waiting?' Brian was wearing headphones and was accompanied by a producer and an engineer with a mobile transmitter. The Duke of Edinburgh joked that Brian looked like a man from outer space.

When they entered King Street the noise from the crowds was considerably louder. Brian forgot royal protocol completely and approached the Duke of Edinburgh to ask whether he would like to say something to the listeners at home. The cheers were so deafening that the Duke could only shout: 'I can't hear myself think!'

Two weeks later Brian was going to be sixty-five and Pauline arranged a special surprise party. On the night before his birthday Clare and I told him to dress up in a dinner jacket because we were going to take him out to dinner. Then he was blindfolded, put in a car and driven across London to an unknown destination. After we had arrived, we led him, still blindfolded, past some surprised onlookers into the mystery building, and it was only when he recognised the tinkling piano of Ian Stewart that he guessed he was at the Savoy Hotel. The blindfold was finally removed to reveal Pauline and the family and about twenty of his closest friends gathered at two large tables in the restaurant. The Savoy Hotel chef had even prepared a special birthday cake with a cricket match sculpted in icing on the top. He was now officially an old age pensioner.

23

Test Match Special

There is no doubt that Brian revitalised *Test Match Special* (hereafter *TMS*) after he became a permanent member of the commentary team in 1970. His extrovert personality may have attracted the listeners, but not everyone enjoyed his schoolboyish sense of humour. Jim Swanton, his former television colleague, was now the regular close-of-play summariser on radio. One day Swanton sat down at the microphone to deliver his summary, which was always off the cuff and with the help of only a few notes. As soon as he started talking Brian grabbed hold of Jim's braces and pulled them back. Swanton had to deliver his whole five-minute summary without knowing when – or if – the braces would snap back. Fortunately Brian did not let go and somehow Swanton managed to keep his concentration. Afterwards his only comment was, 'Oh, Johnston – always fourth form!'

Brian could be serious, however, when the occasion required. During his first year as a freelance commentator in 1973 the West Indies completely outplayed England and won the series 2–0. But the most memorable incident of the summer happened during the third Test at Lord's. About an hour and a quarter after lunch on the Saturday, play was interrupted by the voice of the MCC Secretary, Billy Griffith, announcing over the public address system that a bomb warning had been received from the IRA. Earlier that morning a bomb had exploded in Baker Street so the police were taking the threat seriously and everyone was asked to leave the ground in an orderly fashion. Most of the 26,000 spectators filed calmly out into the streets of St John's Wood. About 5,000, however, chose to join the players and umpires and gathered round the square in the middle of the playing area. Umpire Dickie Bird sat on the covers over the pitch, with his head in his hands, telling himself that at least there was no bomb under *there*.

The pavilion was considered to be one of the most likely targets, so it was evacuated as quickly as possible while the police hunted for the bomb. Brian had been doing the commentary at the time of the announcement, but he simply ignored the order to leave and stayed on the air with Christopher Martin-Jenkins for the next forty-five minutes, describing the events to the listeners at home. At one point the police even carried out a search of the commentary box while they continued talking. 'When the police say everybody out, they mean everybody out,' says Peter Baxter, who began thirty years as the producer of *TMS* in 1973, 'but it would not have occurred to Brian to leave, so we carried on broadcasting.' It must have taken some courage, knowing that in the event of an explosion there would be no escape. Brian typically downplayed the danger, remarking, 'We somehow felt that if a bomb *did* go off we wouldn't have so far to go!'

Fortunately it turned out to be a false alarm and play was resumed after a loss of eighty-eight minutes. A relieved Pauline remarked that Brian should have been awarded a medal for his bravery. Brian simply joked that it was the only time in his career that 'bomb stopped play'!

John Arlott had been part of the radio commentary team at every Test match in England since 1948. For many listeners his gruff Hampshire accent and his poetic turn of phrase represented the true voice of cricket. At first Arlott did not approve of Brian's different approach to the art of commentary. He thought Brian was too much of a good thing and sometimes went over the top. To a certain extent Robert Hudson agreed, but he did not want to ruin the new sense of excitement Brian brought to the programme by asking him to tone it down. Christopher Martin-Jenkins, who succeeded Brian as BBC cricket correspondent in 1973, thinks that Arlott eventually came to recognise that Brian had made the programme more popular and that they were all reaping the reward.

In many ways they needed each other. Arlott's gravitas and imaginative turn of phrase helped to balance Brian's more light-hearted approach, while Brian's jocular style helped to put Arlott's more considered contribution into sharper relief. Peter Baxter agrees. 'Our audience went up when Johnners joined *TMS*,' says Baxter. 'He brought new listeners, attracted by his popular style, who then discovered what a good broadcaster Arlott was.'

Critics of Brian's style of commentary wished that he would stick to describing the cricket, but John Arlott dismissed the idea: 'Some listeners write to say that they only want to hear about the ball being bowled and what happens to it,' explained Arlott. 'We tried that once: the result was 75 per cent silence. There must be other material. Atmosphere varies from ground to ground. To describe it is surely part of the essence of cricket watching.' Surprisingly that was written in 1961, almost ten years before Brian became a full-time member of the radio commentary team.

As far as Brian was concerned, Arlott was in charge of the commentary box; he did not view him as a rival because their styles were so different. 'John Arlott was without doubt the best painter of word pictures we've ever had,' says Trevor Bailey, who first broadcast with Arlott as a summariser on *TMS* in 1967. On the other hand Brian was the better cricketer. 'Arlott knew a lot about the history of cricket,' adds Bailey, 'but he was not a very good player, although he gave the impression that he was. Brian was closer to the game itself.'

The two commentators respected each other professionally but that was as far as it went. 'It's not that Brian didn't like Arlott,' explains Peter Baxter, 'but he would never have chosen him as a friend.' David Rayvern Allen interviewed Brian for his excellent book *Arlott – The Authorised Biography* and Brian told him: 'We were not close friends really. He had a lot of different ideas to me. I used to give him lifts sometimes to a Test match and run him back. We had shouting arguments about South Africa – he felt very deeply about that, and I felt the other way.'

Arlott was quite capable of poking fun at Brian when he felt like it. 'Send as many cakes as you like,' he told the listeners once, and the next day Brian was snowed under with contributions. 'He was a little upset on Friday,' remarked Arlott during another Test match, 'because he didn't get anything, which means that a lot of you are actually eating your own food.' These remarks were said in jest but one suspects that there was an element of genuine frustration behind them. Sometimes it seemed as though more attention was being paid to the cakes than to the cricket.

Brian's name had become almost synonymous with chocolate cakes. It all started quite innocently in the mid-1970s when a lady sent him a chocolate cake for his birthday on 24 June, which was during the Lord's Test match. Being the gentleman that he was, he thanked her politely on the air. To his surprise, someone sent him another cake at the next Test, and then another, until by the 1990s he was receiving three or four cakes a day. Small boys would wait outside the pavilion, holding the latest offering, and say proudly, 'My mum's baked this cake for you, Mr Johnston.'

This led to one of Brian's most famous pranks. In 1977 the veteran Australian commentator Alan McGilvray was a member of the *TMS* commentary team for the Ashes series. During the first Test at Lord's Brian was on the air when he noticed McGilvray come into the commentary box. While he was talking, Brian pointed to a particularly sticky chocolate cake in front of him and invited Alan to take a slice. He waited until McGilvray had a mouth full of cake. 'That ball just goes off the edge of the bat and drops in front of first slip,' said Brian. 'Let's ask Alan McGilvray if he thought it was a catch.' There was a splutter from McGilvray and a spray of crumbs all over the box as he tried to swallow the cake and answer the question. Finally he managed to blurt out a few incoherent words but by then everyone was laughing. McGilvray never really forgave Brian, and after that he would never accept even a biscuit or a sweet in the box.

The cakes became increasingly elaborate, and they were not always chocolate. One year Brian was presented with a coloured icing replica of a famous painting in the Lord's Museum, which shows W. G. Grace batting and King Edward VII and Queen

Alexandra watching in the crowd. It was much too good to eat so Brian took it home and put it in the freezer. When visitors came to the house, instead of inviting them to admire his paintings, he would take them into the kitchen and open up the freezer.

Brian may have encouraged the consumption of food in the box but it was Arlott who introduced alcohol, and he got through a considerable amount of it. Henry Blofeld recalls his first *TMS* at Lord's in 1974 during which Arlott asked him to carry two heavy leather briefcases up to the commentary box. When they reached the top Arlott opened them to reveal seven bottles of claret. 'Well,' he growled proudly to anyone within earshot, 'with any luck, that little lot should see us through to the lunch interval.' Brian did not approve. He was meticulous about not drinking while he was working and thought it was unprofessional. In the end, however, he relented, and he used to enjoy having a glass of dry white wine in the box at midday.

Arlott prided himself on remembering everyone's favourite tipple. He could never understand Brian's preference for white wine but that did not prevent him from being the perfect host. 'John was a most hospitable man,' Brian told David Rayvern Allen. 'If you went to his house – which I didn't do often – always waiting for me was a bottle of Pouilly Fumé – most generous with his entertainment.' In reality, Brian was shocked by the number of bottles of red wine Arlott consumed in an evening. Brian knew when he had had enough. He enjoyed a glass or two of white wine or champagne, and he would always open a bottle at lunch or dinner, but I never saw him drunk in his entire life.

Arlott retired in mid-afternoon on 2 September 1980 during the Centenary match at Lord's. His final words of Test commentary have passed into folklore: '. . . and after Trevor Bailey it will be Christopher Martin-Jenkins.' The whole of Lord's rose to give him a standing ovation, including the entire Australian team and even Geoffrey Boycott, who removed his batting gloves and applauded. It should have been a moment of reflection, of quiet satisfaction, perhaps sadness at the end of an era. But Arlott had something else on his mind. As he left the commentary box he walked over to Don Mosey, who was sitting in the corner, and chuckled into his ear, 'That's stuffed Johnston. He won't be able to retire for at least three years now.' It seems sad, if it is true, that a moment of triumph and acclaim should have ended on such a bitter note. Peter Baxter, however, thinks it may have been intended as a jocular remark and was not meant to be as malicious as it sounds.

There were several new additions to the *TMS* team during the 1970s. Christopher Martin-Jenkins made his first Test match commentary in 1973 and he was followed a year later by Henry Blofeld and Don Mosey. Martin-Jenkins, known to all as CMJ, was only twenty-eight years old when he joined *TMS*. Eleven years earlier, when he was captain of the first eleven at Marlborough, he had written to Brian asking how to become a cricket commentator. To his surprise, Brian had invited him to lunch at the BBC Club, where he had offered some friendly and practical advice. 'He couldn't have been nicer or more fun,' recalls CMJ. The advice must have paid off because, after leaving Cambridge, he joined the BBC's sports news department and, after Brian 'retired' in 1972, he was appointed his successor as the BBC cricket correspondent.

He seems to have escaped being the target of Brian's notorious practical jokes, perhaps in deference to his position. He fell victim to the Johnners sense of humour, however, during a Prudential World Cup match between Canada and England at Old Trafford in 1979. Canada had been dismissed by England for a paltry 45 runs and Brian had been struggling all morning to identify the members of the Canadian team, when CMJ pointed out to Brian that Canada's twelfth man, Showkat Baksh, had just come on to the field. It was a name too far. Brian dissolved into a fit of the giggles, closely followed by CMJ himself. 'We must have been off the air for about a minute,' remembers CMJ, rather embarrassed, 'but fortunately it was such an obscure match that no one heard it.'

Henry Blofeld made his *TMS* debut in 1974 during the first Test against India at Old Trafford. Blowers had been captain of the eleven at Eton and had won a cricket Blue at Cambridge before becoming a writer and broadcaster. His first Test match was almost his last. On the third day Brian was commentating while India were batting and Tony Greig was bowling to Sunil Gavaskar. As Greig walked back to his mark Brian observed: 'Greig . . . as he walks back, polishes the ball on his right thigh.' Gavaskar played the ball to Hendrick at mid-on who threw it back to the bowler. 'And now,' announced Brian, 'to ring the changes, as he walks back Greig polishes his left ball.' There were snorts and suppressed giggles from the back of the box. Fortunately it was Blofeld's turn to take over. 'Over to Henry Blofeld,' spluttered Brian, and poor Blowers had to take over the microphone, trying desperately not to lose his composure, and with it his new job.

Like everyone else, Blowers became used to such pranks over the years. One day he was in full flow at Old Trafford when Brian, sitting behind him in the commentary box, leaned forward with a mischievous grin on his face and pressed the lever on his chair. To his credit, Blowers never missed a beat as his chair suddenly sank underneath him, leaving him about four inches lower, while Brian chuckled happily like a naughty schoolboy.

In contrast to the public school backgrounds of CMJ, Johnners and Blowers, Don Mosey was an ex-grammar school boy, a plain-speaking Yorkshireman in his late forties from Keighley. He had been a producer with BBC North Region and had once helped Brian with a broadcast of the Radio 2 quiz game *Treble Chance* from Lancaster Town Hall. Mosey had seemed so at home amid the dignified trappings of the Mayor's Parlour that Brian had called him 'The Alderman', a nickname which suited him so well that it stuck for the rest of his life.

Brian once described Mosey as 'blunt, honest, obstinate and says exactly what he thinks'. In turn, Mosey did not hide his intense dislike of former public school boys from 'the effete South who seem to achieve success through influence and string-pulling rather than honest toil'. Yet they appeared to enjoy a warm friendship. Mosey found it hard to explain. The main link was a love of laughter. Brian called Mosey 'the worst giggler' in the box and they both had an acute sense of the ridiculous that could swiftly reduce them to helpless giggles. They also shared a love of words and used to while away the hours in the commentary box playing endless rounds of a pencil-and-paper word game that Brian had learned in the office of his family coffee business before the war. Out of season they kept in touch through phone calls, letters and saucy seaside postcards. In the end, Mosey gave up trying to analyse their friendship. 'Obviously we found something in common,' he concluded in his autobiography, *The Alderman's Tale*, 'what need was there for an explanation of it?'

Peter Baxter remembers the day a listener sent in a copy of the Israeli Cricket Association's handbook. Brian was sitting at the back of the commentary box, flipping idly through the book, when he came to the record section. His eye fell on the pair who had made the highest tenth-wicket stand for Israel, Solly Katz and Benny Wadwaker. He tried desperately not to make a noise, but soon stifled laughter exploded from the back of the box. Don Mosey was on air at the time and, without having any idea what was funny, found himself overcome by Brian's infectious high-pitched giggle and was completely unable to carry on.

Another regular on *TMS* throughout the 1970s was Trevor Bailey, the former Essex and England all-rounder, who had been a summariser since 1967. He was a useful man to have in the commentary box because, unlike almost everyone else, it seems, he was able to keep a straight face. At the close of play during one Test match there was an intense discussion in the box about whether a particular captain should make the other side bat again the following day and how he would have the evening to think about it. Brian turned to Bailey and asked innocently, 'Have you ever slept on it overnight, Trevor?' There was a collective gasp from the rest of the commentary box followed by silence on the air as Brian struggled to control his laughter.

Trevor Bailey had to step into the breach. For three minutes he talked about the weather, the pitch, the bowlers and anything else he could think of, until the others in the box had recovered their composure and were able to continue.

Bailey's great colleague as a summariser during the late 1970s and 1980s was Fred Trueman, the former Yorkshire and England fast bowler, who joined the team in 1975. Like Don Mosey, Trueman believed in speaking his mind, especially when it concerned fast bowlers, although sometimes he would get a bit carried away with his criticisms of the modern players. 'I don't know what's going off out there,' he would complain frequently.

Brian encouraged Trueman to be outspoken. 'He said I must never change my style,' says Trueman. 'If I felt something was wrong out there I should say so.' When he became too critical, however, it often took Brian to remind Trueman that the past was not all a bed of roses. 'Of course,' Brian would point out innocently, 'you never ever showed *your* feelings at such moments, did you, Fred?'

The two of them could not have come from more different backgrounds but they forged a good partnership in the commentary box. 'He was very easy to get on with,' says Trueman. 'We both loved stories and, most of all, we loved the game of cricket. I was delighted to work with him.' Even though Brian had never played the first-class game he had seen most of the great Test players before the war. 'He could go back to the 1920s,' continues Trueman. 'He had watched Bradman and Hammond at Lord's, he'd seen legendary players like Wilfred Rhodes and Jack Hobbs. He could talk about all these great players. When you were on the air with Brian it was wonderful because, between you all, you could cover almost a century of cricket.'

Even the great Fred Trueman was not immune from Brian's schoolboy humour. One day he was broadcasting during a Test match at Lord's when he became aware of Brian hovering on his right-hand side. 'If Brian was hovering,' says Trueman, 'I'd been with him long enough to know there was something afoot.' While Trueman was talking, Brian reached over and knocked a chocolate cake off a shelf beside him. 'I caught it in both hands and carried on broadcasting,' relates Trueman. 'He was amazed. His face was a picture!'

The final member of the *TMS* team was, and has been for more than thirty-five years, the statistician Bill Frindall, who joined the programme in 1966 after the death of the former scorer Arthur Wrigley. Frindall's vast knowledge of cricket and his ability to lay his hands instantly on the most obscure cricketing records and statistics soon made him indispensable, while his bushy black beard led to Brian granting him the immortal nickname 'The Bearded Wonder'.

Brian used to delight in trying to catch Frindall out. One favourite trick was to ask him to look up some important cricket record and wait until Frindall was deep in one of his countless books. Then Brian would enquire suddenly, 'How many balls are there left in the over, Bearders?' and chuckle happily as Frindall struggled to answer. After a while Frindall got wise to this ruse and would reply, '*Approximately* two or three,' or whatever the number.

During a Test match Frindall often used to pass notes to Brian and the other commentators with information such as: 'If so-and-so scores another run it will be his highest score in Test cricket.' When Brian was on air he would often glance at such a note and then say casually, 'I'm not sure, my memory is not too good, but I think that if so-and-so scores another run it will be his highest score in Test cricket. Let's ask Bill Frindall if he can check it up in one of his books!' This would produce the required snort from Frindall and a satisfied grin from his tormentor.

Frindall was a keen club cricketer and played with Brian in many charity matches. He once described Brian as 'quite the most bent umpire' he had ever seen, claiming that he would often turn down perfectly good lbw appeals on the grounds that the ball was 'too low' and once called 'no ball' after persuading square leg to field behind him in an illegal position. The final straw, however, came during a match at Fenner's in 1984, when Brian called 'Tea' – and the end of the innings – while Frindall was on 49 and the pavilion clock showed there were still two minutes of play left.

Not everyone approved of the jolly japes in the commentary box. In September 1982 an Edinburgh schoolmaster named E. J. Brack penned a full-page article in *Wisden Cricket Monthly* in which he strongly criticised the direction that the programme had taken since the retirement of John Arlott. He reserved his particular displeasure for Brian:

> Of the present team, some are worse than others, but none annoys me more than Brian Johnston. Apart from his obsessions with juvenile attempts at humour, calling people ridiculous names likes 'Bloers', 'Arl' and 'Alderman' and eating other people's confectionery during commentary, he very rarely keeps to the cricket. Interminable discourses on Fred Trueman's dog, charity matches and the rules of the Primary Club are occasionally interrupted to tell us that Ian Botham reached his century five minutes ago or to inform us in passing that Kim Hughes is out.

In the following month's issue the magazine printed three pages of letters from the 'towering stack' it had received in response to the article. They seemed to be fairly evenly divided, both for and against *TMS*, although Brian was singled out for more criticism: 'The whole programme is being corrupted by one man: Brian Johnston,' fumed a correspondent from Durham. 'It is *his* jokes, *his* sweets, *his* concern for trivial side-issues which destroy the flow of others' commentary and opinion.'

There was a suspicion that David Frith, the editor of *Wisden Cricket Monthly*, had his own agenda. Frith was a close friend of John Arlott's and also thought that Brian made too many references on air to the rival publication the *Cricketer*, of which he was a director. A month later there were still more letters on the subject: '*TMS* is supposed to be a sports programme,' grumbled a reader from Avon, 'not a comedy show.'

Finally in December Don Mosey wrote his own reply to the article, in which he agreed with some of Mr Brack's opinions about *TMS* but strongly defended Brian's position. 'A very large percentage of listeners are housewives enjoying a friendly voice or two about the house while they go about their daily routine,' wrote Mosey. 'Brian gets more listeners' letters than the rest of the *TMS* team put together and they are universally friendly and interested. That has got to mean that Mr Brack's personal distaste is not widely shared.'

In the end, that seemed to be the general consensus and, mercifully, there the correspondence ended. It had made Brian and the rest of the *TMS* team uneasily aware that their style of cricket commentary did not appeal to everyone. But, as Brian invariably pointed out, it is impossible to please all of the people all of the time.

One innovation on *TMS* that did meet with general approval in the 1980s was the introduction of a personality interview conducted by Brian during the Saturday of each Test match. This popular feature was called 'A View from the Boundary', and the tradition started during the first Test against the West Indies at Trent Bridge in 1980, when the farmer and broadcaster Ted Moult was the first guest. These conversations – Brian always insisted they were not interviews – were always with well-known people who shared a love of cricket. They would be invited to spend the Saturday of a Test match in the commentary box with the *TMS* team and when they arrived they would be given a glass or two of champagne to relax them and a bit of food – often an airline-style tray lunch. Then, during the luncheon interval, they would sit and chat to Brian for twenty minutes about themselves and about cricket. It was live, unrehearsed and always entertaining. The list of guests was remarkably diverse, ranging from John Cleese to the Duke of Edinburgh, and included actors, playwrights, singers, politicians, footballers and even a former hostage. Brian's informal, relaxed manner put his guests at ease and seemed to bring out the best in everyone. It was one of the elements of *TMS* that Brian enjoyed the most and proved his theory that the game of cricket crossed all barriers of class, occupation and background.

Over the years Brian became equally well known for his many gaffes in the commentary box. One early classic happened during a match at Hove between Sussex and Hampshire. Henry Horton of Hampshire was batting and he had a most unusual stance at the wicket, crouched very low with his bottom sticking out. Brian tried to describe it to the radio listeners. 'It's going to be Snow to the crouching Henry Horton,' commented Brian, 'who looks as if he is shitting – er – sitting on a shooting stick – er – if you see what I mean!'

On another occasion, when Ray Illingworth was captain of Leicestershire, Brian startled radio listeners when he announced, 'Welcome to Leicester, where Ray Illingworth has just relieved himself at the Pavilion End.'

Another memorable gaffe occurred during the First Test against India at Old Trafford in 1974. It was pouring with rain on the Saturday morning and a group of spectators were sitting huddled together under umbrellas in one of the stands. At 11.30 a.m. the Radio 3 announcer handed over to Brian with the query, 'Any chance of any play this morning, Brian?' 'No,' replied Brian, 'it's raining here and there certainly won't be any play for some time yet.' He peered out of the window and meant to add that he could see a dirty black cloud. Instead he declared: 'There's a dirty black crowd over there!'

When I was compiling the *Johnners at the Beeb* cassette for the BBC I spent hours digging through the radio and television archives and I found recordings of most of his famous slip-ups. There was one noticeable exception. In 1976 England played the West Indies at the Oval. At one point England's Peter Willey was facing the fearsome West Indian fast bowler Michael Holding. What happened next has gone down in cricketing history: 'We welcome World Service listeners to the Oval,' said Brian cheerfully, 'where the bowler's Holding, the batsman's Willey.' Or did he? I think Brian made it up. It was too good a pun to resist but I do not believe that even he could have said it without laughing. The BBC engineers would also have kept a recording of such an outrageous gaffe. More revealingly, Brian never actually said that he had spoken the words on air. He was an honest man and he would not have wanted to tell an outright lie.

Brian used to explain that he had received a letter after the match from a Miss Mainpiece, a name that arouses immediate suspicion. 'We do enjoy your commentaries,' she had complained, 'but you must be more careful, as we have a lot of young people listening. Do you realise what you said the other day?' In later years he would add apologetically, 'I'm still not sure whether I said it or not!' It was the story that his audiences enjoyed the most and it made people laugh. If they wanted to believe it, fair enough.

24

Down Your Way

Nowadays people tend to associate Brian mainly with cricket, but for more than a million radio listeners every week in the 1970s and 1980s he was the friendly voice of *Down Your Way* (*DYW*).

The programme had started in December 1946 and in twenty-five years it had only three main presenters, Stewart MacPherson, Richard Dimbleby and Franklin Engelmann. The format remained essentially the same. Each week the programme would visit a different town or village in the British Isles and talk to six of the local inhabitants about themselves and their area. At the end of the interview, usually about four and a half minutes, they would be asked to choose a piece of music.

The programme had a timeless appeal. In many ways it sounded as if it was stuck somewhere in the 1950s, in a more innocent age when neighbours helped each other out and life revolved around the church and the village post office. 'Whenever we go to a place,' said Brian, 'we try to find out the nice things about it. We don't look under the carpet for scandal or anything controversial.'

The programme went out on Sundays at 5.05 p.m. every week of the year. The routine was always the same. The producer would contact the town clerk at the town or village they wanted to visit and obtain as much information as possible about the history, the industry and any traditional local ceremonies and events. On the Wednesday of the recording the producer would spend the day on location and choose six local characters to be interviewed. They might be the vicar or the village postmistress, the organiser of the annual pancake race, a worker at a local farm or factory, or someone with an unusual job or hobby. If they had the local dialect or accent, so much the better. One criticism of the programme was that the interviewees tended to be elderly, but as Brian explained, they generally knew more about a place and its history and also had usually done more with their lives.

Brian would arrive on Wednesday evening and, if there was time, he would record the first interview that evening. The following day, Thursday, they would record the other five interviews. They allowed an hour for each one and would record them at their home, office, factory, farm or shop. Brian would chat to them for about twenty minutes to put them at ease and then he would announce, 'I'm feeling broody now, what about us recording our conversation?' Once again, it was always a conversation and not an interview. He wanted to be their friend and not their interrogator.

Sometimes they would record two programmes in one week, stockpiling a few reserves so that Brian could take time off for a holiday. It was a small and efficient team, consisting of Brian, the producer and a sound engineer with his portable tape recorder. One day they arrived at a small house in Kirkby Lonsdale to conduct their next interview and a lady opened the front door. 'Oh, hello, Mr Johnston,' she said, 'how nice to see you. Tell me, how big is your equipment?' Brian could not help laughing as he replied, 'Oh, it's quite small. Our engineer is carrying it in his hands.'

It was the perfect programme for Brian. He enjoyed discovering parts of Great Britain that he would otherwise never have visited and, above all, he loved meeting the people. 'We're always told what a wicked and selfish world we live in,' he would say, 'but if you came round with me on *Down Your Way* you'd be amazed at how many good people there are whose main object in life is to help others.' He felt it was part of his mission to shine a spotlight on the 'silent and unsung majority of people' who spent much of their time caring for others, through the Round Table, Help the Aged, the Women's Institute, Meals on Wheels and dozens of other similar organisations.

In February 1975 Richard Burwood broke the news to Brian that *DYW* was going to be dropped 'for economic reasons'. The

BBC were having to make cuts in order to save money and the Controller of Radio 4, Tony Whitby, had decided that he wanted to replace *DYW*, in its prime slot on Sunday afternoons, with a favourite programme of his called *Celebration*. Brian was disappointed because the weekly programme had become a part of his life. It had also become a part of thousands of other people's lives. When the news was announced officially a few days later there was a storm of protest.

There were articles in all the major national and provincial newspapers and the BBC was inundated with hundreds of letters and phone calls protesting against the decision. The Director-General, Sir Charles Curran, even came under fire during a radio phone-in when he turned down a suggestion that *DYW* should continue on BBC local radio.

The only official reason given for taking off the programme was one of economy. *The Times* reported: 'It is believed that the rising cost of travel and accommodation has been a big consideration.' The average cost of making the programme, however, was only about £130 a week, which produced eighty minutes of radio (including the repeat every Tuesday), so this was blatantly untrue. Nevertheless Brian offered to take a cut in his fee if it would help to save the programme. His offer was turned down and his bosses had to admit privately that the cost was not a problem.

The comedian Norman Vaughan wrote to the *Daily Mail*, 'I don't mind things being changed so long as they remain as good or better than they were before. But *Down Your Way* was as gentle and as honest as Sunday cricket on the village green.' Another show business veteran, the entertainer Dickie Henderson, agreed: 'I'm all for change, but why change something which is successful. I found *Down Your Way* not only interesting but educational.'

At the height of the controversy Tony Whitby suddenly died at the age of forty-five and Clare Lawson-Dick was appointed the new Controller of Radio 4. The programme was due to end on 20 April but the new Controller quickly announced that it would return for six episodes during the summer. More was to come.

A few weeks later Radio 4 confirmed that the programme would come back in October on the same regular basis as before. The only difference was that it would now be produced by Anthony Smith, the BBC's radio outside broadcast producer in Bristol.

It was announced to the press on Brian's birthday – 24 June – and in a statement Clare Lawson-Dick said: 'Fans of the programme wrote to us in large numbers asking for it to be restored. We were also greatly touched and influenced by letters from blind and disabled people who were unable to travel and said that *Down Your Way* had been their only means of getting to know Britain.'

The BBC press office told Brian that it was the first time the BBC had publicly admitted to bowing to public pressure on behalf of a programme.

DYW returned in triumph in October 1975 with a cover story in the *Radio Times* and a broadcast from the village of Lacock in Wiltshire. Over the next twelve years, Tony Smith travelled thousands of miles with Brian to every corner of the British Isles. 'I can honestly say that we never had a cross word in all that time,' says Smith. 'The remarkable thing about Brian was that he was always the same person, from me leaving him one week in Glasgow to meeting up with him the next week in Penzance, or wherever. He never changed. He was also so easy to work with. He didn't mind what he did, whether it was going down a coal mine or up in a hot-air balloon. He was game for anything.'

According to Smith, Brian had a favourite trick when they were touring a factory. As they were walking around, Brian would note the nameplate on a particular piece of machinery. After they had moved on a few paces he would turn to his guide and say, 'If I'm not mistaken, isn't that machine back there a such and such? Wasn't it made in Darlington?' The guide would be instantly impressed by Brian's apparent knowledge and, once the microphone was switched on, he would pour out information about his work, eager to share his enthusiasm with such an interested visitor.

It was a long day. One of the problems was that everywhere they went Brian would be offered a cup of tea or coffee and biscuits. Knowing his reputation, many people had often baked him a special cake. It was difficult to refuse without causing offence or embarrassment. The only time it really caused a problem was when they visited Scotland and Brian was invariably offered 'a wee dram'. He hated whisky but was too polite to say no. Fortunately Tony Smith liked it so Brian would pretend to sip from his glass and then switch it with his producer's when no one was looking.

Brian made it sound easy. Tony Smith believes that his secret was that he was always genuinely interested. 'His friendliness could have seemed false,' says Smith, 'but I did hundreds and hundreds of interviews with him and he never treated anyone differently. There was a simplicity about him that allowed him to interact with all sorts of people, and without any doubt he was just as at home in a cottage as in a castle.'

After completing a *DYW* programme, Brian would often say to himself: Well, that's another six friends I've made. He particularly enjoyed meeting the local eccentric characters. One of his favourites was Mrs Emily Brewster from Radcliffe-on-Trent, who had recently celebrated her hundredth birthday. She had been disappointed with her telegram from the Queen. 'Why's that?' asked Brian. 'It wasn't in her own handwriting,' came the reply.

In Biggleswade Brian met Tony Tuthill, the World Ferret-Legging Champion, who conducted his entire interview with a ferret in his trousers. Tuthill had claimed the world record by keeping seven ferrets stuffed down his trousers for a total of six and a half hours. What had he done with himself all that time? 'Oh, I played darts, dominoes, anything you like,' answered Tuthill casually.

Another memorable character was Frank Searle, who ran the Loch Ness Investigations and Information Centre from a caravan on the bank of the loch and had devoted ten years to trying to spot the legendary Loch Ness Monster. He told Brian that he had spent 32,000 hours out on the loch in an open boat and had made thirty-one definite sightings, although the nearest he had ever managed to get to one of the creatures was about three hundred metres. The man was obviously sincere and Brian managed to sound as if he believed every word.

Then there was the vegetarian from Usk in Wales who, during the Second World War in India, had grown mustard and cress in the bottom of his wellington boots every night and eaten it for breakfast; the local rat-catcher in Stockport, Lancashire, who kept about one hundred rats as pets in cages in his garden; and a man from Tenterden in Kent who collected old prams and had more than three hundred of them stored in every room of his house.

In January 1979 Brian persuaded the BBC to allow him to record six editions of *DYW* while he was on holiday in Australia. It was a good excuse to visit his son Andrew, who had been living in Sydney for four years, where he worked as a publishing sales executive for the Hutchinson Publishing Group. Andrew offered to drive Tony Smith and Brian to their various destinations and fitted an armchair in the back of his combi-van, so that Brian could travel around in style.

They recorded programmes in Melbourne, Sydney, Canberra, Adelaide, Wagga Wagga and Alice Springs, where Keith Thomas, the Chief Ranger of the Old Telegraph Station, told Brian about their annual Henley Regatta on the River Todd. According to Smith, Brian could not stop himself from giggling after he heard that the regatta was staged at the height of the summer when the river bed was bone dry. It was the same as any normal regatta, he was told seriously, except that they cut the bottoms out of their boats and ran with them.

My favourite story about *DYW* relates to a visit the programme paid to Brinsworth House, the retirement home for elderly actors and variety artists in Twickenham. Brian was making his way there through Richmond at about 10 a.m. when he saw a policeman directing traffic at a crossroads. 'Excuse me,' said Brian, winding down his window, 'can you tell me the way to Brinsworth House?'

'Certainly, sir,' replied the policeman. 'Go up there, first right, second left, take the right fork, go across the traffic lights and it's up there about two hundred yards on your right.'

'Thank you very much,' said Brian, and went on his way.

He found the house without any problem and recorded the programme throughout the day. He was driving back through Richmond at about 4 p.m. when he saw the same policeman still there at the crossroads. Brian could not resist it. He wound his window down once again. 'Sorry, Officer,' he called out, 'did you say first left or second left?'

Brian loved doing the programme, but eventually the relentless weekly schedule began to take its toll. For almost every week for fifteen years he had been required to leave home at midday every Wednesday and travel to a different location in Britain, returning on Thursday evening, or Friday evening if they were recording for a second day. It had played havoc with his social life. 'People have given up asking us to dinner or the theatre,' he complained. He had also lost out on countless offers of more lucrative engagements because of his radio commitments. Besides, he was nearly seventy-five years old and Pauline had been urging him to slow down for years.

At the end of 1986 he decided it was time to call it a day. He discovered that he had recorded 712 programmes compared with Richard Dimbleby's 300 and Franklin Engelmann's 733. It was then that he came up with the idea of copying the champion steeplechase jockey John Francome. In 1982 Peter Scudamore had been leading the jockeys' table when he fell and broke a collar-bone and was told that he could not ride again that season. John Francome gradually drew level with Scudamore's total of winners and when he reached the same number he announced that he was hanging up his saddle for the rest of the season. He felt that as Scudamore was unable to compete it was only fair that they should finish the season as equal champions.

Franklin Engelmann was also unable to compete, of course, having died in 1972, so Brian decided to retire from *DYW* after equalling Engelmann's total of 733 programmes. The announcement of his departure from the programme was national news and there were articles and features in most of the daily newspapers. 'I am relieved,' Pauline told the *Guardian*. 'It has disrupted one's social life every week.'

Brian was also invited to appear on a number of television programmes to talk about his decision, including *Breakfast Time* with Frank Bough and *Wogan*, where he nearly had the show taken off the air.

After telling Terry Wogan some of his familiar anecdotes, Brian finished with a chorus of 'When I Discovered You' by Irving Berlin, a song he had first performed out in Brazil in the 1930s. It was the first – and only – time he ever sang on television. Wogan's second guest was the comedian Ronnie Corbett, and the conversation turned quickly to golf. Corbett had just told an amusing anecdote about Jimmy Tarbuck when Brian suddenly blurted out, 'Have we got time for Tarby's story?' Wogan looked a bit taken aback but told him to carry on.

'This golfer used to go around with a little white poodle,' said Brian, 'and when he did a good drive or a good putt the poodle got up on his hind legs and clapped with his front paws. So Tarby said to this chap, "What happens if you miss a putt or get in a bunker?" And this chap said, "Oh, he turns a lot of somersaults." Jimmy said, "How many?" And the chap said, "It depends how hard I kick him up the arse!"'

There was a roar of laughter from the audience and a look of stunned amazement on the faces of Ronnie Corbett and Terry Wogan. 'That's not mine, it's Tarbuck's!' said Brian hurriedly. 'That Tarbuck doesn't care what he says,' complained Wogan. 'He's shameless. That's why he works for the other side – as indeed you may do after this!'

Corbett still could not believe what he had heard. 'Is that the first time that word has been said at this time in the evening?' he asked nervously. 'What word?' tempted Wogan. 'A . . .' said Corbett, stopping himself just in time. 'The . . . the bottom word.' 'No, we normally don't go farther than "bottie",' muttered Wogan, before moving swiftly on to the next subject.

Brian redeemed himself at the end of the programme. Wogan invited him to sit in the famous chair used by Ronnie Corbett for his comedy monologues in *The Two Ronnies*. As if he had been doing it for years, Brian put on a pair of fake glasses, perched himself on the chair and delighted the audience with one of his favourite stories:

In 1962 the Duke of Norfolk went to Australia as manager of Ted Dexter's team. A strange chap to have as a manager, a duke, but they loved him in Australia – they called him 'Dukey' – because wherever MCC played he leased a racehorse and ran it in the local meeting.

MCC were playing against South Australia at Adelaide, and about twenty-two miles outside Adelaide there is a racecourse called Gawlor. There's a lovely paddock there with eucalyptus trees and gum trees, very picturesque.

The Duke had a horse running there, so he thought he would go and see it. He spotted it under the eucalyptus tree and walked across the paddock in his pinstripe suit, panama hat and MCC ribbon, very much the duke. As he approached the horse, to his horror, he saw the trainer put his hand in his pocket and give the horse something to eat.

He thought, 'Oh, my God. I'm a member of the Jockey Club at home,' and went up to the trainer and said, 'I hope you didn't give him anything you shouldn't have, Trainer. We don't want any trouble with dope here.'

'No, no, Your Grace,' said the trainer, 'I just gave him a lump of sugar. I'm going to eat one myself. Would you like one too, Your Grace?'

The Duke thought he had better humour him, so he ate the lump of sugar, talked about the race and went off to watch it from the grandstand. Five minutes before the race started, in came the jockeys, waddling as they do.

The Duke's jockey went up under the eucalyptus tree to his horse and the trainer said, 'Look. This is a seven-furlong race. The first five furlongs, keep tucked in behind and don't move. But for the last two furlongs, give him all you've got, and if anyone passes you after that, it's either the Duke of Norfolk or myself!'

DYW had become a national institution. The programme attracted a regular one million listeners on Radio 4 every Sunday, and Henry Stanhope in *The Times* observed: 'an appearance on *DYW* in rural Britain ranks about half way between a gold watch and the British Empire Medal – though clearly below a handshake from the Queen'. Brian recorded his final edition of the programme on 20 May 1987 at Lord's Cricket Ground. When he arrived at the ground he was greeted by a posse of reporters and photographers and a BBC Television camera crew. Up on the Grandstand scoreboard the total was 733 not out – the highest score ever registered on the scoreboard at Lord's, announced Brian proudly, beating Australia's 729 for 6 in 1930.

He interviewed the then President of the MCC, Colin Cowdrey; the Secretary, Lieutenant Colonel John Stephenson; the curator of the Memorial Gallery, Stephen Green; the groundsman, Mick Hunt; and the head of the catering staff, Nancy Doyle. For his final interview on *DYW* he chose his old friend and colleague Denis Compton. The only snag occurred when Cowdrey and Compton both chose 'My Way' by Frank Sinatra as their piece of music. Order was restored when Cowdrey kindly gave way to the Middlesex legend and selected 'Underneath the Arches' instead.

Later Brian said it was one of the happiest days of his life. After the recording MCC gave a lunch in his honour, during which Brian presented Tony Smith with a silver tankard inscribed in his own distinctive handwriting, with thanks 'for so many happy days of fun and friendship'.

During fifteen years and 733 editions of *DYW* Brian had interviewed, or perhaps that should be 'had conversations with', about 4,500 people and, according to him, it had been a joy and a privilege to meet them all.

25

This Is Your Life

At the end of the 1970s Brian concentrated on his radio commitments and made few appearances on television, but in December 1977 he was a guest on *The Generation Game* with Bruce Forsyth and Anthea Redfern. He took part in a game called 'Name the Commentator' with John Snagge, Dan Maskell, Peter Alliss and John Motson. The contestants had to listen to the voices of the various commentators and write down who they were. One team guessed Brian correctly but the other said 'Robertson of *Down Your Way*'. The man apologised to Brian afterwards, saying his mind had gone completely blank. More surprisingly, no one guessed golf commentator Peter Alliss or the veteran Wimbledon commentator Dan Maskell, although one confused contestant put down Maskell's deep, husky voice as Virginia Wade!

Brian had always wanted to be a light comedy actor and he finally got his chance when he was asked in 1978 to appear in an episode of the radio series *The Enchanting World of Hinge and Bracket*. The story was that *Down Your Way* was visiting the village of Stackton Tressle, the home of the two 'dear ladies', Dr Evadne Hinge and Dame Hilda Bracket. According to Michael Craig, the co-writer of the programme: 'The result was a hilarious episode with Brian in and among the laughs, timing his lines to perfection like the best of them (and not having to wear a frock).'

Soon afterwards he made a cameo appearance in another popular comedy series, this time on BBC television, when he was featured in the final episode of *The Good Life* with Richard Briers and Felicity Kendall. The programme was recorded in the presence of the Queen and the Duke of Edinburgh at Television

Centre, the first time Her Majesty had ever watched the recording of a situation comedy. Brian was heard doing a commentary in an episode entitled 'When I'm 65', during which Tom and Jerry challenged each other to a run, before collapsing and having to take a taxi home.

In September 1978 Brian's second volume of autobiography, *It's a Funny Game*, was published, and he was invited to be a guest on *Parkinson*. It was the first time he had been on the programme and he went down well with his well-honed repertoire of funny stories and anecdotes. 'He was a splendid guest because he liked talking,' recalls Michael Parkinson. 'He was modest about his distinguished war record, funny about the early days of broadcasting, hilarious about *Test Match Special* – and he topped it all off with that trick he did with his ears.'

His fellow guests were Manhattan Transfer and the comedian Frankie Howerd, whom Brian had first met in 1947, when he was an unknown comic in a Jack Payne show. At one point Michael Parkinson was discussing Frankie Howerd's lugubrious face. 'Do you think Brian's got the face for a comedian?' he asked Howerd.

'Yes I do. As a matter of fact you look a little like Jimmy Durante,' replied Howerd, turning to Brian. 'I'll tell you why. If I may say so, you have warmth, which is very important. You obviously have a kind of humility. You have a way of expressing yourself. You have a sense of humour – and a sense of humour about yourself – which is very important. I know a lot of comedians who haven't, by the way! And you have a great sense of being able to put over something and appeal to people who are watching you.'

It was a remarkably warm and affectionate tribute from such an established comedian and Brian looked rather embarrassed. 'He also does an amazing trick with his ears,' added Parkinson. 'Let's have a close-up on Mr Johnston, if we can.' When he was a boy, Brian had been taught by Dean, the groom at Much Marcle, how to perform an unusual trick with his ears. As the camera panned in, he tucked the top of his right ear into his ear-hole and then wiggled it until it popped out again. The audience burst into spontaneous laughter and applause. 'Michael,' declared Frankie Howerd, as the laughter died down, 'I can honestly say that in all my years I have never seen a show stolen by an ear!'

Undeterred by his experience with W. G. Greys, Brian was keen to own another racehorse. He saw a golden opportunity in 1979 when he heard from William Douglas Home that his son Jamie was setting up as a trainer at East Hendred in Oxfordshire and had bought a promising young colt in the yearling sales at Newmarket. 'He's a proper gentleman, sir,' said the stable lad, when Brian went down to see him, 'a proper gentleman.' Brian formed a racing syndicate with his old friends Sir Martin Gilliat, Sir Charles Villiers and Lord Orr-Ewing, and they named the horse 'Proper Gentleman'.

At the end of October Brian came down to breakfast one morning complaining that he did not feel very well. When Pauline asked him a question about Proper Gentleman, he said, 'What are you talking about?' He had spoken of nothing else but the horse for weeks and now he had no recollection of it. Pauline rang me to say that Brian appeared to have lost his memory and I feared the worst. After all, he was nearly seventy. He was admitted to the Lindo Wing at St Mary's Hospital in Paddington, where fortunately the problem was quickly diagnosed as a stone in his kidneys, which we were told was causing the memory loss. Painful but treatable. Four days later the kidney stone was removed and his memory returned to normal. But it had been a shock for us all.

Proper Gentleman had his first race at Kempton Park in early May 1980, and to everyone's delight he came third. It turned out to be the highlight of his racing career. Later in August I went with Pauline to see him race at Windsor and lost my one-pound each-way bet when he trailed in a poor tenth. A fortnight later he did manage another third place at Chester, but by then Brian and his friends had decided to cut their losses and they sold the horse at the end of the season.

The highlight of 1980 for the Johnston family was Clare's wedding in March to insurance broker David Oldridge. 'I understand there are some men who do not like cricket,' Brian said once, 'but I would not like my daughter to marry one.' Fortunately

David Oldridge was a keen club cricketer who played for the Old Wykehamists and I Zingari. After David had asked him for his daughter's hand in marriage, Brian joked: 'I told him he had to take the whole girl or nothing at all!'

Clare was the first of Brian's children to get married and he planned the wedding with military precision worthy of an ex-Guardsman. 'He made us stand in a reception line at home,' says Clare, 'and he timed how long it would take for us to greet each guest. He even timed how long it would take me to come downstairs.' The ceremony took place at St John's Wood Church near Lord's. On the day Clare was so punctual that she had to drive around the block until all the guests were seated.

Brian wandered up and down the aisle greeting his friends. I was the chief usher and as I showed William and Rachel Douglas Home and his Old Etonian friend Jimmy Whatman into a pew together, Brian handed them their hymn sheets. Once the service started, William and Jimmy opened their sheets and were startled to see that a busty nude pin-up had been stuck into each of their programmes opposite the first hymn. They looked around quickly to see whether anyone else had noticed and had to sing the opening hymn with the sheets held very close to their chests.

Brian had obtained special permission for the reception to be held in the Long Room at Lord's, and he estimated that it would take about ten minutes to walk at a leisurely pace from the church to the pavilion. The plan was that, after pictures had been taken of the family and guests outside the church, David and Clare would go by car to Lord's, where the photographer would take more pictures of them together. Meanwhile the guests would walk slowly to the pavilion, arriving just as the photography was finished. That way there would be no unnecessary delay or standing around. Unfortunately Brian did not count on the weather. It started to rain as soon as we left the church. Clare and David went in the car as planned but the guests *ran* to Lord's to escape the downpour and arrived within seconds of the bridal couple. The rain-soaked guests had to queue for about fifteen minutes outside the pavilion until Clare and David were ready to receive them.

Brian always enjoyed appearing on radio panel games such as *Just a Minute*, *Quote Unquote* and *Funny Peculiar*, and on the Christmas 1980 edition of *Quote Unquote* he was a member of the panel with novelist P. D. James, Sue MacGregor and Dick Vosburgh. The question-master was Nigel Rees, and he wanted to know who had said: 'Cricket is the greatest thing that God ever created on earth. Greater than sex, although sex isn't bad either. But everyone knows which comes first when it's a question of cricket or sex.'

P. D. James guessed correctly that it was Harold Pinter. 'And I must say,' she added haughtily, 'I find it a very surprising opinion considering the beauty of his wife. If he had said it on the way to the register office with me, I don't think *I'd* have married him.'

Brian politely corrected her. 'What he meant was, you can play cricket and *then* have sex,' he explained, as the audience started to giggle. 'It didn't mean that cricket came before sex, as something better than the other, he meant in time. You go out, you make a hundred, you take a hat-trick, you go home, you have sex!'

In early 1981 Brian made a return appearance on *Parkinson*, where he was joined by Brian Glover and Tommy Trinder. Later he was one of the radio commentators for the first London Marathon, reporting on the race from Tower Bridge. 'I only hope they don't open those twin bascules,' he chuckled as the leading runners came into view. 'I remember once a bus was going over when they opened up the bridge and the chap had to jump it in the bus!'

The major event of 1981, however, was the wedding on 29 July of Prince Charles and Lady Diana Spencer. I was living in Los Angeles at the time and set my alarm for four o'clock in the morning so that I could watch the ceremony on television. After a while I got bored with the American commentary and tuned my crackly short-wave radio to the BBC World Service, where I was delighted to find that Brian was one of the radio commentary team. He was in a marvellous position on a scaffolding platform that had been erected around Queen Anne's statue, outside the main entrance to St Paul's Cathedral, and was able to describe all the coaches and carriages containing the wedding guests as they drew up about six feet in front of him. It was a very emotional occasion, and for a moment he must have forgotten where he was. Along with millions of listeners around the world, I heard him announce:

> I can see Lady Diana coming up Ludgate Hill now in her glass coach with her two escorts. In a minute the coach will stop below me here and a page will open the door. Her father, Earl Spencer, will step out and take her arm, and then they will turn and walk slowly up the steps together, into the pavilion . . . I mean, Cathedral.

One of Brian's friends was a press secretary at Buckingham Palace, and he told Brian of an incident that happened soon after the announcement of the engagement between Prince Charles and Lady Diana. The Royal Family were staying up at Balmoral, and one night the press secretary was invited to join them for dinner. Seated opposite him at the table was Prince Andrew, who had obviously been reading Brian's book *It's a Funny Game*, which included some of his favourite jokes and funny stories. The Prince was telling the Queen how much he had enjoyed the book and proceeded to tell her, and the rest of the table, one of the jokes. They all laughed, so he started to tell them another. Fortunately Brian's friend recognised it as completely unsuitable for the Queen and dared to interrupt Prince Andrew in mid-flow to suggest respectfully that it might be wise not to continue. He probably saved Brian from being sent to the Tower. It was the one about the girl and the chihuahua:

> A lady had a pet dog which was one of those tiny chihuahuas. Its hair began to fall out so she went to her local chemist and asked him if he had anything to stop hair falling out. He went to a shelf and produced a pot of ointment. 'Rub this in twice daily,' he said, 'but there must be no friction, so don't wear a hat for a week.'
>
> 'Oh,' said the lady, 'it's not for my head, it's for my chihuahua.'
>
> 'In that case,' said the chemist, 'I would advise you not to ride a bike for a fortnight!'

At the end of 1981 Brian and Pauline had to move house for the third and final time. After fifteen years, 98 Hamilton Terrace had become too big for them; their four eldest children had grown up and left home, and the house was becoming too expensive to maintain. They found a smaller house a few streets away in the aptly named Boundary Road. Brian soon confirmed the all-important criterion: it was a sixteen-minute walk from Lord's.

Now that John Arlott had retired, Brian was the senior member of *Test Match Special* and his new status was confirmed when he received the Pye Radio Award as Radio Sports Personality of 1981. At the end of the year it was announced that the veteran broadcaster John Snagge was also retiring, and in March 1982 Brian took over from Snagge as the radio commentator of the Boat Race.

He had been involved with the annual event since 1947 when he was stationed on a small floating platform alongside Hammersmith Bridge. After that he had broadcast from a number of different positions on the towpath, including the top of the Harrods Depository building, although after 1952 he was mainly on the steps of Chiswick Bridge, just beyond the finish. This followed the famous incident in 1949 when the BBC launch carrying John Snagge broke down at Duke's Meadow and he was unable to see the end of the race. As luck would have it, that year turned out to be one of the closest races ever, which led to Snagge's immortal words: 'I can't see who's in the lead – it's either Oxford or Cambridge!'

After that, Seymour de Lotbinière decided that there must always be a commentator on Chiswick Bridge so that if anything similar happened again there would be someone to describe the end of the race. For the next twenty-five years Brian played that role and would take over the commentary for a short time when the crews came in sight after Barnes Bridge, before handing back to John Snagge for the finish.

In 1977 Brian was asked to go in a launch for the first time, to act as the link man with the various commentary points along the course. The following year he was on board the launch *Ursula* when the Cambridge crew sank in very rough water shortly after passing under Barnes Bridge. The launch had to stop and rescue the crew, who were struggling in the river. It was a dramatic moment. 'There's a tremendous rescue operation,' shouted Brian excitedly. 'One of the Cambridge crew is being lifted out of the bows. The others are right under the water, you can just see their shoulders. One or two of them are swimming now towards the launch which is taking them on board. You can still see their boat on the surface. The captain is leaving last . . .'

Tom Sutton was the statistician for the BBC broadcasts for thirty years and reveals that the Cambridge crew had been so confident of winning that they had hidden a box of cigars on board to light up at the finish. They went down with the boat.

When John Snagge finally retired in 1981 he had commentated on every Boat Race for fifty years. To many people he *was* the Boat Race, and it was obvious that he was going to be a hard act to follow. However, when Peter Baxter was appointed as the new producer of the radio broadcast he immediately asked Brian to take over the commentary.

'The Boat Race is an event,' explains Baxter, 'and I needed an events commentator.' Having been involved with the broadcast for so long, Brian sometimes knew more about the procedure than his new producer. 'There were shore-based commentary points along the river,' says Baxter, 'in case the race turned into a procession. One year I asked him to hand over to one of them and he hinted strongly that it was the wrong decision.' Baxter adds that Brian's favourite place on the river was always Corney Reach. I wondered why. 'Because it was "corny", of course!'

No one seemed to think it strange that the Boat Race was being described by a cricket commentator, although Brian did have difficulty remembering to call the participants crews and not teams. He shared the commentary duties with Tom Sutton, who supplied all the technical information while Brian concentrated on describing the race. They respected each other's expertise. 'There was a mutual understanding that no one would hog the air,' says Sutton, 'and we automatically knew when to hand over to each other.'

He has fond memories of the hilarity on rehearsal days. On the day before the race each year, Brian would meet up with Tom Sutton, Peter Baxter and the rest of the BBC production crew for a lively lunch at the Star and Garter in Putney. Afterwards they would go out in the BBC launch from Putney to Chiswick and back, testing the outside broadcast equipment and the radio links to Broadcasting House. Brian and Tom Sutton would have to do a mock commentary and, as no one was listening, they would have a little fun. 'We would call the crews Oxbridge and Camford,' recalls Sutton, 'and say silly things like they were rowing in the wrong direction or towing Putney Bridge away.' Sometimes they would add a few spicy comments, and one year a number of people picked up the test broadcast on their short-wave radios. They rang the BBC to complain that they had just heard a very rude commentary – and it sounded just like Brian Johnston! Brian and Tom were ticked off by Broadcasting House.

After the race Brian would usually interview the crews on the towpath. There was intense rivalry between the radio and television producers as to who would speak to the winning crew first. 'It was a huge advantage to have someone that they recognised and gravitated towards,' recalls Baxter. 'They all turned to Brian and not Des Lynam. Afterwards I got angry letters from Television, but I said we can't help it if our man is better known than yours!'

In 1989 Brian decided to call it a day after forty-two years. He felt it was time to let the younger generation have a go. Besides, he was seventy-seven and it could get rather cold and wet standing in the launch. To his delight, Oxford won in his final year. Afterwards Brian was greeted on the towpath by the Duke of Edinburgh, who presented him and Tom Sutton, who was also retiring, with a pair of leather-bound, gilt-edged books on the history of the Boat Race, signed by both the crews and their coaches.

In a sad postscript, a year later Brian was listening at home to the radio commentary of the Boat Race when his replacement in the BBC launch, the veteran Welsh broadcaster Peter Jones, suffered a major heart attack while on air. The shore-based commentators had to complete the Boat Race broadcast and Jones died later in hospital.

Apart from taking over the Boat Race commentary in 1982, Brian had another reason to remember that year. In June he celebrated his seventieth birthday and there was a tremendous amount of publicity, with special programmes on the radio and numerous articles in the press.

Peter Baxter interviewed him for a one-hour programme on Radio 2 called *Johnners at 70*, which incidentally must have been the first time that he was officially referred to as 'Johnners'. The programme nearly did not happen because every time they looked at each other they burst out laughing. Baxter finally had to conduct the interview staring at a pillar in the middle of the room.

In October Brian took part in another revival of *In Town Tonight* to celebrate the sixtieth anniversary of the BBC. He thought it would be a wonderful idea to re-create one of his favourite broadcasting moments, when he sang 'Underneath the Arches' with Bud Flanagan. By a happy coincidence Roy Hudd and Christopher Timothy were starring as Flanagan and Allen in a new musical called *Underneath the Arches* at the Prince of Wales Theatre. Brian arranged with Roy Hudd to interview him 'live' in his dressing room during the show.

Unfortunately, on the night of the broadcast the show was running late and, when Broadcasting House handed over to Brian, Roy Hudd was still onstage. Brian had to conduct a 'live' in-depth interview with Roy's son, who was helping to dress his father during the school holidays. When Hudd finally arrived breathless from the stage he barely had time to say hello before, in keeping with the tradition of the Crazy Gang, he deposited an enormous custard pie on Brian's face.

After the interview Brian had to return to Broadcasting House in a rickshaw (for some obscure reason) and Hudd cherishes the memory of Brian disappearing towards Piccadilly Circus, with custard dripping from his face, calling out, 'Both you Hudders are rotters!'

It may have been the media attention surrounding his birthday which prompted Thames Television to consider Brian as a possible subject for *This Is Your Life*. In many ways it was surprising that they had not featured him on the programme before. Nevertheless, a researcher contacted Pauline and, swearing her to secrecy, asked her to draw up a list of all Brian's closest friends and colleagues who might make suitable guests on the programme. She had been writing out the list one afternoon when Brian came home unexpectedly and noticed the paper on her desk in the sitting room. He spotted the names of all his friends and asked her what it was for. Pauline blurted out that it was her Christmas card list. As this was in the middle of the summer he knew something funny was going on but he did not know what. When we asked him later he admitted that he thought Pauline must be arranging a surprise birthday party for him later in the year. He never suspected for a moment that it was for *This Is Your Life*.

In August I received a telephone call in Los Angeles from Thames Television to ask whether I would like to appear on the programme. They offered to fly me home first class and put me up in a hotel in London for a few days. At the time I was studying at a broadcasting school in Hollywood and working part time as a waiter at a French restaurant called Robaire's, so I did not need to be asked twice.

My brother Andrew had been living in Sydney for about seven years, so they arranged for him to fly to Los Angeles to meet me and on 20 October we flew together to London. On arrival at Heathrow I rang Boundary Road to let Pauline know we had arrived, but Brian answered the phone so I had to put it down quickly.

Thames Television had booked rooms for us at the White House Hotel in central London. There is so much secrecy surrounding the programme that each subject is allocated a code name and only three or four people on the production team know who it really is. Brian had been given the code name Mr Cake – for obvious reasons – and we had to check into the hotel as Barry and Andrew Cake. We were informed that the reason for such tight security was that a receptionist might notice that reservations for the Johnston family were being paid for by Thames Television, guess that Brian was to be the subject of *This Is Your Life*, and leak the story to the newspapers.

That evening we were taken to the production offices at Thames Television for a script conference with Eamonn Andrews. We had all been asked to provide anecdotes, which had been incorporated into the script, and this was our last chance to correct any mistakes and rehearse our contributions. It was a tradition on the programme that friends or relatives from overseas were kept until the end before they made their appearance with the time-honoured words: 'You thought he was in New York/Sydney/Hong Kong, but no, we've flown him ten thousand miles to be here with you tonight . . . you haven't seen him for twenty years . . . it's your long-lost son, Jack!' At which point there would be a roll on the drums and Jack would appear, with floods of tears all round. This was always Brian's favourite part of the programme.

The production staff knew that Brian watched *This Is Your Life* every week and would be wise to such a scheme. They had decided it would be better for Andrew and I to come out near the beginning of the programme, instead of at the end. When we read the script, we said, 'You can't do that, it's his favourite bit!' They explained that if we came out later, Brian would be distracted, wondering when we were going to appear, which did make sense.

The next day Brian was due to record an edition of *Down Your Way* in Chelsea. His producer, Tony Smith, had arranged that there would be a collection of custom-built vehicles in the middle of Sloane Square, and Brian was informed that he would be interviewing the owner of the vehicles. As soon as Brian stepped into the square, a van drew up alongside him and the back doors were flung open. Out of them appeared Tommy Trinder, Michael Denison, Cardew Robinson, Patrick Mower and a host of other Lord's Taverners. Then Eamonn Andrews emerged from the passenger seat and confronted Brian with the famous big red book.

'You've guessed it, Brian,' cried Eamonn, 'the man they never switch off even when the cricket match is rained off . . . ace commentator Brian Johnston, This Is Your Life!' Brian was caught completely unawares. A few minutes later, after he had recovered, he was driven off to the Thames Television theatre in Kingsway.

Once the programme had started, Andrew and I had to wait behind a screen while the rest of the family was introduced. When Eamonn mentioned my name, the doors went back and I walked towards Brian with my arms outstretched to give him a hug. We had not seen each other for eighteen months, but he hated any public displays of affection. He stood up, with his back towards the audience, and as I neared him he whispered, 'We don't kiss, do we?' 'No,' I said as we embraced quickly, 'but Andrew is going to give you a big wet one!' It was a family joke that Brian hated wet kisses. On the programme you could see him looking apprehensive as Andrew walked out towards him. But Andrew knew his father as well as I did, and gave him a firm handshake instead.

There were more than fifty guests on the programme, from Brian's wartime scout-car driver Lewis Gwinnurth to the former Prime Minister Lord Home and cricketing legend Sir Len Hutton. The final surprise guest was Felicity Lane Fox, who had a special reason for wanting to thank Brian. Her brother Jimmy Lane Fox, Brian's best friend at Eton, explained why: 'When we became friends at school,' he said, 'Brian often stayed at my home and became a friend of the whole family, especially my sister, who was six years younger than himself. But when she was twelve, my sister was crippled by polio and Brian took it upon himself to help her live as normal a life as possible. Often he would take her on outings to the cinema and the theatre, carrying her to her seat cradled in his arms. For that kindness and consideration she has always been grateful to him.'

Felicity Lane Fox, who had recently been created a baroness for her services to the disabled, entered in her wheelchair and laughed as she added, 'If anybody asked me why he was carrying me he would say, "Oh, she's drunk again!" and never mention my disability. For which I've always been grateful.'

Afterwards there was a wonderful party backstage during which everyone talked to everyone else at once and watched themselves on-screen as a recording of the programme was replayed on television monitors. It was a memorable day.

The year ended on a high note when Brian learned that he was going to be awarded an OBE for his services to broadcasting in the 1983 New Year's Honours list. He celebrated by flying out to Australia at the end of December for a two-week visit, to spend some time with his son Andrew and to watch the Test match in Sydney.

26

From Tests to Trivia

Brian used to talk sometimes about buying a flat in Sydney and spending the winter months in Australia after he retired. He enjoyed the year-round sunshine and the easy-going attitude to life down under. On his earlier visits he had found that one of the best ways to learn about the country was to travel by taxi. In Sydney you can sit up front with the driver and, like most taxi-drivers, they are great talkers. According to Brian, one day he was riding in a cab in Sydney when he saw a man stagger out of a pub. The man held one finger up in front of his face, stared at it for a second, and then tottered back inside. His driver explained that the man was a 'no-hoper', who would carry on drinking until he could see *two* fingers.

At the end of another taxi journey Brian thought he would try out his Australian on his new friend. 'Good on yer, cobber,' he said to the driver, 'that ride was fair dinkum.' From the look he gave him, Brian related later, the driver must have thought he was a bit 'crook'.

Whenever Brian was in Sydney he would stay with Diana Fisher, who had worked with him at the BBC in London in the 1950s and was now a well-known television personality in Australia. 'He was no fuss,' she says. 'He would make his own breakfast every morning. It was always the same – a boiled egg and a piece of toast – and he would take it out in the garden with the morning newspaper.'

He used to go for a swim at Nielsen Park, which had a large bay and a shark net to protect the bathers. Brian's pleasures were simple. 'He would take a picnic of a plain lettuce sandwich and a banana,' says Diana. 'He loved it.'

Andrew Johnston, like his brother Ian, had grown to be over six feet three and was now visibly taller than his father, who was about six foot. Nevertheless Brian used to enjoy introducing Andrew in Australia as 'my little boy'. One day in 1979 the joke backfired when he went with Andrew to buy tickets for the England–Australia Women's Test match at the Adelaide Oval. Brian asked for one and a half tickets, for him and 'his boy', but when he was handed them he laughed and explained that he really wanted two adult tickets. 'No, you're right, mate,' declared the ticket-seller. 'It's full price for adults and half-price for old age pensioners!'

Brian was now a well-known figure in Australia, and in 1981 he received a letter from Sister Jessie Davies of the Salvation Rescue Mission in Melbourne:

> *Dear Mr Johnston,*
> *Perhaps you have heard of me and my nationwide campaign in the cause of temperance. Annually for the past fourteen years I have made a tour of Australia, delivering a series of lectures on the evils of drinking. On these tours I have been accompanied by my young friend and assistant Claude. Claude, a young man of good family and excellent background, is a pathetic example of life ruined by excessive indulgence in whisky and women.*
>
> *Claude would appear with me at these lectures and sit on the platform drunk, wheezing and staring at the audience through bleary and bloodshot eyes, sweating profusely, picking his nose, belching and passing wind and making obscene gestures at the women, while I would point him out as an example of what over-indulgence can do to a person.*
>
> *This winter, unfortunately, Claude died. A mutual friend has kindly given me your name, and I wonder if you would be available to take Claude's place on my 1981 tour of Australia.*
> *Yours faithfully,*
> *Sister Jessie Davies*

Brian had managed to overcome the Australian's deep-seated

prejudice against toffee-nosed Poms, as Peter Baxter was about to discover. In January 1983 Baxter was producing the *Test Match Special* broadcast from the Sydney Cricket Ground and the day before the match he went to the office at the SCG to ask for some extra passes. 'I need three,' he explained to the burly, gum-chewing official behind the desk. 'One for Trevor Bailey, the great England all-rounder.' The gum-chewing continued. 'One for Mike Denness, the England captain here a few years ago.' Barely a flicker. Baxter began to worry. He played his final card. 'And one for Brian Johnston, the music-hall entertainer.' Suddenly the official's face broke into a wide smile. 'She'll be right, mate!' he said brightly, and handed Baxter the three precious passes.

Baxter remembers Brian turning up at his hotel on New Year's Day wearing a loud Hawaiian shirt and a non-matching pair of shorts. 'Only one thing to do on New Year's Day, Backers,' he had proclaimed enthusiastically, 'and that's to go swimming at Bondi Beach!' Ever since his childhood summers spent in Cornwall, Brian had loved to swim in rough seas. On previous trips to Australia he had picked up a few of the surfing terms and would yell, 'One out the back!' or 'There's too much water in that one!' although he was never quite sure what they meant. Peter Baxter can still picture Brian emerging from the surf after being up-ended by yet another enormous wave, sea water dripping from his bedraggled eyebrows, shouting happily, 'I've been dumped again!'

After he returned to England in January 1983, Brian went to Buckingham Palace with Pauline, Clare and Ian, to be presented with his OBE by Queen Elizabeth the Queen Mother. They celebrated afterwards with lunch at the Hyde Park Hotel, where he and Pauline had held their wedding reception thirty-five years earlier. It was not his only close encounter with the Queen Mother that year. In July Brian was invited to lunch at Clarence House. The Queen Mother's private secretary, Sir Martin Gilliat, had been one of Brian's best friends at Eton and no doubt thought that she would enjoy his lively sense of humour. Brian was a great admirer of the Queen Mother and he broadcast a warm tribute to her at the time of her eighty-fifth birthday. They seem to have enjoyed each other's company because he was invited back on several occasions.

Pauline recalls him going to tea at Clarence House on a hot summer's afternoon. When he arrived there he was greeted by William 'Backstairs Billy' Tallon, the Queen Mother's favourite page, and shown outside to the garden. There, in the shade of a large tree, a table had been beautifully laid out with an antique lace tablecloth and the finest china. Brian could hardly believe it as he sat chatting under the tree with the Queen Mother and Sir Martin Gilliat, while footmen wearing white gloves served them from silver trays with tea and cucumber sandwiches.

Brian may have been in his seventies but he was at the peak of his profession, and later that year his achievement was recognised when he received a Sony Award as the 1983 Radio Sports Personality of the Year. He was a perfect example of the benefits of remaining active in old age, and in October he was invited to take part in a new television series for Channel 4 called *Years Ahead*. It was aimed primarily at the elderly, and the purpose of the programme was to encourage older viewers to stay physically active and to keep mentally alert. Brian was given a regular interview spot, in which he talked to show-business veterans, most of them still working, to illustrate the benefits of not retiring completely. It was exactly the kind of programme he enjoyed, and it provided him with a golden opportunity to reminisce about the good old days with artists such as Larry Adler, Jimmy Jewell and Dame Vera Lynn.

He was always open to new ideas. At the end of 1983 the music impresario Raymond Gubbay had booked the Barbican Theatre in the City of London for his annual Christmas festival of music. He wanted to include something non-musical as a contrast and came up with the concept of putting on a show one afternoon which would attract cricket enthusiasts of all ages. He approached Brian, who thought it was a 'lovely' idea, and *That's Cricket* was born.

The original show took place at the Barbican Theatre on 27

December 1983 and featured some archive film footage and a three-man panel consisting of Jim Swanton, Tony Lewis and Ian Wallace. Brian acted as the chairman, leading the panel on a leisurely discussion of their favourite cricket memories. The Barbican was packed with 1,600 people. 'I'm wearing my Raymond Gubbay suit,' announced Brian cheerfully at the beginning. 'Small checks!'

The show at the Barbican was so successful that Gubbay arranged for *That's Cricket* to go on tour, and over the next two years they performed about twenty-five shows all over the country, selling out large theatres such as the Fairfield Hall in Croydon and the Palace Theatre in Manchester.

The panel changed from place to place but usually included Jim Laker, with either Tom Graveney, Fred Trueman, Ray Illingworth or Trevor Bailey. They travelled about in a mini-coach fitted with aircraft-style reclining seats and a generous supply of dry white wine and smoked salmon sandwiches. According to Gubbay, it was usually Brian who would be first to suggest making a start on the 'Muscers' and the 'Smokers'.

That's Cricket was a regular fixture at the Barbican almost every Christmas for the next ten years. Gubbay described it as 'a summer brightness descending for a couple of hours over the City', and Brian looked forward to it as one of the highlights of the Christmas season.

Brian was always an avid reader, although his taste in literature, as in most aspects of his life, was traditional and uncomplicated. In May 1985 he presented an edition of the Radio 4 programme *With Great Pleasure* in which he was asked to choose his favourite pieces of prose and poetry. The programme was recorded before an invited audience at the Paris Theatre and also featured Ian Carmichael and Julia Foster. It was an informative selection.

As might be expected, there was an extract from *Leave It to Jeeves* by his favourite author P. G. Wodehouse and also from the cricket books *Tales from a Long Room* by Peter Tinniswood, *England, Their England* by A. G. MacDonell and *Close of Play* by Alan Miller. There were also a couple of funny stories by his music-hall heroes Billy Bennett and Max Miller. But Brian also included a speech from June 1943 by his hero Winston Churchill and *The Walrus and the Carpenter* by Lewis Carroll – 'I think this is the first time I ever remember feeling really sorry for anyone,' he revealed. 'Those poor little oysters being conned by two confidence tricksters.'

Another unexpected choice was *The Hound of the Baskervilles* by Arthur Conan Doyle. 'As I grew up,' Brian explained, 'I think, like any boy, I was very keen on comics. Things like *The Little Red Rag* or *Tiger Tim's Weekly*. But by the time I was eight I had already begun to read Conan Doyle's stories of Sherlock Holmes and we were living in Hertfordshire at the time, in the depth of the country. Our garden backed on to a big field and as I read *The Hound of the Baskervilles* I imagined that this field was Dartmoor and was haunted by this terrifying hound.'

The most moving piece was taken from *The Selfish Giant* by Oscar Wilde. 'I have to confess that I blub rather easily,' Brian told the audience, 'whether I am reading, watching the telly or the cinema, and what usually gets me is when a bad man turns good and becomes nice.' True to his word, as Julia Foster finished her reading, he dabbed quickly at his eyes.

In January 1986 Brian paid a return visit to *This Is Your Life* when he appeared as a guest with Pauline and their youngest daughter Joanna. The subject of the programme was Sister June McElnea, MBE, known as Sister Mac, who was retiring after nearly forty years at Great Ormond Street Hospital. Pauline explained to Eamonn Andrews that they had first met Sister Mac at a very traumatic moment when they discovered that Joanna had diabetes. She had taught Joanna how to practise her injections on an orange. 'There were many occasions when Joanna had to go into Great Ormond Street,' Pauline informed Sister Mac, 'and the fact that you were there with your cheerful smile kept our spirits up.'

Brian could not resist telling a joke. 'A mother came to visit her child once,' he told Eamonn, 'and she had rather a bad cough. Sister Mac said, "Let me look at your throat." So she looked down her throat and said, "Yes, you've got a bad cough. Do you ever get a tickle in the morning?" And the mother said, "I used to, but not now they've changed the milkman!"' The audience laughed, although Eamonn looked rather taken aback.

Joanna was wearing an attractive green dress that she had made herself at training college. After she had told Sister Mac about the dress, she suddenly gave her a big twirl. The audience responded with loud applause and as Brian, Pauline and Joanna walked to their seats, Joanna raised her arms in triumph. 'Well,' said Eamonn, as the applause died down, 'that went down better than Dad's joke!'

There was a happy family occasion for Brian and Pauline in July, when their son Andrew returned from Australia to marry Gillian Moon, whom he had met in Sydney. They were married in St Agatha's Church at Llanymynech in North Wales, and for once Brian was content to stay out of the limelight, although I shamelessly pilfered all his corniest jokes for my speech as their best man.

Four days later Brian was back on royal duty when he was stationed on the Victoria Memorial outside Buckingham Palace as part of the radio commentary team for the wedding of the Duke and Duchess of York. When the couple emerged on to the palace balcony there was an enormous roar from the crowd in the Mall who started calling for them to kiss. Brian had to shout to make himself heard, and at times his commentary sounded more as if he were covering a sporting event than a royal occasion. 'We haven't had the kiss yet,' he reported. 'Now they're looking at each other as if to say shall we, shan't we? . . . Sarah is cupping her ear, saying, "What are you shouting at me? I can't hear" . . . There's the kiss! There it is! A very good kiss . . . and I notice his nose is on the left of hers . . .'

Brian had been the question-master on countless radio and TV quizzes such as *Sporting Chance* and *Treble Chance* over the years but he had never been the chairman of a comedy quiz game. Then in 1986 he was approached to host a new radio series. It was to be one of the most popular in his long career.

Trivia Test Match was dreamed up by Malcolm Williamson and Peter Hickey. 'As soon as we had the idea of combining a trivia quiz with the laws of cricket,' says Williamson, 'Brian was the obvious choice.' The team captains were Willie Rushton and Tim Rice, and each week they were joined by two celebrity guests such as Stephen Fry, Paul Merton, Bernard Cribbins and Barry Cryer. 'When I was invited to be a team captain,' recalls Sir Tim Rice, 'and was told it would be with Willie Rushton and Brian Johnston, I said yes right away. It was my dream programme.'

At first *Trivia Test Match* was recorded at the BBC's Paris Theatre in Lower Regent Street. The first two series were well received but did not exactly capture the public's imagination. 'It was a funny programme because it took a while to take root,' says Rice. 'I thought the format was a bit restrictive, but when Brian lost control of the scoring it worked beautifully.' Malcolm Williamson kept the score and had to correct Brian when he got it wrong. 'I don't think Brian ever entirely understood the rules,' he says, laughing, 'but it didn't seem to matter.'

During the second series in March 1987 I made an unexpected appearance on the programme. I was staying at Boundary Road for the weekend and at 7.30 p.m. on Saturday night I was leaving the house to go out on a dinner date when the telephone rang. It was Brian calling from the Paris Theatre. 'Leslie Thomas hasn't turned up,' he said desperately. 'He's got his dates mixed up. We've got a theatre full of people and we're supposed to start recording in a few minutes. Can you get here as quickly as you can?' I could hardly say no, so I drove frantically through the Saturday night traffic and made it to the Paris in less than half an hour. There was nowhere to park so I left my car on a double yellow line and dashed into the theatre. The producer, Paul Spencer, was waiting. 'Thank you for coming,' he said quickly, and ushered me through a curtain on to the stage. There was a polite smattering of applause and I sat down next to Tim Rice. We shook hands, I waved at Brian, and two minutes later the announcer introduced the programme.

I had never heard *Trivia Test Match* and did not know any

of the rules or how it was played. All I knew was that it was a quiz game. We were halfway through the programme before I realised that it was supposed to be funny. When I heard the broadcast a few weeks later I was highly embarrassed to discover that I hardly spoke a word for the first ten minutes. The audience must have wondered why I was there. Afterwards I was thanked profusely for stepping into the breach at such short notice. But I was never invited back. To make things worse, after the recording was finished I went outside to find that my car had been towed away and it would cost me over a hundred pounds to reclaim it. I had to pay for a taxi to take me to my dinner date and arrived to find that she had already polished off more than a bottle of wine and the meal was completely ruined. Apart from that, the evening went quite well.

For the third series, the Paris Theatre was unavailable and the decision was made to record the show at a different cricket club each week. 'It really took off when it went on the road,' says Barry Cryer. 'They were pleased to see us and we were pleased to see them.' The visit of the *Trivia Test Match* team soon became one of the highlights in a cricket club's calendar. 'Brian was like a mythical god appearing in their midst,' says Malcolm Williamson. 'They couldn't believe he was actually in their clubhouse.' The clubs would compete to see who could lay on the biggest buffet and a considerable amount of alcohol was consumed by the audience and the contestants before, after and occasionally during the programme. 'It was a well-oiled machine,' admits Rice, 'but it worked. We all thought we were very witty – both on the stage and in the audience.'

The clubs were mainly in the South so that the participants would not have too far to travel. Willie Rushton recalled one hilarious evening at Windsor Cricket Club. It was normal practice to record two shows in one night and the refreshments were usually served at the end of the recording. 'On this particular night,' related Rushton, 'drinks were brought out *between* the two programmes and it's fair to say that Johnners overdid it.' Everyone wanted to talk to him and he was mobbed by the club members. Perhaps he got a bit carried away with all the hospitality. During the second show he struggled to pronounce his consonants and had terrible trouble with the word 'sarsaparilla'. Malcolm Williamson was sitting next to Brian and continually had to remind him to give the score. 'He kept ploughing on regardless,' says Williamson. 'So I had to nudge him and he would go, "What? What?"' The guest panellists were Bill Tidy and Tim Brooke-Taylor (Brian had to call him 'Brookers') and Rushton said that none of them had ever laughed so loud.

The series began to attract attention. 'People started talking about it for the first time,' says Rice. One of the most enjoyable aspects of the programme was Brian's apparent ability to remain calm amid the surrounding chaos. 'He reminded me of Kenneth Horne on that classic radio series *Round the Horne,*' says Cryer. 'An urbane man in the middle of a lot of idiots. He had that lovely air of not being quite sure what was going on, especially when the answers were a bit naughty. But I think it was a shrewd innocence.'

Trivia Test Match was always funniest when things went wrong. 'Which group of stores was well known for having billiard balls above their shops?' asked Brian. There was a baffled silence until he had another look at the question. 'Oh, sorry,' he cried, 'billiard *halls*!' The audience roared with laughter. 'You made a real halls-up of *that* one!' quipped Barry Cryer.

Bearing in mind that the programmes were recorded in the Home Counties and broadcast on Radio 4, the panellists got away with some amazingly crude remarks. One infamous moment occurred when Stephen Fry was one of the panellists. 'Which part of Napoleon's body were his female servants not allowed to touch?' enquired Brian. The audience immediately started to giggle but no one could guess the correct answer. 'His face,' revealed Brian finally. 'What on earth did they sit on, then?' interrupted Stephen Fry. Everyone collapsed, while Brian pretended not to understand. The audience was in uproar. According to Jon Magnusson, who had taken over as producer in 1990, all the men fell about laughing, while half the women sat stony faced and glared at them. 'The amazing thing is,' adds Cryer, 'they left it in!'

The answers could also be brilliant. Jon Magnusson recalls one example from Willie Rushton. 'If the answer is 9 W,' asked Brian, 'what is the question?' Quick as a flash, Rushton replied, 'Is it true you spell your name with a V, Mr Wagner?'

By the early 1990s Tim Rice had become a major figure in Hollywood and had won an Oscar for his song 'Whole New World' in the Walt Disney film *Aladdin*. He had tremendous difficulty trying to explain to the film executives at Disney why he had to take time off from working on their multimillion-dollar production of *The Lion King* to appear on a radio quiz show for £63 at a cricket club in Surrey. Nevertheless, he returned to England to be on the programme. 'Only Tim would fly back from Hollywood to appear on *Trivia Test Match*!' chuckles Barry Cryer.

The series ran for eight years and Willie Rushton put the longevity of the programme down to Brian's benign but sharp chairmanship. 'It was something he'd never tackled previously,' reflected Rushton, 'but I don't think it occurred to anyone for a moment that he wouldn't make a success of it.'

27

Father Figure

Brian was a creature of habit and liked to get away for some sunshine every year as soon as the cricket season was over. During the 1980s he and Pauline went on a number of holidays to Greece and Cyprus with their friends Ben and Belinda Brocklehurst of the *Cricketer* magazine.

In September 1981 they went for a two-week holiday to the island of Lefkas in Greece. They stayed in a rented taverna in the small fishing village of Nidri and used to join the others for breakfast every morning at a small restaurant on the beach. The *Cricketer* party always included a number of other friends, such as the former England Test cricketer Bill Edrich, Christopher Martin-Jenkins, the ITN newscaster Sandy Gall and Jim Swanton, who liked to go for a quick swim in the sea before breakfast. One morning Swanton forgot to remove his watch and when he got out he found it had stopped working. His wife Ann was furious with him for being so foolish and reluctantly lent him her own watch instead. The following day Swanton had his regular morning swim, only this time he forgot to remove Ann's watch. It also stopped. Swanton was terrified of his wife finding out. When he joined the others at the taverna he tried desperately to keep the broken watch concealed, while all through breakfast Brian pulled his leg constantly, saying, 'I'm sorry, Jim, I seem to have left my watch behind. Do you know what time it is?'

The local restaurant was owned by a larger-than-life character known as Nick the Greek, a former bodyguard of the Greek shipping millionaire Aristotle Onassis. One evening, after a particularly good meal, they all went off to bed except for Pauline and one or two other guests, who stayed up dancing and talking with Nick the Greek until about 2 a.m. When they returned to their taverna one of the women guests found that her husband had locked her bedroom door. She banged loudly and called his name, but he was either in a deep sleep or would not let her in. So Pauline kindly suggested that she sleep in a third bed in her bedroom for the night. The woman accepted gratefully and Brian remained fast asleep as she undressed and slipped into the spare bed.

An hour or so later there was a tremendous thunderstorm with brilliant flashes of lightning. Brian woke up to see a very shapely naked woman standing on their balcony with her arms outstretched, welcoming the dawn. He blinked his eyes, turned to check that Pauline was asleep in the bed beside him, and thought that he must be dreaming. He went back to sleep, and when he woke up later the woman had gone. Subsequently Pauline explained to Brian what had happened, but neither the woman nor her husband ever mentioned it and Brian never revealed to them what he had seen.

While they were on Lefkas they heard a rumour about a mysterious figure known as 'the man in the wheelchair' on the neighbouring island of Scorpios, which was owned by the Onassis family. The rumour was that President John F. Kennedy had survived the assassin's bullet in Dallas but had been left as a vegetable. This was alleged to have been the reason why no proper autopsy was ever carried out on his body. Kennedy was said to have been flown in a private jet by Aristotle Onassis to Scorpios, where he had been cared for in secret for many years, which explained why Jackie Kennedy had paid so many visits to the island. It is certainly true that there was an extraordinary amount of security on Scorpios at that time, with armed guards and killer dogs ensuring that no one came near the island.

Aristotle Onassis had died in 1975 and the island was now largely unoccupied, but the rumour persisted of 'the man in the wheelchair'. The Brocklehursts managed to obtain permission for a friend with a boat to take them out to the island, accompanied by Brian and Pauline, Sandy Gall and his wife Eleanor. Brian thought the whole idea was hysterical. The intrepid investigators scoured the beaches and paths looking for clues but found no sign of any wheelchair tracks. At one point they came to a swimming pool and saw an air pipe sticking out of the water. Brian grabbed hold of it by the end and shouted, 'Are you down there, Mr President?' Adopting his best ventriloquist's voice he replied, 'Yes, I am! Get me out of here!'

Brian's idea of a perfect holiday was to sit in the sunshine and read the English newspapers. He even arranged for the *Daily Telegraph* to be mailed to him every day in Lefkas so that he could do the crossword. There is a marvellous photograph of him sitting in a chair on the beach at Nidri, engrossed in his newspaper, completely oblivious as the incoming tide swirls around his feet. The only problem he had in Lefkas was the food. He hated onions and tomatoes, which can be something of a problem if you are eating out in Greece.

The secret was not to tell him what was in the cooking. 'He used to say, "Euggh! I don't like garlic, onions or tomatoes,"' says Diana Fisher, 'but I would cook him spaghetti bolognese and he loved it!' Brian was once introduced to a member of the Heinz family and complimented him on their Cream of Tomato soup, because it tasted nothing like tomato (which is true). Mr Heinz was said to have been furious.

Every friend of his has a story about his fussy eating habits. Peter Baxter recalls taking him for lunch in his local pub, the Boot. Brian wanted a glass of dry white wine with some bread and cheese. The waiter offered to bring him their special ploughman's lunch with all the trimmings – pickles, salad and dressing. 'Why can't I just have bread and cheese?' protested Brian.

He could not understand why restaurants insisted on serving fancy foreign food. Christopher Martin-Jenkins remembers one evening during a Test match at Trent Bridge when they went out for dinner at the Saracen's Head in Southwell. The waiter brought them a selection of vegetables. 'What are these?' asked Brian suspiciously. 'Mangetouts,' he was told. 'What's wrong with ordinary beans?' he cried.

Even when he was abroad he would never eat the local dishes. 'We were in Hong Kong once,' says Pauline, 'and our friends Cliff and Olive Gillett had booked a table at a Chinese restaurant in Kowloon. Brian and I had never eaten Chinese food before. We took one look at the menu and could not understand a word of it, so Brian said he would order some fish.'

The waiter came back with a bucket containing three live fish. 'Oh my Crippen!' cried Brian, recoiling in horror. He and Pauline each selected a fish, but when the waiter brought them back on a plate they still had their heads and eyes on. 'You should have seen the expression on Brian's face!' says Pauline, laughing.

When Andrew Johnston was living in Sydney he took his father out for a meal one evening. They ordered a plate of mixed vegetables which included zucchini, something Brian had never eaten before. He took one mouthful and spat it out loudly, going 'Yeuucch!' A man sitting at the next table looked up. 'Hello, Brian,' he said cheerfully, 'I thought it was you!'

It made life difficult at home for Pauline, who had to cater for his long list of dislikes. They included: tomatoes, carrots, peas, courgettes, parsnips and turnips, sweetcorn, anything with onions or garlic, cooked cheese and shellfish. He would not eat any kind of hors d'oeuvres, apart from sardines, and for starters he would consider only melon, grapefruit or smoked salmon. Even his lettuce had to be 'honeymoon salad' – without dressing.

'He was no gourmet,' admits John Woodcock. 'Nouvelle cuisine didn't suit the old boy really. He was a great patriot, even when it came to food. He loved English cooking.' His tastes were even more basic than that. What he really liked was schoolboy food. Roast beef or lamb, steak and kidney pudding or pie, any roast bird or game, bangers and mash, fish and chips, and scrambled eggs.

'Honestly,' he would complain, 'I don't see why I am said to be a fussy eater.' His one indulgence was puddings. Treacle sponge, bread-and-butter pudding, spotted dick, summer pudding – he loved them all. Unfortunately Pauline banned him from eating them at home because he was putting on weight.

Sunday lunches were always a time for the family to get

together, even when we had all grown up and left home. Brian would sit at the head of the table cracking jokes and making fun of Pauline's cooking, which, in her defence, had to be fairly plain in order to please him. Sometimes he went too far. After preparing lunch in the kitchen for an hour, Pauline would not be amused to sit down at the dining table and be greeted by sniggers with every mouthful. This went on for some years, until she could bear it no longer and demanded that he stop it.

Apart from those uproarious lunches, none of us has many childhood memories of our father. 'He was never there,' says his eldest daughter Clare simply. It did not help that we were all at boarding school for most of the year. There would be the occasional trip to a TV studio or a cricket match, but during the summer holidays Brian was always working. He used to go down to Swanage with us for a couple of weeks at the beginning of September, but that was it. The one bonus was that he had such a strong personality that when he was around he made a deep and lasting impression.

He had the most extraordinary giggle and he could see the funny side in almost anything. Anyone who has heard the 'leg over' recording will recognise the irresistible combination of wheezes, giggles and yelps that sprang forth from him. You did not need to know what had started it, you simply could not help yourself. You cried with laughter. Many was the time that we would be watching television at home when something would catch his eye. It might be bad acting and corny dialogue or wobbly scenery. It did not really matter. The giggle would start. Soon the whole family would be howling with laughter, tears pouring helplessly down our faces, without really knowing why we were laughing at all.

'My fondest memories are of Swanage,' says his son Andrew. In the 1960s there was a little theatre in Swanage called the Mowlem which used to put on a traditional seaside concert party during the summer. There was a small company that always included a comedian, a singer, a dancer and a novelty act. They would have three or four different programmes of songs and sketches, alternating twice a week, and Brian would take us to see them

14. The BBC staff commentator at another outside broadcast.

15. *Left*: Father figure: Brian shows his two-year-old son Barry how to play *Underneath the Arches* at home in Cavendish Avenue, 1951.

16. *Below*: The controversial new *Twenty Questions* team in 1975. (*Left to right*) Brian, Anona Wynn, Willie Rushton, Bettine le Beau and chairman Terry Wogan. The Social Contract was the Labour government's attempt to restrain pay increases.

"It's abstract! You can't see it! You can't feel it! It doesn't exist!—It's the Social Contract!"

17. The master raconteur gives an after-dinner speech at the Variety Club's dinner for the BBC's 60th Anniversary, 12 July 1982.

18. Inspecting his OBE with wife Pauline and daughter Clare (*right*) outside Buckingham Palace, 1 March 1983.

19. *Down Your Way –*
Down Under in Alice
Springs, Australia,
19 January 1979.

20. Walking up the steps
of the pavilion at Lord's
with Colin Cowdrey, then
President of MCC, after
his 733rd and final *Down*
Your Way, 20 May 1987.

21. Outside the commentary box on the pavilion roof at the Oval with E. W. (Jim) Swanton.

22. With John Arlott during the Fifth Test against South Africa at the Oval, August 1951.

23. *Left*: British Gas appeals for more cake in the commentary box at the Oval, 5 August 1988.

24. *Right*: With Bill Frindall, interviewing an inflatable parrot on *Test Match Special* at Headingley, July 1988.

25. *Below*: With Richie Benaud at the Dragon School, Oxford, c.1967: 'How very sporting to give the batsman so much time to get back.'

26. With Sir Paul Getty in front of the cricket pavilion at Wormsley, August 1993.

27. A champagne moment. Brian and Pauline in their garden at St John's Wood, June 1992.

28. The Johnston family on Pauline's 80th birthday at Wykey House, Shropshire, 9 November 2002. (*Back row, left to right*) Harry, Joanna, Andrew, Gilly (daughter-in-law), Ian, Fiona (daughter-in-law), Rupert, Nicholas; (*middle row*) Sophie, Clare, Pauline, Barry, Emily; (*front row*) Olivia, Georgia, Sam.

29. The weathervane featuring Brian's unmistakable profile on the roof of the cricket pavilion at Sir Paul Getty's ground at Wormsley.

all. After the interval there was a spot where the elderly pianist, 'Frances Buckland at the Pianoforte', would take requests from the audience. The usual favourites would be shouted out: 'Stardust!' or 'Smoke Gets in Your Eyes!' In the summer of 1962 the big number-one hit was 'Come Outside' by Mike Sarne. Brian waited until there was a lull in the requests and then called out from the darkness, 'Come outside!' Frances Buckland looked shocked. 'I'll see you later!' she replied. It got the biggest laugh of the evening.

Brian was not very good with babies or small children. He thought all babies looked the same and small children could not have a conversation with him, so they were no fun. 'I don't think he felt attuned to children,' says Andrew. After my disastrous experience at Eton, Brian rather lost interest in the education of his other sons. Andrew was sent to boarding school at Westminster School, so that he could be closer to home in London. On his first Saturday at Westminster he arrived back at Hamilton Terrace at about 4 p.m. 'What are you doing here?' asked Brian, looking surprised. 'I've come home for the weekend,' Andrew explained, 'I'm a weekly boarder.' His father had apparently not realised this was to be the case.

Brian only really got to know his children once they had started work. We did not share his love of cricket, so it gave us something to talk to him about. 'The first sign of respect I had from him,' says Andrew, 'was when I worked at Foyle's bookshop in Charing Cross Road.' He worked in the sports department and helped to sell a large quantity of his father's books. 'He enjoyed talking about books and publishing,' says Andrew, 'he was interested in how it all worked.' Ian was slightly younger and says he never had a deep discussion with his father. It would be: 'How's everything?' 'Fine.' 'Jolly good!'

Brian acknowledged that Pauline ran the household. 'He always deferred to her if it was anything to do with the family,' says Clare. 'If you asked him whether you could stay out late or something, he would say, "It's all right with me, but you'd better ask your mother."'

He hated any kind of argument or unpleasantness. He wanted people to be happy all the time. 'Don't moan,' he would say to Pauline whenever she found fault with anything. 'I'm not moaning,' she would reply, 'it's normal to complain sometimes.'

One weekend, when I was about eighteen and still living at home, I spent my first Saturday night out at a girlfriend's flat. The next day, dutiful son that I was, I turned up for the traditional family Sunday lunch, but I was several minutes late and looked rather the worse for wear. Brian was not pleased and said he would like a word with me afterwards.

I was in my bedroom after lunch when there was a knock on the door. I thought I was going to be in for a lecture on the facts of life, and they probably were the facts of life as he saw them. 'Look, old man,' said Brian, 'what you get up to with your girlfriend on a Saturday night is entirely up to you. Just don't be late for lunch on Sunday – it does upset your mother!'

It was excellent advice and I have stuck to it ever since. Incidentally, he never did tell me the facts of life. Once again that was left to Pauline, who had handed me a booklet entitled 'The Birds and the Bees' when I was about twelve, and told me to read it very carefully. Brian would have found the whole business far too uncomfortable to talk about.

In the early 1980s I spent four years living and working on radio in California, where people are encouraged to express their feelings. It made an impression on me, and after I returned to the UK I used to tell Brian everything that was happening in my life, from my work as a presenter at BBC Radio Sussex to my latest girlfriend. He admitted later that he really enjoyed the fact that his children felt able to talk to him so frankly, although he could never have done the same himself.

The truth is that Brian was actually quite shy among people that he did not know really well. He was easily embarrassed. It was one of the reasons that he did not like to stay with strangers and would always come home from an evening engagement if at all possible. Pauline recalls them staying in the Lake District during the 1950s, at the home of the BBC television producer

Antony Craxton. Their bedroom was rather a long walk from the bathroom so a porcelain pot had been placed under the bed in case of emergencies. Brian had to use it during the night, but felt that he could not leave the pot for Mrs Craxton or the maid to empty in the morning, so when he woke up he covered it with a towel and carried it discreetly to the bathroom. His route took him along a minstrel's gallery which overlooked the dining room, and as he crept stealthily along, he was horrified to be greeted by a shout from downstairs: 'Morning, Brian! Had a good night?'

'That's it!' he announced to Pauline when he returned to their room. 'I'm never staying in someone else's house again!' In fact there were one or two friends such as William Douglas Home, Charles Sheepshanks and Jimmy Whatman with whom he used to stay from time to time, but significantly he had known them all since he was a boy at Eton.

In May 1985 Brian and Pauline were invited to attend a garden party and to stay overnight at Holyrood House, the Queen's official residence in Edinburgh. They had to sleep in separate bedrooms and Brian was allocated Prince Philip's dressing room. After they had arrived the Queen gave them a guided tour of the royal palace, and when they returned to their rooms Brian was mortified to discover that his suitcase had been unpacked by one of the valets.

It is astonishing to think that someone who made a career out of talking to complete strangers should have been so uncomfortable when asked to stay at someone's house. 'People were always saying, "You must come and stay with us,"' says Pauline, 'but he would always refuse. He would rather stay in a hotel or go home. He was petrified of being caught in his dressing gown walking to the loo at night. It was simply too embarrassing.'

He liked to be at home because he knew where everything was. He enjoyed the company of friends but did not like to go to parties where he did not know anybody. The problem was that everyone wanted to talk to him. 'People would ask him so many questions,' explains Pauline. 'He would have to repeat the same things over and again to each new person that he met.'

Brian was not a passionate man and did not believe in hugs and kisses. He never said, 'I love you.' But he was genuinely kind, honest and sincere, as well as very funny, and his children all adored him. He was a large man and his body was covered with fine dark hair. 'He was like a big bear,' recalls Andrew, 'hairy, with big hands. When we used to go for walks, I remember his hands were always warm.'

After we left school Brian encouraged each of us to pursue our individual dreams, conscious of the fact that his family had put pressure on him to give up his own theatrical ambitions. If we failed, he reasoned, then at least we could never complain that we had not been given the chance. He did not agree with every choice that each of us made in the ensuing years, but in times of trouble it was heartening for us to know that we could always rely on his full support.

He was not a religious man. He thought of himself as a Christian but was not a regular churchgoer, although he enjoyed attending the traditional church services at Easter and Christmas. He professed to believe in God and 'some sort of after-life' but was not entirely convinced. His philosophy of life was simple. It was Christian in principle but was actually based on the character Mrs Do As You Would Be Done By in *The Water Babies* by Charles Kingsley.

Before saying or doing something to someone, Brian would always try to ask himself, 'Would I like to be treated like that?' It explains a great deal about his character and his attitude to life. Everyone I spoke to said that they had never heard Brian say a bad word about anyone. He treated everyone, whether they were friends or strangers, with kindness, consideration and understanding, in the hope that they would treat him the same. If only everyone in the world, he believed, could 'do as they would be done by', our problems would be largely solved.

This makes him sound almost too good to be true. Surely he must have let his guard down once he was at home and lost his temper or kicked the dog occasionally? But no, according to Pauline, the only time he really got cross was when she was late for something, which she admits was quite often. Brian always tried to be five minutes early for an appointment. He particularly hated to be late for the theatre. On countless occasions Brian would be dressed and waiting impatiently downstairs while Pauline was still getting ready. 'The tension in the car would be like a knife-edge,' says Pauline. 'We'd usually arrive in the nick of time, with Brian having driven like crazy, and I would say, "See, I told you we'd make it!"' Everyone agrees that it was the one thing that really annoyed him. 'The strange thing is,' adds Pauline, 'that since Brian died I am now punctual all the time.'

Clare recalls that he would also get upset if someone did not do something that they had been asked to do without a reminder, which was perhaps another legacy of his wartime experience. 'Incompetence annoyed him,' agrees John Woodcock, 'but something had to go pretty seriously wrong for him to get cross.' The worst insult Brian ever delivered to his son Andrew was: 'You couldn't organise a piss-up in a brewery!'

Brian had been brought up not to display his emotions and he was never comfortable talking about his personal feelings, but as he grew older there were signs that he was mellowing. In April 1987 he agreed to be interviewed with me for a Radio 4 series called *Chinese Horoscopes*, presented by the writer and cartoonist Barry Fantoni. The purpose of the interview was to look into the relationship between father and son. Perhaps he was curious about what he might discover.

The premise of *Chinese Horoscopes* was that everyone has a birth sign named after one of the twelve animals that make up the Chinese horoscope. Consequently Brian was a rat and I am a buffalo, which received four out of five stars as a father/son relationship. The analysis of our characters was remarkably accurate. According to Fantoni, the hallmarks of a rat's personality are charm, opportunism and tenacity, all of which applied to Brian. The rat is also naturally gregarious and adores company, can be obsessed by punctuality and tends to have terrible handwriting. All were true.

Brian was clearly less comfortable at answering personal questions. 'I loathe analysing myself,' he told Fantoni, but acknowledged that underneath his cheerful exterior was a steely determination. 'I can direct myself at a point and say I am going to get there,' he said, 'and I will fight quite hard for that, although on the surface I am cracking jokes. I have got to where I wanted to be.'

He revealed that he had felt guilty about sending me to Eton because I had not enjoyed it as much as him, which he had never told me before. He also said that he felt much closer to me now that we were in the same profession and were able to talk about our work. The programme was a fascinating experience for both of us and afterwards he admitted that it was not as bad as he had expected.

Brian may have distrusted foreign food but he liked to travel abroad, especially if it was somewhere hot. In September 1987 he went on holiday with Pauline to northern Cyprus, which they preferred to the southern part of the island because it was less full of tourists. On the second day Brian went down at 9 a.m. to the beach near their hotel and tied their towels around two sunbeds to reserve them. When he and Pauline returned after breakfast they discovered that a German couple had removed the towels and were lying on their sunbeds. Brian gave them a piece of his mind. 'If you can do that,' he fumed, 'you can do anything!'

After his wartime experiences he was not too keen on the Germans, or the Japanese for that matter. This even applied to their cars. He refused to drive a foreign car and nearly always owned a Ford, believing them to be British. He would update his car every few years, progressing from a Ford Pilot to a Zephyr, a Cortina, a Sierra and finally an Escort. We did not dare tell him that in later years many Ford cars were actually built in Germany.

Before arriving in Cyprus he had booked a hire car from the local company and insisted that they supply him with an English Ford if possible. They had only one Ford Escort available, but unfortunately the gearbox was shot; the car would only crawl along, with its engine racing loudly, at about thirty miles an hour.

Brian had to swallow his pride and take the car back. For the rest of the holiday, to his huge embarrassment, he and Pauline drove around Cyprus in a luxury, air-conditioned, Japanese car.

Brian was very aware that he was a public figure. One of the reasons he enjoyed travelling abroad was that he was able to be anonymous. It was impossible for him to go anywhere in England without people shouting, 'Hello, Brian! No cricket today?' As he became more famous, Pauline found it harder to deal with his popularity. He was recognised wherever they went, especially when he spoke. Even more annoying, people would talk to him and ignore her completely.

'Sometimes I'd mutter, don't talk and you won't be seen,' Pauline told the *Observer* after Brian died. 'There was no such thing as a quiet night out with him. It was like being the Royal Family. People would always pester us.'

She says she felt rather like Prince Philip, always having to walk six paces behind Brian while he was greeted by his many admirers. But she loved him dearly. They never had a cross word for longer than ten minutes. 'He taught me a lot,' she added. 'He was very worldly wise. He was my guide and my mentor.'

His family is now scattered around the country but they remain close and keep in constant touch. As you may have gathered, I write and edit books, and produce audiobook recordings for BarryMour Productions, which is based in Sussex. I am married to Fiona and we have two children, Olivia (ten) and Sam (eight). Clare lives in London and has looked after Richie Benaud's UK office for about fifteen years; she is now divorced with three children, Nicholas (twenty), Rupert (eighteen) and Sophie (fourteen).

Andrew lives in Shropshire, where he runs a successful publishing company, Quiller Publishing Ltd, and is married to Gilly, with three children, Harry (sixteen), Emily (fifteen) and Georgia (thirteen). Ian has recently retired as the director of a satellite consultancy company and is unmarried; he lives in Swanage, although he travels regularly to the Far East and other exotic corners of the world.

Joanna lives at a house in Bedfordshire run by the Home Farm Trust and has been engaged to her boyfriend Douglas for seven years. She is currently doing environmental studies and learning French, as well as taking courses in drama and art. Brian would have been proud.

28

Friends and Neighbours

Brian had an extraordinary number of friends and he devoted a lot of his time to keeping in touch with them all. When he was at home he would sit down in the evening and work his way through the several pages of telephone numbers scribbled in the back of his diary, checking that everyone was all right. 'I still miss the phone calls,' says Peter Baxter. 'He would never introduce himself, he would simply say, "What news? What news?" Afterwards I would wonder why he had called, but it was just for a chat.'

In later years, when a number of his friends had died, Brian would continue to phone their widows, maintaining their friendship. Rachel Douglas Home, now Lady Dacre, remembers his compassion. 'He was so wonderful to me after William died,' she says. 'He would ring at least once a week.'

Many of his friends came from the world of cricket. Former Test players such as Bill Edrich and Tom Graveney were regular guests at the annual garden party in St John's Wood. Brian had got to know them back in the 1950s, when the players and the media were much closer than they are today. This was especially true on his first tour to Australia in 1958/59. 'I remember going with him to Melbourne Zoo, where we saw our first duck-billed platypus,' says Trevor Bailey. 'Brian laughed that its nose was even bigger than his. It wouldn't happen now. The TV and press weren't digging for dirt in those days, they were only interested in the cricket.' They even formed a drinking club called 'The Bowers Club', which included Brian and Trevor Bailey, John Woodcock, Godfrey Evans, Frank Tyson and Ted Dexter. They had to wear a bow tie, hence the name, and used to meet every Friday and drink wine. Bailey proudly showed me their club tie, which had a motif of champagne glasses, with a bat and ball resting against some stumps.

The players always knew when Brian had arrived because he used to announce himself by making a noise like a hunting horn. It was heard not only in dressing rooms and hotel foyers; the corridors of Broadcasting House used to echo to the sound of his 'Tally Ho' as he trumpeted his way to and from his office. It became one of his trademarks, along with the chocolate cakes and the brown-and-white corespondent shoes, and merely added to his reputation as a larger-than-life character.

Then, of course, there were the nicknames. Almost no one was safe. The habit had started during the war with friends like Neville Berry, who became known as 'The Hatchet' (as in Berry the . . .), but his practice of adding -ers to the end of people's names became his personal calling card. It was absurd and made all his friends sound like characters out of a novel by P. G. Wodehouse, but it is remarkable how many of his nicknames stuck. John Woodcock became 'Wooders', Henry Blofeld was 'Blowers', Jonathan Agnew was 'Aggers', and so on. It broke down barriers and made everyone feel as if they were members of an exclusive club, to which they were only too pleased to belong.

Sometimes Brian would use the device when he could not remember someone's first name or simply could not pronounce it. When he was in South Africa for the MCC tour in 1964/65 he was doing the radio commentary on a match against Orange Free State at Bloemfontein. The captain of Orange Free State was called D. J. Schonegevel. Brian tried to say his name once or twice but just could not get his tongue around it. 'It's no good,' he said at last, 'he's got to be Schooners!' And 'Schooners' he was from then on. South African radio had never heard anything like it.

Not everyone was in on the joke. Belinda Brocklehurst recalls introducing Brian to her 'very charming, rather smooth' Greek agent Nick Papanicalou. 'How do you do, Nickers,' said Brian instantly. The Greek was aghast. 'Why does that man call me Nickers?' he hissed to Belinda. 'Does he think I am a poof?'

One of Brian's most enduring friendships was with Jim Swanton, who was so often the butt of his practical jokes. Swanton used to complain about Brian's childish behaviour but underlying his disapproval there was a genuine affection. Swanton once described Brian as 'an utterly good, benevolent, cheerful soul', while Brian said of his long-standing colleague that 'he would be one of the first people to whom I would turn if I were ever in serious trouble'. They were never close friends in the same way that Brian and William Douglas Home were, but it is notable that Jim Swanton attended Brian and Pauline's annual summer garden party in St John's Wood without fail for fifty-one years, until he died in 2000.

Everyone has their favourite Swanton story, and the Brocklehursts told me of a Cricketer Cup dinner in 1986 at the Café Royal in London when Brian and Jim Swanton were the guest speakers. Swanton spoke first, and at the end of his speech he gave an outrageous plug for his new book, *Barclays World of Cricket: The Game from A–Z.* 'It's a marvellous book,' declared Swanton, pompously, 'required reading by every student of the game, and it is very good value at only eighteen pounds fifty in all good bookshops.'

Brian was up next. 'I must say I agree with Jim, for once,' he said, 'his book is excellent value for money. When you consider that a new cricket ball costs twenty pounds, if you buy his book you can get a whole load of balls for just eighteen pounds fifty!'

Brian was a loyal supporter of his friends and was not afraid to stand up for what he believed was right. When Rachael Heyhoe-Flint, the former captain of the England women's eleven, applied to become the first woman member of the MCC, Brian was proud to be one of her sponsors. 'I was a guest on *Trivia Test Match*,' recalls Rachael (whom he called Heyhers). 'We were having a drink afterwards and I asked Brian and Tim Rice whether they would support my application.' When they agreed, she wrote off to the MCC for a membership form and signed it R. Flint, so the committee would not realise who the application was from. Her main sponsor was the philanthropist Sir Jack Hayward and her seconder was the former Test batsman Dennis Amiss.

'At the beginning Brian may have thought it would be a bit of fun,' says Rachael. When her true identity was revealed, however, he became an active campaigner for the MCC membership rules to be changed. Rachael's application had caused predictable outrage among the more traditional MCC members, but Brian was a great believer in fair play. 'He realised that women had given a lot to cricket over the years,' she says, 'and he felt they should be allowed to apply for membership, although he did not want them to be granted any special favours.' When Brian was asked in a television interview why he supported Rachael's application, he replied that he felt it was time for the MCC to change their attitudes. He added, however, that he did not believe he would ever see women become members in his own lifetime.

At a controversial AGM in May 1991 Brian and Tim Rice proposed the motion 'that women should be allowed to apply for membership of the MCC'. A two-thirds majority was required to alter the constitution of the MCC but their motion was heavily defeated. Undeterred, Brian continued to support Rachael's campaign. 'He had many contacts,' she says, 'and a lot of lobbying went on behind the scenes.'

Despite his support, Brian understood the strength of feeling at the MCC and in December 1992 he advised her to wait before trying again. 'I still think it should happen but I do not think the time is right,' he wrote. 'The members gave their verdict only two years ago and I think it would be annoying to them and I fear unproductive. Sorry if I appear uncooperative but I think what I think is wise. You are a great girl and I like you! Yours ever, Johnners.'

After renewed pressure from the media and the suggestion that a lottery grant for the new Grandstand might be affected, MCC members finally voted to change their constitution in September 1998. Six months later, Rachael Heyhoe-Flint was made an honorary life member of the MCC, the first time a woman had been allowed to join the club for 212 years. Sadly, of course, Brian did not live to see it. 'It was enormously important to have had someone of his stature supporting me,' she declares. 'It added huge weight to my application. Without his support it would have been dismissed as a zany idea.'

Brian had an ability to get on with almost anyone, but in the summer of 1987 he began a friendship that must have surprised even himself. His youngest son Ian was working as the general manager at Westminster Cable when he was asked whether he could help to install a thirty-foot radio aerial at the apartment of the American oil millionaire John Paul Getty II in Mayfair. It turned out that Getty needed the aerial so that he could listen to *Test Match Special* on Radio 3. When he learned later that Brian was Ian's father, his secretary rang up to see whether they would both like to come round for tea.

Thus began a most unlikely friendship. Brian and Paul Getty shared a mutual love of cricket but, more than that, they discovered that they were both great fans of the Australian soap opera *Neighbours*. They were soon chatting enthusiastically about Harold and Madge, Scott and Charlene, and the other denizens of Ramsay Street. They exchanged phone numbers, and when Brian was at home watching *Neighbours* it was quite common for Getty to ring him as soon as the programme had ended. The two men would then gossip like a pair of old ladies over a fence: 'Did you hear what Jim said to Helen?' 'And what about Mrs Mangel!'

Brian did not like to boast about his high-powered friends and he respected the reclusive tycoon's desire for privacy, so he developed a special code. Whenever he wanted to talk about Getty on *TMS* he would refer to him as 'My friend overlooking Green Park'. Paul Getty, of course, knew exactly whom he was talking about. It would be a while before anyone else realised his identity.

All was revealed two years later when Brian heard that Harold and Madge, or rather their alter egos Ian Smith and Anne Charleston, were due to appear in the pantomime *Dick Whittington* at the Davenport Theatre in Stockport. He immediately persuaded Don Mosey, another *Neighbours* fan, to contact the theatre and book tickets for them both, and a message was sent to Harold and Madge in Melbourne, inviting them to dinner after the show.

They accepted and seats were booked for 11 January 1990. Events began to take a bizarre turn, however, when word came from Paul Getty that he would like to go with Brian and Don Mosey to see the pantomime.

The plan was that Getty would drive up to Stockport with Brian, but two days beforehand he changed his mind about making the two-hundred-mile journey by car and informed Brian that he was trying to hire a helicopter. On the actual day the oil tycoon changed his mind again and decided not to go after all. He felt that renting a helicopter for £2,500 to see a pantomime in Stockport was maybe a bit extravagant, even for a multimillionaire.

By now word had leaked out that one of the richest men in the world was planning to see *Dick Whittington* in Stockport. The national newspapers got hold of the story and sent photographers to obtain pictures of the mysterious millionaire. When Brian and the Alderman arrived, the photographers refused to believe that Paul Getty was not with them and spent most of the performance searching the theatre for him. As Don Mosey commented later, the story they missed was that of an elderly BBC cricket commentator joining hundreds of small children and shouting happily, 'Oh no you won't!' and 'Behind you!'

A postscript to this strange episode was that Brian received a phone call from the producer of the television series *Noel's Addicts*, who had heard about his obsession with *Neighbours* and invited him on to the programme in March 1992. The series was presented by Noel Edmonds and featured various eccentric characters with bizarre obsessions or hobbies, such as collecting barbed wire or vacuum cleaners. 'I've often had half a mind to watch *Neighbours*,' said Edmonds, 'and I'm told that is all you need.' 'Oh no!' replied Brian earnestly. 'They do have a lot of rows, but they are all finished in about a week and they always say sorry, which I think is rather nice.'

To see whether he qualified as a true soap addict, Brian had to answer twelve questions about *Neighbours*; if he got ten answers right he was judged to be an addict. Louis Robinson was the production assistant responsible for setting the questions. 'We wondered whether to make them easy, so as not to embarrass him,' he recalls, 'but we all thought, "No, he'll be fine, let's make them normal."' Robinson was surprised to see how nervous Brian was in the green room before the show. 'He was such a huge fan of *Neighbours*,' says Robinson, 'it obviously meant a lot to him to get the answers right.'

The first question was the name of the suburb of Melbourne where *Neighbours* is supposed to take place. The answer was, and is, Erinsborough, but Brian was completely stumped. As a favour to Brian, Paul Getty had agreed to take part in the programme on the telephone in case he needed help. Even Getty could not guess the correct answer. Noel looked amazed. The production team wondered whether Brian was joking but realised that his mind had gone completely blank. Brian could not answer the next question either. 'He had frozen, like a rabbit caught in the headlights,' says Robinson. 'We did not know what to do.' From then on, things went from bad to worse. Noel asked ten more questions and Brian got almost every one wrong. At the end Noel looked rather embarrassed and did not know quite what to say. It was uncomfortable to watch, and for the first time I wondered whether age was finally catching up with Brian.

He may have been getting older but after he retired from *Down Your Way* he never used a secretary and insisted on answering all his letters personally. He would sit at his desk for a couple of hours every morning, often in his pyjamas, answering his correspondence in his spidery handwriting. He received an enormous amount of post every day but he argued that it was easier to reply himself than to dictate it all to a secretary. If he had been away it would often take him several days to catch up on his mail.

He used to keep in touch with his friends by sending them saucy seaside postcards; he ordered them in bulk from Bamforths and had a large pile of them in the cupboard in his study. His daughter Clare says that he would send her a postcard every week when she was at boarding school, wherever he was in the world, and she has kept many of them in a large box. 'I have a drawer full of his postcards,' admits Neil Durden-Smith, 'some of the filthiest postcards ever manufactured. I take them out occasionally and look at them and they still make me laugh.'

He would send cards to the most unlikely people. There is a marvellous photograph of Lord Home, the former Prime Minister, looking rather weak and frail, laughing out loud at the latest saucy postcard from Brian. 'My father had a third-form wit,' says Caroline Douglas-Home, 'and thought it very funny if someone fell over or got a black eye!' When Lord Home was in hospital in Winchester, following a stroke in the late 1980s, Brian sent him a succession of naughty postcards which he displayed proudly on the shelf next to his bed, in full view of the visiting ex-prime ministers and bishops. Matron did not approve.

Brian's closest friend was probably Lord Home's younger brother, William. They knew each other for more than sixty years and William used to call Brian 'Hook' or 'Hookey', after his large nose. The only time they had a falling-out was during the war when William was court-martialled. Brian admitted later that he felt guilty and ashamed that he had been 'too proud and superior' to help or even write to his friend in his time of need. His excuse was that the war had made him intolerant of anyone who did not conform. After the war was over he found it easier to comprehend William's principled stand and he made an effort to renew their friendship. They got back in touch, and in 1947 Brian was proud to attend the opening night of William's first successful play, *Now Barabbas*, which was based on his experiences in prison.

In his autobiography *Half-Term Report*, published in 1954, William paid this tribute to his old school friend: 'Brian is the only person I know of whom one can truthfully say "He loves life." Some people love children, some women, some themselves – but very few love all their fellow men. But Brian does and his reward on earth is that the world loves him.'

They used to ring each other constantly. When either of them heard a new joke they would immediately be on the phone. They could both remember jokes word for word. The problem with William was that he forgot where he had first heard them. Sometimes he would ring Brian with his latest one and Brian would say, 'Hey, that's mine! I told it to you two weeks ago!' William even used some of Brian's jokes in his work, and included one about a bank manager in his play *In the Red*. 'If there was a bad moment in a play,' admits his widow Rachel, now Lady Dacre, 'William would put in an old chestnut and get a laugh.'

They talked a lot about the theatre and Brian liked to know the latest gossip. He had seen literally hundred of productions in his time and was very knowledgeable about what worked in the theatre, especially comedy. He would often write to William after a first night and suggest a new punch-line or even a new ending. 'He was a very good critic,' says Lady Dacre, 'and he would tell William if he didn't think he had got it right.'

Brian even went so far as to become an 'angel', and in 1959 he invested £100 in William's play *Aunt Edwina*, about a master of foxhounds who has a sex change and becomes a woman. Brian thought it was extremely funny, but when it opened in the West End the critics savaged it. The play came off after only six weeks and Brian lost all his money. Twenty years later, for the second and last time, Brian was persuaded to back another play called *Outside Edge*, by Richard Harris, about a village cricket match. He lost his money again. The play won the Evening Standard Comedy of the Year Award but failed to make a profit in the West End, although it was later adapted to become a highly successful television series.

It was not only humour and the theatre which drew them together, but politics. Pauline says that Brian kept a list of all the Members of Parliament and knew most of their constituencies by heart. 'I wouldn't have minded being an MP,' he remarked once. 'I think I would have enjoyed the club atmosphere.' Pauline believes that he would not have been able to take the criticism. He never talked about politics in public because it was such a controversial subject. With William, however, he could be himself. 'Underneath it all they were two very serious men,' says Lady Dacre. 'They would have long talks about politics. It was another great bond between them.' William listed politics as his hobby, and as a young man he had stood for Parliament on several occasions. According to Lady Dacre, he enjoyed the campaigning and the debate, although he never really wanted to become an MP. 'If I ever win,' he declared, 'I'll be the first man to ask for a recount.'

In later years they used to meet up regularly with their friend Jimmy Whatman to play golf, William and Rachel against Brian and Jimmy. 'It was absolutely hilarious,' says Lady Dacre. 'No one was any good, but they were extremely competitive. The cheating was terrible. Brian would cough when you were about to putt.' They would often play at Liphook and take a break halfway round for lunch in the nearby pub. 'The golf was never very good after lunch,' confesses Lady Dacre, 'we all used to go to pieces.'

Brian was godfather to William's youngest daughter Dinah. On her twenty-first birthday he sent her a cheque for the sum of £99.99. There was a little note attached which read: 'I'm very sorry, but I can't afford a hundred.'

After William Douglas Home died in September 1992 Brian was heartbroken. Pauline says he never talked about it because it was too painful. One of the saddest speeches he ever had to make was at the thanksgiving service for William at St Martin-in-the-Fields. 'I had always hoped that William would do for me,' he began, 'what I am sad but honoured to be doing now for him. I especially wanted him because I knew that he would be kind, generous and witty.'

He concluded with a quote from William's first West End production, *Great Possessions*. 'I remember it had a very sad ending,' said Brian, 'and the dear old nanny walked across the room and looked out of the window. Outside it was raining hard. "I think," she said, "that God must be crying" – and the curtain fell.

'Well, the curtain has fallen now but unlike God we must not cry. William wouldn't like that. Somehow his loss has made the thought of dying oneself that much easier. If ever I get there I can look forward to being greeted by William at the gates of Heaven, asking for the latest joke, which he will then promptly tell to the angels.'

29

It's Been a Long Time

Now that he was in his mid-seventies Brian seemed to take on a new lease of life as a television celebrity, and he kept popping up on the most unlikely programmes. He sang a duet on *Highway* with Harry Secombe in the style of his old music-hall favourites the Western Brothers. He was a regular reviewer of the Sunday papers on TV-AM with David Frost. He appeared on *Noel's House Party* with Noel Edmonds and did a cricket commentary on *Jim'll Fix It* (or, as he wrote in his diary, *Jim'll Fix-up*) for an eight-year-old boy called Russell Doig whose ambition was to bowl for England. He was one of the guests on *This Is Your Life* with Graham Gooch, and later Dickie Bird, and he featured in a long-running television commercial for Yellow Pages, about a cricket umpire at Lord's. The satirical programme *Spitting Image* even featured a hilarious-looking puppet of Brian with bushy eyebrows and a very large nose, usually stuffing his face with chocolate cake.

He also made a cameo appearance in the award-winning series *Inspector Morse* when he was heard in the opening sequence of the episode 'Deceived by Flight'. In a story about a murder at a village cricket match, Morse was listening to Radio 3 in his car and became annoyed when Sergeant Lewis interrupted Haydn's Emperor Quartet to listen to Brian doing a cricket commentary on *Test Match Special.*

Brian loved word games such as Scrabble and Boggle, which he almost always won. One of his favourites was a spelling game that he would play with the family on long car journeys. He would start with a letter, usually 'H', and the next person had to add a letter before or after it without completing a word. It went round the car until someone got it wrong. The loser was 'a rotten egg' – three 'rotten eggs' and you were out. Brian was invariably the winner. So it was no surprise that he became a fan of the word game *Countdown* with Richard Whitely and Carol Vorderman after it was the first programme to be shown on Channel 4 in 1982. Five years later he was delighted when he was invited to appear as the guest celebrity in 'Dictionary Corner'.

'We were thrilled when he agreed to come on the programme,' says Richard Whitely. 'We were not as popular in 1987 as we are now and the fact that Brian was going to be on the programme helped us to be taken seriously. Now everybody wants to be on it.'

'He was very professional,' adds Whitely. 'In those days we did six half-hour shows a day, with a ten-minute break in between. During the break we would change our jackets, or our shirts and ties, to look different for each programme. Brian was such a pro that he would also change his trousers and sometimes even his shoes, although no one could see them behind the desk!'

The guest celebrities in Dictionary Corner sit next to the resident lexicographer and help to supply longer words at the end of each round. They are also required to tell a joke or a story leading into the commercial break. 'Many celebrities come armed with very little to say,' says Whitely, 'but Brian arrived with a wealth of material. He was one hundred per cent involved, even during the numbers rounds, and all through the programmes he kept coming up with little quips and jokes.'

Brian made thirty-seven appearances on *Countdown* over the next few years and he always enjoyed it. When he went on his annual winter trips to Australia or South Africa, he would ask Pauline Matthews, a family friend, to come in to Boundary Road and deal with his enormous post. 'Turn everything down,' he would instruct her, 'unless it is *Countdown*.' His legacy continues in an unexpected but characteristic way. 'I now call Carol Vorderman "Vorders",' reveals Richard Whitely, 'and she calls me "Whiters". That is a direct result of him being on the programme. So we are still under Brian's influence!'

In February 1989 he appeared on the ITV game show *You Bet* with Bruce Forsyth. The other celebrity guests were the motorbike stunt rider Eddie Kidd and the gymnast Suzanne Dando, and they all had to guess whether or not the contestants would succeed in performing some bizarre tricks. One man claimed he could guess the temperature of water to within 1°C by dipping his nose in it (he could), while another claimed he could throw darts and burst one hundred balloons in two minutes (he couldn't). At the end of the show the celebrity with the least number of points had to carry out a forfeit, which normally involved something unpleasant like having to wash a double-decker bus. Brian felt he was getting too old for all that, so he agreed to appear on the show on condition that he could choose as his forfeit to perform a cross-talk act. This was something he had always wanted to do on television and, bearing in mind that he had been doing the same jokes for fifty years, it was not exactly going to be a hardship.

Brian duly emerged as the loser at the end of the programme. Bruce Forsyth was probably expecting him to tell a couple of quick gags but Brian had come prepared. Unknown to Forsyth, he had arranged for his cross-talk act to be written up on cue cards. 'Oh,' said Bruce, looking rather taken aback, 'you've got it all written up!' For the next minute Brian led a bemused Bruce Forsyth in a cross-talk routine which included some of his oldest and corniest jokes:

BRIAN: I've just seen forty men under one umbrella and not one of them got wet.

BRUCE: Forty men under one umbrella and not one of them got wet? It must have been a very large umbrella.

BRIAN: No, it wasn't raining!

At the end of the 1989 cricket season Brian decided to take his four eldest children on a boat trip up the Thames. A few years earlier he had recorded an edition of *Down Your Way* at Wallingford, and he contacted the owner of a boatyard there to hire a boat for the weekend. There were seven of us altogether – Brian and myself, Clare and her husband David, Andrew and his wife Gilly, and

Ian. For the next four days we cruised slowly from Wallingford up to Maidenhead. Very slowly. Brian liked to be in charge and took control of the wheel, wearing an old captain's peaked cap and waving happily to the many passers-by who smiled and pointed at us. After about half an hour we realised that we were dragging the anchor behind us.

When we got to a lock, Ian leaped out to secure the boat, but when he tried to get back on board he fell into the water and had to be dragged out. This was not as bad as on a previous trip that Brian had taken with Andrew, John Woodcock and Jimmy Whatman, when they had tied up their boat on entering a lock. The lock-keeper had come running out to ask what on earth they were doing, as the water started to subside and the boat was left hanging on the side of the lock.

Brian could not bear the smell from the chemical toilet or the noise when it was pumped, so if anyone wanted to use it we had to moor the boat near to a pub or hotel and go ashore, which slowed down our progress even more. The captain's log consisted of a long list of emergency stops for the toilet.

In 1990 Radio 2 launched a new Saturday night programme called *Bob Holness Requests the Pleasure*, based on the format of *In Town Tonight*. It was a mixture of comedy, interviews and music, and Brian was asked whether he would like to contribute a weekly spot similar to 'Let's Go Somewhere'. He suggested an idea he had always wanted to do, which was to visit a different West End theatre each week and interview the stars in their dressing rooms. The spot was called 'Stage Door Johnners', and for eighteen weeks Brian was in his element as he interviewed West End stars such as Nigel Hawthorne, Donald Sinden and Eric Sykes. In reality the interviews were all pre-recorded over a period of several days because Brian had so many other commitments. The interviews highlighted Brian's genuine enthusiasm for the theatre, but the BBC obviously did not think they were worth preserving. Four years later I was commissioned to compile a recording of Brian's best broadcasts and I was disappointed to discover that every single recording of 'Stage Door Johnners' had been destroyed.

The Lord's Taverners celebrated their ruby anniversary in 1990, and on 1 November the then Prime Minister, Mrs Thatcher, hosted a charity reception in their honour at No. 10 Downing Street. Brian and Pauline were among the guests and duly arrived at 6.35 p.m. to be greeted by Mrs Thatcher and her husband Denis in the receiving line. 'Good evening,' she said. 'Good evening, Prime Minister,' replied Brian, but had no chance to say anything else as he found Mrs Thatcher's handshake firmly steering him into the room. Ben and Belinda Brocklehurst were also introduced to the Prime Minister. 'She was smiling,' observed Belinda, 'but I thought she had a steely glint in her eyes.'

Mrs Thatcher stayed for more than an hour, mingling and chatting with the guests. Brian and Pauline left a few minutes after she did. When they walked out of the front door of No. 10 they were met by a battery of lights and television cameras. As soon as the reporters recognised Brian, they all descended on him.

'How was the Prime Minister?' they shouted. 'Fine,' said Brian. 'What was her reaction to Sir Geoffrey's resignation?' they wanted to know. 'What resignation?' asked Brian, bewildered.

It turned out that Sir Geoffrey Howe, the Deputy Prime Minister, had tendered his resignation from the cabinet shortly before 6.30 p.m., signalling the beginning of the end of Mrs Thatcher's eleven years as Prime Minister. Yet five minutes later she had been greeting the Lord's Taverners as if nothing had happened. As soon as she had left the reception she had written her response to Sir Geoffrey, which was then read out on the *Nine o'Clock News*. Brian always considered it a remarkable performance. Four weeks later she was no longer Prime Minister.

The following year started well for Brian. He was awarded the CBE in the 1991 New Year's Honours list and on New Year's Day he and Pauline were invited to Chequers for lunch with the new Prime Minister, John Major. The other guests were mainly from the worlds of politics and cricket and Pauline was surprised to find herself sitting on Major's left-hand side, while Brian was put at the far end of the room with Jim Swanton. She had met John Major when he was Chancellor of the Exchequer and had visited the commentary box at Trent Bridge. He had only been Prime Minister for five weeks. 'He was very nervous,' says Pauline. 'He told me he didn't really know anybody.' Later Brian and Pauline were shown the portraits of the previous prime ministers hanging on the walls and noticed a space awaiting a picture of Mrs Thatcher.

The investiture for the CBE was held at Buckingham Palace on 5 March, and this time Andrew and I were able to attend the ceremony with Pauline. Everyone was requested to be in their seats in the ballroom an hour before the Queen arrived. The awards were handed out in alphabetical order, and by the time Brian's name was called we had been sitting on the hard gilt chairs for about two hours. The actual investiture was all over in a few seconds. As the Queen handed Brian his medal she leaned forward and murmured a few words. Afterwards I asked him what she had said. 'It's been a long time,' he replied. Several hours later he was still puzzling over exactly what she had meant.

In April there was a dinner for Paul Getty at Lord's Cricket Ground. One of the other guests was the cricket umpire Dickie Bird, so Brian invited him to stay overnight at Boundary Road. Bird is notorious for arriving hours early for every appointment and once turned up before 6 a.m. at the Oval for a county match not due to start till 11.30 a.m. After Brian suggested that he join them for tea, Dickie duly turned up at about 2.30 p.m. The next morning he seemed a bit overwhelmed by the hospitality. 'Thank you so much for allowing me to stay,' he said to Brian, as he was leaving. 'How much do I owe you?'

Brian returned to Buckingham Palace in June when he received an unexpected invitation to have lunch with the Queen. The other guests at the private lunch included a university professor and a captain of industry, and Brian was seated next to the Queen. When the cheese and biscuits were served, he was amazed to see her crumbling up the biscuits and flinging them over her shoulder on to the floor. All became clear when a footman opened the doors and the Queen's corgis came scurrying in to help themselves to the crumbs on the carpet. One of the dogs was an unusual shape and Brian asked the Queen what type of breed it was. 'It's a cross between a dachshund and a corgi,' Her Majesty said with a smile. 'We call it a dorgi.'

At the beginning of the 1991 cricket season Don Mosey published his autobiography entitled *The Alderman's Tale*. It caused a sensation. In the book Mosey was highly critical of *Test Match Special* and in particular what he described as the 'public school lot' of commentators. In the past season, he wrote, *TMS* had at times reached such a shambles of personal indiscipline that 'the programme has sounded somewhere between Gussie-Fink-Nottle's speech day address and the Monty Python Twit-of-the-Year contest'. He was bitterly disparaging about the public school backgrounds of Christopher Martin-Jenkins, Henry Blofeld and Peter Baxter. Only Brian seemed to emerge unscathed, although he was by no means beyond criticism.

It was an extraordinary book to publish when he was still a part of the commentary team. When he wrote it, however, Mosey had believed that he was about to be dropped from *TMS* because his style and his Northern accent were so different from the 'bland chorus of public school tones'. Unfortunately for him, he had totally misread the situation. His Yorkshire accent was the very reason that Peter Baxter wanted to keep him on. When Baxter asked Mosey to be a part of the commentary team for the series against the West Indies in 1991, it was too late to stop the publication of the book, and when its contents became public it made the situation in the commentary box almost impossible.

Brian hated to make a scene but he believed strongly in loyalty and friendship. He felt that his colleagues had been stabbed in the back. Shortly after the book was published, Brian, Peter Baxter and Mosey were staying at the same hotel in Birmingham. They had arranged to go out to dinner. Baxter waited in the bar for the other two to appear, but Brian turned up alone. 'I've told the Alderman I can't dine with him,' said Brian simply, 'and he understands.' They went out without him.

That was not the only incident that summer. On the first night of the fourth Test against the West Indies at Edgbaston, the BBC hosted a special dinner for the *TMS* team at the Pebble Mill studios. There was a frost in the air already because of Mosey's book but the atmosphere soon deteriorated even further. The tables had been laid out in an open square, which meant that people sitting opposite each other had almost to shout to be heard. As soon as the dinner started Fred Trueman began a fierce argument with the England manager Mickey Stewart, who was sitting opposite him, complaining bitterly that he had not been consulted about coaching the England fast bowlers.

Mike Lewis, the Head of Radio Sport and Outside Broadcasts, tried to defuse the situation by proposing a loyal toast. That only made matters worse. Everybody stood up except for Pat Murphy, a staunch republican, who stayed firmly rooted to his chair and refused to join in. 'Just exercising my democratic right,' repeated Murphy stubbornly, as the others drank to the health of the Queen. Brian's face was like thunder. He was furious at the disloyalty to the monarch but also at the downright bad manners. Peter Baxter thought he might retire on the spot. He went over to calm Brian down and said, 'I know what you're thinking, but don't do anything now.'

As soon as they had sat down again, Trueman continued where he had left off. 'And another thing . . . !' he shouted at Stewart. Mike Lewis recalls the evening as one of the most embarrassing moments in his BBC career. Two days later he was even more discomfited when the story was splashed across the front page of the *Daily Mirror*.

It was a difficult time for all concerned, especially as the very existence of *TMS* was under serious threat. Mrs Thatcher's government had declared its intention to force the BBC to surrender two of its medium-wave frequencies to the commercial radio operators. One of these was the Radio 3 medium waveband on which *TMS* was broadcast during the summer. As a result the BBC had announced plans for a new education and sports network, Radio 5, which it hoped would become the future home of *TMS*. It did not take a genius to work out that during the summer months cricket would have to compete for airtime on the new BBC network with other sports such as tennis, golf, football and athletics. It spelled the end of guaranteed ball-by-ball commentary on *TMS* after thirty-three years.

There was a public outcry. Questions were asked in the House of Commons and 140 MPs signed a motion deploring the proposed changes to ball-by-ball coverage. Tony Marlow, the Conservative MP for Northampton North, called for an urgent debate on the 'cultural vandalism of the BBC in its proposal to tamper with ball-by-ball commentary on *Test Match Special*'. He told MPs: 'Cricket, cathedrals, "Land of Hope and Glory" and an enduring mistrust of foreigners define classically the best of England. It would be a disaster and a catastrophe if any of these were damaged or destroyed.' John Wakeham, the Leader of the House, declined his request.

The Controller of Radio 5, Pat Ewing, responded to a barrage of letters in *The Times* by trying to reassure readers that there was no possibility of *TMS* losing its unique character, although she rather undermined her argument by admitting that the programme would have to share airtime with other sports.

Gillian Reynolds, the respected radio critic of the *Daily Telegraph*, wrote of *TMS*: 'It cannot be compared with any other kind of commentary. Longer, freer, yet with its own conventions and characteristics, it is an instant poem for six voices, fabricated daily, unique in the world. It could not have happened on any other than public service radio. It is an institution which I believe should be preserved.' As if to prove a point, the young readers of the *New Musical Express*, not previously noted for their devotion to cricket, voted *TMS* on to their list of top five radio programmes.

Matters came to a head when Paul Getty let it be known that he was prepared to buy his own radio station if necessary, in order to keep *TMS* on the air. In November 1991, after three years of constant pressure, the BBC finally relented and announced that ball-by-ball coverage on *TMS* would in future be broadcast without interruption on Radio 3 FM. For the second time in his career, a public campaign had forced the

BBC to change its mind and save one of Brian's programmes from the axe.

After Mosey retired at the end of the 1991 season, the friendly atmosphere on *TMS* soon returned. The following summer there was an endless supply of champagne and chocolate cakes in the commentary box as Brian celebrated his eightieth birthday. On the day itself he launched his third volume of autobiography, *Someone Who Was*, with a press reception at Lord's, and later that evening he treated the whole family to dinner at the Savoy.

To commemorate his birthday and his remarkable career, the BBC commissioned a bronze bust of Brian, sculpted by Neil Andrew, which was unveiled by the chairman of the BBC, Marmaduke Hussey, at a special reception in October. It was only the third time the BBC had ever commissioned such a bust – the other two are of Tommy Handley and Richard Dimbleby – and all three are now on display in the BBC Council Chamber.

He may have turned eighty but his diary reveals that he had few days off that year. In May there was another happy family occasion when I married Fiona Morrison. We had met at BBC Radio Sussex and were married at Southover Grange in Lewes, East Sussex, with my brother Andrew as our best man. We had wanted to get married in April but had to delay the wedding because Brian was so busy.

As well as *TMS* and promoting his new book, he had committed himself to helping out his friend Paul Getty. The oil tycoon had built a new cricket ground at Wormsley, his three-thousand-acre estate in the Chilterns, but he had no experience of arranging cricket matches, so he had turned to Brian for advice. Brian helped to organise everything, from sorting out the problems with the pitch to finding someone to make the sight screens, selecting the teams and arranging the fixtures list. He even advised Getty to serve Bath buns for tea.

The first match was held in May 1992, and for the rest of the summer, whenever he was not commentating on *TMS*, Brian spent his Sundays at Wormsley. As the match manager for the Getty eleven he felt responsible for the success of the operation, and he would be there by 10 a.m. to welcome the teams and their star guests, who might include Michael Caine, Claus von Bulow, Gary Lineker, John Major or even the Queen Mother. Brian was on his feet for most of the day, ensuring that everything ran smoothly. It was hard work, but he did not want to let his friend down.

To express his gratitude, Paul Getty commissioned a special weathervane that is now positioned on top of the pavilion roof. It is a silhouette of Brian's profile surrounded by a laurel wreath and is visible from all parts of the ground. In return, Brian presented Getty with a bronze bell for the pavilion, which is rung at the start of play each Sunday. Visitors have noticed that there is a curious inscription around the bell, which reads TMFOGP. It stands for: To My Friend Overlooking Green Park.

30

Aggers, Do Stop It

I was listening to the radio at home on Friday, 9 August 1991, when I heard an instant classic of radio comedy. Jonathan Agnew, the former Leicestershire and England bowler, had recently joined the *TMS* team as a summariser and was running through the scorecard with Brian at the end of the day. Earlier in the afternoon Ian Botham had got himself out in bizarre fashion by knocking a bail off with the inside of his leg. I was walking out of the sitting room when Agnew mentioned something about Botham not quite getting his leg over. I heard Brian's stifled chuckle and hurried back into the room. I knew he was going to get the giggles. By the time he stopped a minute or so later I had tears running down my face. It was, and still is, the funniest thing I have ever heard.

The original remark was not even Agnew's. He had been in the press box when Botham's wicket fell and John Etheridge of the *Sun* had whispered to him: 'I know what our headline will be tomorrow – Botham cocks it up by not getting his leg over!' In his defence, Agnew has said that he did not originally intend to pass on the comment, but when Brian started to talk about Botham doing the splits, the words just popped into his head. The rest, as they say, is history.

JOHNNERS: Botham, in the end, out in the most extraordinary way.

AGGERS: Oh, it was ever so sad really. It was interesting, because we were talking and he had just started to loosen up. He had started to look, perhaps, for the big blows through the off-side, for anything a little bit wide – and I remember saying, 'It looks as if Ian Botham is just starting to play his old way.'

It was a bouncer and he tried to hook it. Why he tried to hook Ambrose, I'm not sure, because on this sort of pitch it's a very difficult prospect. It smacked him on the helmet, I think – I'm not quite sure where it did actually hit him . . .

JOHNNERS: Shoulder, I think.

AGGERS: Shoulder, was it? As he tried to hook, he lost his balance, and he knew – this is the tragic thing about it – he knew exactly what was going to happen. He tried to step over the stumps and just flicked a bail with his right pad.

JOHNNERS: He more or less tried to do the splits over it and, unfortunately, the inner part of his thigh must have just removed the bail.

AGGERS: He just didn't quite get his leg over!

JOHNNERS: Anyhow (*chuckles*) . . . (*tinkle of china as Bill Frindall drops coffee cup into saucer in shock*) . . . he did very well indeed, batting one hundred and thirty-one minutes and hit three fours . . . (*Agnew buries face in hands and starts to giggle helplessly*) . . . and then we had Lewis playing extremely well for forty-seven not out . . . Aggers, do stop it . . . (*Frindall laughs loudly in background*) . . . and he was joined by DeFreitas who was in for forty minutes, a useful little partnership there. They put on thirty-five in forty minutes and then he was caught by Dujon off Walsh.

(*Snort from Frindall*) Lawrence, always entertaining, batted for thirty-five . . . (*Johnners starts to wheeze*) . . . thirty-five . . . (*gasping*) . . . minutes . . . hit a four over the wicket-keeper's h . . . (*high-pitched giggle*) . . . Aggers, for goodness' sake stop it . . . he hit a f . . . (*dissolves into uncontrollable laughter. Peter Baxter hisses at Agnew to say something.*)

AGGERS: Yes, Lawrence . . . extremely well . . . (*complete collapse*).

Both men are now speechless with laughter, tears rolling down their faces. Agnew turns desperately for help to Tony Cozier, sitting at the microphone on his left, busily writing an article on his word-processor. Cozier looks up, winks at Agnew, grins and carries on with his typing. Brian tries gamely to continue with the scorecard.

JOHNNERS: *(hysterical)* . . . He hit . . . *(his voice getting higher and higher)* he hit a four over the wicket-keeper's head and he was out for nine . . . *(crying and dabbing at his eyes with a large handkerchief)* . . . and Tufnell came in and batted for twelve minutes, then he was caught by Haynes off Patterson for two . . . *(calming down gradually)* . . . and there were fifty-four extras and England were all out for four hundred and nineteen . . . I've stopped laughing now . . .

Afterwards Brian used to claim that it was the most professional piece of broadcasting he had ever done because he tried to keep on talking, in spite of everything. But at the time he was furious with himself for losing control and felt that he had been badly let down by his colleagues. 'Brian was appalled,' says Peter Baxter, 'and so was I. He was very professional and expected others to be so. That is why it upset him.' Brian was cross with Tony Cozier for not coming to his rescue. 'It did flash through my mind at the time,' says Cozier, 'but only for a split second.' Like countless others he had been a victim of Brian's practical jokes and he admits that he took a special delight in turning the tables for once.

The next morning Baxter was surprised to discover that BBC engineers had made secret copies of the giggle and it had already been played on several radio breakfast programmes. Later it was selected for *Pick of the Week* on Radio 4 and someone even suggested that it be entered for a Sony Award. 'How can you enter a mistake for an award?' wondered Baxter.

The letters and phone calls started to flood in. Thousands of drivers had been listening in their cars on their way home and many of them had been forced to pull into the side of the road until they had calmed down. Tim Rice laughed so hard that he thought he was going to endanger his fellow motorists. Ronnie Corbett rang to say that his wife Ann had to stop on the hard shoulder of the M1. A listener called Paul Brookbanks wrote that he was laughing out loud when he pulled up behind a police car at some roadworks in Peterborough. The policeman got out of his car and walked slowly back to the driver to ask him exactly what he found so amusing – just as Brian returned to normal. The poor man tried to explain that he had been listening to a cricket commentary on the radio, but he could tell that the policeman did not believe a word of it.

Another listener, Jane Wardman from Leeds, had been confined to bed for several weeks with pneumonia. She was feeling fed up and depressed. Then she heard the 'leg-over' incident on the radio and for the first time in many weeks, wrote Jane, 'laughed until the tears streamed down my face'.

There were even reports of a two-mile tailback at the entrance to the Dartford Tunnel on the M25, because some drivers were laughing so much that they were unable to go through the tollbooths.

On the Monday following the broadcast the BBC's Head of Litigation, Diana Adie, received an urgent fax from Tony Alexander, a solicitor with a firm called Heffrons in Milton Keynes. It read as follows:

> *Dear Sir,*
> **Re: Cricket Commentary – Friday 9 August 1991**
> *We have been consulted by Mr Wally Painter and his wife Dolly. On Friday evening our clients were in the process of redecorating their hallway. Mr Painter was perched on a ladder in the stairwell of his house, whilst Mrs Painter held the ladder steady. Our clients' aquarium with assorted tropical fish was situated at the foot of the stairwell.*
>
> *Our clients are keen cricket enthusiasts, and were listening to the summary of the day's play on Radio Three, when Mr Brian Johnston and Mr Jon Agnew were discussing Mr Ian Botham's dismissal, which apparently involved some footwork which Mr Botham failed to consummate.*
>
> *The ensuing events caused a vibration in the ladder and, in spite of Mrs Painter's firm grasp, Mr Painter fell off the ladder, landing awkwardly on the partial landing, thereby dislocating his left wrist. The ladder fell on Mrs Painter, who suffered a contusion to her forehead.*
>
> *The 5 litre drum of Dulux Sandalwood Emulsion fell and*

crashed through the aquarium, which flooded the hallway,
depositing various frantically flapping exotic fish onto a Persian
rug. The Painters' pedigree Persian cat (Mr Painter spent many
years in Tehran as an adviser to the late Shah) grabbed one of
the fish, a Malayan red-spined Gurnot, and promptly choked
to death.

The water seeped down into the cellar where the electricity
meters are located. There were several short circuits, which
resulted in (a) the main switchboard being severely damaged
and (b) the burglar alarm (which is connected to the local police
station) being set off.

Meanwhile, Mr and Mrs Painter were staggering towards
the bathroom, apparently in paroxysms of hysterical laughter
despite their injuries. Within minutes, the police arrived, and
believing the Painters to be vandals and suspecting, as both
were incoherent, that they had been taking drugs, promptly
arrested them.

We are now instructed to inform you that our clients hold the
Corporation liable for:–

(a) Their personal injuries.

(b) The loss of the aquarium and various exotic fish collected
over several years.

(c) The damage to the Persian rug.

(d) Damage to the electrical installation and burglar alarm.

(e) Death of the cat.

However, they are prepared to settle all claims for damages
in respect of the above provided that you supply them with a
recording of the discussion between Mr Johnston and Mr Agnew,
together with an undertaking from Mr Johnston and Mr Agnew
that they will not in future discuss Mr Botham's footwork or
lack of it, while Mr and Mrs Painter are decorating their
property.

Yours faithfully,

Heffrons

I am happy to report that they received their tape.

After that Peter Baxter made sure that Brian and Jonathan Agnew were never on air at the same time. All went well until about a year later, when Baxter thought it would be safe to try them together again. One afternoon Brian and Aggers were answering listeners' letters during the tea interval. As the umpires were coming out Jonathan picked one final letter from the pile and started to read it out. 'Can you please explain why in the game of cricket an appeals procedure is necessary or justifiable,' he began. 'This comes from . . .' He caught sight of the name and sniggered. '. . . Berkshire!'

Agnew handed the letter quickly to Brian, who tried to take over. 'It's not the Prime Minister William Pitt . . .' he chortled, suddenly spotting the name. '. . . but this is William H. *Titt* . . . and he says . . .' It was too much for him. He collapsed in silent mirth, tears pouring down his face. For a moment the only sounds to be heard over the airwaves were wheezes and giggles. Fortunately this time Trevor Bailey was at hand.

'The umpires are coming out,' he said, stepping in firmly. Brian was still unable to speak. 'Yes, here they are, Johnners,' said Agnew, calming down. 'You move over. I'll do some commentary.' As the game restarted out on the pitch, Brian had to be helped, still weeping, from the box.

As he approached eighty Brian found it harder to control himself. The slightest hint of anything risqué would get him going. Jonathan Agnew recalls an incident during the fifth Test against Pakistan at the Oval in 1992 when Waqar Younis beat Mike Atherton outside the off-stump. 'Fine delivery that,' commented Agnew. 'Yes,' replied Trevor Bailey, sitting alongside him. 'It's remarkable how he can whip it out just before tea.' Total collapse of Johnners at the back of the box, making commentary on the next delivery, according to Agnew, 'a supreme effort'.

Brian received hundreds of letters from listeners every summer and Peter Baxter says that more than half the *TMS* postbag used to be addressed to Brian. One day he was proud to receive a letter all the way from Iraq. 'I've got a letter here, Aggers,' said Brian, 'from a Mr Richter in Baghdad. He says he loves listening to the cricket commentary as it keeps him in touch with home. Well, Mr Richter, thank you for your letter. It must be lovely in Baghdad at this time of year. Plenty of sunshine, nice and hot . . .' Brian continued in this same vein for a while before moving on to the next topic. The next day he received another letter, from the Friends of Ian Richter, pointing out that the poor man had been languishing in an Iraqi jail for more than five years on a false spying charge and was tuning in to the World Service from his tiny prison cell.

Brian was terribly embarrassed and apologised profusely on air for his mistake, but the story had a happy ending. Richter was released by the Iraqis in November 1991, and the following summer he was able to join Brian in the commentary box at Old Trafford as his special guest on 'A View from the Boundary'.

Brian was renowned for his practical jokes in the box but his fellow commentators would occasionally get their own back. The stakes seem to have been raised when Jonathan Agnew joined the team as the new BBC cricket correspondent in 1991.

At first Agnew was a summariser, so he and Brian would frequently be on air together, which provided plenty of opportunity for them to play jokes on each other. When Agnew moved on to being a commentator, however, they usually broadcast at different times. This meant that any practical jokes required advance planning.

Neville Oliver was the popular Australian commentator, promptly renamed 'Dr NO' as soon as Brian saw his initials listed on the commentators' rota. During the 1993 Ashes series Agnew recruited the Doctor to help him to pull off a classic practical joke. They had received a list of the people who would be making the presentations on the pavilion balcony after the match. Agnew talked his idea over with the Doctor and then surreptitiously typed an additional name at the bottom of the list, photocopying the page to make it look more realistic. Before the presentation ceremony he handed the paper over to Brian, who proceeded to read the list out on the air, including the surprise announcement that also present on the balcony was the managing director of the Cornhill Insurance Group, Mr Hugh Jarce. The laughter in the box was long and loud, and Brian enjoyed it as much as anyone. As Neville Oliver would observe later, it was a rarity to catch Brian so perfectly.

Before the start of the regular *Test Match Special* broadcast that summer there was an extra half-hour programme at 10.30 a.m. on Radio 5, presented by Jonathan Agnew. It began with an upbeat signature tune which required Jonathan to give a summary of the state of play in exactly seven seconds, sounding more like a Radio 1 disc jockey than a Radio 3 cricket commentator. He used to practise it over and over in order to get the timing right and Brian always found it most amusing.

On the Sunday morning of the Test match at Headingley, Brian was the first one in the commentary box as usual, when Peter Baxter rushed in to say that Agnew was going to be late and he would have to do the Radio 5 programme instead. With only minutes to spare, Brian had to write and rehearse his seven-second summary, speaking ever faster over the signature tune, as Baxter kept urging him to do it one more time. 'Still a bit long, Johnners . . . need to lose another second if you can . . .' After several, increasingly frantic, attempts it was time to go on air and, being the consummate professional, Brian did it perfectly.

It was only then that Agnew burst laughing into the box and Brian realised that he had been had. There *was* no Radio 5 programme on Sunday morning. The engineers had recorded the whole episode and for the rest of the day Agnew gleefully played the tape to anyone who would listen, saying that Brian had been unable to get the summary right. 'In fact he was spot on first time,' recalls Baxter, 'as I knew he would be.'

'It made up into a brilliant tape,' says Richie Benaud. 'It was funny and a very good practical joke which Brian took in good part. Trouble was, Aggers wanted to tell the world about it. I thought at the time that this could be a very dangerous thing to do.'

Brian did not wait long to extract his revenge. 'He worked on the basis of never get angry, just get even,' adds Benaud, 'and when he played a joke it was always a beauty. The one he came up with during the next Test at Edgbaston was a ripper. It remains my favourite.'

On the Saturday morning of the match Keith McKenzie, the producer/director of BBC TV cricket, approached Agnew and asked him whether he would record an interview for *Grandstand* during the lunch interval. The subject was to be England's lack of fast bowlers. The interview had to be precisely ten minutes long and hard hitting in content. McKenzie also dropped a hint that there might at some stage be a place for someone new in the television team.

Agnew readily agreed and that lunchtime he sat in front of the cameras with Fred Trueman and Jack Bannister, both former fast bowlers and now respected cricket experts, to record the interview. Trueman was puffing on a huge cigar and blew smoke over Agnew just before they began. Undeterred, Agnew put his first question to Bannister, who replied bluntly, 'I've got no idea.' He turned quickly to Trueman, who took another long puff on his cigar and muttered darkly, 'Don't know.'

Agnew began to sweat, not helped by Keith McKenzie yelling in his earpiece that it was the worst interview he had ever seen. The minutes ticked slowly by. Trueman, when asked about pitches, wandered off into a dissertation on fly-fishing and its benefits to fast bowlers in the strengthening of the shoulder muscles. Bannister contributed an unrelated story about the wrist spinner Eric Hollies and how he almost won a game against Lindsay Hassett's Australian side in 1953. The final straw was when Trueman began talking about damp-proof courses.

At the end of the longest ten minutes in his life, Agnew handed back to the mythical *Grandstand* studio in despair, saying, 'I don't think we have answered too many questions there, gentlemen.' He sat stunned in his chair, imagining his television career to be in ruins. Suddenly his earpiece crackled into life. 'I think the veteran long-nosed commentator might have got his revenge!'

chuckled a well-known voice. Brian had been sitting alongside Keith McKenzie throughout the interview.

He had persuaded the whole of the BBC TV outside broadcast team to give up their lunch break, simply to set up Agnew. You did not beat the master that easily.

31

An Evening with Johnners

At the beginning of 1993 the England cricket team were due to undertake a short tour of India. It was one of the few places in the world where Brian had never commentated on a Test match. Trevor Bailey and his wife Greta were organising a group of about twenty people to watch two of the Tests, and he persuaded Brian and Pauline to join them. Brian's main concern, as one might expect, was the food, but once Bailey had reassured him that the modern Indian hotels would be able to cater to his fastidious tastes, he agreed to go.

Brian and Pauline were very nervous about going to India. There had been riots and killings in Bombay in the previous weeks and they were both petrified of catching the dreaded 'Delhi belly'. Brian did not drink whisky but he had been told that a drop of Scotch each day would kill any lingering bugs, so he bought the largest bottle he could find in the duty-free shop at Heathrow Airport.

After a delayed flight to Delhi, they finally got into bed at their hotel, the Taj Palace, at 3 a.m. Three hours later Brian and Pauline had to get up again because they had booked a car to take them to see the Taj Mahal. Still half asleep, they left at 7 a.m. in thick fog for the four-hour drive to Agra. This was their first sight of India, and they were shocked by the chaotic traffic on the roads. Their driver kept his hand permanently on his horn as he narrowly avoided crashing into lorries, cars, bicycles, people, cattle and even a team of camels.

After two hours Pauline had endured enough. She told Brian that they must have been mad to have considered doing the journey. 'He agreed with me,' she believes, 'but he wouldn't admit it!' They were appalled by the poverty and the squalor. 'Every building looked a wreck, as if nobody cared any more,' says Pauline. 'All along the sides of the road were shacks and tarpaulin-covered sheds, crumbling houses, crumbling shops – not a sign of decent habitation.'

When they arrived at the Taj Mahal the fog lifted at last to give them a glimpse of its cool, majestic splendour. They had to admit that it did look spectacular, but after lunch in a nearby hotel they had to undergo another four-hour journey back again.

'India was a mistake,' says Peter Baxter. 'Brian was not happy. If you've never seen India before, it is crazy to drive from Delhi to Agra. It took a lot out of him.'

The next morning they had to be up early again at 3.15 a.m. to catch their flight to Madras. They arrived at the airport to find that their flight had been delayed because of the fog. Their group were stranded all day with barely any information, few refreshments and nowhere to sit. Brian's extraordinary ability to remain cheerful at all times raised everyone's spirits. 'No airport is a good place to spend eight hours,' remarks Trevor Bailey, 'especially Delhi, but Brian kept everyone amused under the most difficult circumstances.'

He may have cheered everyone else up but he must have been exhausted. He was eighty years old and had spent more than two days either travelling or sitting around in airports.

For the next few days in Madras they watched the second Test match. Brian did two sessions of commentary a day, fulfilling his ambition to broadcast from India. This was the infamous Test during which the England players went out for a prawn curry on the first night of the match and half the team, including the captain Graham Gooch, came down with food poisoning. Brian and Pauline were given a packed lunch by their hotel but took one look at it and decided to eat just the bread roll. They studiously avoided all salads, fish and spicy food and stuck mainly to omelettes, chicken and meat cutlets, which they suspected were actually goat. Every night Brian would take a dose of his whisky, which he drank like medicine. 'He hated it,' says Peter Baxter.

At least the tour produced a new joke. 'They've introduced a new dish especially for the English,' Brian told everyone on his return. 'It's called Boycott Curry. You still get the runs, but more slowly!'

After a week in Madras they flew to Bombay for the third Test. In spite of all their efforts, Pauline succumbed to a bad case of Delhi belly. She managed to visit Gandhi's house but spent most of the week in her hotel bathroom. When the Test was over they were both glad to leave for Goa, but once again they were delayed at the airport when it was discovered that Greta Bailey had thrown away their air tickets. Trevor had to borrow money from the rest of the group to buy some new tickets before they could leave.

At first, Goa looked marvellous. They stayed at the Taj Holiday Village, which consisted of individual cottages and apartments alongside miles of golden, sandy beaches. Brian and Pauline's apartment was set slightly apart from the rest, and every morning their waiter would cycle out to their apartment, carrying their English breakfast on a large tray balanced carefully on his shoulders.

On their final night in Goa, Pauline was woken by the noise of scratching in their room. She got up and searched all round the room with her torch but found nothing. 'Go back to sleep,' murmured Brian, and turned over. The next morning they were packing their suitcases after breakfast. Brian always packed his own case, very neatly. He had emptied the top and second drawers and opened the bottom drawer to remove his shirts. Out leaped a huge rat. They both screamed as it shot across the room and under their twin beds.

Brian grabbed the telephone and called for help. Soon afterwards a man turned up on a bicycle carrying a carpet brush and a dustpan. While Pauline stayed firmly outside, Brian and the man cautiously entered the apartment. They tipped up the twin beds and found rat droppings all over the floor – and the rat. For the next few minutes Brian shouted hysterically as the man chased the rodent around the room, hitting it and eventually killing it with the back of the brush. Finally he emerged triumphantly from the apartment, holding the rat up by its tail. 'I don't know who looked whiter by this time,' says Pauline, 'Brian or me!'

They arrived back in England on 4 March. 'We did not enjoy our first trip to India and Goa,' reflects Pauline sadly, 'but perhaps we were just unlucky.' It had been a gruelling experience, but Brian had no time to recover. A week later he would embark on a new venture.

Since his retirement from the BBC in 1972 he had been inundated with offers to speak at cricket clubs, ladies' luncheons, Rotary Clubs, business dinners and other events all over the country. His diary was so full that he had to turn down as many as he accepted, but still he averaged about forty after-dinner speeches a year. He loved to make people laugh and it was an opportunity to earn some decent money for the first time in his life. Unfortunately, sometimes the venue left a bit to be desired.

Peter Baxter recalls Brian telling him about a speech he had given at Old Trafford. It was a stag dinner shortly before Christmas. From past experience Brian knew that these evenings tended to get a bit out of hand so, when he arrived, he asked the chairman of the dinner whether he could go on early. He was assured that everything would be all right. After the coffee and brandy had been served the first speaker was introduced, a local comedian, who spoke for about twenty minutes. As he sat down to warm applause, Brian turned to the chairman. 'Am I on now?' he whispered. 'In a minute,' he was told.

Another comedian was introduced. He also spoke for about twenty minutes before sitting down to enthusiastic applause. 'Am I on now?' urged Brian. 'Very soon,' he was promised. Next came the auction, which went on for about half an hour. By the end of it Brian was becoming increasingly impatient. 'Now?' he asked, preparing to stand up. 'Won't be long,' came the reply, as two strippers in Father Christmas outfits entered the room. Accompanied by a chorus of loud, drunken cheers, the girls proceeded to take off all their clothes before circulating round the tables, where they sat on everyone's laps, cuddling the guests and letting them fondle their boobs. When the girls finally left the room they received a thunderous reception. By now it was after midnight. 'Now,' announced the chairman, as the hubbub died down, 'the moment you've all been waiting for. Brian Johnston!'

'How did you get on?' enquired Peter Baxter curiously. 'I died a death,' replied Brian.

The booking agents for his after-dinner speeches were Dabber and Paddy Davis, who ran the Associated Speakers lecture agency in Hayes, Middlesex. 'Regular as clockwork, Brian would phone up on the morning after every booking,' chuckles Dabber. 'He would report in as if he was returning from some secret assignment. "All went well, Dabber," he would say. "Mission accomplished!"'

In 1983 Brian was approached by a theatre in Evesham to see whether he would be interested in doing a one-man show, 'An Evening with Brian Johnston'. Dabber thought it would be a good idea and encouraged Brian to do it. For the first half of the show he talked about his life and career, mixed with a liberal helping of old jokes and anecdotes, and in the second half he answered questions from the audience. It went well, and over the next few years he performed several more 'Evenings with . . .' at theatres up and down the country. He had so many stories to tell that after a while he dropped the questions and answers and carried on talking for the whole show.

Dabber Davis recalls going to see one performance at the Sevenoaks Festival in June 1989. Brian was so used to appearing at cricket dinners and business functions that he asked Dabber whether he should wear a dinner jacket. Dabber replied that if he did he would probably frighten half the audience to death. As usual, the evening went down well, although Dabber remembers driving home afterwards with Brian seeking constant reassurance: 'Was that all right? Did they like it? Are you sure?'

After Brian celebrated his eightieth birthday in June 1992 he showed no sign of slowing down. He had the energy and sharpness of mind of a man ten – or even twenty – years younger, and could look back on a full and varied life and an extraordinary career, but there was one ambition left unfulfilled. He had always dreamed of being a stand-up comedian. He was now about to get his chance from a most unlikely source.

During the summer I had a call at Radio Sussex from an old friend of mine, Jeff Watts. Jeff had been the bass player for my group Design back in the 1970s and was now working with the concert promoter John Martin. He wanted to know whether I thought Brian would be interested in doing a nationwide tour of his one-man show. Brian was intrigued by the idea and said that if Jeff could find any theatres to book him, he would give it a try.

'We decided to call the tour "An Evening with Johnners",' says John Martin. 'We thought that would make it sound more light hearted and chatty – more like him.' The first show was at the Hawth Theatre in Crawley on 11 March 1993. 'When I arrived at the theatre,' says John Martin, 'Brian was already up on the stage briefing the lighting people, as if he'd been doing it for years. I was surprised at his professionalism. He knew exactly what he wanted.'

I went to see the show at Crawley. I had heard all the stories at least a dozen times before but soon found myself laughing out loud along with the rest of the audience. In the words of the comedian Frank Carson, it was the way he told them. Brian had a natural gift of comic timing and delivered a punch-line with such obvious delight that you could not help but laugh, no matter how corny the gag.

'From what I can see of the audience,' he used to begin, 'I am willing to bet that I am the oldest man in the theatre tonight and I am going to warn you about what's going to happen when you get to my age. Three things happen: first thing is you lose your memory . . . (pause) . . . and I can't remember what the other two things are!'

The audience loved it. He had no props. He sat on a high wicker stool, with a table alongside him for his glass of water, and occasionally a vase of flowers. That was it. No notes or lists to jog his memory. Everything was in his head. For two hours he would tell his jokes and stories with wit and style, with no hesitation and no mistakes. It would have been a bravura performance for a comedian or an actor of any age, but Brian was then nearly eighty-one years old.

He made it look so easy that it seemed unrehearsed, but he was always trying to improve his act. Jeff Watts says that, in the car on the way home, Brian would go over that night's performance, checking whether the audience had enjoyed it. After I saw him in Crawley, the first thing he wanted to know was which jokes had not worked. There was one story about Eton which I thought had fallen a bit flat. He never told it again.

The tour was a tremendous success. Between March and May Brian performed twenty shows, from Richmond in Yorkshire to Taunton in Somerset. 'He sold out everywhere,' says John Martin, 'I don't think there was a single theatre that was not full.' The Chichester Festival Theatre held more than 1,300 people and sold out in record-breaking time. Patrick Garland, then the artistic director of the Festival Theatre, told Dabber Davis it was the best one-man show they had ever put on there. 'I'll tell you how good he was,' said Garland. 'We had Dustin Hoffman here three weeks ago and the place was only half full!'

'We really thought he would get a mainly male, cricket audience,' adds John Martin, 'but we underestimated the popularity of *Down Your Way*. There were a large number of middle-aged and elderly ladies and many of them were on their own. There were also plenty of younger men who knew him from *Test Match Special*. It was a real cross-section of all ages.'

Brian treated the tour as an excuse to catch up with his friends, and his tour manager Joe Palmer would often have to pick him up several hours early so that he could have lunch or tea with someone on the way. It made the day seem more like fun than work. There was only one stipulation: he must not miss *Neighbours*. Joe had to plan his itinerary carefully so that he would collect Brian after the lunchtime edition of *Neighbours* or else get him to a friend's house or a hotel in time to watch the teatime edition.

Brian liked to arrive at the theatre early so that he could get a feel for the stage. He would sit on his stool and chatter away until he felt comfortable. Then he would retire to his dressing room, where he made himself at home, listening to his radio, doing the *Daily Telegraph* crossword and enjoying cups of tea and a plate of biscuits.

One of the shows was at the King's Lynn Arts Centre in Norfolk. There was some time to spare before the performance, so Joe Palmer and his son decided to go out for something to eat. 'Where are you going?' enquired Brian. 'McDonald's,' replied Joe. 'I'll come with you,' said Brian, who had never been near a Big Mac in his life. Afterwards Joe told John Martin that he had felt highly embarrassed at taking Brian Johnston to McDonald's but that he had seemed to enjoy the experience.

After the performance Brian would go round to the front of the theatre to sign books and meet the audience. He must have been tired after two hours onstage but, even though he wanted to go home, he always made time for his fans. Jeff Watts says that the phrase he remembers Brian uttering the most was 'people are so kind'. In spite of his years of experience, Brian never got over the fact that complete strangers were prepared to go out on a cold, wet and windy night and pay to hear him talk for a couple of hours.

I was so impressed with what I had seen at Crawley that I arranged for a recording of the show to be made a month later at the Marlowe Theatre in Canterbury. I thought it would be something to play to my children or grandchildren in years to come. When I listened to the recording, however, it sounded as good as any comedy record I had ever heard. I had formed a production company called BarryMour Productions with my former BBC radio producer Chris Seymour, so I approached Roger Goldbold at Listen For Pleasure, the EMI spoken-word label. He thought it would be a great idea to release the recording of 'An Evening with Johnners' as an audio cassette.

Brian was unsure at first. He worried that if people could buy a cassette of his best anecdotes, there would be no need for them to buy tickets to see him in person. I persuaded him that the performance was so good that it would encourage people to see him even more. In the end he conceded, probably more as a favour to me than because he believed it was true. Chris Seymour and I edited the recording and EMI agreed to release it to coincide with the second tour in October.

The final night of the first tour was at the Pavilion Theatre in Worthing. 'We wanted to take him out for a meal in a restaurant,' says John Martin, 'but he didn't seem very interested. I think he was a bit fussy about his food. We had heard that he liked Bollinger champagne, so on the last night I presented him with a magnum of Bollinger.' Brian was sitting in his dressing room, chatting with Colin Cowdrey before the show, when John Martin walked in with the magnum. Brian's eyes lit up when he saw the bottle.

'Thank you very much,' he said gratefully. 'At the end of the next tour, will there be something similar?'

32

The Light Fades

The morning after his first tour of 'An Evening with Johnners' ended at Worthing, Brian had to drive up to Manchester for the start of the cricket season, with a series of one-day internationals followed by six Test matches against Australia. He also had a new series of *Trivia Test Match* to record every week, and in June there was the launch of the paperback edition of *Someone Who Was*, which involved a number of book signings and interviews.

On top of all this he was still committed to helping Paul Getty with his cricket matches at Wormsley. He was up early every Sunday to undertake the fifty-minute journey to Buckinghamshire, arriving at about 10 a.m. and never leaving before about 7.15 p.m. He did not have a single Sunday at home all summer.

On the surface he seemed to be coping well, but Peter Baxter noticed there was something different about him. 'He started to leave things behind,' says Baxter, 'like a raincoat or a pen. It was something he didn't do. Others forgot things but never him; he was always so efficient. I was surprised and I thought, Oh, he must be getting old.'

None of his colleagues had noticed anything. 'At eighty-one, he was still at his peak,' says Trevor Bailey. Brian, however, was becoming concerned about his age and worried that he might be outstaying his welcome on *TMS*. At the end of the cricket season he wrote to Mike Lewis, the Head of Radio Sport and Outside Broadcasts, to ask whether it might be a good time for him to step aside. On 5 November 1993, Mike Lewis replied, assuring him that his job was secure. 'As far as your future on *TMS* is concerned,' he wrote, 'it is very simple. Peter [Baxter] and I want you to be a part of the team for as long as you feel fit and think it is a fun thing to do. Age does not come into decisions we take about the commentators. We want you to lead the team for as long as possible, so please don't even consider stepping aside. You are a National Treasure but one that is still in full working order. Long may that continue!'

I wondered whether Mike Lewis had ever considered that Brian was too old to continue as a cricket commentator. 'No,' he says, 'we all agreed that he sounded as good as ever. Brian wanted me to promise to tell him if I felt his standards were slipping. I would have done, but I feel sure that he would have recognised it himself long before me.'

Brian's final Test commentary was at the Oval on 23 August 1993 and, although he was not to know it, he ended as he would have wished, with a memorable England victory by 161 runs against Australia. As soon as the cricket season was over in early September he escaped down to Swanage for two weeks and then flew out to Hong Kong with Pauline for the World Sixes Tournament at Kowloon. He had been invited to do the television commentary for the international knockout competition, which was won unexpectedly by England. His last words as a cricket commentator were on 2 October 1993: 'And they'll get two. And England have won!'

A friend who was on the same flight home said that Brian looked tired and uncomfortable. He was suffering from sciatica down his right leg and the pain was getting him down. He had been examined by a doctor but they could not find the cause. For the first time he was beginning to look his age.

Two days after returning from Hong Kong in early October Brian started his second tour of 'An Evening with Johnners'. This time there would be thirteen shows spread over two months. He was planning to add one or two new stories so Chris Seymour and I went to record the fifth show at the Orchard Theatre in Dartford. In the dressing room beforehand Brian told me that he was going to try out a new joke: 'What do you call a cat that has just eaten a duck? A duck-filled fatty-puss!'

The first half of the show went as planned but during the second half, when he tried to tell the joke, he could not remember the punch-line. 'A duck-billed . . . no, a fat-filled . . .' In the end he had to give up and, with an embarrassed chuckle, he went on to the next joke, which received a big laugh. But he looked shaken and so was I. It was the first time I had ever seen him forget his words onstage. It was a sign that he was getting tired.

A week earlier I had been contacted by a researcher from the daytime TV programme *Kilroy* to see whether Brian and I would like to take part in an edition about 'Fathers and Sons'. He had heard that we got on well together and thought that we might add a note of optimism to the programme. Brian agreed, rather to my surprise. As I have explained earlier, he did not like talking about relationships and he certainly did not need the £150 fee. At that time I was presenting a late-night programme on Radio Sussex and I suspect that he thought it might help my career.

On 21 October a car took us to Teddington Studios for the recording. The programme is normally 'live' but it was explained to us that this edition would be recorded for transmission at a later date. We sat in the front row of the audience and listened as Robert Kilroy-Silk questioned several of the other guests about the problems they had encountered with their fathers.

After a while Brian turned to one of the other guests and remarked, 'I found it very touching when you said to your father "I love you" and he said "I love you too", because I'm ashamed to say I don't think I have ever said to Barry "I love you". I hope I've shown it by my kindnesses, maybe.'

Robert Kilroy-Silk looked astonished. 'Why not?' he asked.

'I don't know,' answered Brian. 'Reserve? I say it to my wife!'

The audience started to laugh. 'I hope you say it to your wife,' said Kilroy-Silk. 'Are you conscious that you feel the love?'

'Oh, yes,' responded Brian.

'But you're conscious that you've never said it?' enquired Kilroy-Silk.

Brian struggled to explain. 'I thought, "Actions speak louder than words,"' he replied, 'and I hoped that I was kind.'

'You've definitely shown it,' I reassured him.

'Tell him,' Kilroy-Silk urged Brian. 'Tell him.' Brian looked hesitant.

'I love *you*,' I told my father at last, 'so that's all right.'

'I love you too,' he said, laughing, as the audience applauded, 'but that's the first time we've said it!'

It was extraordinary that such a private man should have been so open about his feelings for the first time on national television. I think that afterwards he could not quite believe he had actually said it. Pauline says she remembers us both walking in when we returned to Boundary Road for lunch after the programme, clearly feeling very emotional.

In a very English way, we had always known that we loved each other and had never felt the need to say it. But I am very glad that we did. The programme was shown as a tribute to Brian two days after he died.

A week later we appeared onstage together for the one and only time. It was a charity show at the Wimbledon Theatre to raise money for the Home Farm Trust, which cares for Joanna, and was billed as 'Brian Johnston and Son – an afternoon's entertainment with Brian and his son Barry'. For about two hours we took turns telling jokes and anecdotes. I played and sang some Noël Coward songs on the piano and in the second half we combined to re-create Brian's old cross-talk act with John Ellison from *In Town Tonight*. We ended the show with a spoof version of the old 'Yes/No' game from *Take Your Pick*, with Brian pretending to be Michael Miles. The audience seemed to enjoy it and we made a small profit for the charity.

Afterwards Brian told me that he would like us to do it again. He had another tour booked for the spring of 1994 and he proposed that we do a few of the dates together. It sounded like fun.

The audio cassette of *An Evening with Johnners* had been published in early October. Roger Godbold at Listen For Pleasure had explained to us that spoken-word recordings generally took a long time to make a profit. If we were lucky, he said, we might be able to sell about five thousand copies in the first year. To his amazement, and Brian's, the cassette sold more than five thousand copies in the first two months.

Meanwhile the second tour continued. Normally Brian performed on an empty stage or in front of a curtain, but at the Theatre Royal in Windsor the stage was set up for the following week's performance of the play *The Happiest Days of Your Life* starring Patrick Cargill. The set was a school hall with steps leading up to a balcony. Brian could not resist it. At the end of the performance he told the audience, 'Thank you very much. Now I'm going up to bed,' and walked up the steps and out of sight.

On 21 November he played the Richmond Theatre in London. Jeff Watts says it was the only time that he saw Brian nervous before a show. The Richmond is a large theatre and seats about 850 people. Brian had been there many times as a young man to see his favourite comedians and often used to go to the pantomime at Richmond. He had never dreamed that one day he would appear on the stage himself. On top of that the tickets had sold out in record time, so he felt a particular responsibility to be at his best.

Chris Seymour and I recorded the show for a special broadcast on Radio 2, and later it was published on CD and cassette as *An Hour with Johnners*. Maybe it was nerves, or maybe he was feeling tired, but for the first few minutes Brian seemed uncomfortable and stumbled over his words, something he normally never did. Then he came to one of his favourite jokes:

> A friend of mine was celebrating his sixtieth wedding anniversary, his diamond wedding. He and his wife decided to have a second honeymoon – to go to the same town, same hotel, same bedroom, same bed.
>
> They got into bed and the wife put her arms around his shoulders and said, 'Darling, do you remember how romantic you were sixty years ago? You bit me in the neck, you bit me in the shoulder, you bit me in the breast,' and he leaped out of bed and went to the bathroom.
>
> She said, 'What are you doing?' and he said, 'Getting my teeth!'

The audience greeted the punch-line with generous applause and you could feel him relax. After that he gave the performance of his life and the recording of *An Hour with Johnners* was nominated for Best Contemporary Comedy in the 1995 Talkies Awards.

Whenever I had spoken to Brian about the tour he had said how much he was enjoying it. He did not want to do any more after-dinner speeches in future, he declared, they were too tiring. What he had neglected to mention was that he had already agreed to speak at a series of sportsman's lunches that autumn during the tour. 'We were shocked when we found out later,' says John Martin. 'We were very conscious of his age and had tried to group the tour dates around weekends so that he would have time off. We didn't know that he was taking bookings for lunches as well. He didn't tell us, and it was not our business. But these were supposed to be his days off.'

He had not told Pauline either. She was furious when she found out, but he assured her the money was for the grandchildren, to help pay for their education. He did not like to turn such work down; he felt responsible for his large family. Pauline felt that he was being used by unscrupulous agents who had no concern for his welfare. He told her politely to 'mind her own business'.

'He was doing too much,' says Trevor Bailey. 'I thought it was a mistake. It was easy money but he didn't need it. The thing was, he wasn't doing it for himself.' John Woodcock disagrees. 'He loved being out and about and being recognised,' he says. 'I never saw him suffer from any stress. He enjoyed his work. I don't think work killed him, but if he had stopped, it might have.'

On 30 November Brian attended a special luncheon at the London Hilton to celebrate the eightieth birthday of sports agent Reg Hayter. After the lunch, Fred Trueman had to go back to Lord's and offered to share a taxi with Brian to St John's Wood. 'He said he was going to give up the after-dinner speeches,' says Trueman. 'I suggested we do a theatre tour together and he thought it was a good idea. He said he would think about it. When I came home I said to my wife Veronica that it was the first time I had ever seen anything wrong with Brian. She asked me what I meant. I said he had lost that boyish enthusiasm about him.'

In the first two weeks of December he had been booked to speak at seven lunches as far apart as Bristol and Liverpool. After January 1994 he had accepted bookings for fourteen more lunches and eighteen more sold-out shows of 'An Evening with Johnners' before the start of the cricket season.

Something had to give.

33

End of the Innings

On 2 December 1993 Brian was woken at 7.15 a.m. by a phone call from the *Today* studio to remind him that he was going to be asked for his opinion about the proposed change of name for the Bat and Ball pub at Hambledon. As was his habit, he carried out the interview sitting up in bed in his pyjamas, while Pauline lay half asleep beside him.

After the interview he shaved and had a bath and then went down to the kitchen to have his breakfast. Pauline was still in bed, so he carried up her breakfast on a tray, with a copy of the *Daily Mail*, and mentioned that he had a spot of indigestion, which was unusual for him. She gave him one of her Bisodol tablets to suck. He was due to speak at a sporting luncheon in Bristol so he dressed in his light brown checked suit. He gave Pauline a kiss goodbye and told her he would be home at 'about 6 p.m., I hope', complaining that he still had the indigestion in his chest. Pauline gave him another pill to chew in the taxi, which arrived at 9.10 to take him to Paddington Station.

Ten minutes later Pauline was reading the paper when the telephone rang beside her bed. It was the minicab office. 'Your passenger has been taken to Maida Vale Hospital,' said a man's voice, 'because he became ill in the taxi.' Frantically she looked up the number of the hospital in the phone book and rang them, to be told that Brian was on his way in an ambulance to St Mary's Hospital in Paddington.

The taxi had gone only half a mile and had been heading down Hamilton Terrace when the driver, a large, friendly Nigerian called Akim Akimode, heard choking noises from the back seat. Akimode was a football fan and was unaware of the identity of his elderly passenger, but he could tell that he was seriously ill. He drove as fast as he could, ignoring two sets of red traffic lights, to the Maida Vale Hospital two blocks away. It was a neurological hospital and did not have a casualty department, but it was the nearest one that he knew. By the time he arrived Brian's heart had already stopped and he had to be brought back to life on the floor of the hospital entrance. He was then transferred immediately by ambulance to the accident and emergency unit at St Mary's.

Back at Boundary Road, Cally was due to arrive at 9.45, so Pauline got dressed and waited for her, then drove the short distance to St Mary's, still unaware of exactly what had happened. A nurse met them outside the intensive care unit and warned them not to be shocked by Brian's appearance. He was lying on a stretcher bed, eyes wide open, staring blankly, plugged into a number of machines, with a mouthpiece inserted and a heart monitor beeping quietly next to him. 'I said to myself, "That's *not* Brian, it can't be,"' recalls Pauline. 'But it was, less than an hour since we'd said goodbye at home. I couldn't believe what was happening.'

A doctor came to see Pauline in a small room, while Cally waited outside. He explained that Brian had been deprived of oxygen for several minutes before being resuscitated, which meant that there might be some brain damage. They could only hope for the best, he tried to reassure her; time would tell.

Pauline drove home in a daze. She rang Brian's agent Dabber Davis and cancelled his luncheon engagement in Bristol. Then she called the BBC press office and told them that Brian had collapsed from exhaustion – she did not want anyone to know that he had suffered a heart attack – and it was reported on the eleven o'clock news.

She called me at home and stressed that she did not want the world to know how ill Brian really was. Soon afterwards I was phoned by the *Sun* and the *Daily Express* and a news agency, all trying to find out whether it was a heart attack. I lied shamelessly, and the next morning I was relieved to see that almost all the newspapers reported that he had 'collapsed from overwork', with only the *Daily Telegraph* claiming that it had been a heart attack.

I went with my wife Fiona to see Brian the next day. He was still unconscious and hooked up to a ventilator. He looked a shadow of his former self. It was almost impossible to believe that he was the same man, so full of life and energy, whom I had spoken to only a few days before.

The following morning I returned to the hospital. After being unconscious for more than forty-eight hours, Brian had finally woken up. He smiled when he saw me at his bedside and held my hand tightly, as if frightened to let go. I had heard that his cassette of *An Evening with Johnners* was number one in the W.H. Smith best-seller chart, so I passed on the good news and tried to cheer him up by saying that he would soon be back onstage telling all his old jokes. A nurse standing on the other side of the bed looked up and smiled as I told him, but Brian suddenly gripped my hand more tightly and I will never forget the look in his eyes. It was a mixture of panic and pleading. 'Don't worry,' I said quickly, 'if you can't remember all the stories, I'll be able to help you.' He seemed to relax a little, but I was deeply disturbed. He was trying to tell me that he could not remember any jokes. There was never going to be another show.

On Sunday, 5 December, Brian came off the ventilator and was moved into Thistle Ward with about eight other intensive care patients. The next day I was a special guest at the Lord's Taverners' Christmas lunch at the London Hilton in Park Lane. Everyone was very kind about Brian and I was introduced to Prince Edward, the President of the Lord's Taverners that year, who expressed his sympathy. I was going to see Brian immediately after the lunch so I asked one of the committee members of the Taverners, who was looking after Prince Edward, whether he could ask His Royal Highness to write a 'get well' message on one of the lunch menus. I thought it might give Brian a bit of encouragement. He said he would bring it to me later.

During the lunch a toast was proposed to Brian's health and several hundred Taverners and their guests stood and raised their glasses, wishing him a speedy recovery. Afterwards I waited until almost everyone had gone, but there was no sign of the committee member. The waiters had started clearing the tables when I finally tracked him down and asked whether Prince Edward had managed to sign a menu. 'Ah, no,' he said, looking guilty. 'After all, if he did it for you, he would have to do it for everybody!' I was speechless. How many other octogenarian cricket commentators were recovering from severe heart attacks? I am not sure whether Prince Edward ever knew of my request or whether the committee member was simply too scared to ask him, but I felt it would have been a small gesture of support from the President of the Lord's Taverners to one of the club's oldest and best-known members.

After the lunch I went to see Brian, but he seemed confused and did not appear to know where he was or what had happened to him. For the next few days Pauline spent an hour with him every morning and evening. She got him to repeat his name and address over and over again, and the names of his children and grandchildren, to see whether it would jog his memory. At other times Joanna sat with him and played simple card games or encouraged him to count up to ten, twenty or thirty, like a child. The doctors said they were pleased with his progress but it felt more like one step forward and two steps back.

Pauline asked Peter Baxter from *Test Match Special* to visit Brian to see whether he would help to revive his memory, but that did not work either. 'He had a huge stack of get-well cards and it was bothering him,' says Baxter. 'He kept saying, "What are we going to do about these?" In the end I had to hide them behind a curtain. On the way out I asked the sister whether she thought Brian would ever be able to commentate again. "Oh yes," she replied. But I knew he wouldn't.'

After a few days Brian was transferred to Nightingale Ward, a mixed-sex ward of about twenty beds. I visited him on 10 December with Fiona and our baby daughter Olivia, and it was terribly sad to see him sitting silently on a chair next to his bed, surrounded by strangers. People would walk past and stare at him and say, 'How's the cricket going, Brian?' without realising that he had no idea what they were talking about. I think he had only a vague idea of who we were.

On 14 December Brian was moved to the King Edward VII Hospital for Officers. By now it was common knowledge that he had suffered a heart attack, so in order to avoid further intrusion from the press en masse Pauline rang the Press Association and arranged for a photographer to be there as he was leaving St Mary's. The next morning there were several pictures in the national newspapers of Brian sitting in a wheelchair, alongside nurses Caroline Kembery and Claire Witcher, and clutching a large 'get well' balloon in the shape of a roly-poly doctor. He looked as if he had aged ten years.

For the next few days he had a small private room at the Edward VII. It was near the nurses' desk, so they could keep an eye on him, but at least he had some dignity. Pauline took him to see the heart specialist, Dr Swanton – no relation to Jim – at the Weymouth Clinic. His brother Christopher visited him, as did Sir Edward Ford, John Woodcock and Christopher Martin-Jenkins on separate days, but he did not remember who they were or that they had been to see him. 'Even though he wasn't making sense,' says Martin-Jenkins, 'he was still on auto-pilot, making polite conversation. "We've just got back from Australia," he would say cheerfully. It was rather poignant.'

On Sunday, 19 December, the whole family had been due to meet for a pre-Christmas lunch at Boundary Road but, for obvious reasons, Pauline had no time to prepare a meal for fifteen, so the venue was changed to Clare's house in Balham. I was driving up the M23 from Sussex with Fiona and Olivia when we joined a tailback of cars on the slip road to the M25. Suddenly a Volkswagen Golf slammed into the back of us at about seventy miles an hour, before ricocheting backwards. After the driver staggered out the Golf burst into flames. Fortunately we were all wearing seat belts and were also not seriously injured, but our car was a write-off. I called Balham to let them know that we were being taken in an ambulance to East Surrey Hospital. Pauline burst into tears. What else could possibly go wrong?

In the days leading up to Christmas Pauline continued to visit Brian at the Edward VII. He seemed a little stronger but he began to have strange hallucinations. 'Have you arranged the service?' he would enquire anxiously. 'What service?' she would ask. 'You know,' he would reply, 'our wedding service.' At other times he would say, 'I've just had tea with Mummy and Michael [his eldest brother].' Pauline would try to explain that they had both died a long time ago but it made no difference.

Meanwhile she was being inundated with cards, letters and flowers. In the weeks following his heart attack Pauline received more than 600 'get well' cards and replied personally to 250 of them. One of the most touching cards was addressed 'To a wonderful human being, on behalf of London's 25,000 taxi drivers'. She also received 350 Christmas cards.

Two days before Christmas Brian was finally allowed to go home, and a young New Zealand girl called Sarah Hutchinson moved in to Boundary Road to help care for him. At first Pauline was relieved to see him back in his favourite armchair in the sitting room, but he just sat there, hardly saying a word. He had always loved doing the *Daily Telegraph* crossword every day, but he no longer showed any interest in the newspapers or television. His youngest daughter Joanna played simple card games and Scrabble with him, which he managed quite well.

Every morning he would go into his study and try to remember what he was doing there. At the back of his mind he knew that he had a diary filled with speeches, dinners and other engagements. He would collect books, pens, writing paper and his diary and take them downstairs to the sitting room. Several times he packed a suitcase because he thought he had to catch a train or fly somewhere, especially to Adelaide. One day he gave Pauline a big hug. 'Help me, darling,' he said, 'I'm in a great big hole and I can't get out.'

Christmas Day was a dismal occasion. Brian, Pauline and Sarah sat quietly at the table with one cracker each. Brian was only half there and had little appetite. 'It was the saddest day I'd ever had,' says Pauline. Over the next few days one or two friends popped in to see him. Brian was still talking about his mother and brother Mick being with him. As Pauline reflected later, maybe they were.

On New Year's Eve she decided to take Brian for a walk round Lord's Cricket Ground to see whether it would help his memory. She drove up to the Nursery entrance but Brian had lost so much weight that the attendant did not recognise him. She had to explain why they were there before he would let them in. They walked slowly under the deserted Grandstand. Pauline could not help thinking back to all those Test match days when the bars underneath the Grandstand had been packed with a seething mass of drinkers, all shouting, 'Hello, Johnners!'

As they walked on they could see the Pavilion. Pauline pointed up to a balcony. 'What's that?' she asked.

'The team balcony,' said Brian.

She pointed higher, to a window at the top of the Pavilion. 'What's that?' she asked again.

There was a pause before Brian replied simply, 'Test Match Special.'

He seemed to be getting weaker. On 4 January I went up to London to see him and arrived at Boundary Road to find that Pauline had called for an ambulance. She had decided that he must go back to hospital.

I followed the ambulance to the Edward VII, where Brian was taken upstairs to a room. While Pauline went to talk with the nurses I pulled up a chair alongside him and for about ten minutes I told him all my news since I had last seen him. I explained about the car crash, which Pauline had kept hidden from him, and asked whether I could borrow his car for a while. I talked about his ten-month-old granddaughter Olivia, and my new programme at BBC Radio Solent, which I was due to start the following Monday. I am not sure how much he understood, but he seemed happy to sit quietly and listen, the two of us alone together.

After a while Pauline and the nurses returned and I had to leave. My neck and my back had been hurt in the accident and

I had booked an appointment with a doctor in Brighton for later that afternoon. As I got ready to go, Brian stood up shakily. I put my arm round his shoulder and gave him a kiss on his left cheek. 'Take care,' I said, 'I'll see you soon.' As I walked out of the door, he called out, 'Bye, Barrel!'

The next morning I was woken up by the telephone. I knew before I had answered it. It was my brother Andrew.

During the night Brian's condition had worsened and he had been moved into the intensive care ward. At one stage he looked at Pauline and said, 'This is the hardest day's work I have ever done,' and then he smiled at her. Those were his last words. At 6.40 a.m. on 5 January 1994 Brian Johnston breathed a deep sigh. His long innings was over.

34

Summers Will Not Be the Same

The BBC announced Brian's death at 11 a.m. that morning. The news was carried on every radio and television bulletin throughout the day and almost every report concluded with a few seconds of the now famous 'leg-over' giggle. I did not know whether to laugh or cry and usually ended up doing both. Tributes poured in from around the world. Within a few hours Pauline had received a telegram from the Queen and Prince Philip at Sandringham and another from the Prime Minister, John Major. The Queen Mother's private secretary wrote a letter on her behalf, saying that she was 'so very distressed' to hear of his death and remembered his many visits to Clarence House when he 'was always most entertaining!'

The next morning Brian's death was front-page news in almost every national newspaper. *The Times* carried five separate items about him, and there were four pieces in the *Daily Telegraph*, including an editorial which described him as 'a landmark of English culture'. On the front page Christopher Martin-Jenkins wrote a moving tribute:

> I have lost a personal friend whose irrepressible wit and sense of fun enriched my life. It was because of Brian Johnston's particular magic as a broadcaster that literally millions of people will be feeling the same this morning. For wives and mothers engaged in household chores, he was the cheerful presence in the corner of the room, comforting as a fire in the hearth; for car-bound businessmen he was the companion in the next seat, a constant source of amusement; for the blind, to whom radio means so much, he was a lifeline.

It is hard to believe that anyone in the history of broadcasting has induced such widespread affection. His secret was simply that, in front of a microphone, he was himself, the greatest natural broadcaster of them all.

The newspapers gleefully recalled his many gaffes, especially the occasion when the South African bowler Peter Pollock slipped and turned an ankle on his run-up. 'Bad luck on Peter,' Brian had commented. 'He's obviously in great pain. It's especially bad luck as he's here on his honeymoon with his pretty young wife. Still, he'll probably be all right tomorrow if he sticks it up tonight!'

John Major was widely quoted with his own tribute: 'Brian Johnston was a giant among commentators. Over recent years he became almost the personification of cricket. He was a man who enjoyed life hugely and shared that enjoyment with millions. Summers will not be the same.' This led to an amusing cartoon by Geoff Thompson in the *Independent* which showed a man looking puzzled by John Major's final remark: 'Aggers, Fredders, Blowers . . . who the hell is Summers?!'

The funeral took place in Swanage on Monday, 10 January. Brian and Pauline had chosen a particular corner plot at Godlingston Cemetery three years earlier. The cemetery is a very peaceful place on the outskirts of Swanage, surrounded by fields, the only sounds coming from the birds in the trees, a pair of horses in the adjoining meadow and the distant whistle of the Swanage Steam Railway.

Brian was buried wearing his favourite Bunbury Cricket Club sweater and his *Test Match Special* tie. His headstone is carved from the local Purbeck stone and is engraved with crossed cricket bats and a BBC microphone. At the bottom it reads: GONE TO THE GREAT PAVILION IN THE SKY.

The outpouring of warmth and affection following Brian's death took Pauline and the family by surprise. Over the next few weeks she received more than 1,500 letters and cards of condolence from all over the world. Paul Getty kindly loaned his secretary to help sort them out and to type replies. Pauline had expected that Brian would be missed but not that his death would become such a media event.

The audio cassette of *An Evening with Johnners* broke all records and was awarded a gold disc for sales of over 100,000. The CD version entered the Top 50 album charts at number 46 and, according to *The Guinness Book of Records*, this made Brian the oldest person ever to record a chart album (he was eighty at the time). In May 1995 it was replaced at the top of the spoken-word charts by *Johnners at the Beeb*, a compilation of Brian's best broadcasting moments, which was voted the Spoken Word Recording of the Year by the Music Industries Association.

On 16 May 1994 a memorial service was held at Westminster Abbey. 'Ever since Richard Dimbleby died and had his service there,' says Pauline, 'I had dreamed of Brian also having one at the Abbey. I often told him so, but he just pooh-poohed it!' Pauline was determined that it would be a happy and joyful service, a true celebration of Brian's life, and spent many hours discussing every detail of the service with the Dean of Westminster and Sir Roger Cary from the BBC, who later broadcast the ceremony on Radio 2.

The Abbey was packed, with extra seating having to be provided on all sides. The congregation was a glorious mixture of cricketers and celebrities, friends and colleagues, and those who simply felt they knew him from the radio. The music before the service was played by the Band of the Grenadier Guards. Pauline had requested some of Brian's favourite melodies and the congregation filed in to the strains of 'The Eton Boating Song', 'We'll Gather Lilacs' and the signature tunes from *In Town Tonight* and *Down Your Way*.

Brian's brother Christopher and Peter Baxter from *Test Match Special* each read a psalm. A choirboy sang 'O for the Wings of a Dove' and Melvin Collins, a blind listener, recited his own poem. Michael Denison read an extract from the autobiography of Sir Neville Cardus; Lord Runcie, the former Archbishop of Canterbury, said a prayer; and Richard Stilgoe caused laughter to echo round the Abbey with his brilliant poem written especially for the occasion.

There were also tributes from his three sons. Andrew read an extract from Brian's book *Someone Who Was* and Ian read Bud Flanagan's amusing foreword to the book *Let's Go Somewhere*. I chose a poem by William Douglas Home called 'A Glorious Game, Say We', which he wrote in the 1920s after going to an Eton and Harrow match at Lord's. After the service I received a very moving letter from a woman asking whether she could use it at her own father's funeral service, and a year ago John Barclay also read it at the service of thanksgiving for Colin Cowdrey:

> Though we sit tired out by the hours of play
> When the shadows of evening fall
> We have watched through the dancing heat of the day
> The struggle 'twixt bat and ball;
> For we love the changes and chances of cricket
> Though the bat succeeds or fails,
> Though the ball is striking the fatal wicket
> Or the white pavilion rails;
> For cricket's a glorious game, say we
> And cricket will never cease to be.
>
> Yes, cricket will live till the trumpet trumps
> From the wide, pavilioned sky,
> And time, the umpire, lays low the stumps
> As his scythe goes sweeping by—
> Till the mighty seed of humanity fails
> At the light of another birth,
> And God stoops down to remove the bails
> From the dark deserted earth;
> Yes, cricket's a glorious game, say we
> And cricket will live in eternity.

Pauline had asked Sir Colin Cowdrey to give the address but he had felt nervous about undertaking such an important role and asked his good friend John Major to share it with him. The Prime

Minister gave a warm and affectionate address and brought a lump to many throats with his closing words: 'Whenever I met Brian Johnston or saw him or heard him, I smiled. It was impossible not to and I know that sentiment was shared by millions. That was the gift he gave us and it is one that will not be easily or rapidly forgotten. His memory will live on. For there are children not yet born who one day will captain England.' The Prime Minister paused, clearly moved, before adding quietly, 'Even then, the talk will still be of Brian Johnston.' After that, several people were seen to dab their eyes.

At the end of the service my mother felt nervous at having to face so many people, so I held her hand as we walked down the aisle. Earlier she had made a special request for the theme tune from _Neighbours_ to be played as we were leaving the Abbey. The Dean of Westminster had raised his eyebrows and paused, momentarily stunned by the suggestion, and then said solemnly, 'Mrs Johnston, you may of course have this played after the choir has processed down the aisle. But please don't expect _me_ to process to the tune of _Neighbours!_' When the Band of the Grenadier Guards launched into the familiar music it was wonderful to see the looks of puzzlement among the congregation turn to smiles of recognition.

We stood just inside the Great West Door while the congregation filed slowly past us and hundreds of people came up to shake Pauline's hand and to say a few words. They were rather taken aback to see a table beside the door, on which sat an iced cake in the shape of a pair of brown-and-white corespondent shoes, which had been presented to Brian on his eightieth birthday by the Riff-Raff Club. The Dean had granted special permission for it to be displayed in the Abbey.

Finally we emerged into the sunshine to the clamorous sound of the Abbey bells. It was a uniquely British occasion which Brian would have thoroughly enjoyed. Hundreds of people stood around chatting outside the Abbey, in the midst of whom could be seen the Prime Minister and Fred Trueman side by side, happily signing autographs. I heard an American tourist ask a policeman why the Abbey bells were pealing. He was told that it was for a cricket commentator. The tourist looked baffled and walked away, none the wiser.

After the memorial service we expected that the public interest in Brian would gradually fade, but if anything the reverse was true. During the third Test against South Africa in August 1994, Pauline officially opened the new Brian Johnston Broadcasting Centre at the Oval. In November the St John's Wood Society planted a tulip tree in his memory in St John's Wood churchyard. The following day Britannia Airways named a new Boeing 767 after him, and at Durlston Country Park in Swanage the park rangers reclaimed a field and seeded it with wild flowers in his memory. The Grenadier Guards introduced an annual Brian Johnston Cup, a silver rose bowl, for the Bandsman of the Year. In 1997 New College at Oxford built the Brian Johnston Sports Pavilion. The following year Paul Getty sponsored a new Brian Johnston Memorial Film Theatre at the Lord's Museum.

Few people are granted so many permanent memorials. One of the proudest moments was when Pauline opened the Brian Johnston Centre, a purpose-built nursery for blind and partially sighted children at Dorton House School at Sevenoaks in Kent. It was the first of its kind in the country and had been funded largely through donations from the Primary Club, which had benefited so greatly from Brian's on-air appeals on *Test Match Special.*

As for *TMS*, Brian is remembered every Test match with the award of the Brian Johnston Champagne Moment to the player who has contributed the most outstanding moment of the match. His name is often mentioned and sometimes it is easy to believe that he is still sitting there at the back of the commentary box, going through his mail and chuckling softly, waiting for his next stint at the microphone.

After Brian died, Pauline wanted to give something back to the game that he had loved so much, and in 1995 she founded the Brian Johnston Memorial Trust, perhaps his greatest legacy. The patron is Sir Paul Getty and the vice-patrons include Richie Benaud, David Gower and John Major. The object of the charity is to award annual Brian Johnston Scholarships to promising young cricketers who are in need of financial assistance to fulfil their potential, and to support cricket for the blind.

Since December 1999 the Brian Johnston Memorial Trust has been administered by the Lord's Taverners. The awards are now funded mainly through an annual grant from the Lord's Taverners, membership of the Johnners Club, and the Johnners Club Dinner at Lord's in the spring of each year.

Every year the trust awards scholarships to twelve promising boys and girls nominated by the England and Wales Cricket Board national coaches and the women's under-19 coach. In addition the trust pays for three young wrist spinners to go each year for coaching with Terry Jenner at the Australian Cricket Academy in Adelaide. Several Johnners scholars are now being talked about as future England players. Blind cricketers have also been helped with a number of donations, including new kit for the England Blind Cricket Squad at the World Cup in India in December 2002.

If you had asked Brian what his greatest legacy would be he would probably have said his family. He was always very proud of his five children and his seven (now eight) grandchildren. His eldest grandson Nicholas Oldridge is a talented wicket-keeper and batsman. He was vice-captain of the eleven at Stowe School and for the last two years has played for the Surrey under-19s.

Maybe, just maybe, a member of the Johnston family will walk down those pavilion steps at Lord's one day.

Epilogue

On 11 April 2002 I was woken at about 7 a.m. by the telephone. You just know it is going to be bad news at that hour in the morning. It was. 'Hello?' said a man's voice, yelling into a mobile phone. 'Is that Barry Johnston? This is your mother's milkman. Her house is on fire!' Fortunately Pauline had managed to escape and was unharmed.

The fire engine arrived within a few minutes and the fire was soon under control. The actual fire damage was confined to the sitting room but the thick black smoke had gone throughout the house. Luckily the door of Brian's former study was closed, so all his papers and other memorabilia were unharmed. But the rest of the house was ruined by the smoke damage and had to be completely redecorated from top to bottom. It was a year before Pauline was able to move back in again.

When the firemen had extinguished the blaze they looked around the smoke-blackened room. Paintings, porcelain figures, ivory ornaments and many other valuable items had all been destroyed by the intense heat. But in the far corner of the room, underneath the sideboard, they spotted a curious-looking white object wrapped in polythene. Somehow it had survived the fire unscathed. When they brought it out they were surprised to see that it was a large iced cake in the shape of a pair of brown-and-white corespondent shoes.

Acknowledgements

This book would not have been possible without the assistance of dozens of Brian's family, friends and colleagues who have kindly shared their personal memories of Brian with me. I would like to thank them all for their hospitality and their support and for their many wonderful stories.

While researching my previous book based on Brian's letters from 1926 to 1945 I talked to a number of people whose memories proved invaluable in writing this biography, so I would like to repeat my grateful thanks to Fred and Peggy Duder, Vera Franks, Sir John Hogg, Lord and Lady Howard de Walden, Heck Knight, Anne Lane Fox, George Thorne, Ken Thornton and Major Peter Lewis, the former Regimental Archivist of the Grenadier Guards.

For help with Brian's family background and early years I am most grateful to Brian's brother Christopher Johnston and also to Margaret Blyth, Sir Edward Ford, Anne Hanbury, Anthony Johnston, Francis Johnston, Pat Scott and Phyllis Welch.

I am indebted to Simon Wright, the archivist at Temple Grove School, for his informative research, and to John Crump for allowing me to read his excellent memoirs of Temple Grove in the 1920s. Thanks to Michael Meredith, College Librarian at Eton College, Penelope Hatfield, College Archivist, and Nick Baker, Collections Administrator, for their generous help and advice. Thanks also to Lord Carrington, George Cross, Brigadier Peter Prescott, Alfred Shaughnessy and Lord Wigram, who assisted me greatly with details of Brian's army career, and Captain D. Mason of the Grenadier Guards.

For memories of Brian's early years at the BBC and as a cricket commentator on TV and radio, I must thank Trevor

Bailey, Peter Baxter, Raymond Baxter, Richie Benaud, Henry Blofeld, Margaret Cormack, Bryan Cowgill, Peter Dimmock, Neil Durden-Smith, Diana Fisher, Robert Hudson, Oggie Lomas, Christopher Martin-Jenkins, John Pawle, Ken Spencer, Fred Trueman, Peter West and John Woodcock.

For their help with Brian's life and career from the 1970s onwards I am grateful to Ben and Belinda Brocklehurst, Michael Craig, Barry Cryer, Lady Dacre, Dabber Davis, Caroline Douglas-Home, Jamie Douglas-Home, Rachael Heyhoe-Flint, Mike Lewis, Jon Magnusson, John Martin, Michael Parkinson, Sir Tim Rice, Louis Robinson, Tony Smith, Tom Sutton, Jeff Watts, Richard Whitely, Malcolm Williamson and Terry Wogan.

My grateful thanks to Vicky Mitchell at the BBC Commercial Agency for kind permission to reproduce various extracts from the BBC sound archives. Colin Cowdrey, William Douglas Home, John Ellison, Seymour de Lotbinière, E. W. Swanton and Lord Whitelaw were all featured on *It's Been a Lot of Fun*, produced by Roger Thompson for BBC Radio 4 in 1974.

Many thanks to Emma John at *Wisden Cricket Monthly* for her kind assistance and for permission to use excerpts from the magazine's correspondence about *Test Match Special*. Thanks to Lady Dacre for permission to reproduce 'A Glorious Game, Say We' by William Douglas Home; and to Christopher Martin-Jenkins for permission to reproduce his tribute to Brian in the *Daily Telegraph*. Grateful acknowledgement is made to Tony Alexander for the use of his letter about the Ian Botham 'leg over' incident.

The Enemies of Promise by Cyril Connolly © 1938 and 1948 is reproduced by permission of The Estate of Cyril Connolly, c/o Rogers, Coleridge & White Ltd, 20 Powis Mews, London W11 1JN.

Amongst other books consulted, particular use was made of: Jonathan Agnew: *Over To You, Aggers*; David Rayvern Allen: *Arlott: The Authorised Biography*; Peter Baxter and Phil McNeill: *From Arlott to Aggers*; Henry Blofeld: *A Thirst For Life*; Tim Card: *Eton Renewed*; Paul Donovan: *The Radio Companion*; William Douglas Home: *Half-Term Report*; *Mr Home Pronounced Hume*; *Sins Of*

Commission and *Old Men Remember*; Bernard Fergusson: *Eton Portrait*; Tim Heald: *Brian Johnston: The Authorised Biography*; Robert Hudson: *Inside Outside Broadcasts*; Brian Johnston: *Let's Go Somewhere*; *It's Been a Lot of Fun*; *It's a Funny Game*; *Chatterboxes*; *Down Your Way* and *Someone Who Was*; Brian Johnston and Barry Johnston, ed.: *An Evening with Johnners* and *Letters Home 1926–1945*; Christopher Martin-Jenkins: *Ball By Ball*; Christopher Martin-Jenkins and Pat Gibson: *Summers Will Never Be the Same*; Don Mosey: *The Alderman's Tale*; and Terry Wogan: *Is It Me?*

For their memories of Brian as a father I must offer sincere thanks to my brothers Andrew and Ian Johnston and to my sisters Clare Oldridge and Joanna Johnston. I would also like to express special thanks to my mother Pauline Johnston for allowing me to use extracts from her personal memoirs of her life with Brian, especially her diary of their engagement and marriage and the events surrounding Brian's final year.

I am extremely grateful to Rupert Lancaster at Hodder & Stoughton for his encouragement and for his excellent advice, and to my copy editor, Ian Paten, for his consideration and skill in correcting the manuscript.

Finally I must thank my dear wife Fiona and our two lovely children Olivia and Sam for their patience and understanding. It feels as if I have spent most of the last year sitting in front of the computer. Now you know what I have been doing!

PHOTOGRAPHIC ACKNOWLEDGEMENTS

Photographs are from the Johnston Family Collection, except the following: Army PR Photo Section HQ Berlin(British Sector)/photo Leo Chrzanowski: 36. Associated Newspapers/Atlantic Syndication: 38. BBC: 33, 39, 41, 60. Bishop Television News Service: 27. British Railways Southern Region: 23. Derek Chamberlain: 58. Patrick Eagar: 52. E.H. Emanuel: 37. Eton College Library: 11, 12, 14, 19. Graphic Photo Union: 26. Halksworth Wheeler, Folkestone: 28. Hertfordshire Mercury: 55. Mirrorpix: 29,30. Photo-Reportage: 34. R.A.F. Crown Copyright Reserved: 35. A.Whittington/John Bull: 32. John Woodcock: 54.

Every reasonable effort has been made to contact the copyright holders, but if there are any errors or omissions, Hodder & Stoughton will be pleased to insert the appropriate acknowledgements in any subsequent printing of this publication.

The Brian Johnston Memorial Trust

The Brian Johnston Memorial Trust was founded in 1995 and the objects of the charity are:

- The award of Brian Johnston Scholarships to promising young cricketers in need of financial support to fulfil their potential
- The support of sport for the disabled, particularly cricket for the blind

These awards are funded mainly through membership of the Johnners Club and the annual Johnners Club dinner at Lord's in the spring of each year.

If you would like more information on how to become a member of the Johnners Club or if you would like to apply for a Brian Johnston cricket scholarship, please contact:

The Brian Johnston Memorial Trust
10 Buckingham Place
London SWIE 6HX
Telephone: 020 7821 2821
E-mail: bjmt@lordstaverners.org

Or you can find out more about the charity by visiting the official Brian Johnston website at: www.johnners.com

Index

Adam, Kenneth 189–90
Adamson, Joy 216
Adie, Diana 309
Adler, Larry 264
Agnew, Jonathan 'Aggers' 286, 309–15
    and 'leg over' incident 306–8
    practical jokes on BJ 312–13
    BJ's revenge 314–15
Akimode, Akim 332–3
Alderman's Tale, The (Mosey) 230, 301
Alexander, Tony 309–10
Alexandra, Queen 226–7
Alington, Dr Cyril 31–2
Alington, Elizabeth (Lady Dunglass, Lady
    Home) 32, 91
Allan, Elkan 207
Allan, Nick 118
Allen, Chesney 73, 148, 256
Allen, Katie 'Putty' 24–5
Alliss, Peter 247
Allsorts sports club 48, 52–3
Almanzora (ship) 78, 79, 86
Alston, Rex 126, 186, 196
Alt, Brian (uncle) 9
Alt, Elizabeth (grandmother) 9
Alt, Pleasance (*see Johnston, Pleasance*)
Alt, Col. William (grandfather) 9
Ambrose 73
Ambrose, Curtly 307
Amethyst, HMS 172
Amiss, Dennis 287
Ammonds, John 213
Andrew, Neil 304
Andrew, Prince, Duke of York 252, 267
Andrews, Eamonn 191–2, 258–9, 266–7
Annandale, Marquis of 8
Anne, Princess 212
Annesley, Dodo (cousin) 17

Annesley, Sheila (cousin) 17
Arlott (Rayvern Allen) 225
Arlott, John 185, 233, 253
    review of BJ's autobiography 212
    and BJ 224–8
    last commentary 227–8
Armstrong-Jones, Anthony (Earl of
    Snowdon) 187
Arsenal 90
Asher, Jane 201
Askey, Arthur 128
Astaire, Adele 35
Astaire, Fred 35
Astil, Margaret (Mrs John Carter) 82–3
Astor, David 53
Astor, Michael 90
Astor, Nancy, Viscountess 53
Atherton, Mike 311
Attlee, Clement, later Earl 157

Bachelors' Club 73
Bader, Sir Douglas 26
Baerlein, Anthony 42–3, 63
Baerlein, Edgar 63–4
Baerlein, Mrs 63
Bailey, Greta 316, 318
Bailey, Trevor 220–1, 263, 265, 325, 330
    and *TMS* 225, 227, 230–1, 311
    on tour with BJ 285–6, 316, 317, 318
Baker, Josephine 214
Baker, Nigel 107
Baksh, Showkat 228
Baldwin, Stanley 84
Balfour, Eve 72
Bamforths (postcards) 291
Bannister, Jack 219, 314
Barclay, John 343
Barclay, Paymaster-Lt. 17–19

Barclays World of Cricket (Swanton) 287
Barkers, of Earls Barton 180
Baroda, Maharajah of 15
BarryMour Productions 283, 323
Bates, H. E. 192
Bates, Master 55
Bates, Mrs (landlady) 55
Baxter, Peter 274, 285, 317, 319–20, 325,
     335, 342
   and *TMS* 224, 230, 263, 301, 302,
     311, 313
   on BJ and John Arlott 225, 228
   and 'leg over' incident 307–8
   and Boat Race 254, 255, 256
Baxter, Raymond 161–2, 173, 186,
     189, 195
   and Monte Carlo Rally 161
Beatles, The 192, 201
Beckwith, Misses 23
Bedser, Sir Alec 130, 197
Bedser, Eric 130
Bell, Arthur 172
Bellamy, M. 24
Belloc, Hilaire 39
Benaud, Richie 190, 204, 283, 313–14,
     345
   and BJ on TV 179–80, 183–4
   plays cricket with BJ 196, 197–8
   and Kerry Packer 221
Bennett, Billy 266
Benny, Jack 157
Berlin, Irving 244
Berry, Neville 286
Bertram Mills Circus 173
Bird, Dickie 224, 295, 300
Black, Peter 188
Blofeld, Henry 'Blowers' 218, 227,
     286, 301
   and BJ on *TMS* 228–9
Bly, Lou 196
Blyth, Margaret (née Edwardes-Jones,
     cousin) 4, 13, 19
Bolsover, Mike 85
Boodles Club 73
Borotra, Jean 131
Botham, Ian 233, 306–7, 309, 310
Bough, Frank 244
Boycott, Geoffrey 227, 318
Brack, E. J. 232–3, 234
Braden, Bernard 163

Bradfield College 193
Bradman, Sir Donald 90, 138, 231
Brewster, Mrs Emily 241
Brian Johnston Memorial Trust 345–6,
     351
Briers, Richard 247
Britannia Airways 345
Brocklehurst, Ben and Belinda 217–18,
     272, 273, 286, 287, 299
Brookbanks, Paul 308–9
Brooke-Taylor, Tim 270
Brown, David 219–20
Brown, Tricia 219
Browning, Lt.-Col. Frederick 34, 68
Browning, Lt.-Gen. Sir Frederick
     (Tommy) 'Boy' (cousin) 93, 114
Browning, Nancy (née Alt, aunt) 34, 35
Buckland, Frances 277
Bude (Cornwall) 16–20, 60–2, 82,
     112, 174
Bullingdon Club 53
Bulow, Claus von 305
Bunbury Cricket Club 341
Burwood, Richard 215, 238
Butt, Dame Clara 34
Butterflies cricket club 48
Bygraves, Max 128
Byng, Douglas 73

Caine, Sir Michael 305
Callander, Mrs Ella 'Cally' 188, 200,
     202, 333
Callander, Jack and Ann 188
Campbell, Patrick 211
Canberra (ship) 180
Cardus, Sir Neville 342
Cargill, Patrick 329
Carmichael, Ian 265
Carr, W. A. K. 'Bushey' 52
Carrington, Peter Carington, 6th Baron
     101, 111, 114
Carrington, Rupert Carington, 5th
     Baron 62
Carroll, Lewis 266
cars, owned by BJ 63, 72, 155, 194, 282
Carson, Frank 321
Carter, Charles (nephew) 103
Carter, David (nephew, godson) 103
Carter, Howard (nephew) 83
Carter, Hugh 54

Carter, John (brother-in-law) 82–3
Cartwright, Lt.-Col. G. H. M. 'Buns' 64, 73
Cary, Sir Roger 342
Chalmers, Judith (Mrs Neil Durden-Smith) 191
Chamberlain, Neville 91, 92, 97
Chaplin, Charles 40
Chapman, Graham 206
Charles, Prince of Wales 251
Charleston, Anne 289
Chichester, Sir Francis 192
chocolate cake, and BJ 37, 226–7
Churchill, Sir Winston 97, 105, 108, 266
 BJ meets 73–4
Cleese, John 206, 234
Cliff, Laddie 34
Close of Play (Miller) 265
Coco the Clown 173
Collins, Arthur 172–3
Collins, Melvin 342
Compton, Denis 77–8, 130, 193, 246
 and BJ on TV 177–8, 181, 183, 184
Conan Doyle, Sir Arthur 266
Connolly, Cyril 46–7
Cooper, Sir Henry 172
Cooper, Tommy 213
Corbett, Ann 308
Corbett, Mr & Mrs and family 94
Corbett, Ronnie 244, 308
Cormack, Margaret 195
Cornhill Insurance Group 313
Corrie (schoolboy) 24
Courtneidge, Dame Cicely 128, 213
Cove-Smith, Dr R. 199
Coward, Sir Noël 114, 328
Cowdrey, Colin, later Lord 181, 193, 246, 324, 343
 at church service with BJ 181–2
 owns greyhound with BJ 202
Cowgill, Bryan 204–6
Cozier, Tony 307–8
Craig, Michael 247
Crandall, Bill 50, 54
Crawley, Aidan 175
Craxton, Antony 279
Craxton, Mrs 279
Crazy Gang 135, 147–8, 256
Crease, Chief Petty Officer 27, 28
Cribbins, Bernard 268

cricket, BJ as player 26–7, 41–2, 57, 62, 66, 82, 195–8
 fails to make Eton 1st XI 42–3
 captain of New College 57
 at Bude Cricket Club 62
 hangs up gloves 197–8
Cricketer, The 217–18, 233, 272
Crippen, Dr 142
Crisp, Gert 89–90, 91, 93, 102
Crisp, Tom 'Crippen' 89–90, 93, 102
Cross, George 112
Crump, John 23, 24
Cryer, Barry 268, 269, 270–1
Curran, Sir Charles 239
Curtis, Mrs 16

Dacre, Lady 250, 285, 293–4
Dad's Army 106
Dando, Suzanne 297
Davies, Sister Jessie 262
Davies, 'Mad Johnny' 144
Davies, Rex 79
Davies, Rupert 192
Davis, 'Dabber' 320, 322, 333
Davis, Diana *(see Fisher, Diana)*
Davis, Paddy 320
Dawn 213
Day, Frances 114
Dean (groom) 33, 248
Dean, Captain 57
De Freitas, Philip 307
de Gaulle, General Charles 105
Deighton, Charles 'Jerry' 87
Deighton, Dorothy 87
de Jaeger, Charles 134
de Lotbinière, Seymour (Lobby) 128, 130, 131, 153, 160, 179, 253
 offers BJ a job at BBC 124–6
 and BJ's first broadcast 127
 on BJ's commentary style 176
de Manio, Jack 186–7
de Montmorency, Ann *(see Swanton, Ann)*
de Montmorency, R. H. 30
Denison, Michael 258, 342
Denness, Mike 215, 263
Derby Day (film) 159
Derwen Training College 201
Design 213, 214, 321
Dexter, Ted 181, 285
Diack, Phil 169

Diana, Princess of Wales 251–2
Dimbleby, David 191
Dimbleby, Richard 162, 171, 186, 237, 243, 304, 342
  Monte Carlo Rally with BJ 161
Dimmock, Peter 175, 186, 187, 204–6
Doig, Russell 295
Dorton House School for the Blind 345
Douglas-Home, Sir Alec, Lord Dunglass, later 14th Earl of Home 32, 91, 194, 259
  and postcards from BJ 292
Douglas-Home, Caroline 194–5, 292
Douglas-Home, Charles, 13th Earl of Home 56, 64
Douglas-Home, David, Lord Dunglass, later 15th Earl of Home 194–5
Douglas-Home, Dinah (god-daughter) 294
Douglas-Home, Elizabeth *(see Alington, Elizabeth)*
Douglas-Home, Jamie 249
Douglas-Home, Meriel (god-daughter) 91, 194
Douglas-Home, Rachel *(see Dacre, Lady)*
Douglas Home, William 32, 44, 64–6, 75, 119, 188–9, 215, 249, 250, 343
  at Oxford 49–50, 52, 53–9
  in rooms with BJ 89–91, 93
  and Kathleen Kennedy 94
  wartime 94–5, 96, 101–2, 103–4
  court-martialled, gaoled 114–15
  friendship with BJ 279, 285, 287, 292–4
  death 294
Doyle, Nancy 246
Drusilla's Zoo 54
Duder, Fred 79–81, 83, 84, 85, 86, 114
  torpedoed 106
Duder, Helena (Mrs Robert Hunt) 85
Duder, Vera 'Nip' (Mrs Franks) 83, 85, 87–8, 106
Duffield-Jones, Major 'Buffer' 27
Dujon, Jeffrey 307
du Maurier, Sir Gerald 35
Duncan, Peter 14–1, 154
Duncan, Reverend 34
Durante, Jimmy 'Schnozzle' 157, 248
Durden-Smith, Emma 191
Durden-Smith, Neil 191, 203–4, 291–2
Durlston Country Park 345
D'Utra Vaz, Dr 87

Edds, Reginald 141–2
Edgbaston 178, 180, 302, 314–15
Edmonds, Noel 290–1, 295
Edrich, Bill 130, 272, 285
Edward (footman) 71
Edward VII, King 226
Edward VII, King, Hospital for Officers 173, 336–7, 338
Edward VIII, King
  as Prince of Wales 40
  and Mrs Simpson 84
Edward, Prince, Earl of Wessex 334–5
Edwardes-Jones, Gaie (née Johnston, aunt) 4, 19
Edwardes-Jones, George 4
Edwardes-Jones, Margaret *(see Blyth, Margaret)*
Edwards, Jimmy 146
Elder Tree Cottage (house) 93, 103, 120
Elizabeth (assistant matron) 25
Elizabeth II, Queen 221, 246, 247–8, 252, 302, 340
  as Princess Elizabeth 97, 106, 134, 159
  BJ meets 279, 300–1
Elizabeth the Queen Mother, Queen 219, 305, 340
  as Queen 106, 160
  invites BJ to Clarence House 263–4
Elliott, Canon W. H. 94
Ellison, John 127–8, 135, 137
  shares office with BJ 130–1
  and *In Town Tonight* 140, 142, 145, 149, 150, 154, 155, 328
Elwes, Polly 191
Emery, Dick 192
Enemies of Promise (Connolly) 46
Engelmann, Franklin (Jingle) 207, 237, 243
England and Wales Cricket Board 346
England Blind Cricket Squad 346
England, Their England (MacDonell) 265
E.N.S.A. (Entertainments National Service Association) 114
Etheridge, John 306
Eton College 9, 14, 52, 54, 215, 322
  BJ at: 28, 30–33, 35–47
  in Officer Training Corps 35–6
  awarded School Field colours 38
  fails to get into 1st XI 42–3
  elected to 'Pop' 43–4

housemaster's reports 45–6
and Barry Johnston 192–3, 277, 282
Eton College Musical Society 213
Eton Portrait (Fergusson) 35
Eton Ramblers 42, 57, 62–4, 66, 69, 73,
94, 129, 172
Evans, Godfrey 285
'Evening with Johnners, An' (one-man
show) 15, 321–4, 325, 326–7, 329–31
recording 323–4, 328, 329–30, 334, 342
Ewing, Patricia 303
Eyres, Rev. Charles (great-grandfather) 9
Eyres, Lt. Walter 17–19

Fantoni, Barry 281–2
Fender, Percy 175
Fenwick, Lieutenant 106
Fergusson, Bernard 35
Feversham, Lord and Lady 107
Field, Sid 116
Fields, Gracie 171
Fingleton, Jack 180, 196
Fisher, Diana (née Davis) 157–8,
261, 274
Fisher, Archbishop Geoffrey 158, 159
Fisher, H. A. L. 49
Fisher, Humphrey 158
Fisher, John 214
Flanagan, Bud 73, 148, 160, 213, 256
foreword to BJ's book 148–9, 343
Fleming, Doug 166–7
Flexford House (school) 200
Ford (butler) 34
Ford, Sir Edward 63, 90, 172, 336
cross-talk act with BJ 132–3
Forsyth, Bruce 247, 297
Fortune, Charles 203
Foster, Julia 265, 266
Fox, Sir Paul 189
Fox, Roy 73
Francome, Johnny 243
Franks, Vera *(see Duder, Vera)*
Fraser, Gen. Sir David 120
Frindall, Bill 232, 307
Fritche, A. E. 24
Frith, David 233
Frost, Sir David 295
Fry, Stephen 268, 270
Funny Way to be a Hero (Fisher)
213–14

Gaekwar ma *(see Baroda, Maharajah of)*
gaffes, BJ's broadcasting 177–8, 180, 185,
229, 230, 234–6, 251–2, 306–8, 341
Gall, Eleanor 273
Gall, Sandy 272, 273
Gandhi, M. K. 318
Gardner, Charles 190
Garland, Patrick 322
Gatehouse Learning Centre 200
Gavaskar, Sunil 229
George V, King 36, 40
George VI, King 84, 96, 106, 132
. BJ does commentary for 159–60
state funeral 162–3
Gershwin, George & Ira 35
Getty, Sir John Paul 300, 303, 341, 345
friendship with BJ 289–91
Wormsley cricket ground 304–5, 325
Gibbons, Carroll 73
Gibson, Prof. James 51
Giles, Mrs 166
Gillett, Cliff & Olive 275
Gillett, Sir Robin 221
Gilliat, Sir Martin 219, 249, 263–4
Gledhill, Cecil 83
Glendenning, Raymond 126, 135,
137, 167
Glover, Brian 251
'Glorious Game, Say We, A' (Douglas
Home) 343
Goat, Mr 161
Godbold, Roger 323, 328
Goebbels, Dr Josef 76–7
golf, BJ playing 48, 211, 294
Gooch, Graham 295, 317
Goodfellow, 'Splendid Chap' 95
Gower, David 345
Grace, W. G. 226
Graveney, Tom 265, 285
Graves, Peter 159
Green, Stephen 246
Greene, Edward 70
Greig, Tony 220, 229
Grenadier Guards 133, 134, 342, 344
BJ serves in 93, 95–120
and discipline 100–1, 112
military campaign 109–116
memorial to BJ 345
Gridiron Club 53
Griffith, Billy 223

Grimond, Jo, later Lord 89, 215
Grisewood, Freddy 126
Grover, Mr (tutor) 33
Guards Armoured Division 107, 109, 110, 112, 113, 115
    formed 103
    Churchill and de Gaulle visit 105
    officially disbanded 116
Gubbay, Raymond 264–5
Gwinnurth, Lewis 259

Hackforth, Norman 216
Half-Term Report (Douglas Home) 292
Halifax, Earl of 94
Hammond, Walter 90, 231
Hampton (schoolboy) 27
Hancock, Tony 161
Handley, Tommy 304
Hankey, Anne (Mrs Richard Hanbury, cousin) 71–3
Hankey, Joanah 71
Hankey, Mildred (née Johnston, aunt) 72
Hankey, Percival 72
Harbin, Robert 146
Harding, Gilbert 126
Harewood, Princess Mary, Countess of 63
Harewood, Earl of 40
Harmsworth, Jim St John 57, 66–7
Harper (butler) 39
Harris, Richard 293
Harrison, Noel 61
Harrison, Sir Rex 61–2
Harrow School 40–1, 66–8, 196
Harvey, Neil 180
Hassett, Lindsay 314
Hawthorne, Sir Nigel 298
Hay, Will 114
Haynes, Desmond 308
Hayter, Reg 330
Hayward, Sir Jack 287
Headingley 176, 180, 313
Headlam, G. W. 'Tuppy' 32, 54
Hearn (schoolboy) 27
Hearne, Jack 26
Heinz, Mr 274
Hellens, Much Marcle (house) 33–4, 60
Henderson, Dean 49
Henderson, Dickie 239
Hendren, Patsy 26, 77–8
Hendrick, Mike 229

Heyhoe-Flint, Rachael 287–9
Hickey, Peter 268
Hill, Benny 213
Hill, Graham 192
Hill, M. D. 32–3
Hill, Trevor 144–5
Hinge & Bracket 247
Hitchcock, Sir Alfred 171
Hitchcock, Joe 143–4
Hitler, Adolf 76, 91, 92, 95, 97, 115
Hobbs, Sir Jack 231
Hoffman, Dustin 322
Hogg, Sir John 'Pig' 44, 89, 91
    at Oxford with BJ 51, 54–5
    on BJ as cricketer 62
    cross-talk act with BJ 66
Holding, Michael 235
Holdsworth, Michael 134
Hollies, Eric 314
Hollinshead, Reg 219
Holloway, Stanley 34
Holness, Bob 298
Home, Countess of 56, 65
Home, 13th Earl of 56, 64
Home, Lord *(see Douglas-Home, Alec)*
Home Farm Trust 201, 284, 328
Homewell, Bude (house) 60, 82, 83
Hone, Brian 57
Honey, Sid 'Bunch' 48
Hope, Bob 157
Hopetoun, Earl of 42
Horne, Kenneth 167–8, 171, 270
Horrocks, Lt.-Gen. Sir Brian 116
Horton, Henry 234–5
The Hound of the Baskervilles (Conan Doyle) 266
Howard, Trevor 196
Howard de Walden, John Scott-Ellis, 9th Lord 39
Howard de Walden, T. E. Scott-Ellis, 8th Lord 39
Howe, Sir Geoffrey 299
Howerd, Frankie 128, 248–9
Hudd, Roy 256–7
Hudson, Robert 126, 160, 175, 177
    as staff commentator 186, 187, 195
    on BJ being sacked by TV 204, 205
    on BJ and *TMS* 206, 224
Hughes, Kim 233
Hulbert, Jack 128

Hunt, Mick 246
Hunt, Robert 79, 84
Hurdie (cook) 72–3
Huson, A. C. 32, 38–9, 41, 42, 44
  school reports on BJ 45–6
Hussey, Marmaduke 304
Hutchinson, Leslie (Hutch) 213
Hutchinson, Sarah 337
Hutton, Betty 157
Hutton, Sir Len 259

I Zingari 57, 250
Idle, Eric 206
Ilha das Palmas (Johnston's Island) 69
Illingworth, Ray 235, 265
Inside Outside Broadcasts (Hudson) 186
It's a Funny Game (Johnston) 248, 252
It's Been a Lot of Fun (Johnston) 97, 208,
  212, 214

James, Alex 90
James, P. D. 251
James, Sid 161
Jenner, Terry 346
Jewell, Jimmy 264
John XXIII, Pope 184
Johnners at the Beeb 235, 342
Johnson, Dame Celia 171
Johnston, Alice (née Eyres, grandmother)
  9
Johnston, Andrew (son) 207, 297, 300,
  304, 339, 343
  birth 169
  Westminster School 193, 277
  in Australia 242, 260, 262, 275
  This Is Your Life 257–9
  marriage 267
  relationship with BJ 276–7, 280, 281
  family 283
Johnston, Anne (sister, Mrs John Carter;
  Mrs Sharp and Mrs Hall) 9, 11, 12, 34,
  54, 207
  and father's drowning 16–17, 19
  divorce 82–3
Johnston, Audrey (née Hankey, wife of
  Alex) 71–2, 89
Johnston, Barry (son) 144, 149, 173, 219,
  222, 250, 267, 297, 298, 300, 306, 347
  birth 156
  at Eton 192–3, 277

in Design 213–14, 321
in USA 251, 257, 278
This Is Your Life 257–9
Trivia Test Match 268–9
Chinese Horoscopes 281–2
radio career 257, 278, 304, 321,
  327, 338
BarryMour Productions 283, 323
'An Evening with Johnners' 321–2,
  323–4, 326–7, 328, 329
Kilroy 327–8
relationship with BJ 170, 278, 281–2,
  327–8
marriage 304
family 283
charity show with BJ 328
and BJ's heart attack 333–6
last words with BJ 338–9
thanksgiving service 343
Johnston, Bertram (great-uncle) 69, 70
Johnston, Brian:
  family background 7–9
  birth 9–10
  childhood 10–13
  at Temple Grove 14–16, 23–29
  father drowns 4, 16–22
  at Eton 28, 30–3, 35–47
  mother's remarriage 33
  at Oxford 46, 48–59
  with family coffee business 74–87,
    91, 92–5
  in Germany 75–7
  in Brazil 79–87
  acute peripheral neuritis 87
  in Grenadier Guards 93, 95–120
  marriage proposal rejected 97
  in France and Germany 98–120
  awarded MC 118
  joins BBC 124–6
  first broadcast 127
  and broadcasts from theatres 128
  as sports commentator 129, 138
  marriage to Pauline 133–9
  on 'Let's Go Somewhere' 141–55
  radio and TV programmes 156–7,
    159–73, 186–92, 211–17, 247–9,
    251–60, 264–71, 295–8,
  and children 156, 158–9, 169–70,
    199–201, 283–4
  mother's death 174

as TV cricket commentator 175–84
first BBC cricket correspondent 183
and politics 188–9, 293–4
sacked as TV cricket commentator
  203–6
retirement from BBC staff 206–7
on *Down Your Way* 207–8, 237–46
writes autobiography 208, 212–13
and Kerry Packer 220–1
on *Test Match Special* 206, 223–36,
  306–15
awarded OBE 260
and food dislikes 274–6
family life 276–8
personal character 278–83
friendships 285–94
awarded CBE 299–300
and 'leg over' incident 306–10
one-man show 319–24, 326–31
heart attack 332–3
convalescence 334–8
death 339
tributes to 340–1
burial 341
thanksgiving service 342–5
memorials to 345–6
Johnston, Charles Edward (great-uncle) 9
Johnston, Lt.-Col. Charles (father) 7, 11,
  12, 14, 23, 46, 174
marriage and family 9
and Great War 11, 27, 118
and family business 7, 9, 11, 69–70, 123
drowning at Bude 4, 16–22
Johnston, Christopher (brother) 60, 71,
  74, 193, 336, 342
childhood 9, 10, 12, 13, 33–4
and Temple Grove 14, 15, 23
and father's death 16, 18, 19–21
at Eton and Oxford 30, 36, 39, 44, 48
army career 58, 59
Johnston, Clare (daughter, Mrs David
  Oldridge) 222, 263, 297, 336
birth 158–9
in Australia 215
marriage 249–50
relationship with BJ 276, 277, 281, 291
family 283
Johnston, Edward & Co. 7
founding in Brazil 8, 69
London office 9, 70

BJ under pressure to join 44, 58, 59
BJ works for 74–8, 80–1, 83, 87, 91, 92
centenary lunch 105–6
BJ considers leaving 90–1, 95, 123
Johnston, Edward (great-grandfather) 8,
  9, 69, 70
Johnston, Elizabeth (née Ellis, ancestor)
  8
Johnston, Emily (granddaughter) 283
Johnston, Fiona (née Morrison, wife of
  Barry) 283, 304, 334, 335–6
Johnston, Francis (né Johnstone) 8
Johnston, Francis Alexander 'Cousin Alex'
  (godfather) 7, 10, 70–2
pressure on BJ to join business 44,
  58–9, 70
BJ stays with 70–1, 89
Johnston, Geoffrey (uncle) 11, 21, 70
Johnston, Georgia (grandaughter) 283
Johnston, Gilly (née Moon, wife of
  Andrew) 267, 283, 297
Johnston, Hamil (uncle, guardian)
  21, 44, 46
Johnston, Harry (grandson) 283
Johnston, Henriette (née Moke, wife of
  Edward) 8
Johnston, Ian (son) 170, 262, 263, 283,
  289, 297, 343
birth 169
Bradfield College 193
relationship with BJ 277
Johnston, Joanna (daughter) 199–201,
  214–15, 284
birth 199
Down's Syndrome 199–200
This Is Your Life 266–7
helps BJ after heart attack 335, 337
Johnston, Michael (brother) 9, 26, 34,
  174, 337, 338
at Eton 30
poor health 59
Johnston, Olivia (granddaughter) 283,
  335–6, 338
Johnston, Pauline (wife) 138–9, 156, 181,
  182–3, 188, 202, 208, 219, 222, 224,
  249, 263, 264, 287, 293, 294, 328
as Pauline Tozer 133–7
honeymoon 137–8
and *Let's Go Somewhere* 142, 144, 145,
  148, 151

children 156, 158–9, 169–70, 199–201,
    283–4
relationship with BJ 169–70, 277–9,
    280–1, 283, 330
holiday homes 174, 211
abroad with BJ 182–3, 207, 217, 272–4,
    275, 282–3, 316–19, 326
and daughter Joanna 199–201, 214–15,
    266–7
on *Down Your Way* 243
This Is Your Life 257, 266–7
and BJ's food dislikes 275–6
at No. 10 and Chequers 299–300
and BJ's heart attack 332–333, 335–9
after BJ's death 340, 341–2, 343–5
fire at Boundary Road 347
Johnston, Pleasance (mother, née Alt,
    later Mrs Scully) 10, 11, 23, 26, 36–7,
    43, 44, 62, 63, 74, 81, 102, 115, 144,
    337, 338
first marriage and children 9
husband's death 16, 18, 19–22
second marriage 33–4, 60
divorce 83
in Brazil 86, 87
at Elder Tree Cottage 93, 103
death 174
Johnston, Reginald Eden 'Granny Pa'
    (grandfather) 9, 19, 92, 123
Governor of Bank of England 7, 9, 70
at Terlings Park 12–13
death 21–2
Johnston, Sam (grandson) 283
Johnstone, Francis (ancestor) 8
Johnstone, James (ancestor) 8
Joint, James 85
Jones, Mickey 198
Jones, Peter 216
Jones, Peter 256
Juliana, Princess, of Netherlands 65

Katz, Solly 230
Kaye, Danny 145–6
Keegan, John 119
Keller, Frau 80
Kembery, Caroline 336
Kendall, Felicity 247
Kenfield Hall (house) 211
Kennedy, Jacqueline (later Mrs Onassis)
    273

Kennedy, President John F. 94, 188, 273
Kennedy, Ambassador Joseph P. 94
Kennedy, Kathleen 'Kick' 94
Kentish Kipper (greyhound) 202–3
Kerans, Lt.-Cdr. 172
Kidd, Eddie 297
Kilroy-Silk, Robert 327–8
Kingsley, Charles 280
Kitter, Roger 214
Knight, Guy 109
Knight, Heck (*see Loyd, Hester*)
Knott, Alan 197
Knox, Teddy 147–8
Köhl, Herr 80
Kok, M. 67
Korner, Herr 75

Laker, Jim 197, 203, 204, 265
Lambton, Lord 202
Lane Fox, Anne 92, 136
Lane Fox, Col. Edward 172
Lane Fox, Felicity, later Baroness 83,
    259–60
Lane Fox, Jimmy 83, 94, 136, 138, 172
President of 'Pop' 44
at Oxford with BJ 55, 57, 62
and Grenadier Guards 93, 95, 112
This Is Your Life 259
Lawrence, David 'Syd' 307–8
Lawson-Dick, Clare 239–40
Leame, Captain 17
Leave it to Jeeves (Wodehouse) 265
Le Beau, Bettine 216
Lebus, A. H. H. 41
Lee, Vanessa 213
Legge, Wickham 49–50
Let's Go Somewhere (Johnston) 141,
    148, 343
Lewis, Chris 307
Lewis, Mike 302, 325–6
Lewis, Tony 265
Lightfoot, Alan 118
Lindwall, Ray 197
Lineker, Gary 305
Little Offley (house) 10–12, 21
Llewelyn-Davies, Nico 165
Lloyd-George, David 49
Lomas, Oggie 137, 143
London, BJ's homes in
    Queen's Gate 71–2, 89

South Eaton Place 89–91, 93, 102
Gloucester Place 126
Westbourne Crescent 138–9
Cavendish Avenue 156, 188, 195, 201
Hamilton Terrace 202, 253, 277
Boundary Road 253, 268, 300, 328,
  333, 336, 337–8, 347
London Palladium 73, 115, 157
BJ on stage at 146
and Barry Johnston 214
Lord's Cricket Ground 77, 139, 142, 156,
  183, 185, 193, 201, 202, 205, 218, 253,
  295, 300, 304, 330, 346
  Eton v. Harrow match 40–1, 42–3,
    66–8, 129, 196, 343
  Test matches at 90, 129, 136, 137, 175,
    176, 184, 221, 223–4, 226, 227, 231
  BJ's first TV commentary 175
  bomb scare 223–4
  final *Down Your Way* 246
  Clare's wedding reception 250
  BJ's last visit to 338
  memorial to BJ 345
Lord's Taverners 183, 197, 258,
  299, 334–5,
  and Brian Johnston Memorial Trust 346
Loyd, Hester 'Heck' (later Mrs Knight)
  92–3, 97, 109
Loyd, John 109
Lynam, Des 255
Lynn, Ralph 35
Lynn, Dame Vera 264
Lyttelton, Humphrey 192

McCartney, Sir Paul 201
MacDonald, Ramsay 74
MacDonnell, A. G. 265
McElnea, Sister June 'Sister Mac' 266–7
McGibbon, '3-Goal' 129
McGilvray, Alan 226
MacGregor, Sue 251
Mackenzie, Sir Compton 171
McKenzie, Keith 314–15
MacPherson, Stewart 107, 124, 126,
  130–1, 137, 237
Magnusson, Jon 270–1
Major, John, 305, 340, 345
  at Chequers 299–300
  tributes to BJ 341, 343–4
Manhattan Transfer 248

Margaret, Princess 97, 106, 132,
  160, 187–8
Marlow, Tony 303
Marshall, Howard 101
Marson, Lionel 138
Martin, John 321, 322, 323, 324, 330
Martin-Jenkins, Christopher 'CMJ' 272,
  274, 336
  and *TMS* 224, 227, 228, 229, 301
  tribute to BJ 340–1
Marvin, Hank B. 171
Mary, Queen 40, 84, 127
Marylebone Cricket Club (MCC), and BJ
  57, 68, 287–9
Maskell, Dan 247
Matthews, Pauline 296
Max-Muller, Charles 173, 179, 181, 184
May, Peter 178
Melford, Michael 'Mellers' 181, 202
Merton, Paul 268
Metro Club 218
Michelmore, Cliff 166–7
Miers, John 85
Miles, Michael 203, 328
military, and BJ:
  and Cadet Corps 27–8
  Eton College Officer Training Corps
    35–6
  against army career 58
  Grenadier Guards Officer Cadet
    Reserve 93
  officer training 95–7
  Transport Officer 99–103
  Technical Adjutant 104–116
  army revues 106, 108, 117–18
  scout car FUJIAR 109–10
  overseas 109–120
  promoted major 118
  awarded MC 118–120
  demobbed 118, 120
Miller, Alan 265
Miller, Keith 197
Miller, Max 73, 117, 266
Mills, Bernard 173
Milton, Arthur 202–3
Mitford, Colonel 27
Moke, Henriette *(see Johnston, Henriette)*
Monkman, Phyllis 34
Montgomery, Field-Marshal Viscount 98,
  108, 110, 117

BJ meets 163, 171
Monty Python's Flying Circus 206
Moody, Vic 'Spud' 141
Moon, Gillian *(see Johnston, Gilly)*
Moore, Lt.-Col. Rodney 111
Morecambe and Wise 213
Morrison, Fiona *(see Johnston, Fiona)*
Mosey, Don 'The Alderman' 228, 231, 289–90, 304
  friendship with BJ 229–30
  writes in support of BJ 233–4
  criticism of *TMS* 301–2
Moss, Stirling 171
Motson, John 247
Moult, Ted 234
Mountbatten, Earl, of Burma 163–4
Mower, Patrick 258
Much Marcle (Herefordshire) 33–4, 60
Muir, Frank 211
Munro, Jock 79, 85
Murphy, Pat 302

Nancy (cook) 194
Napier, Lord 8
Neagle, Dame Anna 159, 202
Neighbours 289–91, 322, 344
Neilson-Terry, Phyllis 39
Nervo, Jimmy 147–8
New College, Oxford 48–59, 127
  BJ's entrance 46
  captain of cricket XI 57
  Brian Johnston Sports Pavilion 345
Nick the Greek 272–3
nicknames, BJ and 51, 89, 95, 100, 229, 232, 286
Nixon, Richard M. 188
Norfolk, Bernard Fitzalan-Howard, 16th Duke of 99, 172, 245
Norton, Betty 54
Novello, Ivor 148
Nuffield, William Morris, Viscount 84

Old Trafford 181, 228–9, 235, 312, 319
Oldfield, Peter 57
Oldridge, Clare *(see Johnston, Clare)*
Oldridge, David (son-in-law) 249–50, 297
Oldridge, Nicholas (grandson) 283, 346
Oldridge, Rupert (grandson) 283
Oldridge, Sophie (granddaughter) 283
Oliver, Neville 'Dr NO' 312–13

Onassis, Aristotle 272, 273
Orr-Ewing, Ian, later Lord 129, 175, 249
Ottea, Morgiste 12, 13
Oval 129, 175–6, 177, 235, 311, 326
  Brian Johnston Broadcasting Centre 345
Oxford Authentics 57
Oxford University 9, 20, 44–5, 66, 70, 72, 168
  BJ at New College 46, 48–59
  practical jokes & pranks 50–2, 55–8
  degree awarded to BJ 50

Packer, Kerry 220, 221
Paget, General Sir Bernard 106–7
Paine, Reverend 62
Painter, Wally and Dolly 309–10
Palmer, Joe 322–23
Palmer, Lilli 62
Papanicalou, Nick 286
Parkinson, Michael 248
Patterson, Patrick 308
Patton, Gen. George S. 110
Pawle, John 67, 196
Payne, Jack 248
Peck, Geoffrey 129, 131, 135
Pendry, Mr 32–3
Peten, Madame 115
Philharmonia Orchestra 213
Philip, Prince, Duke of Edinburgh 134, 159, 169, 247, 279, 283, 340
  BJ interviews 221, 234
  presents award to BJ 255
Phillips, Arthur 207
Phillips, Capt. Mark 212
Pinter, Harold 251
Pitt, William 311
plays, revues, shows:
  Annie Get Your Gun 128
  Aunt Edwina 293
  Call Me Madam 158
  Carousel 128
  Come and Get It 106
  The Co-optimists 34–5
  The Eyes Have It! 117–18, 165
  Funny Face 35
  The Ghost Train 86, 123
  Great Possessions 294
  The Happiest Days of Your Life 329
  Happy and Glorious 116
  In the Red 293

Interference 35
It's All Laid On 108
The Little Victims 95
Now Barabbas 292
Nuts in May 85
Oklahoma! 128
Outside Edge 293
South Pacific 128
Smoky Cell 40
Something in the Air 62
Song of Norway 128
Strike It Again 116
Together Again 147
Under the Counter 128
Underneath the Arches 256
What About It Then? 118
Plomley, Roy 212
Polden, Polly 130
Pollock, Graeme 203
Pollock, Peter 341
postcards, saucy, BJ sends 162, 291–2
  to Lord Home 292
Powell, Dilys 171
Powell, Mr & Mrs 33, 37
Pratts Club 73
Prescott, Brig. Peter 111–12
Primary Club 219, 233, 345
Prince of Wales Theatre 115, 256
Pye Radio Award 253

Quaglino's 166–7
Quarry Cottage, Swanage (house)
  174, 211
Queen's Park Rangers 129

racehorses, part-owned by BJ
  Proper Gentleman 249
  W. G. Greys 219–20, 249
radio, BJ on:
  Boat Race 149, 168, 253–6
  Bob Holness Requests the Pleasure 298
  Brass Band Championships 160
  Chinese Horoscopes 281–2
  Desert Island Discs 212–14
  Down Your Way 211, 219, 237–46, 247,
    258, 291, 297, 322, 342
    BJ takes over from Engelmann 207–8
    programme cancelled 215–16, 238–9
    public protests and return 239–40
    eccentric characters 241–2

  in Australia 242
  BJ announces retirement 243–4
  final programme 246
Enchanting World of Hinge & Bracket
  247
Funny Peculiar 251
Hancock's Half Hour 161
Housewives' Choice 194
In Town Tonight 140–55, 217, 256, 298,
  328, 342
Johnners at 70 256
Just A Minute 251
'Let's Go Somewhere' 141–54, 156,
  157, 217
  night in Chamber of Horrors 141–2
  attacked by Alsatian 144–5
  on stage with Crazy Gang 147–8
  lies under Golden Arrow 150
  hypnotised 150–1
  The Piccadilly Incident 152–3
Let's Go Somewhere 165–8
'Many Happy Returns' 171
Married to Fame 192
'Meet a Sportsman' 172
Monte Carlo Rally 161
Olympic Games 138
'On The Job' 140
Open House 212
Quote Unquote 251
Round the Halls 128
Roundabout 172
Royal Variety Performance 157, 159–60
royal weddings 251–2, 267
Saturday Night at the London Palladium
  157
Sporting Chance 189, 267
Spot the Headliner 172
'Stage Door Johnners' 298
Test Match Special 185, 208, 218, 219,
  223–36, 248, 253, 263, 295, 301–4,
  322, 325–6, 335, 345
  BJ joins 204, 206, 223
  commentary team 224–232
  criticism in *Wisden Cricket Monthly*
    232–4
  and Sir Paul Getty 289, 303
  threat to ball-by-ball coverage 302–4
  'leg over' incident 306–311
  giggles and practical jokes 311–313
  BJ's last commentary 326

Today 171, 186–7, 194, 212, 332
Treble Chance 190, 194, 200, 229, 267
Trivia Test Match 267–71, 287, 325
Twenty Questions 171, 186, 216–17
'View From The Boundary, A'
    234, 312
What's It All About? 171
With Great Pleasure 265–6
Work's Wonders 129–30
Raw, Rupert 44
Ray, Ted 128
Rayvern Allen, David 225, 227
real tennis, BJ plays 48
Redfern, Anthea 247
Redhead, Brian 215
Rees, Nigel 251
Reid, Mike 214
Remick, Lee 202
Reynolds, Gillian 303
Rhodes, Joan 146
Rhodes, Wilfred 183, 231
Rice, Sir Tim 308
    Trivia Test Match 268, 269, 270, 271
    and MCC 287, 288
Richards, Barry 203
Richter, Ian 312
Riddell, Henry 150–1, 157, 166
Ridley, Arnold 86
Riff-Raff Club 344
Robertson, Max 157, 161
Robertson-Glasgow, R. C. 175
Robinson, Cardew 258
Robinson, Eric 157
Robinson, Louis 290–1
Rogers, Keith 162
Rommel, Field Marshal Erwin 171
Ronnies, The Two 213, 244
Roxburghe, Duke of 172
Roy, Harry 73
royal palaces, BJ's visits to
    Buckingham Palace 263, 300–1
    Clarence House 263–4, 340
    Holyrood House 279
rugby football, BJ playing 27, 46, 48,
    52
    scores try in a macintosh 57–8
Runcie, Lord 342
Rushton, Willie 216, 217, 268, 269,
    270, 271
Russell, Audrey 126

Ruston, Frank (batman) 115, 118

St John's Wood Society 345
St Paul's Cathedral 221, 251–2
Salmon, Ross 170, 181
Salote, Queen, of Tonga 163
Sandhurst 58, 60, 95–6
Santos (Brazil) 69, 79–88, 106
Sargent, Sir Malcolm 213
Sarne, Mike 277
Savoy Hotel 188, 222, 304
    BJ stays at 103, 116
Sayers, R. S. 9
Schonegevel, D. J. 286
Scott, Pat 60–2, 82
Scott-Ellis, John *(see Howard de Walden)*
Scott-Johnston, Alastair 216
Scudamore, Peter 243
Scully, Col. Marcus (stepfather) 36,
    44, 58, 60
    attempt to rescue BJ's father 17–20
    marries BJ's mother 33
    divorce 83
    death 102
Scully, Pleasance *(see Johnston, Pleasance)*
Searle, Frank 241–2
Secombe, Sir Harry 295
Seekers, The 194
The Selfish Giant (Wilde) 266
Sellers, Peter 149
Seymour, Chris 323–4, 326, 329
Shadows, The 171
Sharp, E. G. 'Daddy' 15
Sharp, Terry 83
Shaughnessy, Alfred 89, 93, 111, 123
    on BJ at Eton 43, 44
    wartime revues with BJ 106, 108, 117
Sheepshanks, Charles 279
Sheppard, Rev. David, later Lord 181–2
Simpson, Mrs Wallis 84
Sinatra, Frank 246
Sinden, Sir Donald 298
Slater, E. V. 38
Smith, Anthony 240–1, 242, 246, 258
Smith, Ian 289
Snagge, John 141, 247, 253, 254
Snow, John 235
Sobers, Sir Garfield 207
Someone Who Was (Johnston) 304,
    325, 343

Sony Award 264
Spencer, Lady Diana (later Princess of Wales) 251–2
Spencer, Kenneth 146, 148
Spencer, Paul 268
Squires, Dorothy 135
Stanhope, Henry 246
Statham, Brian 197
Stephenson, Lt.-Col. John 246
Stewart, David 150
Stewart, Ian 222
Stewart, Mickey 302
Stiffkey, Rector of 64
Stilgoe, Richard 342–3
Stone, Lew 73
Stowe School 346
Sutton, Tom 254–5
Swaebe, A. V. 134
Swanage (Dorset) 208, 214, 283, 326
    holiday homes at 174, 211
    Mowlem theatre 276–7
    BJ's burial at 341
    memorial meadow 345
Swanton, Ann 30–1, 272
Swanton, Dr 336
Swanton, E. W. (Jim) 31, 57, 196, 206, 265, 272, 299
    and BJ's MCC membership 68
    and BJ on TV 175–6, 177
    BJ's practical jokes on 184, 223
    friendship with BJ 286–7
Sykes, Eric 298
Sykes, Herbert 183

table tennis (with Rex Harrison), BJ plays 61
Tales from a Long Room (Tinniswood) 265
Tallon, William 'Backstairs Billy' 264
Tarbuck, Jimmy 244
Targett (butler) 71
Tatham, W. G. 45
Tati, Jacques 158
Tawney, Lily 55–6
Taylor, Mr (schoolmaster) 24
television, BJ on:
    All Your Own 170–1
    Ask Your Dad 170
    Breakfast Time 244
    Call My Bluff 211

Come Dancing 191
coronation of Elizabeth II 163
Countdown 296
cricket commentaries 129, 156, 175–85, 326
Dog's Chance 171
funeral of George VI 162–3
Generation Game, The 247
Good Life, The 247–8
Highway 295
How Do You View? 156–7
Inspector Morse 295
International Ballroom Championships 190
Jim'll Fix It 295
Kilroy 327–8
Lord Mayor's Show 168, 212
Miss World 168
Monty Python's Flying Circus 206
Noel's Addicts 290–1
Noel's House Party 295
Parkinson 248–9, 251
Pebble Mill at One 214
Place in the Country, A 211
Reunion 215
royal weddings 187–8, 212
Saturday Night Out 169
Spitting Image 295
Sporting Chance 189–90
Sportsview 186, 187
This is Your Life 191–2, 266, 295
    BJ as subject of 257–60
What's New 191
Wogan 244–5
Years Ahead 264
You Bet 297
Temple Grove School 11, 13, 14–16, 23–29, 36, 137
tennis, BJ playing 61, 80, 158
Terlings Park (house) 12, 13
Terry-Thomas 156–7
Tetcott Hunt 56
Thatcher, Sir Denis 299
Thatcher, Margaret, later Lady 103, 299, 300, 302
That's Cricket (tour) 264–5
theatre, BJ's love of 34–5, 58, 123, 128, 146, 293, 298
They Were Not Divided (film) 136–7
Thomas, Major Cyril 60, 61

Thomas, Jane (later Duchess of Somerset) 60

Thomas, Jessie 60, 61

Thomas, Keith 242

Thomas, Leslie 268

Thomas, Marjorie (Collette, Mrs Rex Harrison) 60–2

Thomas, Micky 60, 112

Thomas, Mike 219

Thomas, Pat *(see Scott, Pat)*

Thompson, Geoff 341

Thorne, George 41–2, 43, 111

Thornton, Ken 110, 112

Tidy, Bill 270

Tilley, John 73

Timothy, Christopher 256

Tinniswood, Peter 265

Titt, William H. 311

Tollemache, Mrs 50

Tollemache, Tony 50

Tozer, Edward 182–3

Tozer, Eileen (mother-in-law) 159

Tozer, Germaine 136

Tozer, Gordon (brother-in-law) 133–4, 136

Tozer, Pauline *(see also Johnston, Pauline)*
family background 133–4, 182–3
telephones BJ 133–4
courtship 135–6
engagement and marriage 136–7

Tozer, Susan 136

Tozer, Col. William (father-in-law) 133–4, 136, 138

Train, Jack 216, 217

travels, BJ's, to
Australia 178–9, 181–3, 207, 215, 260, 261–3
Brazil 78–88
Cyprus 190, 272, 282–3
Europe 75–7, 92, 94, 109–120
France 77, 92, 94, 109–113
Germany 75–7, 92, 115–120, 190
Greece 217–18, 272–4
Hong Kong 190, 326
India and Goa 316–19
Middle and Far East 180, 190
South Africa 199, 203, 207, 211
West Indies 214

Travers, Ben 35

Trent, Bruce 213

Trent Bridge 177, 184, 234

Trinder, Tommy 116, 128, 251, 258
BJ on stage with 146, 214

Trubshawe, Michael 137

Trueman, Fred 178, 197, 265, 344
and *TMS* 231, 233, 302
practical joke on Aggers 314
on BJ's health 330

Trueman, Veronica 330

Tucker, Sophie 73

Tufnell, Philip 308

Tuke-Hastings, Michael 189–90

Turner, Glenn 185

Turner, Nigel 66

Tuscan Star (ship) 106

Tussauds, Madame 141–2, 168

Tuthill, Tony 241

Tyson, Frank 285

Upjohn, Gerald, later Lord 103–4

Upstairs Downstairs 106

Upwey Manor (house) 21

Vaughan, Norman 239

Vaughan-Thomas, Wynford 130, 135, 137, 157, 160, 190
BJ meets 107, 124
and BJ's BBC audition 125–6
politics 189

Venables-Llewellyn, Lt.-Col. Mike 100

Victoria Palace 147–8, 160

Victoria Station 150, 165–6, 168

Villiers, Sir Charles 44, 99, 105, 132, 249

Villiers, Nick 132

Vincent's Club 53

Vorderman, Carol 296

Vosburgh, Dick 251

Wade, Virginia 247

Wadwaker, Benny 230

Wakefield (chauffeur) 12

Wakeham, John, later Lord 303

Walbrook, Anton 158

Wallace, Edgar 39–40

Wallace, Ian 265

Wallis, Shani 158

Walls, Tom 35

The Walrus and the Carpenter (Carroll) 266

Walsh, Courtney 307

Waqar Younis 311

Ward, Alan 185
Wardman, Jane 309
Warner, Sir Pelham 142, 206
The Water Babies (Kingsley) 280
Waterfield, H. W. 'Bug' 15–16, 24, 28–29
Waterfield, Mrs 'Dame Bug' 15, 25
Watts, Jeff 321, 322, 323, 329
Webber, Roy 181
Welch, Phyllis 20
Weldon, Sir Huw 170
Wells, Bill 112
Wells, Elsa 190
West, Peter 191, 196, 204, 206
    and BJ on TV 177, 181, 184
Western Brothers 295
Westminster, Dean of 342, 344
Westminster Abbey 342–5
Westminster School 193, 277
Whatman, Jimmy 250, 279, 294, 298
Whitby, Tony 215–16, 239
Whitelaw, William, later Lord 103–4
Whitely, Richard 296
Whitworth, Arthur 59, 91, 123
Wigram, Sir Clive 102
Wigram, Neville, later Lord 99–101, 102, 112, 120
Wilcox, Herbert 159
Wilde, Oscar 266

Wilding, Michael 159
Wilkins (butler) 24
Wilkinson, Roger 55
Willey, Peter 235
Williams, Kenneth 161
Williamson, Malcolm 268, 269, 270
Willis, Bob 219
Wilson, Cecil 160
Windmill Theatre 73
Winn, Anona 216
Winton, Nan 190
Wisden Cricket Monthly 232–4
Witcher, Claire 336
Wodehouse, Sir P. G. 48, 265, 286
Wogan, Terry 216, 217, 244
Wong, Anna May 81
Woodcock, John 'Wooders' 175, 197, 202, 286, 298, 336
    in Australia 181, 182, 285
    owns greyhound with BJ 202
    on BJ's character 275, 281, 330
Wrigley, Arthur 232

York, Duchess of 267
York, Duke of *(see Andrew, Prince)*
Young, Mr (tutor) 50
Young, Terence 136

Zeppelins 11, 80